THE
MAGNIFICENT
PENINSULA

THE COMPREHENSIVE GUIDEBOOK TO MEXICO'S

BAJA
CALIFORNIA

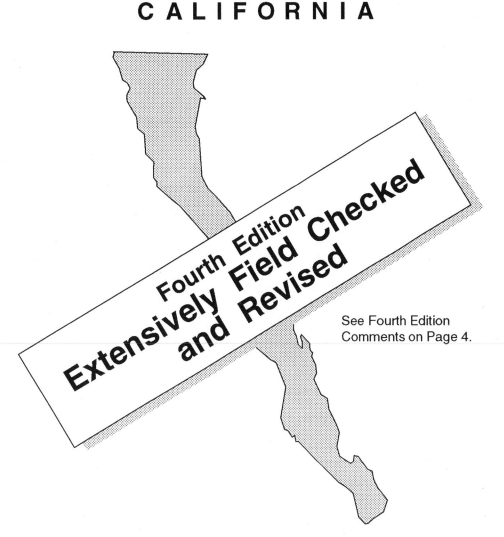

Fourth Edition
Extensively Field Checked
and Revised

See Fourth Edition
Comments on Page 4.

JACK WILLIAMS

Published by
H. J. Williams Publications
P.O. Box 203
Sausalito, CA 94966
(415) 332-8635

Printed by
Publishers Press
1900 West 2300 South
Salt Lake City, Utah 84119-0408
(801) 972-6600 (800) 456 6600

Copyright by H. J. Williams Publications
First Edition — November 1986
Second Edition — April 1987
Third Edition — October 1989
Fourth Edition — Fall 1992

Library of Congress Catalog Card Number 86-90487
ISBN 0-9616843-5-6.

**A "cardonal" of cardon (giant cactus) at
the southern end of Bahia Concepcion.**

CONTENTS

AUTHOR'S PREFACE

The Author's Preface in the original edition of The Magnificent Peninsula presented my qualifications for producing the book. It was essentially an apology for my having had the audacity to become an author in that my past experience in writing had been limited to business letters and the reports and other assorted jargon of the world of bureaucracy. As The Magnificent Peninsula has now met with some modest success, I am perhaps justified in withdrawing the apology. However, still included here is some background material about myself as many readers have expressed interest in the pedigree of their guide.

Initially, I love to travel, and this activity is one of the driving forces of my life. I submit that having such an affliction is the basic requirement for writing a travel guide. By quick tally I find I have expended some 27 months traveling in Mexico, with over three-quarters of this time spent on the Baja peninsula or over its surrounding waters. Perhaps, more importantly, I am a rover, not lingering long in any one haunt. I frequently talk to other people who's knowledge about a particular place in Baja exceeds my own, but perhaps the nature and breadth of my wanderings have provided an overall perspective of Baja shared with only a relative few.

By training and experience I am a forester, although I have now retired from that calling. Being a specialist in trees and forests may seem a strange qualification for delving into the almost totally desert environment of the Baja peninsula. In practice, many foresters find themselves engaged in the far broader task of managing land with all its surface and subsurface resources. We are fortunate in becoming familiar with geology, wildlife, botany, soils, and a variety of other outdoor-oriented subjects.

In addition, many of us become keen observers and interpreters of what we see, whether it be forest or desert.

At the core of my view of travel book writing is the concept that travelers need a source of information concerning the land and all its natural and man-made attributes as a basis for enjoying and appreciating what they see. As a purveyor of such material, I am an expert in very little, but in keeping with my name, I am perhaps a "Jack" of all trades concerning the great outdoors.

My post-retirement activities in Baja started in 1983 gathering data to assist another author in republishing his out-of-print boating guide. The Magnificent Peninsula was written as an act of frustration as I waited for this individual to produce his book. As his project still did not materialize, I produced my own Baja Boater's Guide in 1988. During this five year period from 1983 to 1988 I conducted two complete circumnavigations of the peninsula in my sailboat, retraced this same terrain by aircraft taking over 1,000 aerial photos, and traveled approximately 20,000 miles over Baja's roads and highways.

In presenting these credentials I have so far omitted what may be most important. I have a love affair with Mexico and the Baja peninsula. This is the catalyst that has led me to the perilous task of authorship. Hopefully, this infatuation will not overly cloud my objectivity. It is my sincere wish that these efforts will enhance your ability to plan, and to savor traveling in Mexico's Magnificent Peninsula. If perchance it does, or if you can offer the path to improvement, it would be a pleasure to hear from you.

Jack Williams, P. O. Box 203, Sausalito, CA 94966.

FOURTH EDITION REVISIONS — Changes in this book's 2nd edition were limited to correction of a few errors. In contrast, the 3rd, and now this 4th edition reflect a revisitation of nearly all of the places reported on in PART III THE GRAND TOUR. PARTS I and II are also revised as needed.

The most important change has been to the book's maps and graphics. All of the 62 maps, and some of the tables and other graphics have been totally reconstructed using EPS (Encapsulated Postscript) computer software. They represent a considerable improvement in readability and accuracy over those in previous editions.

The road logs in PART III have been revised as needed and all hotels have been revisited and recent developments added to the hotel list. Finally, significant changes have been made in chapters 3 - Transportation, 4 - Recreation Vehicles and Camping, and 13 - Our Developing Country Neighbor.

In the 3-years between the 3rd and 4th editions there has been continued urbanization in the coastal corridor between Tijuana and Ensenada. Extensive new development has also occurred in the Cape Area at and between San Jose del Cabo and Cabo San Lucas.

Most of the vast remainder of the peninsula has experienced relatively little new recreational development although revision of this book was clearly in order.

The way to maximize profits from a travel guide is to make as few changes as possible after the initial edition. A page change, no matter how small, requires that page be rephotographed by the printer. Changes made early in a book may force all subsequent pages to be reformatted.

All of this is expensive. It is for this reason that many travel books, including some on Baja, are kept in print long after many conditions have changed. Some books are simply reprinted with little or no change, except on the cover, which announces a "New Edition" so as to delude the reader into believing they are purchasing an up-to-date guide.

I have decided that needed changes will be made in this book regardless of their effect on costs. I sincerely hope that the book's ultimate financial reward will emanate from its reputation as being reliable and up-to-date, and not as the result of compromises made to reduce production costs.

ACKNOWLEDGMENTS

Where does one begin? I have no big names to drop, but many people have made big contributions to *The Magnificent Peninsula*. My thanks go to:

My daughter, Barbara Williams, who was the first to review the manuscript in the office and who sat at my side as we checked the GRAND TOUR in the field. The changes made at her suggestion are immense; —— —— Robert Pawlak, who produced a professional cover design while tolerating my cost-cutting maneuvers; —— Ken Reimer, for contributing the poetry, a welcome touch of class; —— Alan Lamb, a true friend and excellent companion during La Patricia's circumnavigation of the Baja peninsula and for his office and field review of the manuscript. (Putting up with the vile moods of the skipper takes a special kind of person;) —— June Siringer, for a masterful job of editing a manuscript where the spelling was inspired by the political philosophy of Abraham Lincoln: "Some of the words were spelled wrong all of the time, and all of the words were spelled wrong some of the time, but mercifully all of the words were not spelled wrong all of the time;" and where the author looked upon commas as a cook looks on salt, "something to be sprinkled on at random in the process of preparation."

And a special tribute to my wife, Patricia Williams, for endless hours of help and understanding in many forms. Without her, there would have simply been no La Patricia, no The Magnificent Peninsula, and perhaps, no Jack Williams. H. J. Williams Publications is now truly a joint endeavor for the two of us.

My thanks also to Lyn Gladstone for hunchs, and counsel, (my thin skin will never be the same); to Peter Schultz for guidance through the strange and wonderfull world of printing; to Ellie Lamb for reviewing the manuscript in the field; to my parents, Henry and Margaret Williams whose energy and frugality produced the initial financial resources to publish the book; and to Leland Lewis, who provided the motivation and opportunity for my venture into writing. Sometimes it is not what you do, but what you don't do that is important. Thus it was with Leland.

My gratitude to Chet Sherman, President of the Vagabundos del Mar for extensive cooperation in bringing this book to the attention of the members of his fine travel club.

Finally, thanks to an endless number of travelers in the Magnificent Peninsula who have offered their counsel; to Mexican officials who have struggled with my poor Spanish in answering my questions; and to the wonderfully warm and friendly Mexican people who share their land with we travelers from the north.

Thank you all.

Dedication
To Patty

Baja California...legendary land
* Of the warrior women,*
Of precious pearls...;
* Stepchild appendix*
Of a great continent...,
* Where the sands of time*
Mark the ages languidly,
* as she dreams on and on*
In her siesta 'neath the sun.

BAJA CALIFORNIA
By Ken Reimer

On October 15, 1524, Hernan Cortez wrote the king of Spain. The conqueror of New Spain reported on a legendary island that was populated only by women. It was also said to be rich in pearls and gold. These reports no doubt inspired Cortez to dispatch expeditions in search of this romantic land. They also provide the background for Ken Reimer's poem. (More poems by Ken on pages 75, 110, 164, and 173.)

"Siesta 'neath the sun" at Playa el Coyote.

CHAPTER 1
INTRODUCTION

Few places in the world so perfectly fit Webster's definition of a peninsula: "A portion of jutting land nearly surrounded by water." From the United States-Mexican border to Baja's tip at Cabo San Lucas is a straight-line distance of nearly 700 miles, a length greater than that of two of the world's other well-known peninsulas, Florida and the Italian boot.

This enchanting land is also unique in another manner. Baja is largely a wilderness. Except for La Paz and the border towns, it is little developed and lightly visited. It has always amazed me that such an area is located adjacent to one of the most densely populated metropolitan centers in the world. It is as if there were a magic line separating the two, and of course there is, the international border. There can be little doubt that the face of the peninsula would bear slight resemblance to what one finds today if it were a portion of the United States. Those of us who love Baja are unanimous in expressing gratitude for the presence of that border.

THE COMPRENHENSIVE GUIDEBOOK

It is perhaps a bit brazen for an author to maintain that his book is THE COMPREHENSIVE GUIDEBOOK when several other volumes on the same topic may be readily acquired. Making such a statement is a good marketing technique, but in the final analysis it will succeed only if it is true. I submit here the reasons why I believe the claim is correct, and at the same time tell you how the volume is organized and present the basic ideas on which it is founded.

Most of the space in many travel books provides descriptions of specific attractions and locales. Relatively little space is devoted to more broadly based background material concerning the total area under consideration. *The Magnificent Peninsula* devotes approximately equal attention to these two arenas. PARTS I and II provide the background. PART III, a GRAND TOUR through the entire peninsula, stresses and relies upon the PARTS I and II information. I believe it is the nature and use of this background material that makes the book comprehensive.

We will now move to a brief discussion of the three parts of this book.

PART I
BACKGROUND AND PLANNING

It is one of my principal objectives to paint the big picture rather than to provide overly finite details that may be of limited value. I hope to bring Baja alive so that you can visualize it as a whole and obtain a grasp of its major attributes and recreational attractions. But don't be misled. This does not mean you will be reading a cluster of broad generalities. As in many subjects, even the big picture can be quite complex. So it is with Baja.

The seven chapters in PART I are designed to provide BASIC background information that every visitor to Baja should know. I suggest you use PART I as a planning tool to help decide if you want to go, where you want to go, how you will travel, and in what activities you will engage. Obviously it should best be read before undertaking a visit to the Magnificent Peninsula.

In PART II we will move on to a HIGHER level of background material.

PART II
HIGHER NEEDS

Psychologists have long recognized that all human animals share certain BASIC needs for things such as food, safety, protection, care, gregariousness, love, respect, standing, status, and self-respect. Famous psychologist Abraham Maslow stresses that these elements seem to arrange themselves in a hierarchy of importance and that the demand to fulfill a particular need usually rests on some prior satisfaction of those that fall lower on the scale. Maslow also contends that at the apex of this hierarchy there is a still HIGHER group of needs which relate to the sheer quest for knowledge, understanding, and such aesthetic factors as beauty, symmetry, simplicity, and order.

OBTAIN COPIES OF THIS BOOK IN BAJA FROM

ENSENADA -- The *BAJA SUN* newspaper. 1099 Obrigon Street. See Ensenada map in Ch. 17.

SAN FELIPE -- The Papeleria 2001. On Mar de Cortez Street. See San Felipe map in Ch. 15.

MULEGE -- Mulege Divers. On Madero #45. See Mulege map in Ch. 21.

La PAZ -- La Tienda Gift Shop. Across from the Cabanas de Los Arcos. See La Paz map in Ch. 22.

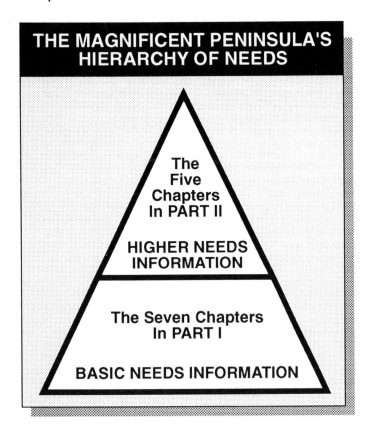

THE MAGNIFICENT PENINSULA'S HIERARCHY OF NEEDS

The Five Chapters In PART II

HIGHER NEEDS INFORMATION

The Seven Chapters In PART I

BASIC NEEDS INFORMATION

As before, it appears that these HIGHER needs only come into prominence when the BASIC list has been adequately serviced. I submit that it would be relatively easy to defend the proposition that most American and Canadian citizens who have the leisure and financial resources to visit Baja California have their BASIC needs reasonably well in hand. It follows that the fulfilling of Maslow's HIGHER needs is an important objective for many of Baja's visitors.

It is the objective of PART II of *The Magnificent Peninsula* to provide the data needed to gratify this human quest for knowledge, understanding, and the search for beauty. It does this by discussing subjects that relate to what is in plain view when one travels through Baja: land, vegetation, wildlife, places of historic interest, the people and their works. I suggest that its five chapters be read or reviewed a few days prior to making your trip so that its material will be fresh in mind. You can ignore PART II and still have a fine trip to Baja, but I urge you to absorb its contents in your quest for Maslow's higher ground.

4th EDITION NOTE — In writing the above paragraphs in the 1st edition of this book I was fearful that many readers would not share my enthusiasm for the subject matter in PART II. To my pleasant surprise, these pages have proved to be the book's most popular segment. Maslow was right.

PART III
THE GRAND TOUR

The long, craggy finger of the Baja peninsula is dominated from a transportation standpoint by the Transpeninsular Highway

(Highway 1) which extends over 1,000 miles from the international border to within a mile of the famous arch at the tip of Cabo San Lucas. In PART III, the reader is taken on a GRAND TOUR of the Baja peninsula along the highway from north to south and is directed to dozens of side trips along the way. It also includes tours of the border towns, the San Felipe area, and numerous other highways and roads.

The GRAND TOUR is packed with elements of real interest which will enhance your trip. Often these items are based upon the background material presented in PARTS I and II. PART III goes well beyond simply keeping you from getting lost and recommending where to spend the night. It features a thirty stop POINTS OF SPECIAL INTEREST Tour and other unique features which are outlined in more detail in the INTRODUCTION to PART III.

PART III is designed to be read as you make the GRAND TOUR. Of course, it may be perused as part of the planning phase prior to departure.

A FEW GROUND RULES

Preparation of *The Magnificent Peninsula* has been based on two cardinal rules.

1. I REPORT WHAT I HAVE SEEN. — This book has been written almost exclusively from my own notes and observations, supplemented in a few cases by those of trusted associates. I have reviewed the works of the authors who have preceded me but I have not pirated their accounts. In some instances I have visited coastal areas by boat but have not traveled the back roads to reach these same locations. I will alert you to these situations. In all other cases I have personally seen or investigated everything that is described. In preparing PART II, it has been necessary to base the background for much of the material on scientific literature relating to the subject in question. This is particularly true for the chapter on history. However, the specific points of interest that are noted in relation to these subjects all reflect my own observations.

2. I CONCENTRATE ON WHAT THE TRAVELER CAN SEE. — A majority of the information presented relates to objects that can easily be seen while traveling in the Magnificent Peninsula. I have refrained from relating lenghty accounts of the geologic past, the activities of nocturnal or rare desert animals or other phenomena that no one is likely to see. The history chapter provides the principal exception to this rule, but even there a special effort has been made to relate the historical account to the sites where events took place and which you may visit.

It has been a constant temptation to refer to citizens of the United States as *Americans*. I am aware that Canadians and Mexicans rightly consider that they too are Americans. To avoid offending these people, the term *North Americans* is frequently used when referring to everyone who visits Baja from *north of the border*. These terms apply to the two peoples and countries of Canada and the United States collectively.

Use of the word *California* also presents a problem. For several centuries California was everything *over there* west of the mainland of New Spain (Mexico). With the establishment of the Franciscan missions in what is now California in the United States, the northern area became *Alta California* and the name *Baja California* was applied to the peninsula itself.

The Magnificent Peninsula refers to the present State of California as Alta California, or California in the United States, in deference to our Mexican friends who might otherwise feel that the name of their land has been usurped. The peninsula as a whole is usually referred to as *Baja*, as this is a term universally used north of the border. I apologize to those in Mexico who feel that the full name Baja California is more appropriate. Also, the names Baja and the Magnificent Peninsula are used interchangeably. *The Magnificent Peninsula* is printed in italic when it refers to this book.

It has recently come to my attention that some individuals refer to Baja California as "The Baja," meaning "The Lower." I am sure most true Baja lovers would join me in endeavoring to discourage this practice.

Finally, place names in Baja are presented in Spanish. Thus, *Bahia Escondido* is not referred to as *Escondido Bay* or *Hidden Bay*. The exceptions to this rule are the *Pacific Ocean* and the *Sea of Cortez* because they are so well known in their English versions. A list of words such as *cape, bay,* and *beach*, which are frequently used in geographical place names, is given in both Spanish and English in the GLOSSARY.

SOME PERSONAL OPINIONS

Travel book authors, as a breed, tend to paint enchanting pictures of the realms they are describing. Their third person descriptions sometimes take on the tone of indisputable truths or natural laws laid down by the gods. "The place has a magic charm and is a veritable heaven on earth" not because the author says so, but because that's the way it is. Descriptions and advertisements concerning Mexico frequently fall in this category. They describe a carefree land of fiestas, mariachi music, swimming pools, and luxury hotels.

With a title like *The Magnificent Peninsula* before one, a discerning reader might conclude I have fallen victim to this same sleight of hand. Please, forgive me, one must have a catchy title or no one will notice his book. In my defense I draw attention to the fact that I have chosen to write in the first person so it will be clear "from whence comeith the word" in this volume. And now that you have been enticed into purchasing the book, and hopefully cannot retrieve your money, let me present a few personal comments aimed at bringing a note of realism to the Baja peninsula.

First of all, I sincerely believe that the Baja peninsula is magnificent. Its mountains, unique desert vegetation, coastline, people, and culture appeal to thousands of *Baja Buffs*. Others may not find it so. Baja is largely a desert. This is an inescapable reality. If deserts are an uncomfortable environment for you, *magnificent* may seem overly generous. If you have become addicted to all the finely tuned luxuries of the 20th century that are commonplace north of the border, you may be less than enchanted with Baja. What is charming, unique, or challenging to one individual may be an inconvenience to others.

It is also inescapable that the living standards in Mexico are considerably below what many of us are accustomed to in the United States and Canada. A great majority of the Mexican people you will meet are fully engaged with activities lower on Maslow's scale of needs than those at its summit. The traveler can simply overlook this situation or, preferably, will adapt a frame of mind that accepts what one encounters as part of a culture that provides a foreign country with its charm. Regrettably, I know people who find what they view as poverty in Mexico is personally offensive, even when seen from the window of a luxury hotel. Should you be one of these, your travel plans might best be directed at places other than Mexico or other developing countries.

Finally, I wish to direct your attention back to a comment presented in the opening lines of this introduction. It concerns the fact that except for the border towns, Baja is relatively unvisited. Thousands of vacationers visit Baja every year. Many return over and over, the true Baja Buffs. But their numbers are astonishingly small when one considers the enormous population living next door in the Los Angeles-San Diego area. Why isn't Baja simply overrun with tourists? I believe I know the major answer. It can be expressed in only one word. *Fear.*

At work on the book above the beach on the El Migrino Loop, south of Todos Santos. -- Tough work, but somebody has to do it.

BAJA TRAVEL CLUBS

There are several travel clubs that concentrate their activities on Baja California, plus two others whose membership is broader based. All offer discount auto insurance to their members along with a variety of other services. I recommend you consider membership in one of these organizations.

The oldest, and I believe the largest is the VAGABUNDOS DEL MAR, P. O. Box 824, Isleton, CA 95641 (707) 374-5511. They offer a monthly newsletter and feature a variety of highly enjoyable social events. It is a non-profit club and thus its services tend to be less expensive than the others. See notice on the last page of this book.

DISCOVER BAJA is a new club at press time. It advertises a full range of services. 3065-B Clairemont Dr., San Diego, CA 92117, (800) 727-2252. Other clubs are: DOS AMIGOS, 11313 Edmonson Ave., Moreno Valley, CA 92360, (800) 421-1394; SPORTSMANS, 5431 Ave Encinas, Carlsbad, CA. 92008, (800) 234-0618; MEXICO WEST, P. O. Box 1646, Bonita, CA 92002 (619) 585-3033.

The BAJA BUSH PILOTS specializes in services for the private flyer. It is described in more detail in Chapter 3 under Air Travel.

The two broader based clubs that provide services concerning Baja California are: (1) The AUTOMOBILE CLUB OF SOUTHERN CALIFORNIA, 2601 South Figueroa Street, Los Angeles, CA 90007 which publishes an excellent road map for the peninsula along with many other services, and (2) the RECREATION VEHICLE ASSOCIATION OF BRITISH COLUMBIA, P.O. Box 2977, Vancouver, B. C. V6B 3X4. (604) 581 0745. This organization publishes the R. V. Times and sponsors rallies and other special events for its members.

I have given considerable thought to bringing forth this subject. Is it wise for a travel book author to raise the potential of something negative about the area he is promoting? Obviously I have decided to do so. Proceeding otherwise would be to ignore what is all too apparent; that is, that many people are frightened to travel in Mexico. Some may fear the language barrier or the potential for becoming ill. But many more are concerned with the potential for crime and harassment from dishonest public officials.

To deny that there are such officials, or to proclaim that there is no crime in Baja, would be inaccurate. But the level of anxiety experienced by the North American public is blown far out of proportion with reality. Press reports of crime and violence in the United States and of unrest in Central America lead me to conclude that Baja must be the safest place on this continent.

I have discussed the fear issue with Baja Buffs camped on the beaches and otherwise absorbed in the beauty and remoteness of the Magnificent Peninsula. Many concur that there is a fear problem, but I have been universally and firmly requested not to do anything to remedy the situation. They well know that their favorite haunts will become overwhelmed with tourists if this conceptual barrier is removed.

In closing this issue, I must note that I have stayed the night alone or with a single friend in scores of the most remote coves, beaches, and villages in Baja. I have never been treated with anything but friendship and courtesy, a remarkable record considering that I sport an often unkempt beard and have never been nominated as a candidate for Mr. Neat. Thousands of visitors go to Mexico without fear. I hope you will join us, but please don't tell many others. The Baja Buffs will crucify me.

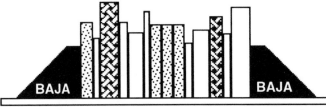

| See the **BAJA BOOKSHELF** in the Appendix | | See the **BAJA BOOKSHELF** in the Appendix |

BAJA BOOKSHELF

The BAJA BOOKSHELF offers the Baja Buff an array of publications concerning Baja California. Some were written specifically about the peninsula. Others are the best available books dealing with subjects related to Baja such as wildlife, Spanish, etc. Each represents my choice of the best title available on the subject.

Order books directly from the BAJA BOOKSHELF in the Appendix, or upon request we will send you more complete information on any book, including new titles that were not available when the THE MAGNIFICENT PENINSULA was published.

Jack Williams

PART I
BACKGROUND
AND PLANNING

BAJA'S FASCINATING CIRIO
BACKED BY OTHER SONORAN
DESERT VEGETATION.

CHAPTER 2
THE BIG PICTURE

Much of the world's information is best understood if presented through the art of classification. For this reason, I will be continually breaking Baja and many of its principal subjects into segments or areas. The first of these will be a vertical slice in which we will examine four zones that run more or less north-south. I say more or less because in reality, the Baja peninsula extends closer to northwest-southeast than true north and south. The four zones are: (1) Baja's Pacific coast, (2) Baja's Sea of Cortez coast, (3) the interior, and (4) Mexico's mainland coast (north half). The last zone may come as a surprise because it isn't a part of Baja. The reason for its inclusion will be explained in due course.

THE VERTICAL SLICE

BAJA'S PACIFIC COAST — Measuring a line drawn along the edge of the many projections of Baja's interface with the Pacific Ocean would disclose a largely deserted coastline of approximately 1,000 miles. Inclusion of the many bays and lagoons would add hundreds of additional miles. The startling fact is how little of this shore is readily accessible to tourists who travel to Baja by conventional two-wheel-drive vehicles and whose temperaments require them to stay on the main roads. This description fits the majority of those who visit Baja by road.

Traveling from the international border to Cabo San Lucas over Highways 1 and 19 is a trip of approximately 1,025 miles. I have inventoried this route in terms of coastal accessibility and found that only some 230 miles of highway provide access to the Pacific Ocean. (See COASTAL ACCESSIBILITY Map.) If anything, these estimates are generous. In most places the ocean is not visible from the highway, and side roads must be used to reach the water's edge. Conditions are similar on the Sea of Cortez coast. As the great majority of tourists traveling to Baja by road are destined for seashore areas, it is important to understand this situation.

There are several sizeable villages and many *fish camps* along those sections of the Pacific coast that are not readily accessible from the main highway. These are regularly visited by yachts making the Baja Passage and by a few land-based travelers whose equipment and interests lead them to explore the hundreds of miles of secondary and lower standard roads. These communities provide a fascinating contrast with life as we know it north of the border. Visiting them, one finds it hard to believe they are so close to the metropolitan centers of southwestern United States.

Several other subjects must be presented to complete the big picture of the Baja peninsula's Pacific coast. The first concerns the weather. Most travel south from the border towns in Baja takes place in late fall, winter, and early spring. (Most of the principal tourist areas are a bit hot during summer and early fall.) These travelers are seeking escape from a variety of adverse weather conditions north of the border. Unfortunately Baja's Pacific coast north of about Bahia Magdalena does not present a significant contrast to the weather in coastal areas of southern and central Alta California. Clearly, rain decreases as one travels south, but temperatures remain cool. Fog or low clouds often prevail. It is not the warm *swimsuit-lie-in-the-sun* weather most people are seeking in sunny Mexico.

The next big picture subject for the Pacific coast concerns the ocean itself. While the coast is largely deserted, there is much activity on the surface and within the ocean waters. Each year thousands of yachtsmen cruise from San Diego to Cabo San Lucas and beyond. Mexican fishing vessels in the 70-foot class are numerous, and these in turn are far outnumbered by shorter range, outboard-powered

Typical section of Baja's Pacific Coast where the surf pounds on rocky, sparsely vegetated cliffs. — Photo taken north of Playa los Cerritos. (See Chapter 24.)

COASTAL AREAS ACCESSIBLE FROM PRINCIPAL HIGHWAYS

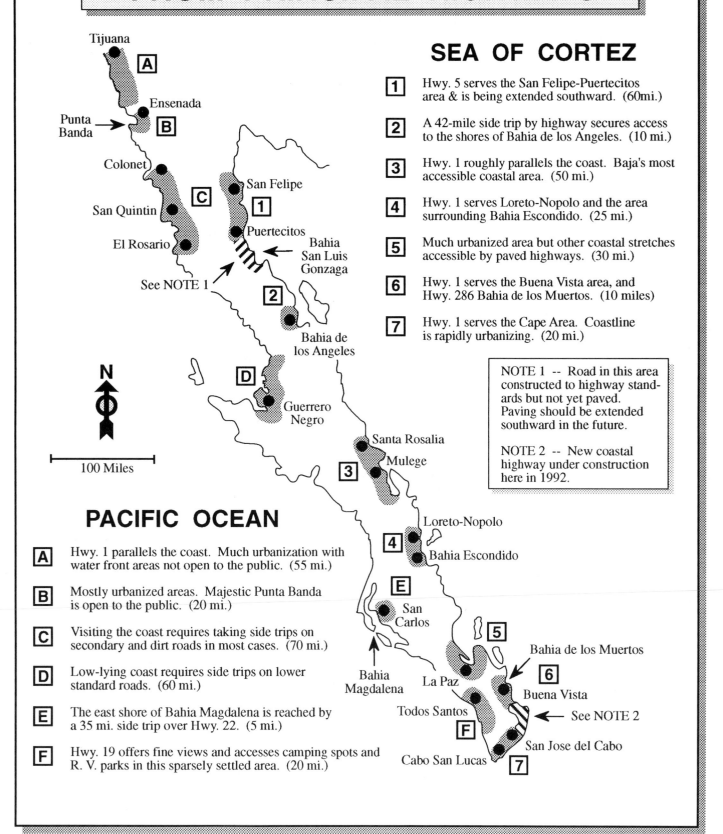

SEA OF CORTEZ

1 Hwy. 5 serves the San Felipe-Puertecitos area & is being extended southward. (60mi.)

2 A 42-mile side trip by highway secures access to the shores of Bahia de los Angeles. (10 mi.)

3 Hwy. 1 roughly parallels the coast. Baja's most accessible coastal area. (50 mi.)

4 Hwy. 1 serves Loreto-Nopolo and the area surrounding Bahia Escondido. (25 mi.)

5 Much urbanized area but other coastal stretches accessible by paved highways. (30 mi.)

6 Hwy. 1 serves the Buena Vista area, and Hwy. 286 Bahia de los Muertos. (10 miles)

7 Hwy. 1 serves the Cape Area. Coastline is rapidly urbanizing. (20 mi.)

NOTE 1 -- Road in this area constructed to highway standards but not yet paved. Paving should be extended southward in the future.

NOTE 2 -- New coastal highway under construction here in 1992.

PACIFIC OCEAN

A Hwy. 1 parallels the coast. Much urbanization with water front areas not open to the public. (55 mi.)

B Mostly urbanized areas. Majestic Punta Banda is open to the public. (20 mi.)

C Visiting the coast requires taking side trips on secondary and dirt roads in most cases. (70 mi.)

D Low-lying coast requires side trips on lower standard roads. (60 mi.)

E The east shore of Bahia Magdalena is reached by a 35 mi. side trip over Hwy. 22. (5 mi.)

F Hwy. 19 offers fine views and accesses camping spots and R. V. parks in this sparsely settled area. (20 mi.)

100 Miles

pangas engaged in fishing and lobstering. I am convinced that there is considerably more traffic on these waters than off the Pacific coast of the U.S. mainland.

Below the surface there is abundant fish life. The ocean off the central portion of the Baja peninsula is the most productive fishing area of the entire Mexican Pacific coast. These waters are also the winter home of the California gray whale which uses Baja's protected lagoons as its calving grounds.

South of the Ensenada area there is an almost total absence of the small, tourist-owned, sportfishing boats which are common-place in the Sea of Cortez. The reasons for this situation are the lack of launching ramps and surf conditions which make launching over the beach and use of the ocean itself a bit hazardous. Swells sweep onto the peninsula from the northwest unobstucted for thousands of miles. While they severely limit the use of small boats, they make the Pacific coast a fine area for surfing. It is also a scenic coast with its rocky outline and pounding surf. You will find the small boating and surfing situations reversed on the calmer waters of the Sea of Cortez.

Finally, as a by-product of the conditions just mentioned, the Pacific coast south of Ensenada has few tourist-oriented facilities, although this situation is changing south of Todas Santos. The few hotels and trailer courts are usually not visited as destinations in themselves but only as stopping points on the journey to the east coast or the peninsula's tip. The people in the towns along the Pacific side make their living from farming, cattle raising, fishing, and mining. Relatively few serve the traveling public. These towns offer little of the architectural and landscaping charms common in the more tourist-oriented areas.

BAJA'S SEA OF CORTEZ COAST — We will now proceed across to the eastern coast of the peninsula. The body of water between Baja California and the Mexican mainland is referred to as the Gulf of California on most maps, even those printed in Mexico. However, to most Mexicans and many North American tourists it is known as the Sea of Cortez (Mar de Cortez) in honor of conquistador Hernan Cortez, and that is what it will be called in this book.

Traveling south to Cabo San Lucas entirely on the Transpeninsular Highway (Highway 1) is 34 miles longer than is the combination of Highway 1 and Highway 19 through Todos Santos. Taking the former route provides access to the Sea of Cortez. An inventory of accessibility, as was done for the Pacific side, shows that 145 miles of coast are made accessible by the main highways. An additional 60 miles can be reached in the San Felipe area and this will be increased as paving of Highway 5 continues southward. Fortunately, many additional miles of the coast are made accessible by secondary and lower standard roads. Also, on the positive side is the fact that hundreds of miles of unroaded peninsular and offshore-island coast is available to boaters as a result of good boating conditions in the Sea of Cortez.

Because of the differences in the two coasts, the mileages presented are of minimal value when compared directly with each other. The key point is that relatively few miles of the main

SUMMARY COMPARISON OF PACIFIC OCEAN & SEA OF CORTEZ		
ITEM	**PACIFIC OCEAN**	**SEA OF CORTEZ**
OCEAN WATERS	Heavy northwest swells. Boat launching difficult. Good surfing. Water is cold.	Seas flat except in high winds. Easy boat launching. Good wind surfing and swimming.
HOTELS & TRAILER COURTS	Numerous from Ensenada north. Few south of Ensenada & little visited as destination points.	Numerous at San Felipe and in the southern half from Santa Rosalia to Cabo San Lucas.
TOURIST SEASON WEATHER	Cool north of Bahia Magdalena, warmer to south. Some fog. Northwest winds.	Generally warmer and dryer than the Pacific coast. Winds from the north.
CAMPING	Some camping spots, but most are lightly used due to cool ocean and weather conditions.	Numerous camping spots. Many heavily used because of good weather and ocean conditions.

highways provide direct coastal access on either shore. Obviously the traveler needs to know where the principal tourist areas are located. This information is presented later in this chapter.

One shoreline condition applies to both coasts. Baja is a mountainous land. Where these mountains meet the sea both coastlines are rocky, steep-faced, and majestic. Beaches are small but picturesque. This situation is typical of some 75-80 percent of the Baja coast. Vegetation is sparse and there is little soil. The mountains stand out sharply with their geologic features clearly visible. The colors and textures of their rocks are readily apparent. These coastal sections are beautiful to behold, particularly when viewed from the sea itself.

The remaining 20-25 percent of the coast consists of low coastal plains fronted by scores of miles of deserted beaches. Most of these are seldom visited and are on the Pacific side. In any event, you may be assured that there are miles of beautiful, although generally smaller, beaches at all of the popular tourist areas.

Campers on the beach north of Punta Chivato on the Sea of Cortez. — Photo taken on a windy day at an exposed location but swells are low and gentle compared to those on the Pacific coast.

It is important for the traveler to realize that there are marked differences in the surf conditions between the two coasts. The Sea of Cortez lacks the pounding swells which are an ever-present condition on the Pacific side. The peninsula's picturesque rocky tip at Cabo San Lucas is generally considered to be the dividing point between the Pacific Ocean and the Sea of Cortez. The Pacific swells dissipate rapidly beyond the cape and disappear completely approximately 50 miles to the NE. With few swells in the Sea of Cortez, it is relatively easy to launch small boats over the beach, and swimming is far safer than on the Pacific side. While this is good news for boaters and swimmers, surfing enthusiasts will be disappointed along with those travelers who enjoy the picturesque breaking of waves on a rock-bound coast. Except during high wind conditions, the water's edge on Baja's east side takes on the characteristics of a large inland lake.

From what has been presented, you may have concluded that the Sea of Cortez coast provides home for most of the principal tourist areas in Baja; if so, you are correct.

THE INTERIOR — A prominent backbone of mountains dominates the entire western edge of the continents of North and South America, with large bellies of flatter lands to the east. The mountains of Baja parallel these ranges, but in Baja the terrain is mostly backbone with relatively little belly.

One more or less continuous chain of mountains runs the full length of the peninsula with only one brief interruption, near La Paz (See GEOLOGIC PROVINCES map in Chapter 9). The crest of this chain rims the eastern side of the peninsula with most of the flat land found along the southern half of the Pacific

coast. It is, however, important to qualify these remarks for those of you who plan to drive to Baja. While the peninsula is mountainous, traversing Baja's highways is not an arduous task for a variety of reasons that will be discussed in Chapter 3. Many of you will be exposed to artists' renditions of the peninsula's mountains on the covers and pages of maps and guidebooks. A considerable number of these are badly exaggerated and could easily frighten the faint of heart into staying home. There are many highways in the United States and Canada that traverse far more difficult terrain.

Almost all of Baja's significant cities and towns are located within a few miles of the coasts. Few are in the interior. The area's most dominant feature is man-made: the Transpeninsular Highway. By North American standards it is a modest accomplishment, but its completion in 1973 was of monumental importance for the future of Baja. It is the principal way for the tourist to travel by land to the peninsula's primary destination areas along the southern portion of the Sea of Cortez.

The interior of the peninsula also provides habitat for the best of Baja's outstanding desert vegetation. Neither coast can match the higher lands in this regard.

MEXICAN MAINLAND COAST / NORTH HALF The area under consideration lies directly opposite the Baja peninsula and is the eastern shore of the Sea of Cortez. It is shown on the TRANSPORTATION Map in Chapter 3.

Any map that depicts topography will show that most of this coastal area is composed of flat terrain. This condition extends south from the mouth of the Rio Colorado for about 1,000 miles to near the town of Tepic, south of Mazatlan. While sailing along this coast, one is confronted with hundreds of miles of deserted and monotonous sandy beaches backed by sparsely vegetated, low coastal plains and marshes. From a scenic standpoint, the two Baja coastlines are hands-down winners over their mainland neighbor. The mainland highway from the United States, Highway 15, offers almost no views of the coast or the Sea of Cortez.

Still, there are some scenic areas on the mainland, the principal ones being at Bahia Kino, Guaymas, and Mazatlan. These three areas, along with Puerto Penasco to the north, attract almost all the North American tourists. Guaymas, more accurately the town of San Carlos just to the north, has a large winter tourist population. It is a Mexican Phoenix, a haven for retirees and others escaping the northern winter. Mazatlan also is a fine town with excellent beaches and many tourists.

Why do so many people choose the mainland instead of Baja? It is partly a matter of transportation routes. It is closer to the mainland than to Baja from the United States intermountain west. Its cities are large and provide abundant trailer courts and hotels. Because people are attracted to other people, they feel more secure in such places. Perhaps, most importantly, Baja is remote, unknown, and *over there*.

The point of this discussion is to give you the information needed to make a choice. I don't wish to downgrade the mainland, but alas, the scenery in Baja is better, the boating and camping areas are far more extensive, the choice of destination points is larger, the hotels are more charming, etc., etc., etc. However, should you crave the company of large numbers of your fellow North Americans in a trailer court atmosphere or at highrise hotels, and the amenities of large nearby cities, the mainland may be best for you.

SIX PRINCIPAL TOURIST AREAS

Having sliced Baja vertically, we will now reassemble it and classify the peninsula into six principal tourist areas. (See SIX PRINCIPAL TOURIST AREAS Map). These are:

1	—	Tijuana-Ensenada Area
2	—	San Felipe-Puertecitos Area
3	—	Bahia de los Angeles
4	—	Central Coast
5	—	La Paz
6	—	The South Coast

1 TIJUANA / ENSENADA AREA — Poised at the international border and eager to entice North American tourists are the city of Tijuana and the smaller town of Tecate. Ensenada lies sixty-eight miles south along the Pacific coast. Between the two large cities are numerous tourist-oriented subdivisions and other developments. The number of visitors to these communities is very sizeable. Tijuana boasts of being visited by more people from a foreign country than any other city in the world.

The large city of Mexicali also lies on the international border. Many people living and working in adjoining areas in the United States visit here, but it would appear that much of their activities are not related to tourism. At least in my view, Mexicali is not a tourist-oriented city.

Here are the highlights of this area:

(a) The most accessible area from the United States. Many visitors walk across the border to visit Tijuana. The place to go if you have only a day or two. Otherwise, head south.

(b) A bonanza for buying gifts and Mexican handicrafts of all kinds. Many of these items are typical tourist fare, but there is also much quality merchandise available.

(c) Excellent party-boat sportfishing at Ensenada.

(d) Several trailer courts, hotels, and thousands of second, and some first, homes for North Americans along the coast south to Punta Banda. There are very few places left for camping outside the developed trailer courts.

2 SAN FELIPE-PUERTECITOS AREA — San Felipe is the northernmost communitiy along the Sea of Cortez. The town is modest in size but heavily tourist oriented and provides all essential services. There are several good hotels. There are miles of beachs lined with housing developments, trailer courts and more modest *campos*. Visitation to this area will greatly increase when the paving of Highway 5 is completed south to Highway 1 (See discussion at the beginning of Chapter 15).

(a) The quickest way for most North Americans to hit the beach on the Sea of Cortez. It is 127 miles by highway from the border at Mexicali.

(b) Winter temperatures not as balmy as farther south, and it is hot in the summer.

(c) Many long-term trailer sites, but also a good spot for the long weekender.

(d) Puertecitos, a small town of Norte Americano homes 48 miles south of San Felipe, is accessible over a paved highway.

(e) A few low hills near San Felipe provide a scenic coast, but much of the shoreline is one continuous long sandy beach backed by low coastal plains. The desert vegetation is relatively unattractive. Thus the scenery is not as good as other areas to the south, although the towering Sierra San Pedro Martir mountains are in view to the west.

(f) No nearby offshore islands, and tidal differences of up to 20 feet make small boat launching difficult.

3 BAHIA DE LOS ANGELES — Located here is a sizeable bay with miles of beaches protected by several offshore islands. A small village offers modest services.

SIX PRINCIPAL TOURIST AREAS

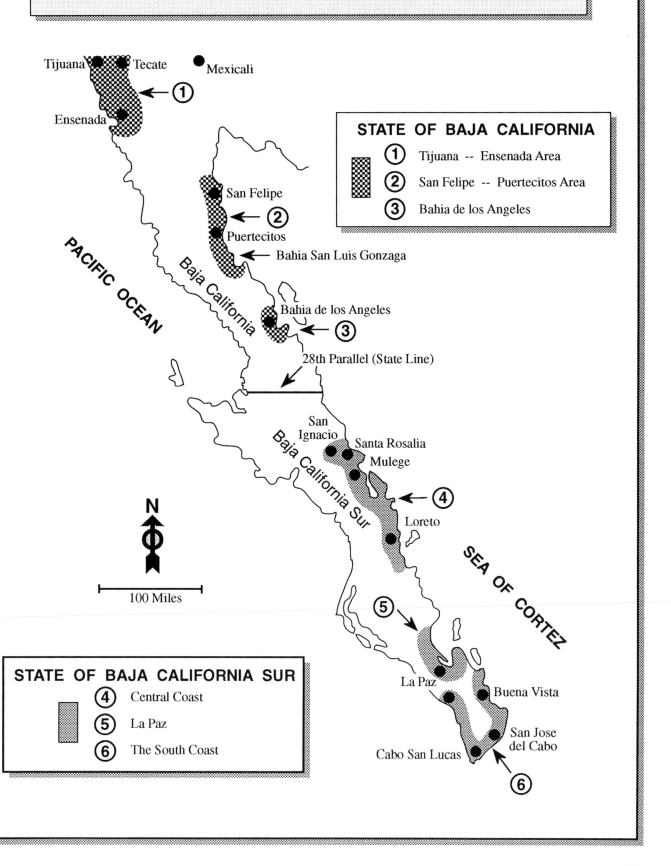

Tijuana · Tecate · Mexicali

① (arrow)

Ensenada

STATE OF BAJA CALIFORNIA

① Tijuana -- Ensenada Area

② San Felipe -- Puertecitos Area

③ Bahia de los Angeles

San Felipe

② (arrow)

Puertecitos

Bahia San Luis Gonzaga

PACIFIC OCEAN

Baja California

Bahia de los Angeles

③ (arrow)

28th Parallel (State Line)

San Ignacio · Santa Rosalia · Mulege

Baja California Sur

④ (arrow)

Loreto

N

100 Miles

SEA OF CORTEZ

⑤ (arrow)

La Paz · Buena Vista

San Jose del Cabo

Cabo San Lucas

⑥ (arrow)

STATE OF BAJA CALIFORNIA SUR

④ Central Coast

⑤ La Paz

⑥ The South Coast

(a) Two hotels and several trailer courts. There are also several miles of undeveloped beaches north of the village offering camping sites.

(b) Reaching the area requires a 42 mile side trip from the Transpeninsular Highway. The total distance to Tijuana is 415 miles, making it a very long one-day trip from the border.

(c) A scenic mountainous area with a good mixture of beaches and rocky coast but with relatively unattractive desert vegetation. The nearby coast and offshore islands contain many coves and provide good boating and fishing.

(d) The least visited of the six principal tourist areas.

4 CENTRAL COAST — This is one of the principal destination areas in Baja. It features three coastal, and one inland town. (Santa Rosalia, Mulege, Loreto, and San Ignacio.)

(a) Each town has its charms and all are worth exploring.

(b) The late winter and spring weather is balmy. This is what you came to Baja to experience.

(c) Several first-class hotels and other more modest ones, but fewer than farther south. Served by an international airport at Loreto.

(d) Many trailer courts and minimum facility beach parking areas. The most popular R.V. and camping area in Baja.

(e) Good combination of beaches and rocky coast backdropped by the most scenic mountains in Baja. Numerous offshore islands and coves. Fine area for fishing and overnight trips by small boat.

5 LA PAZ — A fine, large, modern community and the capital city of Baja California Sur. Thought by many, including myself, to be the finest large city in Mexico.

(a) Several fine luxury hotels served by an international airport. A large new hotel development is planned south of town.

(b) City fronts the beach on a protected bay, but the main attraction here is the weather and the city itself.

(c) There are several trailer courts, but the central and south coasts are superior if your objective is to enjoy the beach and the out-of-doors.

(d) Excellent modern stores. The only really good shopping area south of the border towns although there are many tourist oriented shops at Cabo San Lucas.

(e) Good, but sometimes windy, winter weather. Winter weather not as good as in the Cape Area.

(f) Sportfishing boats are available. You can use your own small boat but other areas are better suited for such craft.

6 THE SOUTH COAST — The U-shaped area capping the peninsula's southern tip has developed into three distinct zones. These are;

THE CAPE AREA -- At the peninsula's tip and between the small communities of Cabo San Lucas and San Jose del Cabo is Baja's principal hotel, condominium, and golf course area. This development has been going on for over 10 years and the end is no where in sight. It is served by an international airport. There are several good trailer courts but only one is on the beach. On-your-own camping on the beach is a thing of the past.

THE EAST CAPE -- On the right side of the South Coast-U is the East Cape. There are several good but modest-sized hotels, and trailer courts at and near Buena Vista. It is the place to go to experience the older Baja hotel charm without the jet-set-bustle that has developed at the Cape Area. There are many undeveloped camping sites south of Buena Vista but an oiled highway is currently being extended from north to south along the coast which will change the complexion of the area.

Both the Cape Area and the East Cape are famed for their marlin and other big-game fishing. This fishery is amongst the best in the world.

THE WEST CAPE -- This section of coast was basically undeveloped until Highway 19 was completed in 1984. There is one small hotel in Todos Santos and several trailer courts and fine beach camping areas between there and the Cape. This is the area to go for free-lance beach campers who have been forced out of the Cape Area by urban development.

BAJA'S CLIMATE

Two circumstances dominate the climate of Baja California. As is obvious to any visitor, the peninsula is an arid land. The reasons for this situation are discussed in the BAJA'S DESERT LANDS Section in Chapter 10 VEGETATION. The low level of precipitation is key in determining vegetational characteristics.

Of equal but less apparent importance is the variability of the climate from one area to another, from season to season, and from year to year. Most of the time the peninsula receives no rainfall because it lies outside the normal influence of any of the major weather systems in this part of the world, but by a twist of geographic fate it lies near the outer edge of several such systems. It is the occasional impact from these entities that creates climatic variability in Baja.

Baja lies (1) at the southern edge of the winter storms that bring plentiful rainfall to the west coast of the United States and

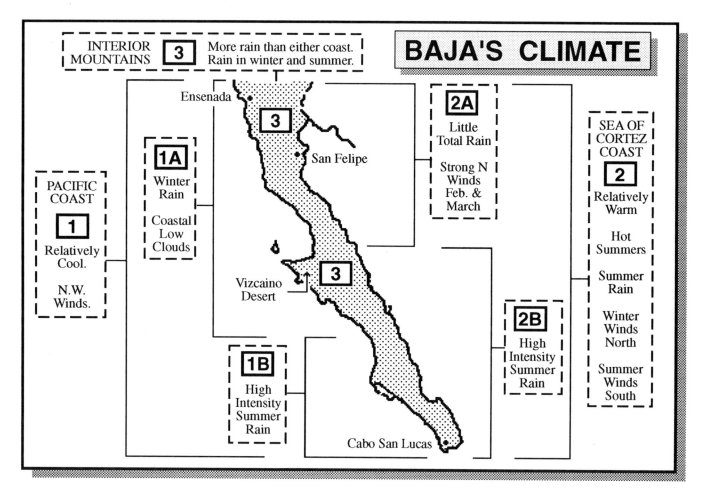

BAJA'S CLIMATE

INTERIOR MOUNTAINS **3** More rain than either coast. Rain in winter and summer.

2A Little Total Rain — Strong N Winds Feb. & March

SEA OF CORTEZ COAST **2** Relatively Warm — Hot Summers — Summer Rain — Winter Winds North — Summer Winds South

PACIFIC COAST **1** Relatively Cool. N.W. Winds.

1A Winter Rain — Coastal Low Clouds

1B High Intensity Summer Rain

2B High Intensity Summer Rain

Ensenada

San Felipe

Vizcaino Desert

Cabo San Lucas

Canada, (2) at the western perimeter of the monsoons formed over the Gulf of Mexico that bring precipitation to northern Mexico and southwestern United States in the summer, and (3) at the northeastern fringe of the region of tropical storms and hurricanes that form off the west coast of the Mexican mainland in late summer and fall.

The overall effect of these systems is summarized on a map labeled BAJA'S CLIMATE. The following statements relate to the zones depicted on this map.

1. The air temperature along the full length of Baja's Pacific coast is relatively cool as the result of prevailing northwest winds which move inland over the cool waters of the Pacific Ocean.

1A. The northern segment of the Pacific coast receives its rainfall during winter from the southern edges of the same storm systems that impact the coast of the United States and Canada. The average annual rainfall at Ensenada is about eleven inches, but from here south to Bahia Magdalena records show only three to four inches per year. The vegetation in the Vizcaino Desert at the midpoint of the peninsula is extremely scant.

1B. Rainfall picks up along the southern Pacific coast with Cabo San Lucas receiving an average of over nine inches per year. In contrast to area 1A, this precipitation comes mostly from high-

intensity tropical storms that breed in the warm waters to the south during late summer and fall.

2. The Sea of Cortez coast is much warmer than that on the Pacific side. Some of the hotels in the Cape Area close during summer. To the north, San Felipe has the highest summer temperature of any of Baja's tourist areas.

2A. During the winter, temperatures at San Felipe are almost as chilly as at Ensenada. This coolness is aggravated by strong northerly winds funneling down the Sea of Cortez from southwestern United States. This is Baja's driest area, but what little rain does fall comes in the winter.

2B. As on the Pacific coast, most of the rainfall comes from high-intensity tropical storms in the late fall and summer. Winter months windy.

3. Baja's interior mountains receive considerably more rainfall than either coastal area. Also, they are battered by storms in both winter and summer. The winter systems are the same as those that dampen area 1A. The summer rain comes from systems in the Gulf of Mexico that also pass over the Mexican mainland and SW United States.

A final note concerning *El Nino*, an unusual warming of Pacific ocean waters off Central and North America every few years.

Lost again, but we found a tall friend, Senor Cardon.

The winter of 1991-92 was an El Nino year. Southern California in the United States received near record rain storms and the Baja peninsula received abundant winter precipitation. This occurred not only in the northern area but in the southern portions which normally receive their rainfall in the late summer.

The result was a less than fully desirable vacation to Baja for tourists seeking endless sunshine. Travel on back roads was also hazardous due to muddy conditions. On the bright side was a wonderful display of lush desert vegetation and flowers. So keep alert to the occasional occurrence of El Nino and brace for unusual weather conditions in Baja.

In evaluating all this material, keep in mind the key factor of variability. One can only hope that you will not find yourself recovering from a trip through the arid desert one day and hiking ankle deep in the runoff from a tropical storm the next. And remember, I am not in charge of the weather. Contact *You Know Who*.

WHEN TO VISIT

1 — Be alert, that most tourists visit Baja in the winter months (November through March). That is not when the peninsular weather is at its best, but it is when conditions at home north of the border are at their worst, and when escape is most needed. After Easter, there is a dramatic drop-off of tourism in Baja.

2 — I recommend April, May, and June as the best months to visit Baja's east coast and cape areas. Temperatures are warm, and the often chilly winter winds that sweep down the Sea of Cortez have ceased. Many beaches and other camping areas are uncomfortably cool and windy in the winter months. And there are far fewer other tourists with whom to contend after Easter.

3 — If fishing is your primary goal, go south in the summer (July through October). Air temperatures are hot, and sea waters warm. The latter condition induces the game fish to migrate north into the Sea of Cortez. Summer is also the time to visit the many isolated camping and fishing areas along the cooler Pacific shore south of Ensenada.

BAJA'S TWO STATES

There are two states in the Baja peninsula. The dividing line is the 28th parallel of northern latitude. (See SIX PRINCIPAL TOURIST AREAS Map.)

There is little question that the southern state is *Baja California Sur* (south). Its capital city is La Paz. In contrast, there is much confusion about the name of the northern state with its capital in Mexicali. I have investigated this matter in considerable depth and can guarantee with absolute certainty that its name is *Baja California* (probably). This is the name used on state documents, stationery, license plates, and many other places. Government officials have assured me that this is the proper name.

Other officials firmly attest that the name is *Baja California Norte* (north). I have seen this title on the doors of government offices and in official publications, travel guides, and numerous other places. You may call it what you choose. I believe Baja California is correct.

BAJA BOATER'S GUIDE

The two volume BAJA BOATER'S GUIDE contains 350 low level, oblique aerial photos of all important areas along both Baja coasts. It is thus a valuable tool for all seashore travel whether it be by land or water. See Chapter 5 for more details.

CHAPTER 3
TRANSPORTATION

By now, the reader will have little difficulty in forecasting that it is possible to travel to Baja by land, sea, or air. These alternatives will be discussed in that order.

LAND TRAVEL

The Magnificent Peninsula provides information concerning all methods of transportation, but the great majority of its readers are looking for data on the land itself and how to travel to Baja by road. Thus, much of the remainder of the book is devoted to these subjects.

THE TRANSPENINSULAR HIGHWAY — The Transpeninsular Highway is Mexican Federal Highway 1 and 1-D. Officially it is La Carretera Transpeninsular Benito Juarez. It traverses the full length of the peninsula from the international border to Cabo San Lucas, a distance of 1,057.468 miles to the inch. How do I know so accurately? I have consulted five references to the length of the highway, each of which is different. I have added all these offerings together and divided by five, a method I'm sure will be understood by my high school mathematics instructor who gave me a D in his subject.

The five sources provide answers from 1,042 as a low to a high of 1,067. For the balance of this book I will use 1,059 miles as this is the distance given on the widely used map distributed by the Auto Club of Southern California. It has to be close.

Baja's citizens waited through many decades of promises by Mexico's presidential candidates before witnessing completion of the Transpeninsular Highway. At long last, on December 1, 1973, President Luis Echeverria Alvarez fulfilled his promise to build the road and dedicated its completion at the 28th parallel near Guerrero Negro. The actual completion had taken place when road building crews from north and south met the previous October near what is now named Catavina in the plateau lands some 75 miles south of El Rosario. The President was apparently motivated to action after being treated to a trip over the old road, known to its travelers as "The Trail." By all accounts such a trip was an adventure. The new highway is a monumental leap forward.

Prior to describing Highway 1, I will repeat an opinion expressed in this books introductory chapter. There I promised to be realistic in my descriptions of the beauty and charms of Baja, as I feel that many authors stray from reality in their use of adjectives and in their efforts to achieve literary merit. Even more disconcerting to me are those authors who create literary horror stories when providing cautionary advice. This often becomes the case when they are describing the Transpeninsular Highway. I have seen articles which would frighten even the most stout-hearted traveler into staying home. What are, in truth, reasons for caution become blown out of proportion by overly poetic adjectives and a sense of the dramatic. I will steer for the middle ground.

The Transpeninsular Highway is paved its entire distance. It is well engineered. Appropriate banking and curves allow for adequate visibility if you drive at reasonable speeds. Some 44 percent of its length is over hilly terrain but grades (steepness) are modest and not overly demanding for vehicles that are adequately powered. The remaining 56 percent passes over level ground. The highway is generally well maintained. One frequently sees crews doing everything from cutting roadside weeds to applying new oiled surfacing. Sections of the highway may be seen in several photos in this and other chapters.

But Highway 1 does have its shortcomings, any of which can result in serious accidents or inconvenience if you violate one of two cardinal rules. These are, (1) don't drive at high speeds and (2) don't drive at night. Here is a list of the negative features:

1. — With the exception of the northerly most 80 miles, the highway is narrow. Most of it has a travel surface only 24-feet wide. Its narrowness is heightened by the almost total lack of a shoulder. There is little margin for error and if you slip off the travel surface you face the very serious threat of rolling over, particularly if you are in a recreation vehicle with a high center of gravity. Thus what is otherwise a fine highway is compromised by its lack of width.

2. — A large part of Baja is open range. Thus the roadside is not fenced, and cattle and other animals may be encountered, particularly at night when they are attracted by the warmth of the road surface.

3. — There are few turnouts or other places to move off the travel surface. It is not uncommon to come upon a vehicle blocking one lane of the highway while the driver is engaged in some roadside activity or correcting a mechanical problem.

4. — The major arroyo crossings have been bridged; however, hundreds of the lesser crossings are designed to let water flow over the highway during storms. These dips (*vados*) provide no problem most of the time, but they can be full of water, rocks, and soil during and after heavy storms.

A typical segment of the Transpeninsular Highway (Highway 1) north of Bahia Concepcion.

5. — There are occasional potholes which can be very hard on tires if hit at high speeds. I have found that areas of potholes encountered one year have been repaired the next, but others take their place.

6. — Finally, for the person of environmental sensitivity, there is one unfortunate problem with the Transpeninsular Highway. All new roads in Baja are constructed by first clearing the right-of-way of all vegetation with a bulldozer or grader. In most places various plants are returning but there is an almost total lack of the larger and more picturesque species that make the Baja desert spectacular. The vegetation is often outstanding but unfortunately is a few yards removed.

Traveling the Transpeninsular Highway can be a safe and rewarding experience if it is driven at reasonable speeds during daylight hours. Insurance industry data indicate that some 80 percent of the accidents on Baja's highways occur at night. And, what are safe speeds? A travel time estimate provided by one of the Mexican insurance companies indicates that it would take 23-3/4 hours to drive the 991 miles from Ensenada to Cabo San Lucas. This equates to 42 miles per hour. I would have estimated 40 miles per hour. You can do it faster, but you should not.

BAJA'S OTHER ROADS — From 1973 until about 1983 there were few paved roads other than the Transpeninsular Highway. The location of this road appears to have been planned to connect the peninsula's principal communities over the most cost effective route. As stressed in Chapter two, it provides little direct access to the seaside areas most sought after by tourists.

From 1983 until about 1989 many additional miles of highway standard roads were constructed along with hundreds of miles of

gravel surfaced secondary roads. The new highway routes are clearly designed to access currently undeveloped coastal areas. As of 1992 some of these highway standard roads were completed and oiled while other sections were left unfinished and unsurfaced. The majority of these new highways are in six places with the location of the unfinished sections shown with question marks (?) on the TRANSPORTATION Map in this chapter.

My inspection of the peninsula in spring 1992 disclosed that little new highway or road construction of interest to the tourist had taken place since 1989, and five of the six new highway routes remained unchanged. The sixth route between La Ribera and San Jose del Cabo in the East Cape area was rapidly being complete (See Chapter 23 for details).

Completion of all six new highways will make major changes in recreational travel and will divert travelers from Highway 1 to coastal areas. In particular, the completion of Highway 5 south of San Felipe will provide a totally new approach road to southern Baja which will bypass the northern 1/3 of the Transpeninsular Highway and the congestion of the Tijuana and Ensenada areas. Many travelers will also be able to skirt the maddening and dangerous Los Angeles and San Diego freeway systems. "Let's hear it for Highway 5." (See Chapter 15 for more details.) You should be alert to additional construction activity in all six areas just noted even though my most recent inspection showed limited current activity.

As a result of the recent road construction activity just discussed, Baja's roads may be classified rather neatly into four classes. These are described below.

HIGHWAYS (PAVED) — There are approximately 800 miles of main paved highways in Baja in addition to the Transpeninsular Highway. Roughly 550 miles are in the northern state of Baja California, with the remaining 250 in Baja California Sur. These figures do not include a considerable additional mileage of paved roads within the Valle de Mexicali agricultural area adjoining the international border and occasional short roads in other places.

I have driven all 800 miles of these highways and have concluded that they have all been engineered to approximately the same standards as the Transpeninsular Highway. Thus, they are all adequate facilities and in general are safer than the Transpeninsular Highway as there is often less traffic and fewer wide trucks, buses, and recreational vehicles. Most of these 800 miles of highway are shown on the TRANSPORTATION Map in this chapter.

HIGHWAY STANDARD (NOT PAVED) — In Baja, all construction work up to final paving is usually completed

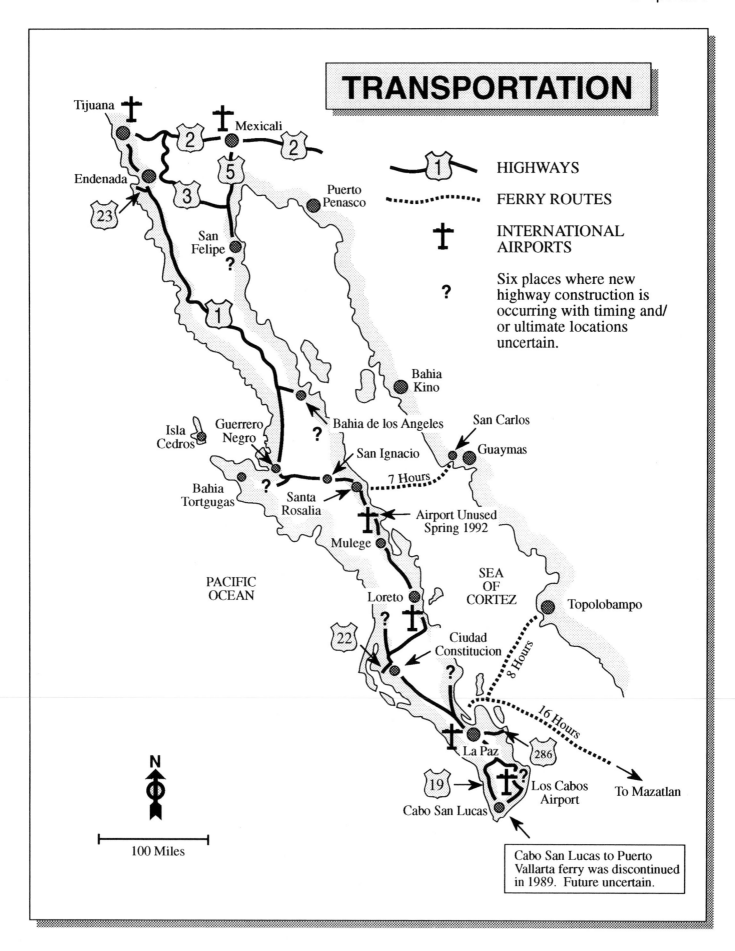

TRANSPORTATION

HIGHWAYS

FERRY ROUTES

INTERNATIONAL AIRPORTS

? Six places where new highway construction is occurring with timing and/or ultimate locations uncertain.

Tijuana

Mexicali

Endenada

Puerto Penasco

San Felipe

Bahia Kino

Isla Cedros

Guerrero Negro

Bahia de los Angeles

San Carlos

Guaymas

San Ignacio

7 Hours

Bahia Tortgugas

Santa Rosalia

Airport Unused Spring 1992

Mulege

PACIFIC OCEAN

SEA OF CORTEZ

Topolobampo

Loreto

8 Hours

Ciudad Constitucion

16 Hours

La Paz

To Mazatlan

N

Los Cabos Airport

19

Cabo San Lucas

100 Miles

Cabo San Lucas to Puerto Vallarta ferry was discontinued in 1989. Future uncertain.

A portion of the secondary road in steep mountain country between Loreto and the famous mission at San Javier. Most secondary roads are located on far more level terrain.

several years before surfacing is applied. At press time there were about 250 miles of these roads, fully constructed to highway standards, but still awaiting finished grading and their oiled surface. They are the six projects noted earlier in this section.

The pit-run gravel used for the subsurface of these projects is often quite coarse, as it is not intended as the final surface. Thus, these roads quickly become very rough and badly washboarded. Travel speeds are usually substantially less than over much lower-standard dirt roads. After traversing all of these projects to prepare this account, my companion noticed a dump truck loaded with 8-to-10 inch diameter stones destined for someone's rock wall. He noted, "There goes a load of road gravel." It's not that bad, but be prepared for a bumpy ride. As with the secondary roads described below, this class of roads are best suited for pickups and vans.

My experience is that new surfacing is completed in sections of from 5-to-10 miles. Unfortunately, the oiled surface of Baja's highways is very thin, and previously paved sections are sometimes allowed to deteriorate badly while work is advancing up ahead. But hope springs eternal, and perhaps all will be finished when you arrive. Keep me posted. My long-suffering pickup is getting tired.

SECONDARY ROADS (UNPAVED) — A decade or so ago, one could say that there were only two standards of roads in Baja (1) the paved highways and (2) all the others, which were of the *two tracks in the desert* variety. As previously noted, this is no longer the case. There are now hundreds of miles of dirt and gravel-surfaced roads of intermediate standard. The majority have been built to provide improved road access to Mexicans

living in small towns or ranches. In many cases they also serve the needs of the recreational traveler who wants to get away from the more heavily used areas. As these areas become more and more crowded, these secondary roads will become increasingly important.

These roads are 1 1/2-to-2 lanes in width. Some sections are wider and some are narrower. In most places, you can pass an oncoming car, but slowing down and keeping well to the right are often necessary. The surface is sometimes composed of native soil and gravel; in other places, a better grade of gravel has been imported. In all cases, the travel surface has been constructed by earthmoving equipment and is free of large rocks and similar obstacles. With few exceptions, secondary roads are those shown as "Graded Dirt Road" on the road map produced by the Southern California Automobile Association.

Secondary roads are infrequently graded. When recent maintenance has occurred, one can travel in the 20-40 mph range. More often you will be greeted by miles of washboarding and occasionally by rutting caused by erosion and wet weather use. As this rough road surface is common, consider letting some of the air out of your tires to soften the washboard shock.

You will also be faced with a choice dictated by the 4-40 rule. That is, drive slowly (4 mph) to cooperate with the surface, or fly over the tops of the ridges at 40 mph. Most owners of the vehicle they are driving will choose the former alternative. (You actually will average in the 10-20 mph range.) However, brace yourself for meeting some of the local citizens flying low with the fishing-co-op pickup .

These secondary roads have been *engineered*. By that I mean that the surface may have been built-up (turnpiked) above the natural terrain and there are often hard surfaced arroyo crossings and an occasional culvert. Also, there are occasional kilometer posts and usually directional signs where these roads join the main highways. Curves and grades are modest; in most cases these roads have been constructed in areas of gentle topography. If you become alert to these characteristics of an engineered road, you can be reasonably assured that you are on the type of facility that I am describing and that washboarding will be the worst of your troubles. Be careful after storms, however, as even these engineered roads will become slick and sometimes impassable when wet.

My impression of such roads is the same as for the main highways; that is, that they all seem to have been constructed to about the same standard. To a large degree, when you have seen one, you have seen them all, and you can develop confidence in using them for recreational travel. Keep in mind that while the chief problem with the main highway system is lack of width, the weak points of secondary roads are washboarding and slick or muddy surfaces after storms.

The GRAND TOUR in PART III provides maps and details concerning such roads and the places they serve. These routes will be referred to as *secondary roads*. This term will not be used for lower standard facilities.

OTHER ROADS (DIRT SURFACE) — There are thousands of miles of lower-standard dirt roads in Baja. Some have been built by a bulldozer pushing its way through the desert. Typically, the surfaces of such roads are lower than the surrounding terrain. They are not built-up as indicated for the secondary roads. Other roads simply developed as the result of vehicular use. Such roads provide access to scores of isolated ranches, fish camps, and miles of coastline. They are generally unsuitable for sedans and large recreational vehicles; however, for those with vans and lightly loaded pickups, these roads offer endless possibilities. Often their travel surfaces are smoother than are those of secondary roads and unpaved highways, but they will be narrow and harbor steep trouble spots at arroyo crossings. Directional signs are rare. These roads will be referred to as *dirt roads*.

FOUR-WHEEL-DRIVE TRAVEL — Do you need four-wheel-drive in Baja? The answer is "No." I have visited scores of isolated villages and ranches by land and sea and seeing a Mexican with a four-wheel-drive vehicle is very unusual. The workhorse of the economy is the standard pickup truck and all of my investigative work has been done with such a vehicle. One can go almost everywhere with two-wheel-drive. But keep in mind that I just said almost everywhere. If you have a 4x4 vehicle, by all means take it to Baja, as it will add a positive new dimension to your travels.

The comments that follow have been prepared in consultation with Bob and Jean Evans, longtime members of the Vagabundos del Mar, and 4x4 travelers in Baja since 1965. They report that 98 percent of their off-highway travel in Baja is in standard drive, but it is that remaining two percent that makes the difference for them. With only standard drive one must frequently stop just short of that special place to camp. A 4x4 vehicle allows one to travel onto the beach, out on rocky ledges overlooking the sea, or into sandy arroyos seeking the shade of the desert's only trees. Four-wheel power allows for a steady climb up steep pitches where other vehicles have scraped deep ruts while spinning their tires. But most importantly to the Evans is the peace of mind they have in knowing that their vehicle will take them to the places they really want to go.

Accompanying these comments is a table showing Bob and Jean's recommendations for twelve 4x4 adventures that provide a cross section of the type of experiences that Baja has to offer. They vary from a very short side trip at Morro Santo Domingo to a loop trip along the Pacific shore of over 100 miles. These trips will be noted in further detail when they are encountered in PART III of this book. (I have not personally traveled these routes.) Each will be highlighted by the "BOB & JEAN 4X4" logo shown in the upper corners of the table. With few exceptions they involve travel over existing roads. I do not recommend cross-country travel which frequently results in damage to Baja's sensitive desert environment.

FUEL AND REPAIRS — Two problems concerning travel in Baja do not relate directly to the roadways. These are vehicle repairs and fuel supplies. Except when driving in the heat of summer, there is little reason why a vehicle should have more repair problems in Baja than north of the border. The difficulty arises when something does happen. With the exception of Ensenada, Ciudad Constitucion, La Paz, and the border cities, good repair facilities and parts stores are few and far between. The prudent driver will always carry spare belts, hoses, filters, and a tool kit. Should you have a serious breakdown, the most expedient course of action may be to return to the United States by some means and acquire the needed parts on your own.

On one of our trips, my wife and I gave a lift to a young lady whose car had serious engine trouble. We delivered her to the machine shop (*taller mecanico*) in Loreto. Its floor was the

BOB & JEAN 4X4	4X4 RECOMMENDATIONS By Bob and Jean Evans	BOB & JEAN 4X4

1 --	Canons Diablo & Diablito	Rugged canyons with waterfalls, pools, and entrancing vegetation.	Ch. 15
2 --	Pacific Coast Loop	An isolated section of coast - Puerto Catarina to Santa Rosalillita.	Ch. 19
3 --	El Volcan	Crystal forming spring near the famous El Marmol onyx mine.	Ch. 19
4 --	Mission Santa Maria	One of Baja's least visited mission ruins in a lovely palm canyon.	Ch. 19
5 --	Morro Santo Domingo	A short 4x4 trip provides spectacular camp spots along the Pacific.	Ch. 19
6 --	Cerro San Francisco	Prehistoric cave paintings at Cerro San Francisco.	Ch. 20
7 --	Candelaria	Prehistoric cave paintings at Candelaria.	Ch. 21
8 --	Punta Concepcion	Drive the eastern shore of Bahia Concepcion to Punta Concepcion.	Ch. 21
9 --	Arroyo de La Purisima	The old canyon road to La Purisima through Arroyo de la Purisima.	Ch. 21
10 --	San Javier Loop	Rugged desert mountain scenery & the historic town of San Javier.	Ch. 21
11 --	Mision San Luis Gonzaga	Visit the 1737 stone mission plus numerous rugged mountain roads.	Ch. 22
12 --	Agua Caliente	Hot spring and camping by a large pool at the foot of the mountains.	Ch. 23

native surface and there was very little roof. Its benches and the surrounding area were littered with tools and the remains of automotive disasters of previous decades. These wrecks serve as the "parts department." We did our best for our friend but do not know how she fared.

At a similar facility in another town, I was in need of a tire pressure gauge and asked the owner if I might borrow one. When he headed for the refrigerator I thought I had been misunderstood. Alas, the refrigerator had long outlived its original calling and now served as a tool cache, the only place in the entire facility that would remain dry in the event of rain.

The favorable news is that I have found the mechanics to be good at their trade. They have to be, in a land where new cars in top running order are relatively few in number. I have also found them to be friendly and eager to help, in sharp contrast to what one often finds you-know-where. The other saving feature is the Green Angels (*Angeles Verdes*), a service of the Mexican government. They patrol the Transpeninsular, and other main highways, in their green-and-white pickup trucks. There is usually a crew of two, one of whom speaks English. They carry a limited supply of spare parts, gasoline, oil, and water and perform minor repairs at no charge. Parts are sold at cost. While you may have to wait a few hours, help is always on the way.

Mexico's fuel supplies are another subject where some travel authors rejoice in painting an unrealistically pessimistic picture. I sometimes feel that the poor conditions that were present in the past are copied from one author to the next and passed on like old wives' tales. Their most common accusation is that Mexican fuel is filled with impurities. I am sure some drivers have experienced this problem, but I have motored my diesel-powered sailboat over 10,000 miles on Mexican fuel and changed a filter only once. I have never had to change a filter in my pickup. It stands to reason that the highways would be lined with stalled vehicles if unclean fuel were a serious problem.

Also good news is the fact that gasoline and diesel prices are the same almost everywhere because fuel is sold through a government marketing monopoly. Each station bears the same sign, PEMEX (*Petroleos Mexicanos*). If all else fails, look for the pumps. The silver pump is for MAGNA SIN, a 92-octane unleaded fuel. The blue pump dispenses NOVA, which is an 82-octane regular gas containing tetraethyl lead. Diesel fuel, spelled the same in English and Spanish, comes from the red pumps.

Finally, you may be happy to find that station attendants actually pump gas for you, the self-service era not having penetrated south of the border. Young boys also often climb on your hood to wash the windows for a few pesos. Contribute to the cause. But now for some not-so-good news. Here is the list.

1. — Tests indicate that actual octane ratings are lower than advertised. Your engine will let you know if this is the case. You may experience pinging or your motor may decline to stop when the key is turned off. In spite of this problem, most vehicles get along reasonably well, particularly if you use one of the readily available gasoline additives.

2. — In the past gas stations were not always open for a variety of reasons and there was difficulty obtaining fuel along the 221-mile section of Highway 1 between El Rosario and Guerrero Negro. In recent years both of these problems have greatly improved but it is still wise to never let your fuel supply drop below the halfway point.

3. — You can almost always count on a PEMEX station having NOVA gasoline; however, a few do not carry, or are out of, the lead-free MAGNA SIN. The same is true for diesel. As an aid to tourists, PEMEX has now placed signs along the main highways advising how far it is from the town you are leaving to the next station carrying MAGNA SIN.

A recent study in the United States disclosed that 16 percent of vehicles designed to run on lead-free gas were being driven illegally with leaded gas. It is obvious that they will run with such fuel. If you own such a vehicle, I recommend you inquire into what adverse effects it and its smog control system might encounter if you use leaded gasoline. You might have to make a decision to use such fuel as the alternative to considerable inconvenience while driving in Mexico.

MAPS AND ROAD DIRECTIONS — The maps and directions contained in this book are fully adequate for recreational travelers using the main highways and principal secondary roads. However, I strongly recommend that you attempt to obtain the *Baja California Road Map* published by the Automobile Club of Southern California (AAA). This is an outstanding publication, but it is available only to club members. It shows all four classes of roads described in this chapter. Obtain road maps before going to Baja as they are hard to find once you are in the peninsula.

RAILROADS — Baja was linked to the Mexican mainland by railroad in 1948. This line now proceeds north from Mexicali into the United States and eventually returns to Baja at Tecate and then to Tijuana. This Tecate to Tijuana segment appears to receive very little use. In contrast, trains from Mexicali make regularly scheduled runs southeastward to the Mexican mainland.

The Mexicali train links up with the main line from Nogales to Mexico City at Benjamin Hill. The trip to Mexico City is scheduled to take about 48 hours, although I am advised that connection problems in Guadalajara add an extra day. En route, it passes through Guaymas, Mazatlan and Guadalajara. The line then continues east from Mexico City to the Yucatan peninsula and its Mayan ruins.

I have made this run from Mexicali as far as Guadalajara, and can recommend it for the not to faint of heart. I have also made, and can thoroughly recommend, a related side rail trip from Los

Mochis to Creel near Copper Canyon. The Pullman and other passenger cars are of 1940 vintage, which actually allow you to open up the windows; no choking from the air conditioning. You won't see much of Baja, but Mexicali is the starting point for these railroad adventures. Train reservations may be acquired through Romero's Mexico Service, 1600 West Coast Highway, Newport Beach CA 92663, (714) 548-8931.

BUSES — Several bus companies provide frequent service between Tijuana, Mexicali, and mainland Mexico along Highway 2. They operate from the Central de Autobuses (Central Bus Terminal) located near the airport in Tijuana. (See Tijuana map in Chapter 14). Two of these lines, Tres Estrellas de Oro (Three Stars of Gold) and ABC (Autobuses Baja California) also traverse Highway 1 from Tijuana to La Paz. The trip takes about 26 hours.

Bus service in Mexico is rated as super deluxe, deluxe, first, second, and third class. The third-class buses are affectionately referred to as *chicken buses* as they often are used to transport members of the animal kingdom other than man. Tourists are advised to utilize only the first class or higher services. Seats on these buses are reserved, but you must acquire your reservations and tickets in person.

There are usually two drivers on the longer runs. One drives while the other rests. I have found the service and quality of Mexican buses to be very good. If I were asked to compare the overall deportment and other characteristics of the people on Mexican buses with those in the United States, I would cast my vote for south of the border.

RENTAL CARS — Rental cars are available in Tijuana, Mexicali, Loreto, La Paz and at the Cape. The major companies are the same as those serving the United States and Canada. Reservations may be made by calling these firms' 800 telephone numbers. It is not normally possible to rent a car in Tijuana and drop it off in the southern part of the peninsula.

Tourists renting a car at La Paz or the two Cape communities can easily make the Hwy 1- Hwy 19 loop and return their car at the point of origin.

OCEAN TRAVEL

OCEAN LINERS — Thousands of people make the passage to Baja each year in pleasure craft of various types and sizes. This fascinating means of seeing the world will be examined in some detail in Chapter 5. At the opposite end of the ocean travel spectrum is the growing number of tourists who can now experience a few hours stopover at Cabo San Lucas while their ocean liner lies at anchor in the bay. As it has been for centuries, Cabo is a natural stopover point for vessels plying the sea. Its inner harbor provides tourist facilities at the water's edge

but is too small and shallow for the large cruise vessels. Passengers make the trip to and from the anchorage in ships' launches.

During a trip to Cabo San Lucas my wife and I encountered an elderly lady who had arrived in this manner. The lady asked how we had made our journey. We replied that we had driven in our camper. Her response was, "You mean there is some kind of giant bridge to this island?" My wife provided a brief geography lesson. In an act of great restraint, I refrained from advising her that the Spanish explorer Francisco de Ulloa discovered that the Baja peninsula was not an island in 1539.

In contrast to Cabo San Lucas, Baja's Pacific coast port city of Ensenada can accommodate ocean liners at dockside. In recent years, liners have made the run from San Pedro (near Los Angeles) to Ensenada on a regular basis.

In 1991 a passanger dock and terminal suitable for large ocean liners was completed within the harbor of Pichilingue 10 miles from the city of La Paz in an effort to lure the ocean cruising trade to that community. Contract your travel agent for details concerning ships to both Ensenada and La Paz .

The 143 foot, 80 passenger *Pacific Northwest Explorer* provided cruises into the Sea of Cortez in past years. This service was discontinued at press time but it may reappear in the future.

FERRY SERVICE — The Sea of Cortez ferry routes are shown on the TRANSPORTATION Map in this chapter. The SAMPLE FERRY SCHEDULE summarizes the overall operation of the system. Keep in mind that this schedule changes from time to time. Also, there may be lengthy delays and cancellations of reservations when the ferries do not operate due to storm conditions or mechanical breakdowns. Fog at the entrance to the Topolobampo harbor on the Mexican mainland, and constricted entrance conditions at Santa Rosalia often cause

The La Paz, a typical vessel of the Mexican ferry system. Here she is docked at Pichilingue near La Paz.

delays in the run between these two ports. Wise travelers will maintain a flexible schedule when planning to use the ferry system.

The Santa Rosalia ferry terminal is located inside the man-made harbor at this community. The La Paz ferry docks within the natural harbor of Pichilingue located 17 Km (10.5 miles) from downtown La Paz over a blacktop highway. There is also a ferry terminal inside the man-made harbor at Cabo San Lucas but the service from there to Puerto Vallarta was discontinued in 1989.

About 1990 the ferry system was sold by the Mexican government to private interests (Grupo SEMATUR de California). As a result the formerly subsidized prices have risen sharply. Rates for vehicles are based upon their length and as of spring 1992 ranged from $126 to $214 between Mazatlan and La Paz; $77 to $131 between Topolobampo and La Paz; and $89 to $151 between Guaymas and Santa Rosalia. Reservations may be made by phone to any of the ferry offices or at the toll free national (Mexico) number 91 800 6-96-96.

The ferry system has become the lifeline for southern Baja California. Food and endless other commodities are carried on large trucks, and truck containers transported from the mainland by ferry. It is thus becoming increasingly more difficult to secure ferry reservations for recreational vehicles. Passenger traffic has also increased and I have had reports of tourists having to buy tickets from scalpers at dockside.

Procedures for using the La Paz ferry are a bit complex as the ferry terminal and the La Paz reservation office are not at the same location. Using the system at Santa Rosalia is simpler as the two facilities are in one building. (See Santa Rosalia and La Paz maps for locations of the ferry offices.)

There are three passenger classes. Salon Class passengers are entitled to one of the numerous seats located throughout the ferry. Reservations are given for this general seating area. Advance reservations are required for Turista Class (cabins with toilet facilities outside the room) and Cabina Class (cabins with toilets).

A temporary export permit is required for any vehicle using the ferry system. It is best to take care of this procedure at Tijuana or the other ports-of-entry. In La Paz, it may be obtained at the office of the Registro Federal de Vehiculos located near the corner of Belisario Dominguez and 5 de Febrero.

AIR TRAVEL

Air travel has both increased and decreased in importance as a means of transportation to Baja since the early 1970s. This seeming contradiction is explained by the fact that commercial jet travel has substantially grown due to the construction of international airports and many new hotels in the peninsula's southern half. In contrast, the completion of the Transpeninsular Highway in 1973 has considerably lowered the tourist industry's reliance on travelers who transport themselves in small private aircraft.

COMMERCIAL AIR TRANSPORTATION

AIRPORTS — There are five airports that serve modern jet aircraft. A sixth has been constructed south of Santa Rosalia but has yet to be utilized. (See TRANSPORTATION Map.) Two of these accommodate the border area at Tijuana and Mexicali, but these two cities are seldom the destination points of North Americans traveling to Mexico by jet.

The three airports in the peninsula's southern half receive nearly all the tourist traffic from the United States and Canada. The La Paz airport has been in existence for some time, while those at Loreto and Los Cabos were constructed since 1975 in tandem

SAMPLE FERRY SCHEDULE
Schedule in effect spring 1992. It can be expected to be modified in the future.

| ROUTE | | DEPARTURES | | TRAVEL TIME |
FROM	TO	DAYS	TIME	
GUAYMAS	SANTA ROSALIA	Daily exc. Tues & Fri.	8 A.M.	7 Hours
SANTA ROSALIA	GUAYMAS	Daily exc. Wed & Sun.	8 P.M.	7 Hours
TOPOLOBAMPO	LA PAZ	Daily exc. Sun & Tues.	10 A.M.	8 Hours
LA PAZ	TOPOLOBAMPO	Daily exc. Sat & Thur.	8 P.M.	8 Hours
MAZATLAN	LA PAZ	Daily exc. Sat.	3 P.M.	16 Hours
LA PAZ	MAZATLAN	Daily exc. Sat.	3 P.M.	16 Hours
The Cabo San Lucas to Puerto Vallarta ferry was discontinued in 1989				

with major new resort facilities sponsored by FONATUR, a government tourist development agency. The Los Cabos airport has now been enlarged so it may accommodate jumbo jets

Almost all of Baja's cities and towns have airstrips, and several of these are served by propeller-driven aircraft on a scheduled or nonscheduled basis. The more prominent of these places are Ciudad Constitucion, Ensenada, Guerrero Negro, Bahia Tortugas, Mulege, Santa Rosalia, Isla Cedros, and several of the larger southern hotels. Relatively few tourists travel using these facilities, but it is comforting to know that they are available in case of emergencies.

AIRPORT TAX — As in most places in the world, there is an airport tax. In flying into Mexico, it somehow is magically taken care of in the cost of the ticket; however, in leaving the country one must pay the tax at an airport ticket stand, and the price may be quoted only in pesos. This system causes considerable distress to some tourists who do not understand Spanish, have spent all of their pesos, and suspect that the whole process may be a local extortion operation. It is best to find out the amount of the tax in advance and save a few pesos for that purpose. It's all quite simple, although why they don't combine the tax with the ticket price is a great mystery, except perhaps to the ticket seller's union.

AIRLINES — Mexican-operated Aeromexico, Mexicana and Aero California are the principal regularly scheduled jet-equipped airlines serving Baja's resort areas from points in the United States. U. S. carriers join in the peninsular market from time to time. The two Mexican airlines fly a variety of American-made aircraft, and the service is as good or better than it is north of the border. See your travel agent for details.

AIRPORT GROUND TRANSPORTATION — Most air travelers know that getting to and from the airport is often more complex and tiring than the flight itself. At the three southern

Baja airports there is ample van-type transportation to all tourist facilities. Prices are moderate and are often included in hotel accommodation packages. Taxis also are plentiful and one is required to use them to return to the airports as a concession to the taxi unions. As a result both taxis and vans run empty during half of the airport round trip.

The Loreto airport is only three miles from the main resort areas. From Los Cabos airport it is about ten miles to the San Jose del Cabo resorts and 27 miles to Cabo San Lucas. The La Paz airport is about five miles from the downtown area.

PRIVATE FLYING — People flying to Baja in small private aircraft share with the ocean cruisers a means of savoring the peninsula's truly unique features. Unfortunately their choice of landing strips has been greatly reduced in recent years as the Mexican government has closed many of the smaller landing fields as a means of combatting drug traffic.

For many years the pilot's bible for flying in Baja was a detailed book titled *Airports of Baja California and Northwest Mexico* by Arnold Senterfitt. At press time this book is out-of-print but Arnold still operates his Baja Bush Pilots organization at P.O. Box 34280 San Diego, CA 92163, (619) 297-5587 or 6450. This is the best source of information on general aviation flying and Mexican aircraft insurance.

FLY-IN HOTELS — The HOTEL LIST presented in Chapter 6 HOTELS shows that a considerable number of the peninsula's hotels and resorts have nearby landing strips. Other small, isolated, overnight facilities that cater to the fly-in trade are beyond the scope of this list. The traveler's aircraft can often be tied down within a few yards of their lodging, and management takes special pains to attend to those who fly in. Virtually all Baja towns have a community airstrip; thus almost all of the peninsula's hotels and resorts are readily available to the small plane pilot.

CHAPTER 4
RECREATION VEHICLES AND CAMPING

This chapter was entitled *Camping* in earlier editions of this book. I have adapted the present title as the passage of time in Baja has made it evident that camping with tents and minimum facility vehicles, and the use of motor homes and larger recreation vehicles, are two quite different activities. Likewise, for the most part, they take place at different places and provide different recreation experiences.

RECREATION VEHICLES

Recreational vehicles make up a significant portion of the traffic one sees on Baja's highways. While increasing numbers of tourists are traveling to Baja in private automobiles, such vehicles do not dominate the scene as they do north of the border. Recreational vehicles that travel south include bicycles, motorcycles, vans, pickup campers, trailers, and motor homes of all sizes. Most of you will travel to Baja in the vehicle you already own and will not venture forth to buy one based on reading this book. However, you need to understand the relationship of your particular R.V. to conditions in Baja.

All of life is a compromise. The owner of an R.V. must choose between accessibility and accommodations. Smaller, lighter vehicles can go far more places than their larger cousins. Obviously there are more creature comforts in the larger motor homes and trailers. While these conditions are also true in the U.S. and Canada, the contrast is considerably greater in Baja. This is why the marked differences between the different classes of roads were stressed in the previous chapter.

Most larger R.V. users do not stray far from paved highways and tend to congregate in developed R.V. parks. The risk of an accident is also increased when these large, top-heavy rigs have to pass oncoming vehicles on the narrow highways. In contrast, the smaller vehicles commonly use all classes of roads. As a result, their owners can see much more of the Magnificent Peninsula and can escape the more heavily used areas that are close to the paved highways.

Remember, also, that the principal negative feature of unpaved highways and secondary roads is their rough surface. If you are willing to subject your motor home, its passengers and contents to washboard shock treatment, there is little other reason why larger rigs cannot be driven on many of these roads in dry weather. In fact, one occasionally finds them in the strangest places, although it is very unusual to see a trailer on such roads.

To complete this discussion, I need to convey a definition of *smaller R.V.* and *larger R.V.* as these terms will be used fre-

quently throughout the book. Motorcycles, vans, and pickup trucks with low, shell-type campers clearly fall into the former group. Most single-purpose motor homes and trailers are clearly in the latter. My own vehicle is a 3/4-ton pickup truck with a powerful 454-cubic-inch engine. The photo presented in Chapter 2 shows it equipped with a 8-foot cab-over camper. Such an arrangement falls midway between the small and large R.V. groups.

In the past I frequently used this pickup-camper combination on secondary and unimproved dirt roads but occasionally found myself in places where I wish I had not ventured, due primarily to the top-heaviness of the camper. I simply could not drive over many other unimproved roads which I wanted to explore.

For these reasons I have switched to a lightweight shell-type camper. I can now travel almost everywhere and enjoy camping in secluded settings. Obviously creature comforts are minimal and when I have to stay at a trailer court I am ill at ease sitting on my tailgate while large motor homes tower over me on either side. These comments clearly illustrate the decision you need to make between accessibility or accommodations for camping in Baja.

R.V. PARKS

In Baja, the term *R.V. park* applies to several types of facilities. These are:

1. — Permanent mobile home subdivisions. There are many of these on the Sea of Cortez from the San Felipe area south to Puertecitos and along the Pacific coast from Tijuana south to the La Jolla area SE of Ensenada. In these places North Americans have leased a small site and placed a recreation vehicle on it, usually adding a roof of some kind along with a variety of other attached structures. The result has usually been a community that is considerably less than luxurious. In most cases, the structures are now permanent. These are de facto recreation vehicle-second home tracts.

In more recent years similar places have developed farther south in Mulege, Puerto Escondido, Buena Vista and Cabo San Lucas. Some of these are more pleasing to the eye than those in the north. Many started out as transient parks and gradually converted to all permanent residents.

2. — Courts that serve most travelers only for a night or two while the R.V. is in transit from one place to the other or for short weekend trips in the border areas. During the mid-1970s the

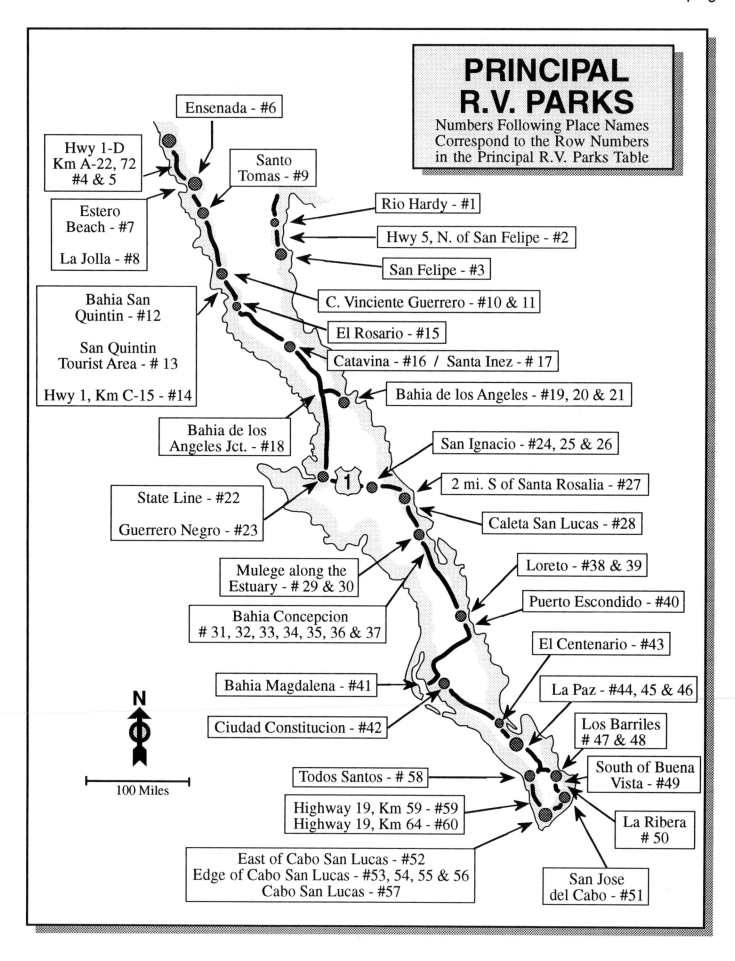

PRINCIPAL
R.V. PARKS
Numbers Following Place Names
Correspond to the Row Numbers
in the Principal R.V. Parks Table

Ensenada - #6

Hwy 1-D
Km A-22, 72
#4 & 5

Santo
Tomas - #9

Estero
Beach - #7

La Jolla - #8

Rio Hardy - #1

Hwy 5, N. of San Felipe - #2

San Felipe - #3

C. Vinciente Guerrero - #10 & 11

El Rosario - #15

Bahia San
Quintin - #12

San Quintin
Tourist Area - # 13

Hwy 1, Km C-15 - #14

Catavina - #16 / Santa Inez - # 17

Bahia de los Angeles - #19, 20 & 21

Bahia de los
Angeles Jct. - #18

San Ignacio - #24, 25 & 26

State Line - #22

Guerrero Negro - #23

2 mi. S of Santa Rosalia - #27

Caleta San Lucas - #28

Loreto - #38 & 39

Mulege along the
Estuary - # 29 & 30

Puerto Escondido - #40

Bahia Concepcion
31, 32, 33, 34, 35, 36 & 37

El Centenario - #43

Bahia Magdalena - #41

La Paz - #44, 45 & 46

Ciudad Constitucion - #42

Los Barriles
47 & 48

South of Buena
Vista - #49

Todos Santos - # 58

Highway 19, Km 59 - #59
Highway 19, Km 64 - #60

La Ribera
50

East of Cabo San Lucas - #52
Edge of Cabo San Lucas - #53, 54, 55 & 56
Cabo San Lucas - #57

San Jose
del Cabo - #51

N

100 Miles

1

PRINCIPAL R.V. PARKS
* Indicates Full Hookups.   See text for description of TYPE.

	Ch	LOCATION	NAME	TYPE	COMMENTS
1	15	Rio Hardy	Several Campos	2	Used mostly as camps for bird hunting & river fishing.
2	15	Hwy 5, N. of San Felipe	Many Campos on Beach	1,2,3	A mixed bag of beach camping and permanent sites.
3	15	San Felipe	8 Trailer Courts	2&3a	7 in town, 1 South of town. See San Felipe map.*
4	17	Hwy 1-D, Km A - 22	KOA Trailer Court	1&2	Pleasant hillside location. Lots of transient spaces.*
5	17	Hwy 1-D, Km A - 72	Baja Ensenada	2&3a	High-class & expensive. On the beach. Club House.*
6	17	Ensenada	Campo Playo	2&3a	Only court in downtown Ensenada. Pleasant.*
7	18	Estero Beach	Estero Beach Resort	2&3a	First-class court adjoining hotel. On lagoon near ocean.*
8	18	La Jolla	2 R.V. Subdivisions	1	Permanent leased sites but with parking area for transients.
9	18	Santo Tomas	El Palomar Trailer Court	2	Caters to weekend groups. Pleasant spot in olive grove.*
10	18	C. Viciente Guerrero	Don Pepes	1&2	Restaurant. A mixture of permanent and transient sites.*
11	18	C. Viciente Guerrero	Posada Don Diego	2	Restaurant. A large area used as a stopover by caravans.*
12	19	Bahia San Quintin	Old Mill Motel	2	Under construction in 1992. Next to the Old Mill Motel.*
13	19	San Quintin Tourist Area	Cielito Lindo Trailer Ct.	2	Poor facilities because of ocean flooding but near the beach.
14	19	Hwy 1, Km C-15	El Pabellon	2	Unaesthetic court but parking OK near fine nearby beach.*
15	19	El Rosario	Sinai	2	A simple parking area behind the Sinia Motel in town.*
16	19	Catavina	Government Court	2	A pleasant, safe, landscaped place to park but no facilities.
17	19	Santa Inez near Catavina	Rancho Santa Inez	2	A cleared area for parking near small motel and cafe.
18	19	Bahia de los Angeles Jct.	Government Court	2	A pleasant, safe, landscaped place to park but no facilities.
19	19	Bahia de los Angeles	Villa Vitta R.V. Court	3a	Unaesthetic court but on the beach.*
20	19	Bahia de los Angeles	Guerrmo's Trailer Court	3a	Unaesthetic court but on the beach.*
21	19	Bahia de los Angeles	Government Court	3b	Pleasant, landscaped place to park near beach. No facilities.
22	20	State Line	Government Court	2	A pleasant, safe, landscaped place to park. Modest facilities.
23	20	Guerrero Negro	Several courts in town	2	Parking areas adjoining motels N-side of highway into town.*
24	20	San Ignacio	Government Court	2	A landscaped parking area. Modest facilities. Near PEMEX.
25	20	San Ignacio	R.V. parking area	2	Pleasant parking area in palms on road into town.
26	20	San Ignacio	El Padrino R.V. Park	2	Pleasant park in palms on road into town.*
27	21	2 mi. S of Santa Rosalia	El Palomar	2	Nice park along highway with small restaurant.*
28	21	Caleta San Lucas	San Lucas R.V. Park	3a	Little landscaping but directly on the water.*
29	21	Mulege along the estuary	Huerta (Orchard) Court	3a	Pleasant court in palms between highway and the estuary.*
30	21	Mulege along the estuary	Maria Isabel Court	3a	Pleasant court in palms between highway and the estuary.*

PRINCIPAL R.V. PARKS

* Indicates Full Hookups.   See text for description of TYPE.

No	Ch	LOCATION	NAME	TYPE	COMMENTS
31	21	Bahia Concepcion	Playa Punta Arena	3b	R.V. parking directly on the beach. No hookups.
32	21	Bahia Concepcion	Playa Santispac	3b	R.V. parking directly on the beach. Restaurant - no hookups.
33	21	Bahia Concepcion	Posada Concepcion	3b	A few transient sites adjoining an R.V subdivision.*
34	21	Bahia Concepcion	Los Cocos	3b	R.V. parking directly on the beach. No hookups.
35	21	Bahia Concepcion	La Burra	3b	R.V. parking directly on the beach. No hookups.
36	21	Bahia Concepcion	Playa El Coyote	3b	R.V. parking directly on the beach. No hookups.
37	21	Bahia Concepcion	Playa Buena Ventura	3a	Court directly on the beach with restaurant and hookups.*
38	21	Loreto	Las Palmas	3a	Pleasant court among many palms directly on the water.*
39	21	Loreto	Loremar R.V. Park	3a	Little landscaping, directly on the water.*
40	22	Puerto Escondido	Tripui R.V. Resort	2	Small transient area next to permanent sites in R.V. Resort.*
41	22	Bahia Magdalena	Las Palapas R.V. Park	3b	Parking along the beach next to a small motel & cafe.
42	22	Ciudad Constitucion	Camperstre La Pila	2	Parking area near grassy pool area adjoining working farm.*
43	22	El Centenario	Oasis de Aripes	3a	A pleasant court on the water 10 miles NW of La Paz.*
44	22	La Paz	El Cardon	3a	A pleasant court with pool on the Hwy. entering La Paz.*
45	22	La Paz	Aguamarina Trailer Ct.	3a	A pleasant court with pool in residential area of La Paz.*
46	22	La Paz	La Paz Trailer Court	3a	A pleasant court with pool near the water in La Paz.*
47	23	Los Barriles	Martin Verdugos	3a	Very good shaded park on the beach.*
48	23	Los Barriles	Playa de Oro	1&3a	Good park on the beach but most sites are permanent.*
49	23	South of Buena Vista	Capilla Trailer Court	3a	Very good park on the beach in rural area.*
50	23	La Ribera	Correcaminos	3a	Pleasant court in mango orchard. Short walk to the beach.*
51	23	San Jose del Cabo	Brisa del Mar	3a	Pleasant court, pool, restaurant on the beach at edge of town.*
52	23	East of Cabo San Lucas	Villa Serena	3a	Near water with fine view of the Cape. Pool, etc.*
53	23	Edge of Cabo San Lucas	El Arco	3a	On the Hwy entering town from the E. Pool, etc.*
54	23	Edge of Cabo San Lucas	Cabo Cielo	3a	On the Hwy entering town from the E. Pool, etc.*
55	23	Edge of Cabo San Lucas	San Vicente	3a	On the Hwy entering town from the E. Pool, etc.*
56	23	Edge of Cabo San Lucas	Vagabundos del Mar	3a	On the Hwy entering town from the E. Pool, etc.*
57	23	Cabo San Lucas	El Faro Viejo	3a	Older court in a residential area of town.*
58	24	Todos Santos	El Molino Trailer Court	2&3a	In town, very pleasant. Caravan destination. Sun. Brunch.*
59	24	Highway 19, Km 59	San Pedrito R. V. Park	3a	On fine beach. Pool in palm grove.
60	24	Highway 19, Km 64	Government Court	3a	On fine beach. Desert landscaping and active management.*

The Tripui Trailer Court at Puerto Escondido 16 miles south of Loreto. Note the pool, store, restaurant area at the right center. — The Sierra Giganta lies in the background.

Mexican government built eight trailer courts at various places. They were nicely landscaped and were enclosed with chain-link fences. Most of them were promptly abandoned. They now provide good places for overnight parking and five of them are being operated by local Mexicans on a charge basis.

There are now several other privately developed parks that serve the same purpose. Some are quite nice while others are little more than parking lots adjoining a motel.

3. — Courts whose clientele are R.V. tourists who spend extended periods of time at the same spot. They are of course available for short-term use if space is available. There are two sub-types of such parks.

3a -- The most common are developed parks with full hookups. Some are rather austere while others are well landscaped with swimming pools, restaurants and good toilet facilities. Some are in town and others lie on the beach although only a few choice sites are directly on the water. Rent is paid by the week, month, or season, but the visitor has no long-term legal rights to the site. There is often considerable competition for choice sites, and advance reservations are frequently made. One can easily recognize the pecking order in these places.

3b -- One of Baja's most popular camping areas is the eastern shore of Bahia Concepcion south of Mulege (see Chapter 21). In this area are located six beaches that become lined with recreation vehicles each winter season. There are no facilities except rather primitive pit toilets and trash barrels. But the R.V. people love them because everybody gets to park directly on the beach and the camping fee is low, $3.00 to $4.00 per day during my last visit.

Some of the courts serve only one of these functions, while others provide for two or all three. Also there is a clear trend of leasing the better sites at courts throughout Baja on a long-term basis. This arrangement best serves the economic interests of the land owner. Unfortunately the result is that the best properties are occupied most of the time by vacant improvements while the current tourist has difficulty finding a nice place to stay.

You will recall that I have promised not to oversell the charms of Baja and to stay as close as possible to reality. In this spirit, I have to note that in my view, many of Baja's R.V. parks leave something to be desired. Vegetation is often scarce, there is very little space between sites, and often the sanitary facilities would bring tears to the eyes of a journeyman plumber. In spite of these features, most courts are well visited and the folks you meet seem content. I am sure that the communal activity that occurs in such places is one of their positive features. Also, please weigh my remarks with the knowledge that given the choice between an R.V. park and the beach I would invariably choose the latter.

Having made the above negative comment I am compelled to note that some of the newer parks are well landscaped and quite pleasant, and while I prefer the more remote areas, the parks do have their charm. They have also improved with age as landscaping has grown in size and Mexican owners have become more proficient in filling the aesthetic needs of their clients.

The first park that I stayed in many years ago had an approach road fenced off by a rope. Adjoining this road on the driver's side, a tall packing crate was upended with a window cut out facing incoming vehicles. This structure served as the manager's office. When he saw us coming he entered the box and took our money through the window. While still inside, he lowered the rope barrier to let us pass. A marvel of efficiency and the high point of our stay. The advantages of such a system are obvious when compared to our park systems up north where the first $100,000 of taxpayer's money goes into a fancy entrance station.

My most recent stop at the place mentioned above showed that it is now even more efficient. The packing crate and rope fence were gone and were replaced by a sign that read "Pick Your Spot — Collection at 5:00 P.M." In another court, a similar sign notes "If caretaker is absent, please suit yourself. We catch you later. Thanks." Now that I think about it, R.V. parks aren't all that bad.

Tables in this chapter list all of the principal R.V. parks in Baja. The numbers in the TYPE column refer to the several classes of parks described above in the text. The locations of these parks are shown in a map on page 31. (Most are also shown on larger scale maps in PART III THE GRAND TOUR.) The site numbers on the map correspond to the same parks listed in the tables.

SEASIDE CAMPING

By the term *camping*, I am here referring to staying overnight in a natural setting with the use of tents or minimum facility vehicles such as vans and pickup trucks will camper shells.

If one visits Baja's main R.V. parks and beaches it is easy to conclude that the camper is now far outnumbered by the owners of larger R.V.s. But one still sees many smaller rigs on the highways indicating that there are still many true campers around hiding out in the lesser known and harder to reach areas. The balance of this chapter is dedicated to these people.

If you are a veteran camper you will know that in most places north of the border you are not permitted to camp because you are on private land or are restricted to developed sites on public lands. In the latter areas, you will be accustomed to graceful loop roads and parking spurs all neatly lined with barriers to keep you in your place. These facilities come complete with camp tables, stoves, restrooms, and a sign, or an attendant at the gate who will tell you in great detail the rules of the camp and how to pay your fee. In Baja, forget all that. Camping here is a unique experience and the rules are quite simple. They are: (1) find campsite, (2) camp.

Much of the land in Mexico is federally owned, and in all cases the shoreline is open to the public. Even where the land is privately owned, no one will bother you unless you are in their front yard. Exceptions are the cities and towns and the water-front area between San Jose del Cabo and Cabo San Lucas. In the latter place the beaches themselves are open to the public but camping is most difficult for the tourist. In other places, unless there is some obvious reason why you should not camp, you are free to do so. If someone is authorized to charge a fee, they will seek you out.

I have frequently camped in close proximity to remote seaside fish camps. One waves at the fishermen on the way in and out, but unless I initiate it, there is usually no other contact. If someone does come by, it is simply out of curiosity and to say hello. Travelers from north of the border may expect to be told "you are on private property, get out." I have never had this happen.

Campgrounds north of the border are almost always built some distance from the feature you came to see. Camping at the edge of the stream, on the beach, or at the rim of the canyon is next to impossible. Much of this practice is justifiable, but I am also convinced that campground planners take great pleasure in separating the public from what they came to enjoy. In Baja, you may camp as near as you like to the shoreline. You may need plenty of sea water for dish washing and the sensible camper will not expend excess energy in carrying it too far.

On a recent trip to Baja's Pacific shore, I pulled my camper to within 10 feet of the edge of a cliff overlooking the surf pounding over a rock-lined coast. There were majestic views for 20 miles in both directions. Baja is one of the few places in North America where you can camp in this manner. I believe it is this freedom to spend time in such sites, free from the restraints placed on us by more civilized portions of our continent, that make travelers to Baja return again and again. On the same trip I met a Canadian lady camping in this type of isolated area. She was obviously enthralled by Baja. I asked her why. She said, "I really don't know, there's just something about the place!"

There has been a continuing evolution in camping at Baja's seaside areas. Prior to 1973 and the completion of the Transpeninsular Highway, camping and traveling south of San Quintin required a tough, lightweight vehicle capable of enduring miles of rough roads. After the highway was finished, the larger R.V.'s took over and soon began to line the beaches near the highway. Today most of the beach areas near the Transpeninsular Highway have been taken over by hotels, residences and the several types of R. V. parks described earlier in this chapter.

There are still countless uncrowded shoreside camping sites on the peninsula, but many are accessible only by secondary and lower standard dirt roads. Thus, as in many parts of the world, true campers must search out the lesser known and harder to access spots to fill their needs.

THE LAST HUNDRED YARDS

What follows is a discussion of the fine art of getting stuck in the sand, followed by some suggestions on how to reverse the

Beach camping at Santispac on Bahia Coyote. It is one of the most heavily used beaches in Baja as it directly adjoins Highway 1 and is used as a overnight stopover point.

Camping on the sand spit at El Requeson on the west shore of Bahia Concepcion.

process. As noted above, many camping spots are undeveloped, and foremost among the features that are missing are adequate roads for the last few yards to that spot that you are simply in love with only 20 feet from the ocean. In many places, you will be driving on the natural surface that has not been compacted adequately to support a vehicle. The problem is compounded by the fact that shoreline camping spots will usually be at a lower elevation than the main road. Thus, you drive downhill to your campsite but must return uphill. Spin-outs in loose sand are a frequent result, followed by "Henry, I told you this would happen."

Most people camp in one location for many days, weeks or even months, so the pain of extracting one's vehicle from a place that has provided so much pleasure may be a small price to pay. Many veterans know full well what will happen and are well versed in the extraction process.

The prudent traveler to Baja's beaches will carry a shovel and tow chain or nylon line. Others are equipped with several buckets for carrying sea water to wet down the surface on which the drive wheels will travel. This should be done prior to moving a vehicle; however, the best method of which I am aware is to let some, or nearly all, of the air out of your tires. The increase in traction is miraculous. For this reason, don't travel in Baja without some means of pumping up your tires after returning to firmer ground. Most U.S. auto parts stores carry small, inexpensive tire pumps that operate by plugging into your vehicle cigarette lighter. Others function from engine compression and require the temporary removal of one spark plug. Don't leave home without one.

Obviously use of four-wheel-drive vehicles is the ultimate answer to the problem of "The Last 100 Yards," although sometimes even drivers of these vehicles overextend themselves and become mired down. Then one really has trouble.

CAMPFIRES

I have always been intrigued with the fascination that the human animal has with such things as the shoreline of a body of water, a flowing stream, attractive vegetation, and an open fire. Because of this latter attraction, I will devote a few words to fire building in the hope that it will improve your camping experience.

If you are expecting to hear that firewood is scarce in Baja you would be in error. As long as the land is covered with woody desert vegetation, there will be plenty of firewood. This is the situation in most of Baja. Unfortunately, the individual pieces of wood are small, and they will be well picked over near camping areas. The keys to success in gathering firewood in Baja are one or more large cloth or canvas sacks and a pair of gloves. Before you reach your camping site, stop near an area of heavy vegetation, wander through the desert, and fill up your sacks. Wear the gloves for protection from the ever-present thorns.

Many desert plants have dead branches near their bases, and the inside skeletal structure of dead cactus is excellent firewood. I have never had to use an axe in Baja. In most places, it's only a matter of a few minutes work to gather all the wood needed for several days. The pieces will be small, but they will be dry, full of energy, and easy to gather.

I also recommend matching your small pieces of wood with a small fire. Lay several flat rocks in two rows about six inches apart with their long axis in the same direction as the wind. Digging a trench between the rocks is also useful. A fire built within such an enclosure will conserve energy and use relatively little fuel. The rocks also can be used to support a small grill for outdoor cooking.

My old 1942 Boy Scout manual offers very sound advice. "A cooking fire is a small fire." The same should also apply to a fire used just to look at. Remember the counsel of the old Indian who said, "White man build big fire and stand way back, Indian build little fire and get up close." Spoken no doubt by a man who was running low on squaws to gather his firewood.

Finally, keep in mind that wildfires do occur in Baja. The brushy areas in the California Vegetative Region of northern Baja are as highly flammable as similar places in southern California in the United States. Deserts can also burn, and I have seen several large devastated areas in Baja where centuries will have to pass before revegetation occurs. PLEASE BE CAREFUL WITH FIRE.

CHAPTER 5
WATERSPORTS

I really do not exaggerate in telling you that Baja, and in particular the coast of the Sea of Cortez, is a paradise for watersports. This is especially true for windsurfers and the owners of small trailerable or car-top boats who are confronted at home with the bone-chilling temperatures and heavy swells of the Pacific Ocean off the United States and Canada. North of the border the use of small boats is limited almost exclusively to inland lakes, reservoirs, rivers, and protected ocean bays. In the Sea of Cortez deep-sea fishing and other watersports can be enjoyed in ocean waters that have mild temperatures and light swells.

BOATING

BAJA BOATER'S GUIDE — My interest in writing about Baja California started in 1983 when I circumnavigated the peninsula in my sailboat gathering data to assist in the revision of the out-of-print *Baja Sea Guide*. The book you are reading, *The Magnificent Peninsula*, was written as an act of frustration while I waited for the *Sea Guides* author to prepare the new edition. Alas, it never appeared. I thus set about producing my own *Baja Boater's Guide*, having had my fill of joint endeavors.

The *Baja Boater's Guide* was designed to be by far the most comprehensive marine guide ever produced for the Baja penin-sula. It evolved into a two volume production totaling 476 pages, with 178 charts and 455 photographs, most of them aerial views. I recommend it for the serious boater along with a compilation of U. S. government maritime charts published as *ChartGuides Mexico West*. Both are available from the BAJA BOOKSHELF in the Appendix. They are further described in notices in this chapter. Because of the availability of these detailed guides, only a broad overview of boating is presented in this chapter.

BOAT CLASSIFICATION — It is important to understand the relationship of several different classes of boats to conditions in Baja. The message is that not all boats may be transported to, or used in Baja. Here are the details. (The four-boat classification system is my own creation. See BOAT CLASSIFICATION Table.)

CLASS 1 — Sail and power vessels that have the fuel capacity, crew capabilities, and design characteristics for ocean conditions can make the Baja Passage from San Diego around the peninsula's southern tip and into the Sea of Cortez. Hundreds make this trip every year. See the OCEAN-CRUISING Section in this chapter for further discussion concerning the use of such boats.

BAJA BOATER'S GUIDE

By JACK WILLIAMS

PHOTOS -- 350, low-level, oblique, aerial photos allow for easy identification of every prominent bay, cove, promontory, island, and harbor in Baja. Plus many general interest photos and sea level profiles of prominent points of land.

CHARTS -- 178 charts covering every inch of the Baja coast and every important bay, cove, and island. Most charts electronically traced from highly accurate Mexican government topographic maps. No pencil sketches as in previous guides.

PRINTING SPECIFICATIONS -- Black and white - High gloss paper for top photo reproduction - Stitch binding for durability - Film laminated cover.

VOLUME I -- THE PACIFIC COAST
212 Pages - 201 Photos - 81 Charts
VOLUME II -- SEA OF CORTEZ
264 Pages - 254 Photos - 97 Charts

Get your copy from the BAJA BOOKSHELF in the Appendix

CHARTGUIDE MEXICO WEST

Exact reproductions of dozens of U. S. nautical charts from San Diego to Guatemala including all of the Baja peninsula and the Sea of Cortez. Many are no longer available from the government.

Charts in the Baja Boater's Guide show large scale outlines of coastal features but have no underwater detail and they are not suitable for navigation. The U. S. nautical charts are needed to meet these needs.

The price of U. S. nautical charts at press time is $11.50 each. Duplicating the coverage provided by the CHARTGUIDES MEXICO WEST package would cost many times more than its $58.00 price.

Get your copy from the BAJA BOOKSHELF in the Appendix

CLASS 2 — An unfortunate problem lies in the fact that the marinas of the United States and Canada are overflowing with boats that are either too small, have insufficient fuel capacity, or are underdesigned for the ocean passage. At the same time, they are too large to be easily trailered or launched under Baja conditions. The majority of such vessels are powerboats in the 20-to-35-foot cabin cruiser category. They should not be taken to Baja. Please read the material to follow concerning ocean cruising and review the description of the Transpeninsular Highway if you are inclined to ignore this advice.

CLASS 3 — Two classes of boats can be transported to Baja by highway. First are those that because of their weight must be floated from a trailer into the water by use of a launching ramp. There are few locations in Baja that have ramps and many of these have one or more shortcomings. (See BOAT LAUNCHING RAMPS Table in this chapter.)

Once in the water, these larger vessels enjoy distance and water condition capabilities greater than lightweight class 4 boats, so I don't discourage your taking them south. Simply keep in mind that they can only be launched at a limited number of locations and that you must face the risks of towing engendered by the narrowness of the Transpeninsular Highway.

CLASS 4 — Finally, there are those boats which are light enough to be manhandled over the beach. In most cases, this involves carrying the outboard motor separately. Inflatable rubber dinghies and lightweight aluminum boats in the 13-to-17-foot range make up the majority of this class. My observation is that the great majority are carried in or on top of vans or on pickup truck racks. A few are transported by trailer.

Various types of inflatable boats are also common and in the final analysis may be the best and safest way to enjoy the water.

SMALL BOATS — By small boats, I am referring to the class 3 and 4 vessels just described.

SMALL BOAT LAUNCHING — Since first publishing this book in 1986, the number of boat launching ramps in Baja has

BOAT CLASSIFICATION

NO.	DESCRIPTION	COMMENTS
1	Ocean-going sail and powerboats having the capabilities for travel by sea.	LONG RANGE Great experience. Travel almost anywhere.
2	Boats without long-range ocean capabilities, but too big to trailer safely.	UNUSABLE IN BAJA
3	Heavy trailer boats that require a launching ramp to enter the water.	MEDIUM RANGE Sea access limited due to shortage of launching sites.
4	Light trailer or car-top boats which can be launched over the beach.	SHORT RANGE Maximum flexibility due to ease of launching.

significantly increased. Details are shown in the BOAT LAUNCHING RAMPS Table in this chapter.

The ramps at about half of these locations have rough concrete surfaces which have rather obviously been poured by hand. A ready-mix concrete truck in Baja is not a common sight. Because of the difficulty in getting concrete to set after the tide comes in, some of these ramps do not extend far enough toward the water to be effective at low tide.

As previously noted, those boaters with craft that are light enough to be manhandled over the beach will be able to use their boats in far more places than those who require a ramp. Boats 18 feet and larger usually require a hard-surfaced ramp.

Other boaters abandon the boat-trailer method altogether and, after lowering their boat to the ground, maneuver it in and out of the water by hand or on various types of rollers. Also, rolling devises can be purchased that attach directly onto the hull of small boats. Many veteran Baja fishermen rely solely on lightweight 13-15 foot aluminum boats because of the ease of launching such craft over the beach.

SMALL BOAT CRUISING — I approach this subject with a considerable degree of trepidation, fearing that what I write might encourage the use of small boats in waters beyond their capabilities. I am proceeding simply because the cruising of small class 3 and 4 boats in the Sea of Cortez is already a common practice. These adventures range from a simple overnight camping trip to extended voyages involving many weeks and hundreds of miles. Some utilize the heaviest possible trailer boats with on-board sleeping and cooking facilities. At the other extreme, lengthy voyages are undertaken in kayaks and small, center-board sailboats not over 12 feet in length.

Few owners of ocean cruisers would trade their vessels for such craft, but the little fellow does have some clear advantages over the bigger boats. Most small powerboats have a greater speed than the 4-to-8 knots of the average ocean cruiser. They can thus traverse a considerable distance in a short time taking advantage of windless periods. During some months, the wind blows heavily during all but a few hours per day. Also, small shallow-draft boats can be easily hauled onto the beach almost anywhere if the weather kicks up, and they can be anchored in coves too small or shallow to offer protection to larger vessels. These advantages open up the potential of isolated camping in scores of charming and pristine hideaways.

For the very adventuresome, I need to note that some skippers of large trailer boats launch their vessels at Kino Bay on the Mexican mainland and make the 100-plus mile crossing of the Sea of Cortez to Bahia de los Angeles. Others launch at San Carlos and cross to Bahia Concepcion. The former

trip is the safer as the Midriff Islands lie en route and offer wind and sea protection and potential stopping points. Also, increasing numbers of small boat owners are launching at the ramps in Bahia de los Angeles and cruising south along Baja's eastern coast. The return trip is made by hauling the boat north on the Transpeninsular Highway.

I strongly advise that no one undertake any of these ventures in a small boat without having tested it in sea conditions similar to those encountered in the Sea of Cortez. Keep in mind that the prevailing wind during the cruising season is from the north and blows down the long axis of the peninsula. Crossing the Sea of Cortez at right angles to these winds puts one's boat in the belly of the seas, a dangerous and uncomfortable exercise. Any of these trips should best be undertaken in April through July. The winter months are windy.

Boaters interested in small boat cruising should consider membership in the Vagabundos del Mar (see notice on the last page of this book). This club frequently organizes such events in the Sea of Cortez and at Bahia Magdalena on the Pacific side.

OCEAN-CRUISING — Records at the office of the port captain at Cabo San Lucas show that over 1,000 foreign yachts check in at that port each year. Most of these vessels arrive from the United States and Canada and return north after the winter cruising season. Some overwinter at protected spots in the Sea of Cortez. A few are making longer passages to the South Pacific or are en route to or from the Panama Canal.

Most readers will not be fortunate enough to make an ocean voyage to Baja. Nevertheless, this section on ocean-cruising is presented for two reasons. First, many of you who visit Baja by land will see the cruisers' vessels at various locations. They are part of the Baja scene and you may be interested in their way of life. More importantly, this brief exposure might encourage

A heavy trailer boat (class 3) at a natural surface ramp. Very few boats larger than this one are towed to Baja.

BOAT LAUNCHING RAMPS

LOCATION		COMMENTS
GENERAL	**SPECIFIC**	🛶 Ramps shown on maps with this symbol.
SAN FELIPE	Three ramps. Ruben's R.V. park - Motel el Cortez - Club de Pesca. (P-151)	Ramps used only at high tide due to extreme fluctuation of water level.
PUERTECITOS AREA	Near north entrance to Puertecitos Cove & at Papa Fernandez Resort. (P-148)	Both are concrete ramps but they are usable only at high tides.
ENSENADA	A concrete ramp near the sportfishing piers within the harbor. (P-163)	Good concrete ramp but access may be constricted by new building construction.
ESTERO BEACH	At the Estero Beach Hotel, 6 miles S of Ensenada on Estero de Punta Banda. (P-167)	Concrete ramp. After launching, boats must cross estero entrance bar to access the ocean.
LA JOLLA	2 ramps at La Jolla Beach camps on the Pacific. 8 Miles W of Maneadero. (P-167)	Directly on Pacific Ocean. Concrete ramps are unusable in windy weather or low tide.
LA BUFADORA	Near the head of the cove east of the La Bufadora blowhole. (P-167)	A steep, concrete ramp leading to gravel beach. Constructed in the bottom of a short, narrow arroyo.
PUERTO SANTO TOMAS	In arroyo bottom at the west end of the fish camp. (P-166)	A steep concrete ramp. Unusable when ocean swells are heavy.
SAN QUINTIN	At the Old Mill Motel, and at the Pedregal subdivision. North end of bay. (P-172)	Old Mill ramp is hard-packed natural surface. Widely used.
BAHIA DE LOS ANGELES	Three neighboring concrete ramps run by the hotels and R.V. parks. (P-184)	Hotel Villa Vita ramp built from a rock breakwater and reaches deeper water than the other two.
CAMPO RENE (ESTERO COYOTE)	The beach at small Campo Rene resort on the shore of shallow Estero Coyote. (P-189)	A natural-surface (sand and shell) beach. Fishing inside the bay or access to the open Pacific.
CALETA SAN LUCAS	Ramp is inside the grounds of the San Lucas R.V. Park. (P-195)	A natural surface launch area, but well protected inside the cove at Caleta San Lucas.
PUNTA CHIVATO	200 yards NW of the Hotel Punta Chivato. 16 mile dirt road E from Hwy. 1. (P-196)	Rock and concrete ramp. The hotel staff will help out if a problem arises.
MULEGE	3 ramps at R.V. parks & hotel on S. side of estuary, plus ramp near lighthouse. (P-198)	Concrete ramps (lighthouse ramp is packed sand), but there is no water in the river when the tide is out.
PLAYA BUENAVENTURA	At the Playa Buenaventura R.V. Park on Bahia Concepcion. Km F-94 on Hwy. 1. (P-196)	A wide concrete ramp run by the R.V. park. Plenty of parking and easy approach.
LORETO	Inside breakwater-lined harbor and on the open water at the Las Palmas R.V. Resort. (P-204)	Good concrete ramps. There is a large public parking area adjoining the harbor.
PUERTO ESCONDIDO	At south end of the inner harbor and adjacent to the entrance channel. (P-210)	A good concrete ramp accessible by oiled highway. One of the most heavily used ramps in Baja.
BAHIA MAGDALENA	1 Mile S of San Carlos on a Bahia Magdalena side lagoon. (P-213)	A concrete ramp. Does not extend far enough at low tide, and flooded at high tide. Try mid-tide.
LA PAZ	4 ramps. Fedepaz - Aquamarina R.V. - Marina de La Paz - Palmira marina. (P-216-217)	All are good concrete ramps leading into the quiet waters of Canal de La Paz.
PICHILINGUE	In small cove north of Puerto Pichilingue. Off Highway 11 north of La Paz. (P-216)	Two good, side-by-side, concrete ramps in a protected cove.
BUENA VISTA AREA	Over the beach launching at R.V. parks and hotels in Buena Vista and Los Barriles. (P-223)	Launch over the beach using 4x4 trucks owned by R.V. parks and hotels.
CABO SAN LUCAS	Two ramps in the inner harbor. One at north end and one at the south. (P-228)	Good concrete ramps. The north ramp is operated by the marina.

See notice for Mike Bale's LAUNCH RAMPS book on page 235. It contains a wealth of additional information on the ramps shown in this table.

some of you to seek an opportunity to make such a voyage. Twice in my life I simply quit work for four months and sailed south to sweep away the cranial cobwebs. These two trips motivated me to give up the office entrapment altogether and return for two more voyages completely around the peninsula.

There is no set way to make the passage from San Diego to Cabo San Lucas. Some cruisers simply make their way many miles offshore where the winds are stronger, and don't touch land until rounding the cape. However, the majority stay closer to land following the *Baja Passage* shown on the BOATING IN BAJA Map.

The BOATING IN BAJA Map shows several points that provide the principal anchorages along the Baja Passage. At two, there is no possibility of obtaining fuel except from other boaters. At most of the other places, fuel can be obtained only by carrying it over the beach in cans if you can persuade the local inhabitants into giving up some of their own hard-earned supply. The only reliable fueling point, and the only one actually in the business of servicing the cruiser, is Bahia Tortugas. This well-protected port and community lies approximately midway between San Diego and Cabo San Lucas. Even here, you must anchor off the pier while fuel is gravity fed from barrels.

Bahia Tortugas is 340 miles south of San Diego. The journey from Bahia Tortugas to Cabo San Lucas is 460 miles. For this reason the rule of thumb is that you should not make the Baja Passage in a powerboat that carries fuel for less than 600 miles. This allows a reasonable margin of safety for the passages to and from Bahia Tortugas. You frequently see large, gas-guzzling sportfishing boats with 55-gallon drums lashed in their cockpits to stretch their tankage for the passage. This fuel situation is one of the principal reasons why many mid-sized powerboats (class 2) should not be cruised to Baja. Those broad, open-to-the-sea aft cockpits are another. It is easy for a following sea to invite itself aboard.

Keep in mind that the prevailing wind is northwest along the west coast of Baja during the entire cruising season. With energy from both wind and swells coming from this direction, more or less parallel with the coast, the *downhill* voyage south is usually a delight. The return trip north is *uphill* into the wind and swells. Even sailboats make this return trip almost entirely under power. The pounding the boat and crew takes on the way north is the price to be paid for a sunny winter in Baja. Crews to make this uphill run are often in demand, and skippers with Captain Bligh tendencies may find themselves without help.

Ocean-cruisers, like the trailer court folks are often a gregarious breed. Thus, it is a bit ironic that people who have the transportation capabilities to visit anywhere they wish tend to congregate at certain ports. These places are: Cabo San Lucas, La Paz, Puerto Escondido, and across the Sea of Cortez at San Carlos.

Launching car-top (Class 4) boats at the concrete launching ramp at Cabo San Lucas.

The two last mentioned ports host large numbers of cruising boats whose owners have decided to spend the hot summer in Mexico. Both are well protected and are north of the tracks of a great majority of late summer hurricanes. Because of these intense tropical storms most sensible cruisers will not venture into southern Mexican waters during summer. The safe cruising season in Baja is from December to May.

Please consult the *Baja Boater's Guide* for more details on ocean-cruising. Volume I, The Pacific Coast, contains extensive background material on the subject.

MARINAS AND FUEL — Until recently the subject of marinas in Baja could have been covered in three words: "there aren't any." Now five locations offer marina facilities. These are:

ENSENADA — Three small marinas are in place at the northern end of the harbor. One of these is operated in conjunction with a small craft shipyard.

CABO SAN LUCAS INNER HARBOR — The entire inner harbor has been constructed by dredging. After a wait of over a decade an excellent marina was constructed about 1990. The harbor, well protected from winter weather and Pacific swells, provides easy access to the open sea.

LA PAZ — Prior to 1985, there were no marinas in La Paz and obtaining fuel was not a simple task. There are now three fully functional marinas with diesel fuel. Gasoline is delivered from town.

PUERTO ESCONDIDO — The area immediately inside the entrance channel has been dredged and reformed and a major resort area with hotels, condominiums, and marina awaits construction. In spring 1992 the only boating facility completed was the launching ramp.

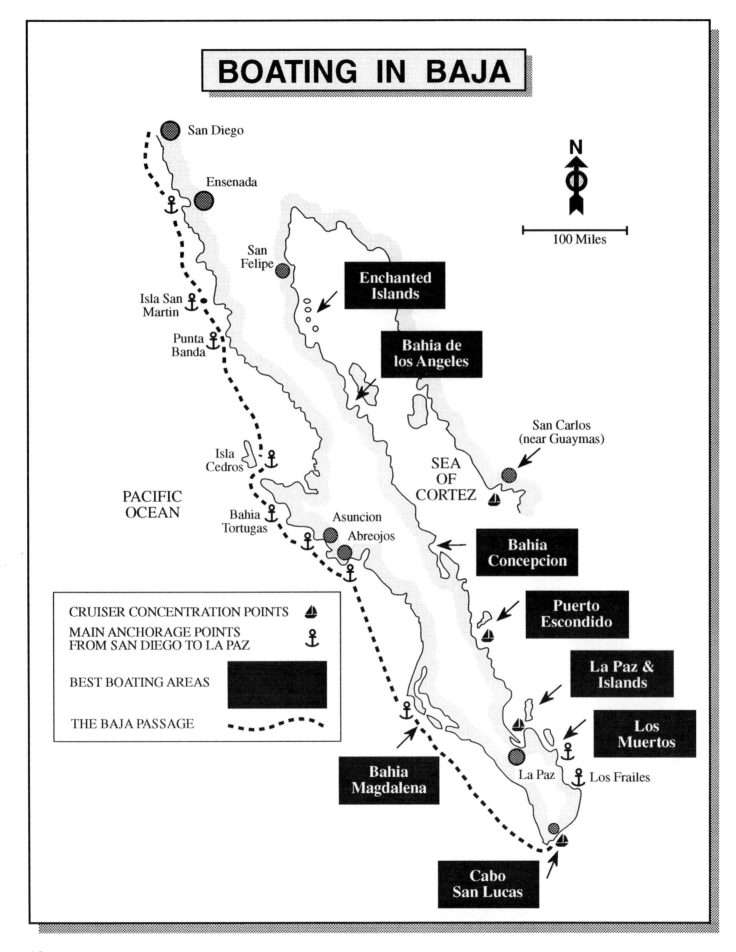

BOATING IN BAJA

San Diego

Ensenada

San Felipe

Enchanted Islands

Isla San Martin

Punta Banda

Bahia de los Angeles

San Carlos (near Guaymas)

Isla Cedros

SEA OF CORTEZ

PACIFIC OCEAN

Bahia Tortugas

Asuncion

Abreojos

Bahia Concepcion

Puerto Escondido

CRUISER CONCENTRATION POINTS

MAIN ANCHORAGE POINTS FROM SAN DIEGO TO LA PAZ

BEST BOATING AREAS

THE BAJA PASSAGE

La Paz & Islands

Los Muertos

La Paz   Los Frailes

Bahia Magdalena

Cabo San Lucas

N

100 Miles

SANTA ROSALIA — There is a small, but very adequate marina inside the breakwater lined harbor at this community. Plans call for its being enlarged in the future.

There are long range plans for marinas at many other places. In 1989 the Mexican Director of Tourism announced that marinas will be constructed every 150 miles along the Pacific coast of the country. By 1992 nothing new had occurred. My only recommendation is "Don't hold your breath."

It must be clear by now that obtaining fuel for your boat in Baja is not a simple matter of gliding alongside the nearest fuel dock. Therefore, in most places the boater must obtain fuel from the land-based PEMEX stations and transport it to the launching site. Serious fishermen carry a drum of gas in the back of their pickups.

BEST BOATING AREAS — The BOATING IN BAJA Map shows the locations of what I believe are the eight best boating areas in Baja California. See the *Baja Boater's Guide* for details on all of these areas.

WINDSURFING — The sport of windsurfing has rapidly gained in popularity in Baja in recent years. Windsurfers crave strong winds in the 15-30 knot range that blow parallel to the takeoff area. As noted in Chapter 2, northerly winds that meet these requirements are common along the entire Sea of Cortez coast in the winter season. When the breeze is uncomfortably strong and cool for most campers, it is just right for the windsurfers.

Individual windsurfers will be seen at many locations on the Sea of Cortez and windsurfing equipment is often for rent at the hotels on the outer harbor at Cabo San Lucas, at Nopolo and La Paz. There are, however, three areas of special interest.

THE EAST CAPE — The Buena Vista-Los Barriles area along Baja's East Cape has become one of the most popular windsurfing destinations in North America. The area has long sandy beaches impacted by the wind conditions noted above, and being near the peninsula's tip, air temperatures are warmer than farther north. Even so, many sailors prefer to wear shorty or full summer wetsuits when spending much time on the water.

Starting about 1987, U. S. windsurfing groups organized an annual Baja International Boardsailing Regatta at the East Cape each January. This event attracts hundreds of young enthusiasts who camp on the beach north of Los Barriles where I rather suspect things get a little wild.

These same organizations set up headquarters at the Hotel Playa Hermosa, and Hotel Palmas de Cortez during the entire winter season. Rental equipment, instruction, and repair services are thus readily available.

PUNTA CHIVATO — From December to March a Eugene, Oregon organization offers week long windsurfing fly-in excursions with accommodations provided at the Hotel Punta Chivato. Contact Excursions Extraordinaires, P. O. Box 3493, Eugene, OR 97403.

PUNTA SAN CARLOS — The Sea of Cortez offers windsurfing with surf-less seas. On the Pacific shore, Punta San Carlos attracts the expert surfers with its high winds and breaking seas. I am advised by these hardy souls that it offers the best and most challenging area for their sport on the North American coast. There are no facilities at Punta San Carlos and the trip in from Highway 1 is a rough 40 miles. The access road leaves Highway 1 about 16 miles SE from El Rosario.

SURFING — Surfing in Baja is limited to the peninsula's Pacific coast and the Cape Area. There are normally no swells or surf on the Sea of Cortez side. Several surfing hotspots are the Islas Todos Santos near Ensenada, and Puntas Rosarito and Santa Rosalillita about 50 miles north of Guerrero Negro.

To my knowledge there is no authoritative written guidebook about surfing in Baja. A *Baja-Mexico Surf Map* is available from Mountain & Sea, Redondo Beach, CA 90277 (310) 379-9321. It covers the entire west coast of Mexico. It lacks the precise detail needed to pinpoint exact sites, but it contains the best information available.

KAYAKING — Ocean kayaking is a sport of rapidly growing popularity in Baja. My own observations indicate that there are far more kayaks on the Sea of Cortez at any one time than there are cruising sailboats.

Ocean kayaking enthusiasts can cruise within feet of Baja's rock-bound coast, and camp, fish, and explore at small idyllic coves and beaches that are too confining for use by larger boats. Kayaks can easily be car-topped on conventional vehicles and launched almost anywhere. The small single seat vessels weigh a scant 50 pounds while two person, 20-foot-long models weigh about 75 pounds. They are quite stable.

Experienced kayakers have traversed the full length of both Baja coasts. The trip from San Felipe to La Paz in the Sea of Cortez is frequently accomplished in 25-to-30 days. The most popular areas for shorter trips are the Bahia de los Angeles, Puerto Escondido, and the Bahia Concepcion areas. On the Pacific side, kayakers use Puerto Lopez Mateos as a base for trips into the Magdalena lagoons for whale-watching expeditions.

Kayaks can carry sufficient food and gear for extended voyages, but many kayakers take advantage of package tours offered by various outfitters. In these instances supplies are transported to prearranged camping sites by pangas which also provide added safety for trips to islands a bit beyond the range of kayakers alone. Contact Sea Trek, P.O. Box 561, Woodacre, CA, (415) 488-1000. Sea Kayak South, 2803 Morningside Terrace, Escondido, CA 92025 (619) 747-3615, or Baja Expeditions, 2625 Garnet Ave., San Diego, CA 92109, (619) 581-3311. This latter organization also runs other types of boat trips.

The modern Marina de La Paz at La Paz.

DIVING — Many locations around the Baja peninsula offer excellent sites for scuba diving. The authoritative manual for this sport is the *Baja California Diver's Guide* by Michael and Lauren Farley. It pinpoints and describes the best diving locations. It is available from the BAJA BOOKSHELF in the Appendix. Full-service diving shops are located in Ensenada, Cabo San Lucas, La Paz, Loreto, and Mulege. Live-aboard diving charter boats operate from the Marina de La Paz in La Paz and are offered by the Baja Expeditions organization noted above under kayaking.

NOTE — See Chapter 11 WILDLIFE concerning whale-watching in Baja waters.

FISHING

One rarely encounters reports concerning fishing that do not extol the virtues of the area being discussed. Certainly this is true for Baja California. The advertisements for the Cape, and East Area hotels claim the "world's finest big-game fishing." One peninsular fishing book maintains that fishing "is unequaled anywhere in the world," and everything else one can read boasts of the outstanding qualities of the catch in a particular area. In preparing this book, I endeavored —with limited success — to determine if all of this were true. What follows results from readings in the scientific and popular literature, and my own observations.

RATING BAJA'S FISHING — I have been unable to find any author who makes direct qualitative comparisons of the world's fishing areas. I suspect those who claim the *world's best* for Baja may be on shaky scientific ground and could be guilty of what is known in the advertising world as *puffing* (an over-emphasis of a product's good points). Nevertheless, there are several sound reasons for believing that the fishing in the waters surrounding the Baja peninsula is of high quality. Here they are:

UPWELLING — There are several relatively isolated sections along the western coasts of the world's continents where the prevailing winds have the effect of forcing the surface waters offshore. The result is an upwelling of colder waters from below that bear rich concentrations of nitrates, phosphates, and other nutrients. Their presence allows the development of enormous quantities of microscopic plants and animals known as plankton. Plankton, in turn, is the base of the food chain that results in large numbers of game fish.

This condition exists off the north-central portion of Baja's Pacific coast. The nutrient qualities of these waters are not as high as in similar areas adjacent to Peru and at the tip of South America, but they are considerably better than average. Cool water upwelling also occurs off Baja's East Cape and in the Midriff island area east of Bahia de los Angeles due no doubt to the islands forming a constriction to the flow of tidal currents in the narrow Sea of Cortez. Upwelling conditions rarely occur on the eastern coasts of the world's continents.

WATER TEMPERATURE — The world's oceans are classified into several temperature zones. Those adjoining the coasts of North America are shown on the WATER TEMPERATURE ZONES Map. As can be seen, tropical waters are found in the Sea of Cortez and at the tip of the Baja peninsula. Tropical seas represent the most ideal environment for life on earth. Fish tend to be larger, more abundant, and of different species than those found in cooler waters. Baja's Pacific waters are classified as subtropical and represent a transition between the tropics and the temperate area to the north. Near the shore, they are often cooled by the upwelling noted above.

As a result of these temperature factors, the Sea of Cortez offers the abundance of sea life common to tropical waters. It is the closest body of such waters to people living in much of western Canada and western United States. At the same time, the presence of cooler, subtropic and upwelling conditions on the Pacific side result in a wide variety of fish species being available to the Baja fisherman.

COASTAL HABITAT — Many species of smaller game fish thrive only where they are protected by rocky shores and reefs. As previously noted, much of Baja's coastline is mountainous and rocky. In addition, there are a considerable number of coastal islands with similar shoreline characteristics. The peninsula thus offers favorable marine environments for those who fish from, or close to, the shore.

OBSERVATION — In cruising off the coasts of Baja, one is seldom out of sight of a Mexican fishing vessel of some type. These boats do not fish hundreds of miles out to sea but near the land. There are fishing camps and villages in scores of locations. Fish processing plants are to be found in most larger communi-

BAJA CALIFORNIA DIVER'S GUIDE

By Michael B. & Lauren K. Farley

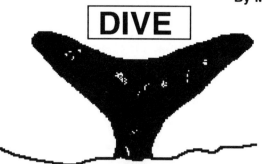

DIVE

THE authoritative book on diving in Baja's ocean waters.

The Farley's guide is the result of over 10 years of diving in Mexican waters. Included are all diving sites along both coasts of the Baja peninsula. There are numerous maps, drawings black and white photographs, and the names and addresses of diving speciality shops in Baja.

220 pages including 16 pages of brilliant underwater color photos of tropical plants and animals. A MUST FOR BAJA DIVERS.

Look for the **DIVE** symbol on the charts in the Baja Boater's Guide.

Get your copy from the BAJA BOOKSHELF in the Appendix.

---

ties. It is a simple matter of observation to conclude that there is abundant marine life in the surrounding waters.

OVERFISHING — Sadly, this heavy commercial fishing has significantly decreased the quality of sportfishing in Baja waters in many locations. The heaviest impact has come from Mexico's own fishing vessels based at Ensenada and La Paz on the peninsula, and at Guaymas, Topolobampo, and other ports on the Mexican mainland. Mexican officials have even licensed foreign fleets to fish in Baja waters sacrificing long-term good for quick profit.

Neil Kelly laments the adverse effects of commercial fishing in his book *The Baja Catch*, noting particularly the areas around San Felipe, Bahia de los Angeles, Loreto, Mulege, and Ensenada.

The sportfishing fleet operators at La Paz readily concede that the waters immediately adjoining their city have been fished-out, and several resort owners have asked me if there is anything I can do about the heavy commercial fishing. In spite of all this, sportfishing in Baja is still outstanding although it is not as good as it once was in some places.

FISHING ALTERNATIVES — Fishermen have a wide range of alternatives for enjoying their sport in Baja waters as indicated in the outline below.

LARGE CHARTER BOATS

    Party Boats
    Sportfisher Charters
    Extended Trip Charters

MEDIUM CHARTER BOATS

PANGA CHARTERS

FISHERMEN OWNED BOATS

    Ocean-Cruisers
    Trailer Boats

LARGE CHARTER BOATS — Vessels in the 40-60 ft. range.

Party Boats — At many Pacific coast ports in the United States, individual fishermen may pay to join 15-to-30 others for a day's sport. Fishing gear may be rented, or you may bring your own. The advantage of such trips is their relatively low cost made possible by the large number of fishermen making each trip.

Many party boats are based in San Diego at the Commercial Basin on the north side of Shelter Island. Some of these fish in

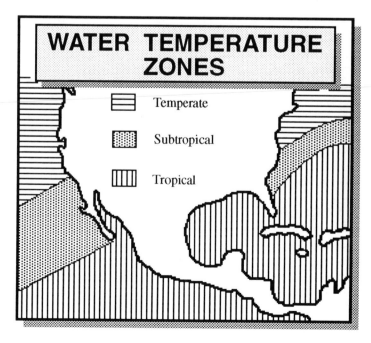

WATER TEMPERATURE ZONES

▭ Temperate

▩ Subtropical

⊪ Tropical

Mexican waters surrounding the Coronado Islands. Others offer more extended trips farther south. Ensenada is the only port offering true party boat service in Baja. Fishing, here, is in Bahia Todos Santos and around the Islas Todos Santos. Mexican fishing licenses are usually included in the cost of the Ensenada trips. Many species caught off Ensenada are seldom taken farther north.

Sportfisher Charters — "Sportfisher" is the name applied to any number of fast, open-transom powerboats in the 40-60 foot range. They normally accommodate only 2-4 anglers at a time who sit in fancy chairs in the boat's stern and haul in the large glamour fish. Trips are normally on a day basis only as overnight accommodations are limited.

Numerous sportfishers are based at Cabo San Lucas and reservations may be made at any of the local hotels or from U. S. agents in Southern California. In the past, many of these craft have been operated by U. S. skippers without formal authority from the Mexican government. I am advised that this practice may be coming to an end, but certainly sportfishing boats will be available at Cabo through one means or another. A smaller number of sportfisher vessels operate out of La Paz.

Extended Trip Charters — There are three ports in Baja that offer ocean-going vessels large enough to provide overnight accommodations for multiday fishing, whale-watching, and general enjoyment adventures. These are ENSENADA contact Ensenada Clipper, 8194 Havasu, Buena Park, CA 90621 (714) 994-1872 — SAN FELIPE Tony Reyes Fishing Tours, contact The Long Fin, 4010 E. Chapman Ave. Suite D, Orange, CA 92669 (714) 538-8010, or The Poseidon, P.O. Box 974, Calexico,

CA 92231 (619) 239-6123. The Tony Reyes trips are 6-day adventures to the Midriff Island area. — LA PAZ Baja Yacht Charters, contact Frazer Charters Inc, P.O. Box 60099, San Diego, CA 92106 (619) 225-0588. The Tony Reyes vessel is moved from San Felipe to La Paz during January and February.

As the agents for these charter vessels will change with time, you might consult advertisements in *South Coast Sportfishing Magazine* for current information.

MEDIUM CHARTER BOATS — Most of the larger vessels discussed above were manufactured in the United States. Dozens of smaller flybridge cruisers in the 25-35 foot range have been produced by small Mexican boatyards in the southern portion of the peninsula. They are less sumptuous than the U. S. products.

The majority of these boats make up the fishing fleets of the hotels from Cabo San Lucas to San Jose del Cabo and the Buena Vista-Los Barriles area. Another fleet operates out of the Hotel los Arcos in La Paz. Chartering these vessels is usually less expensive than the larger vessels. Contact any of the major hotels in the areas noted.

PANGA CHARTERS — No discussion of boating in Baja would be complete without reference to the panga, a heavy fiberglass open boat powered by an outboard motor. They are made in La Paz and were designed by Mac Shroyer a former math teacher from the United States who now manages the Marina de La Paz in La Paz. They range from 18-to-24 feet in length. There is hardly a Mexican fisherman on the Sea of Cortez who does not operate from such a boat. About 2,500 have been constructed (see picture on this page). You will see them everywhere Mexican fishermen gather.

Most pangas are used for commercial fishing by the members of fishing cooperatives. However, more and more they are being offered for charter to sportfishermen. At La Paz, pangas make up the fishing fleet operated by Bob Butler. Contact the Hotel Los Arcos, or P.O. Box 6688, Crestline, CA 92325. In Bahia de los Angeles a small fleet is maintained by Guerrmo's Trailer Court. In most other places one contacts the individual operators of the pangas who will be waiting by their boats.

Concentrations of pangas available for hire may be found in the inner harbor at Cabo San Lucas, at the fisherman's landing at the small town of La Playa 1 mile east of San Jose del Cabo, near the trailer courts in Loreto, immediately south of the lighthouse in San Felipe, at the mouth of the river in Mulege, and in scores of other less visited locations. Even if a panga fishermen is not normally in the sportfishing business, his boat can usually be hired for that purpose. Hard cash is hard to turn down.

Some sportfishermen have purchased Mexican pangas made in La Paz. Here one is being launched at the Fisherman's Landing launching ramp at the mouth of the estuary at Mulege.

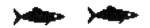

THE BAJA CATCH

By NIEL KELLY AND GENE KIRA

There are too many travel books on the market that reflect very little of the authors personal experiences. And too many fishing books are long on "fish stories" and short on solid information. These two fellows did it right. The went down to Baja and fished. The BAJA CATCH is crammed with the "wheres" and "hows" of enjoying one of Baja's biggest attractions - FISHEN.

NUMEROUS MAPS -- 275 PAGES -- FISH ILLUSTRATIONS

Revised and expanded 2nd edition.

Get your copy from the BAJA BOOKSHELF in the Appendix

FISHERMAN OWNED BOATS — We will now discuss the three classes of boats brought south by tourists. The three classes are the same as presented earlier in this chapter.

Ocean-Cruisers — The people coming to Baja on ocean-cruising sailboats usually engage in sportfishing. Some of this is simply bottom fishing from the boat when it is at anchor. More often the ship's tender is used for trolling away from the anchorage. When this occurs, the ocean-cruiser has the advantages attributable to the small class 4 boats described below, plus the range provided by the larger mother vessel.

Trailer Boats — Small car-top and trailerable boats are taken south to Baja by the thousands. They are the class 3 and 4 vessels noted earlier in this chapter. They range in size from small 13 foot aluminum craft to the heavy vessel on the three-axle trailer shown in the photo in this chapter. The larger boat has significant range but lacks maneuverability for fishing in shallow and restricted areas. The 13 footers have maximum maneuverability and can be launched at hundreds of places where there is no ramp. The fisherman's range is thus expanded by moving the boat around on land. The small boat's disadvantages are that it cannot be used in even moderately rough weather and they cannot safely venture far from land.

FISHING LITERATURE — Past books about fishing in Baja waters have been long on fish-stories but short on specifics, even though they have been instrumental in drawing large numbers of fishermen to the peninsula. Fortunately, a fishing manual worthy of the name is now available. This is *The Baja Catch*.

Coauthored by Neil Kelly and Gene Kira, the book documents the extensive fishing exploits of the first named author. Kelly fishes almost exclusively from a small 13 foot aluminum boat. This craft is easily launched over the beach and provides the maneuverability necessary to fish over reefs and close to shore where Kelly believes the best habitats are found. Most of his fishing involves trolling over zigzag courses at 3-to-6 knots using jointed, artificial lures.

The book's subtitle, *An Inshore Fishing Manual for Baja California* alerts you that it is devoted largely to the above described

method of fishing. The coastal areas described are necessarily limited to only a small percentage of the Baja shore, and only a few of its many islands, as these are the areas safely accessible in Kelly's small vessel. However, what is covered is presented in great detail. Explicit recommendations on boats, tackle, fishing tactics, best fishing seasons, and descriptions and drawings of the fifty most common fish species are also included.

Acquire *The Baja Catch* if fishing is one of your primary objectives in visiting Baja. Many of the fishing areas it recommends are shown in the aerial photos in the *Baja Boater's Guide* .

FISHING OVERVIEW — By way of background I present the following overview material.

WHEN TO FISH — There are hundreds of varieties of game fish in the waters surrounding the Baja peninsula. They range in size from giant marlin to small rockfish and triggers. There is considerable variation in the time of year when any given species is present, and this availability also differs from section-to-section of the coast.

Please refer to the graph entitled QUALITY OF FISHING BY MONTHS. It is based on a composite of information for common game fish for all areas of the peninsula. The rating index in the chart's vertical axis is my own invention and has no significance other than to show the relative fishing quality by months of the year. It is designed to show that (1) fishing in Baja is never poor, (2) the best fishing is during the summer and early fall, and (3) the least productive months are during the winter.

In general, the peninsula-wide yearly trend shown in the chart is also encountered in most individual sections, particularly in the tropical waters of the Sea of Cortez. Clearly, the presence of many species increases as the waters become warmer during summer. However there are numerous seasonal variations, particularly if you are interested in one particular species of fish. More data on when to fish are noted in the area summaries below.

UPPER SEA OF CORTEZ AREA — This is the area from north of Santa Rosalia to the mouth of the Rio Colorado. While the waters here are still classified as tropical, there is upwelling of cooler waters near the Midriff Islands lying off Bahia de los Angeles and some of the tropical fish species such as sailfish, amberjack, snappers, and needlefish do not migrate this far north. By way of compensation, the northern area has several species not found farther south. These include the spotted bass and many of the mullet, tortuava, croker, and corvina that spawn in the shallow waters south of the Rio Colorado.

In much of this area fishing is good year-round, but fishermen are faced with two practicalities posed by the weather. The chilly northerly winds present throughout the Sea of Cortez are particularly strong north of Santa Rosalia. Fishing in small boats can thus be both cold and dangerous during these months. In the summer, air temperatures are excessively hot, even more so than areas to the south. Thus, from a practical standpoint, the spring and fall months constitute the best fishing periods. Boat launching is also complicated by the extreme tide fluctuations and severe currents present in these waters.

MULEGE-LORETO AREA — Several of the extremes which confront the fisherman in the upper Sea of Cortez are less of a problem farther south. Winter temperatures are milder and winds, while present, are less severe. And summer temperatures, while hot, are less so than farther north. Tides and currents are not serious problems as they are to the north. However, fisherman need to be alert to the possibility of severe tropical storms that occasionally reach into this area. U. S. Naval Weather Service records indicate the danger period is from mid-August to mid-October.

While fishing is good year-round near Caleta San Lucas, it is more seasonal in such other popular fishing areas as Punta Chivato, Mulege, Bahia Concepcion, and the area around Puerto Escondido. This is because several of the most sought after species are migrators that come and go with the seasons. As examples, yellowtail are prevalent in the winter while July is the big month for dorado and marlin. Consult The Baja Catch for details.

LA PAZ AREA — The fishing fleet advertisements in La Paz stating that their city is Baja's all-season fishing grounds are a bit deceptive. First, fleet operators readily concede that the waters immediately off the city are badly depleted. For this reason they transport their clients either to the northern end of the East Cape area or to the waters around the southern end of Isla Espiritu Santos. In this latter area they can meet the large migratory species moving north into the Sea of Cortez around June.

Thus, La Paz has to reach somewhat far afield to tap good fishing waters and the area is only lightly visited by fishermen in small trailerable boats.

THE EAST CAPE AREA — The East Cape is that section of coast from the southern end of Isla Cerralvo south to Bahia los Frailes (see map in Chapter 23). The areas hotel operators boast it is the finest fishing grounds in the world, and Neil Kelly's *Baja Catch* rates it as the *best-of-the-best* in Baja. There are four basic reasons for this high praise.

(1) While Cabo San Lucas is recognized as the marlin capital of the world, this species is also one of the big draws along the East Cape. (2) The most sought after species of fish along Baja's east coast are migrators which include marlin, tuna, dorado, roosterfish, and wahoo. They move north into the Sea of Cortez in the spring and back south again in fall. Most of this migration takes place close to the Baja shore rather than on the mainland side. It passes on either side of Isla Cerralvo.

(3) Ocean waters over 1,000 feet deep lie only a few miles offshore along much of the East Cape shoreline, and it is in such deep, blue-water areas that marlin thrive. Thus, lengthy trips to sea are not required to reach the large glamour species in this area. The best season is short, however, centering around six-week periods in late May and October, although some of the large species persist in some areas through the summer. (4) While the main marlin periods are limited, the East Cape also has a sizeable population of top-flight resident species so that fishing of some variety is always available.

THE CAPE AREA — There are fewer resident fishes at the tip of the Baja peninsula than in other areas, but fishing for striped marlin and other billfish is unexcelled. They

QUALITY OF FISHING BY MONTHS

See text for discussion of the vertical axis rating scale.

are catchable throughout the year with the best seasons centering around April and November.

As in the East Cape, the deep waters favored by marlin come close to shore at Cabo San Lucas. They may thus be caught only a few miles off the Cape, although many charter vessels take their customers to various *banks* that lie some 20-25 miles offshore. During the winter months the marlin are found on the Pacific side of the Cape and along the Sea of Cortez shore in the summer.

Small boats may be launched at the excellent ramps in the inner harbor at Cabo San Lucas, but surf conditions greatly limit over the beach launching in the Cape area. Each morning there is a mass exodus of sportfishing vessels leaving the Cabo San Lucas harbor. Some are small fishermen owned boats but most are various sizes of charter vessels catering to the areas hotel clients. There is considerable fishing action at San Jose del Cabo, but simple observation will disclose that Cabo San Lucas is the fishing capital of Baja California.

PACIFIC LAGOONS — Much of Baja's Pacific shore consists of the extremely low-lying terrain of the Continental Borderlands Province (see map in Chapter 9). Saltwater lagoons lie behind the barrier-beaches in many places and most have entrances to the sea protected by breaking bars. The larger lagoons support Mexican fish camps and receive light visitation from sportfishermen using small car-top boats.

The lagoons most frequently visited are Puerto San Quintin, Laguna Manuela, Laguna la Bocana, Estero Coyote, Laguna San Ignacio, and Bahia Magdalena and the extensive lagoons north of its main bay. Fishing in these places is rated from fair to excellent. See this books Index for the location of these lagoons, and consult *The Baja Catch* and *Baja Boater's Guide* for more details.

With the exception of Bahia Magdalena, these places are accessed by washboarded secondary roads over level but poorly vegetated planes. Camping sites are austere and often windswept, but avid fishermen will find the lagoons a special and rewarding challenge.

PACIFIC ROCKY SHORES — The GEOLOGIC PROVINCES Map in Chapter 9 shows the mountainous, and rocky portions of Baja's Pacific coast. There is little sportfishing data on these areas as road access is poor and the launching of small boats into the heavy Pacific surf is very difficult. I expect that the Punta Eugenia and Punta Abreojos area will become popular fishing areas when oiling of t highway to Bahia Tortugas is completed.

For now, sportfishing is concentrated in the Bahia Todos Santos area at Ensenada, and at various reefs and Islands to the south which are accessed by three

and four day charter trips out of San Diego and Ensenada. The Coronados Islands may also be reached by larger fisherman-owned boats out of San Diego.

SHRIMP — Tourists at San Felipe and Bahia Concepcion in the Sea of Cortez will frequently observe Mexican fishing vessels in the 40-to-60 foot class. These, in most cases, will be *shrimpers* and may be distinguished from more conventional fishing boats by the large array of often colorful nets hanging from booms when the boat is not actually working. Many shrimpers work at night so you will see them anchored during the day.

Dragging for shrimp takes place in relatively shallow waters along both coasts in the northern half of the Sea of Cortez. I have also seen shrimpers working the waters of Bahia de La Paz. On the Pacific coast shrimp boats will also be seen in Bahia Magdalena and in the shallow waters along the sandy beaches north of this bay.

Because of Mexico's economic problems, the government has decreed that shrimp must be sold on the international market in order to produce foreign currency. Many fishermen will sell shrimp to tourists, but you should recognize the illicit nature of these transactions. There are reports of shrimp being sold to tourists, who are then approached by the salesman's accomplices posing as federal officers looking for *la mordida*.

LOBSTER — Lobsters abound in the waters along the rocky sections of the Pacific coast and its islands. Bahia Magdalena is at the southern end of the lobstering area. Boaters must be continually alert for small buoys attached by line to a lobster trap resting on the ocean floor. As with shrimp, the taking of lobsters by other than Mexican nationals is not permitted and, again, they may not by sold to tourists.

Large sportfishing vessels lying at anchor in front of the Hotel Hacienda at Cabo San Lucas. Scores of such boats make the run from southern California to Cabo each winter.

Landing one of the mammoth glamour fish is commonplace at Cabo San Lucas.

FISHING LICENSES — All tourists 12 years or older must obtain a Mexican Sport Fishing License to fish in Mexican waters. They are issued by the day, week, month, or year. Fees depend upon the length of time involved and fluctuate widely according to the current exchange rate. All persons aboard a tourist's boat must have a license if the vessel is carrying fishing gear or any kind of fish or fish parts. This can become expensive for yachts carrying numerous people on extended voyages.

A fishing license must also be obtained for any boat used for fishing. Here, the fee is based on the length of the vessel. Some guidebooks mistakenly refer to this license as a boat permit. To be on the safe side, it may be prudent to get a boat fishing license if your boat is of the type commonly used for fishing even if you do not intend to use it for fishing purposes. Clearly, you do not need a permit for a surfboard, wind surfer, or similar small craft. A license is also required to fish from the shore in Mexico. These licenses are issued at no charge.

Licenses covering all types of sportfishing are issued by the federal government *(Secretaria de Pesca)* and are thus valid throughout Mexico. They may be obtained at the offices of the Mexican Department of Fisheries in San Diego and Ensenada. Several of the travel clubs noted in Chapter 1 sell licenses through the mail as a service to their members.

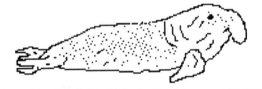

CHAPTER 6
HOTELS

I must alert you that I am in love with Baja's hotels. They are one of her major tourist attractions and provide excellent examples of the blending of man-made features with outstanding natural surroundings. The destination of most of my travels north of the border has usually been an interesting city, a National Park or other enticing outdoor attractions. With few exceptions, the hotels and motels in which I have spent the night offer little more than a place to stay. When you visit Baja's fine hotels I hope you will come to agree that they provide an end in themselves.

I am not a world traveler, but I have been fortunate in recent years to visit the major Caribbean islands, the major South American cities plus England and Spain. Baja's hotels are better than anything I have seen in these places. I will now briefly explain why I believe this is so.

1. LOCATION — Except in the border cities, most of Baja's better hotels are situated directly on the water's edge, thus taking full advantage of mankind's love affair with the seacoast. In some cases, the front yard of your room will be an extensive white sand beach as at San Felipe, Buena Vista, and San Jose del Cabo. In others, the setting blends the hotel with craggy cliffs and small isolated beaches. This latter situation is typical of the fine facilities in the Cape Area at the tip of the peninsula.

Hotel locations run the gamut from busy downtown La Paz to complete isolation. In some cases, there are no other man-made features for miles in any direction. If you are less than enchanted with visiting such sardine-packed resort centers as Acapulco, Honolulu, and the Florida coast, Baja will provide a welcome change.

2. ARCHITECTURAL STYLE — The designers of Baja's fine hotels have achieved an outstanding blending of structural and landscape architecture. Perhaps most importantly, almost all of Baja's fine hotels are low rise. Three stories are usually the limit. These buildings blend with the natural environment. That Wall Street feeling is left behind. North of the border, the hotel guest is greeted by steel, lumber, and sheetrock; in Baja, it is brick, native stone, and tile, with palm thatching in the patio areas. These building materials, combined with the archways, tile corridors, and other trappings of Spanish architecture, provide a charming change for the northern visitor.

Completing the picture are swimming pools, fountains, and attractive desert landscaping. Baja's desert plants seem amazingly tolerant to being transplanted for domestic purposes. They provide peninsula hotels with instant oasis of greenery and shade. If you cannot relax in such a setting you may be beyond relaxation.

3. UNCROWDED SETTING — Only a few of Baja's hotels have as many as 250 rooms. The majority are much smaller. The overall ambiance is usually one of freedom and spaciousness. There is no need to rise at dawn to reserve one's lounge chair from among all the others packed at the rim of the pool, as in many other parts of the world.

Even the best hotels are seldom full except during three-day weekends and immediately prior to Christmas and Easter. (This observation spans all of my travels in Baja. It is as true today as it was 20 years ago when Baja was far less popular than it is presently.) Reservations should be made well in advance for these peak periods. They are advisable at other times but are usually easily obtained.

While this light use is not good news for management, it is pleasant for the patron who benefits by receiving better service under less hectic conditions. The caption on an advertising brochure for the central coast reads "Undiscovered Loreto." This phrase can be applied equally well to Baja hotels in general.

The Hotel Finisterra on the cliffs near the tip of the peninsula at Cabo San Lucas.

It seems all too obvious that there are more hotel rooms than the supply of tourists and more are being built. While this would seem to make very little economic sense for the hotel operators, it results in a relaxed and uncrowded atmosphere for the tourist.

As always, there is also the not-so-good news. Mexican hotels have their shortcomings. There is a rather obvious absence of building codes and standards. Thus, plumbing and electrical fixtures frequently leave something to be desired, even in the best establishments. Furniture, door frames, and other wooden objects are often of poor quality.

On one recent visit I closed the door of my room at one of the best hotels and skinned my knuckle because the door knob had been set too close to the frame. At a smaller motel, the men's restroom contained two urinals beautifully set in tile in the corner of the room. They were located in such a way that a gentleman using one facility would be required to stand in the exact same spot as someone using the other but the setting was extremely attractive! To most visitors, these minor inconveniences are of little consequence in comparison to the charm, fine food, and usually excellent service found at most peninsula hotels. I mention them here only to bring the required touch of realism to these remarks.

TYPES OF HOTELS

Baja hotels and other lodging facilities fall into three categories relating to the traveler's means of transportation and other factors. These are:

    1 — Highway Travel - Overnight Stops
    2 — Fly-in Hotels
    3 — Destination Resorts

Its fine architectural style and great seaside location near San Jose del Cabo make the Palmilla Los Cabos one of Baja's finest hotels.

The HOTEL SUMMARY presented in this chapter classifies each peninsula hotel using this system.

There are several imperfections with this three-category system. Some of the fly-in hotels also qualify as destination resorts. Most fly-in facilities are also accessible by road so that they, as well as the destination resorts, also serve the visitor who drives to Baja. While there are these shortcomings with this arrangement, I hope that it will be of assistance to you in providing the big-picture view of the peninsula's hotels and resorts.

HIGHWAY TRAVEL - OVERNIGHT STOPS — In tandem with the completion of the Transpeninsular Highway in 1973, came the construction, by the government, of a series of paradors and nearby hotels. (*Parador* is derived from the Spanish word *parada* meaning stopping place.) The paradors originally offered fuel, cafeteria-style restaurants, restrooms, and trailer courts. Many of these facilities have been abandoned, but the hotels are all still in operation, all bearing the name Hotel La Pinta (see the hotel logo on page 53).

It is clear that the Mexican government wished to provide modern, first-class facilities for the deluge of tourists that were expected after completion of the highway. The paradors were to fill this need from Ensenada to the Sea of Cortez where there were then few tourist accommodations. The onslaught came, but in the form of recreational vehicle users hellbent on making it south to the beaches in the shortest possible time. Relatively few visitors arrived in automobiles, and as a result, there was only light demand for restaurants and hotels along the highway.

More recently there has been a significant increase in the number of tourists traveling Highway 1 in automobiles and the La Pinta hotels are thus enjoying better business. They are located at, or near, San Quintin, Catavina, Parallelo 28 near Guerrero Negro, San Ignacio, and Loreto. These hotels are modest in size (25 to 65 rooms). and they were being well maintained during my most recent visit. I recommend them to you for an overnight stop.

In recent years small to medium-sized motels have been developed in many of the towns along Highway 1. They are clean and fully usable for an overnight or longer stay but are two numerous to include in the HOTEL DESCRIPTIONS presented in this chapter. The names of the towns having such motels are shown in the HOTEL SUMMARY.

FLY-IN HOTELS — Long before completion of the Transpeninsular Highway, private hotel operators were catering to the North American tourist trade; however, many facilities south-of-the-border cities had to be reached by air. The hotels at La Paz have long been served by an airport suitable for large commercial aircraft in addition to ferry service from the mainland. Most of the other hotels had to provide their own dirt-surface landing strips. Their

Hotel la pinta

The logo of Baja's La Pinta Hotels

patrons were thus almost exclusively people who arrived in small, privately-owned aircraft.

These hotels were scattered along the coast of the Sea of Cortez from Bahia Gonzaga, on the north, all the way to Cabo San Lucas. The majority were isolated from the outside world. Some were very modest, having only a few cabins and a central dining and lounging facility. Others were, and still are, among the most luxurious resorts in all of Baja. They provide a series of little-known Shangri-La's for private pilots who can land in the hotel's back yard and be greeted by familiar faces and surroundings.

Most of these hotels are still in operation, but many are in locations now served by main highways. Fly-in customers must share their old haunts with others who arrive by road. At Cabo San Lucas, not only has the highway arrived but the old beachside airstrip has long ago been dredged away and replaced by a marina. The good news for the pilot seeking solitude has been the construction of a few new facilities at spots that should stay relatively isolated.

While part of Baja's past allure may have vanished for those who remember how it used to be, several facilities still cater to the needs of the fly-in customer. The HOTEL SUMMARY indicates facilities with private airstrips or, as at Bahia de los Angeles, are close to the village airfield. It should also be noted that flyers are welcome at any of the larger international airports.

DESTINATION RESORTS — I offer no precise definition of *destination resort*. In general, I refer to the more luxurious facilities, many of which offer tennis courts and sportfishing fleets along with swimming pools and other activities. Most are served by one of the Baja California Sur international airports, or are within easy driving range of the United States between Tijuana and Ensenada and at San Felipe. They are the kind of places you would go, with the love of your life, to spend a week or two lying in the sun and being pampered. You will find a few of the fly-in hotels included in this category. The majority of destination resorts are concentrated at La Paz and the Cape Area.

FONATUR

Everywhere there are people who are content with the way things are and who resist modernization and change. These feelings often extend to places beyond one's home into areas that have been visited as tourists. Such it is with Baja. Many will look with displeasure as Baja's *Old Mexico* charms are replaced with those of a more modern era. For better or worse, the change has been underway for some time, and at several places tourists of the future will be confronted with markedly different allurements.

The prime mover of these changes is FONATUR, the acronym for *Fondo National de Formento al Turismo* (translated into English as *National Fund for Tourism Development*). FONATUR is an agency created by the federal government in 1969. Its primary function is to encourage and channel the government and private investments needed to establish new centers of tourist activities with the objectives of increasing domestic employment, generating foreign exchange, and promoting regional development.

FONATUR'S initial activities were on the mainland at Cancun on Mexico's Caribbean coast and at Ixtapa on the Pacific coast north of Acapulco. Here, two essentially deserted sections of coast were converted into rows of high-rise hotels, condominiums, and tourist-oriented facilities. International airports were constructed nearby.

During the mid 1970s FONATUR initiated work at two new sites on the Baja peninsula. Actual construction started at Loreto in 1977, and at San Jose del Cabo and Cabo San Lucas in 1978. At both sites, early work consisted of developing such essential facilities as water and power supplies, sewage systems, and offices and housing for employees. New hotels soon followed, along with extensive networks of streets for vacation homes and condominiums. Golf courses were largely complete by 1989.

So far, these developments have not included high-rise buildings; one would hope that this remains true for the future. Their current status is described as they are encountered in the PART III GRAND TOUR.

DESCRIPTIONS AND RECOMMENDATIONS

Below you will find a concise HOTEL SUMMARY that lists the principal hotels. Following that is a HOTEL DESCRIPTIONS list which describes each facility in more detail. I strive to present my honest judgments but have avoided making overly negative comments. You may detect that I have been guilty of damnation through faint praise when describing establishments that are not to my liking. In addition, here are my untarnished recommendations, totally free of personal bias. And keep in mind, that a great view of the ocean is higher on my list of priorities than how quickly the hot water arrives at the shower.

THE CAPE AREA (San Jose del Cabo to Cabo San Lucas) — There are five long-established, modest-sized hotels in this area that I have always rated as Baja's best. They are the Hotels Palmilla Los Cabos, Cabo San Lucas, Twin Dolphin, Hacienda, and Finisterra. Some people would add the Hotel Solmar to this list. All of these hotels were built so that most of the rooms and other facilities face the ocean. They thus have a maximum of seaside ambiance. In more recent years two large Melia hotels have been constructed at Cabo San Lucas and the new resort area of Cabo Real. Other similar larger hotels will shortly follow. I expect to be able to rate most of these new facilities as excellent but to me they will lack the charm of my old favorite top-five. In all cases prices are high.

The Hotel Stouffer Presidente at San Jose del Cabo is the best at this location. The other facilities nearby are lower in quality.

THE EAST CAPE — Cabo San Lucas, San Jose de Cabo and Cabo Real will never be as crowded and hectic as Acapulco and Honolulu, but they are trying their damndest. The Los Barriles - Buena Vista area is more rural and slow paced and should remain that way. The Hotel Palmas de Cortez and the Rancho Buena Vista are my choices.

LA PAZ — None of this city's hotels are up to the Cape Area's best. But the Cape doesn't have La Paz. In my view you pick a hotel in La Paz to visit this attractive, clean, waterfront town. So my top pick is the Los Arcos and its satelite Cabanas de los Arcos because they are downtown where I for one want to be. If you would like to be farther out, the La Concha Beach Resort is the best.

FLY-IN HOTELS — In my view, none of the establishments that I rate as fly-in hotels are quite as good as the best at The Cape. Others will disagree, largely because the fly-ins offer such fine isolated settings, and lets face it, they have a bit of snob appeal. I won't argue, and present the Hotels Punta Chivato, Las Arenas, and Punta Pescadero as the best of this breed.

HOTEL SUMMARY

1 = Highway Travel -- 2 = Fly-in Hotels
3 = Destination Resorts

HOTEL	123	RATING	HOTEL	123	RATING
TIJUANA			Ensenada Travelodge	X - -	Good
Hotel Paraiso Radisson	X - -	Very Good	**SAN QUINTIN AREA**		
Hotel El Conquistador	X - -	Very Good	Hotel La Pinta San Quintin	X X -	Good +
Hotel Fiesta Americana	X - -	Very Good	Cielito Lindo Motel	X X -	Fair +
Hotel Lucerna	X - -	Very Good	Bay-side Motels	X X -	Good
Hotel Palacio Azteca	X - -	Good	**PARQUE NACIONAL SAN PEDRO MARTIR**		
MEXICALI			Meling Ranch (In Mountains)	- X -	Good
Hotel Lucerna	X - -	Very Good +	**CATAVINA**		
Holiday Inn	X - -	Very Good	Hotel La Pinta Cativina	X - -	Good +
SAN FELIPE			Rancho Santa Ines	X - -	Fair
Motel El Cortez	X - X	Good +	**BAHIA SAN LUIS GONZAGA AREA**		
Hotel Aguamarina (Closed 1992)	X - X	--------	Punta Bufeo Tourist Camp	X X -	Fair
Hotel Las Missiones	X - X	Good +	Papa Fernandez	X X -	Fair
PUERTECITOS			Alfonsina's	X X -	Fair
Posada de Orozco	X X -	Fair	**BAHIA DE LOS ANGELES**		
ROSARITO & OLD HIGHWAY 1			Villa Vitta Hotel	X X -	Good
Rosarito Beach Hotel	X - X	Very Good	Casa Diaz	X X -	Fair
Plaza del Mar Spa	X - -	Good	**SAN FRANCISQUITO (El Arco-L.A. Bay Loop)**		
La Fonda Motel	X - -	Good	Punta San Francisquito Resort	- X -	Fair
Hotel Las Rocas	X - X	Very Good +	**GUERRERO NEGRO**		
Hotel New Port Baja	X - X	Very Good +	Hotel La Pinta Guerrero Negro	X - -	Good
ENSENADA AREA			Several Motels in Town	X - -	Fair
Estero Beach Resort Hotel	X - X	Very Good +	**BAHIA TORTUGAS**		
Hotel Agua Caliente (Hot Springs)	X - -	Fair	Vera Cruz Motel	X X -	Fair
Mision Santa Isabel	X - -	Very Good	**SAN IGNACIO**		
Hotel La Pinta, Ensenada	X - -	Good +	Hotel La Pinta San Ignacio	X - -	Good +
San Nicolas Resort Hotel	X - X	Very Good	La Posada Motel	X - -	Fair +
Hotel Villa Marina	X - -	Very Good	**SANTA ROSALIA**		
Corona Hotel	X - -	Good +	Hotel El Morro	X - -	Good
Casa del Sol	X - -	Good	**PUNTA CHIVATO**		
El Cid Motor Hotel	X - -	Good	Hotel Punta Chivato	- X -	Very Good

Hotels listed as they are encountered from north to south.

OTHERS — Some of my other favorites are: Hotel Lucerna (Tijuana and Mexicali); Mision Santa Isabel, San Nicolas Resort Hotel, and Estero Beach Resort Hotel (Ensenada); Hotel La Pinta San Ignacio (best of the La Pinta chain). While the FONATUR development at Nopolo near Loreto has attracted very little attention, its Hotel Presidente is really very nice. I present it as the least known of Baja's better hotels.

OFFBEAT — Finally, lets get down to some places most people never heard of and which offer a special charm at reasonable prices. I hate to mention these hideouts because their owners may get the *bighead* and raise their prices; and then, where am I going to stay? But here they are from north to south:

The Meling Ranch (Parque Nacional San Pedro Martir), La Fonda Motel & Restaurant (Old Highway 1), Bay-side Motels (Bahia San Quintin), Las Casitas (Mulege), Hotel Oasis (Loreto),

Hotel Gardinas (La Paz), Hotel California (Todos Santos), Hotel Palomar (Santiago), and Hotel Mar de Cortez (Cabo San Lucas).

In addition, I recommend that you take advantage of the services of a travel agent. Many Baja hotels offer discount rates for stays of more than two or three days, and lower air fares can frequently be obtained if travel is combined in a package with hotel reservations. These and other advantages can easily be missed if you make your own reservations. Unfortunately, travel agencies will not help you with some of the smaller hotels that do not have toll free numbers or pay agency commissions.

Finally, brace for the fact that some Baja hotels change their names and phone numbers with great regularity. You may have to do some detective work to match what you find here with what appears at your travel agency .

HOTEL SUMMARY

1 = Highway Travel -- 2 = Fly-in Hotels
3 = Destination Resorts

HOTEL	123	RATING	HOTEL	123	RATING
MULEGE			**THE EAST CAPE**		
Hotel Vista Hermosa	X - -	Good +	Hotel Las Arenas	- X X	Very Good
Hotel Serenidad	X X -	Good +	Punta Pescadero	- X X	Very Good
Hotel Terrazas	X - -	Fair	Hotel Playa Hermosa	X - -	Good
Hotel Las Casitas	X - -	Good	Hotel Palmas de Cortez	- X X	Very Good
Motel La Siesta	X - -	Good	Rancho Buena Vista	- X X	Very Good
Hotel Hacienda	X - -	Fair	Hotel Spa Buena Vista	- - X	Good +
LORETO - NOPOLO			Hotel Punta Colorado	X X -	Good +
Hotel La Pinta Loreto	X - -	Good	Rancho Leonero	X X -	Good
Hotel Mision de Loreto	X - -	Good +	**SAN JOSE DEL CABO**		
Hotel Oasis	X - -	Good +	Brisa del Mar Motel	X - -	Fair
Hotel Presidente Loreto	X - X	Very Good	Stouffer Presidente	- - X	Very Good
BAHIA MAGDALENA			Hotel Pasada Real	- - X	Good +
Hotel Alcatraz	X - -	Fair +	Hotel Aguamarina	- - X	Good
CUIDAD CONSTITUCION			Fiesta Inn	- - X	Good +
Hotel Maribel	X - -	Fair	**THE CABO CORRIDOR including CABO REAL**		
Hotel Casino	X - -	Fair	Hotel Palmilla	- X X	Excellent
LA PAZ			Hotel Cabo San Lucas	- X X	Excellent
La Posada	- - X	Very Good	Hotel Melina Cabo Real	- - X	Excellent
Hotel Gran Baja	- - X	Good +	Hotel Twin Dolphin	- - X	Excellent
Hotel Los Arcos	- - X	Very Good	Hotel Clarion Cabo San Lucas	- - X	Very Good
Cabanas de Los Arcos	- - X	Very Good	New excellent hotels under construction at Cabo Real		
Hotel La Perla	X - -	Good	**CABO SAN LUCAS**		
Palmira	- - X	Very Good	Hacienda Hotel	- - X	Excelent
La Concha Beach Resort	- - X	Very Good	Hotel Solmar	- - X	Very Good +
Hotel Gardenias	X - -	Good	Mar de Cortez	X - -	Good +
Club El Morro	- - X	Very Good	Hotel Finisterra	- - X	Excellent
Numerous other motels			Hotel Melina		
TODOS SANTOS			**TOWNS WITH MOTELS NOT LISTED ABOVE**		
Hotel California	X - -	Good	Tecate - Santo Tomas - San Quintin - San Vicente - El Rosaro.		

Hotels listed as they are encountered from north to south.

HOTEL DESCRIPTIONS

Towns are listed as encountered from north to south.

TIJUANA

HOTEL PARAISO RADISSON — 200 rooms, restaurant, bar, pool, Jacuzzi, convention center for 350 people. Blvd Agua Caliente No. 1 adjacent to the Tijuana Country Club. PO Box 431588, San Ysidro, CA 92073. 011-(526)-681-7200. An 8-story modern hotel.

HOTEL EL CONQUISTADOR — 110 rooms, restaurant, bar, pool, sauna, convention center for 300 people. Located near the Tijuana Country Club at 1777 Blvd Agua Caliente. PO Box 4471, San Ysidro, CA 92073. (800) 326-0995. An attractive 2-story motel with old world charm.

HOTEL FIESTA AMERICANA — 422 rooms, several restaurants and bars, pool, sauna and tennis courts. Convention center for 1,200 people. 4500 Agua Caliente Blvd. (800) FIESTA I. Hotel is part of the Plaza Agua Caliente on Blvd Agua Caliente adjacent the Tijuana Country Club. For a skyscraper view of Tijuana, this is the place, as there are 27 floors of rooms in this westerly segment of a modern twin-towered building. Hard to tell it apart from hotels in the major cities north of the border.

HOTEL LUCERNA — 168 rooms and suites, 2 restaurants, bar, pool convention facilities. NW corner of Paseo de los Heroes and Ave Rodriguez. PO Box 437910, San Ysidro, CA 92143. 011-(526) 634-2000 or (800) 582-3762. A modern 6-story hotel in the developing Rio Tijuana area. As a result, the overall atmosphere is less crowded than that in the older sections of town and the interior court is well landscaped.

HOTEL PALACIO AZTECA — 214 rooms, restaurant, bar, pool. On Old Hwy 1 two blocks south of Blvd Agua Caliente. PO Box 434049, San Ysidro, CA 92143-4049. 011 (526) 681-8100. A 6-story hotel which was being extensively remodeled in 1992. Located in the older, more congested, part of Tijuana.

TECATE

MOTELS — There are two motels on the north side of Highway 2 entering Tecate from the west. These are the Motel El Dorado and the Hotel Hacienda. The latter establishment has a restaurant and disco-bar. Its rooms face inward toward a central courtyard. There are no trailer courts in Tecate.

MEXICALI

HOTEL LUCERNA — 200 rooms, restaurant, bar, pool. 2151 Blvd Benito Juarez. 011-(526) 634-2000 or (800) 582-3762. A very nice 6-story hotel with well-landscaped inside courtyard.

HOLIDAY INN — 120 rooms, restaurant, bar, pool. On Blvd Benito Juarez. Toll free (800) 456-4329. A multi-storied hotel with pleasant internal courtyard.

SAN FELIPE

MOTEL EL CORTEZ — 78 rooms, restaurant, bar, pool, and boat launching ramp. PO Box 1227, Calexico, CA 92231. (706) 566-8324. A pleasant motel located on the beach about 1/2 mi. south of the center of town.

HOTEL AGUAMARINA — 140 rooms, restaurant, bar, pool. (*This hotel was closed in 1992 but is included here in the event it reopens.*) This 3-story hotel is built on a sandy hillside adjoining the Sea of Cortez 10 mi. south of San Felipe via paved highway. It is isolated from other developments. The rooms have balconies overlooking the water.

HOTEL LAS MISIONES — 120 rooms, restaurant, bar, tennis court, meeting facilities. PO Box 120637 Chula Vista, CA 92012. (800) 336-5454. A very nice modern 3-story hotel directly on the beach about 1 mi. south of town. Well-landscaped courtyard area.

The Cape Area's Hotel Twin Dolphin

ADDITIONAL MOTELS — There are 5 other very adequate motels within a few blocks of, and south of, the center of town. They are the Motel Capitan, Motel Chapala, Hotel Truncha Vagabundo, Hotel Riviera, and Motel Villa del Mar.

PUERTECITOS

POSADA DE OROZCO — Gift shop. This is facility located near the PEMEX on the beach at the head of the cove. In spring 1989 it was being expanded and modernized as the result of the paved highway being completed south to Puertecitos. Look forward to an improved facility in the future.

ROSARITO AND OLD HWY 1

ROSARITO BEACH HOTEL — 152 rooms (being expanded to 282), restaurant, 3 bars, pool, entertainment. On Old Hwy 1 at the south Rosarito exit from Hwy 1-D. PO Box 430145, San Diego, CA 92143-0145. (800) 343-8582 A 1-story former gambling casino dating from the 1930s. Many of the rooms have been remodeled and the public rooms are also well kept. The hotel is on the POINTS OF SPECIAL INTEREST Tour because of its historic interest.

PLAZA DEL MAR HOTEL SPA — 180 rooms, 5 restaurants, bars, tennis court, entertainment, pool. On Old Highway 1, 0.8 mi. north of the La Mision exit from Highway 1-D. PO Box 434520 San Diego, CA 92143-4520. 001 (526) 685-9152 or (800) 762-6380. A sprawling older but adaquate resort complex on a high bluff overlooking the Pacific. The room construction is poor but the landscaping and overall atmosphere are good. Look for the pyramid in the archeological garden.

LA FONDA — 25 rooms, restaurant, bar, entertainment. On Old Hwy 1, 0.3 mi. south of the La Mision exit from Hwy 1-D. A famous old road-house with great food located on the bluffs overlooking the Pacific. The restaurant is more of the attraction than the motel. No phone or mailing address.

HOTEL LAS ROCAS -- 26 Suites & 46 Rooms, restaurant, bar with life music, conference facilities, pool, tennis court and jacuzzis. P. O. Box 8851, Chula Vista, CA 91912. (800) 733-6394. A new (1991) modern, 5-story hotel on cliffs overlooking the ocean. All rooms with terraces and ocean views. Located on old Highway 1 near Km 38. Fancy.

HOTEL NEW PORT BAJA -- 150 rooms, restaurant, bar, tennis courts, gift shop, pool and jacuzzi. P. O. Box 139 Plaza Patria 22441, Tijuana. (800) 582-1018. A new (1991) modern 3-story hotel on cliffs overlooking the ocean. All rooms with ocean views. Located on old Highway 1 near Km 45. Fancy.

ENSENADA AREA

ESTERO BEACH RESORT HOTEL — 110 rooms, restaurant, bar, tennis court. PO Box 86, Ensenada, B.C. Mexico. 011 (526) 676-6230 or (800) 762-2494. At this location on the shores of Estero Punta Banda are combined an attractive and well-landscaped hotel, trailer court and shops. It is the only Ensenada area hotel which fully meets my standards for a destination resort. Located 6 mi. S of Ensenada's tourist center.

HOTEL AGUA CALIENTE — 50 rooms, restaurant, bar. Large swimming pools heated by nearby hot springs. Adjoining camping area under large live oak trees. The hotel is a bit run-down. A pleasant spa, 5.1 mi. by dirt road south of **Km 26** on Hwy 3 east of Ensenada.

HOTEL MISION SANTA ISABEL — 58 rooms, restaurant, bar, pool. An older, charming, colonial-style hotel at the east end of the *Tourist Row* area. Completely remodeled in 1989. Isabel Travel, (619) 942-9108. P.O. Box 76, Ensenada B.C. Mexico.

HOTEL LA PINTA ENSENADA — 52 rooms, restaurant, bar, pool. Blvd Los Bucaneros. (800) 542-3283. The northern-most of Baja's chain of La Pinta hotels. Built around a central courtyard.

SAN NICOLAS RESORT HOTEL — 150 rooms, restaurant, bar, entertainment, coffee shop, pools, convention facilities for 450 people. Ave Lopez Mateos and Ave Guadalupe. PO Box 437060, San Diego, CA 92143-7060. (706) 676-4070. This is the fanciest of the hotels in downtown Ensenada. It is rated as a destination resort with the reservation that its location on the city streets several blocks from the waterfront leaves a bit to be desired. It is close to the tourist area shops and has a pleasant internal atmosphere.

HOTEL VILLA MARINA — 130 rooms, 2 restaurants, bar, pool. (011) 526 678-3321. P. O. Box 727, Bonita, CA 91908. Ave Lopez Mateo and Ave Castillo. It is Ensenada's only highrise building and has views of the city and the Pacific.

CASA DEL SOL — 46 rooms, restaurant, pool. (800) 528-1234 (Best Western reservation system) or 011 (526) 678-2307. A motel directly on Tourist Row.

EL CID MOTOR HOTEL — 52 rooms, restaurant, bar, pool. PO Box 1431, Ensenada, B.C. Mexico 22800. 011 (526) 678-2402. A motel directly on Tourist Row.

ENSENADA TRAVELODGE — 52 rooms, restaurant, bar, pool and enclosed parking. P. O. Box 1467 Ensenada. (800) 255-3050. A motel directly on Tourist Row.

CORONA HOTEL — 93 Rooms, restaurant, bar, pool. (706) 678-0901 A 4 story hotel at the edge of the harbor area a few blocks from the tourist area.

SAN QUINTIN AREA

HOTEL LA PINTA SAN QUINTIN — 60 rooms, restaurant, bar, tennis court. (800) 542-3283. One of the original parador hotels. See Chapter 19 for directions. All rooms have a private terrace facing the ocean. Winter season often cool and windy. There is an airstrip nearby.

CIELITO LINDO MOTEL — 13 rooms, coffee shop, lounge-bar with dancing. Write Santa Maria, Valle de San Quintin, B.C.N. Mexico. A modest but pleasant motel operated with the nearby Cielito Lindo Trailer Court. Rooms are grouped in several buildings facing a central grassy courtyard. It is a relatively short walk to the beach. Located away from other developments. See Chapter 19 for directions. The lounge has a band and dancing on Saturday nights, and from the way it looked on Sunday morning, a good time is assured. An airstrip is located 200 yards to the east.

BAY-SIDE MOTELS — There are three modest motels which lie on the low bluff near the water's edge along the east shore of Bahia San Quintin. These are Ernesto's, Old Mill Motel, and Muelle Viejo Motel. Each has a restaurant and bar, that touch of rural Mexico flavor, views of the bay and the cinder cones to the west. See Chapter 19 for directions.

PARQUE NACIONAL SAN PEDRO MARTIR

MELING RANCH — The Meling Ranch is a working cattle ranch but with very pleasant accommodations for about 12 guests. There is a dining room and swimming pool. The ranch lies 32 miles east of Hwy 1 on the road to Parque Nacional San Pedro Martir, and 19 miles west of the park boundry. There is a nearby air strip.

CATAVINA

HOTEL LA PINTA CATAVINA — 28 rooms, pool, restaurant, bar, tennis court. . (800) 542-3283. One of the original parador hotels. A pleasant hotel located adjacent to Hwy 1 at Catavina. Perhaps its most appealing feature is its location within the fascinating granite boulders and outstanding desert vegetation present in this area. An airstrip is nearby.

RANCHO SANTA INEZ — A modest facility situated a short distance east of Hwy 1. Cabins and small restaurant. Adjoins a blacktop airstrip.

BAHIA SAN LUIS GONZAGA AREA

ALFONSINA'S — 6 rooms, restaurant (order in advance). A line of very modest rooms along the beach at the north end of the residential development and dirt airstrip at Bahia San Luis Gonzaga. Fronted by an outstanding sand beach.

PUNTA BUFEO TOURIST CAMP — 10 or more stone houses for lease or rent. Small restaurant and 3 small rental rooms. Owned by Francisca Fernandez and sons. This is the northernmost of the fly-in facilities on the Sea of Cortez. It has a dirt landing strip parallel to the beach. A really isolated location with little vegetation, as is typical of the San Felipe

Desert. The last time I saw it was in 1989 . Located near Punta Bufeo, 6 mi. north of Punta Willard. See US nautical chart 21008 for location.

PAPA FERNANDEZ — Cabins and refreshments. A very modest fly-in facility located near the north end of Bahia Gonzaga. The founder, Papa Fernandez, was 94 in 1989. The resort is now run by his son, who bears the same name.

BAHIA DE LOS ANGELES

VILLA VITTA HOTEL — 40 rooms, restaurant, bar, pool, boat rental. Write Jimsair, 2904 Pacific Hwy, San Diego, CA 92101. (619) 298-4958. A very nice modern facility located adjacent to the paved highway as one enters the village. I list this as a fly-in facility as the hotel promptly meets incoming aircraft at the village airstrip about 1 mi. away. They have an excellent boat launching ramp. $20/$40

CASA DIAZ — 15 rooms, restaurant, store, boat ramp, rental boats. Write Antero Diaz, PO Box 579, Ensenada, B.C. Mexico. Not quite as fancy as the Villa Vitta, but this is the original, family-operated, fly-in resort at Bahia de los Angeles and is well liked. Very nice and well run although lacking the desert landscaping common to many Baja hotels. Make reservations in advance for the restaurant, where meals are served family style. The old adjacent airstrip is gone. Aircraft now use the village strip about 1-1/2 mi. distant.

SAN FRANCISQUITO

PUNTA SAN FRANCISQUITO RESORT — 11 cabins with cots, restaurant, central restroom, shower facilities. Write 2004 Newton Ave, San Diego, CA 92113. (619) 239-8872. A modest fly-in facility with poor road access. Also caters to boaters crossing the Sea of Cortez from Bahia Kino. Some visitors fly in, camp on the beach, and use the resort's restrooms and other facilities. One of the key aviation fuel stops for the private pilot.

GUERRERO NEGRO

HOTEL LA PINTA GUERRERO NEGRO — 28 rooms, restaurant, bar. (800) 542-3283. Another of the original parador hotels. Located adjacent to Hwy 1 next to the eagle monument at the 28th parallel. The hotel is modern and comparable to the other La Pinta facilities, but its setting in the flat, relatively barren desert is less attractive than those of its sister hotels.

The are several small motels on the right side of the road entering the town of Guerrero Negro. Of particular note is the Malarrimo restaurant and motel.

BAHIA TORTUGAS

VERA CRUZ MOTEL — 8 rooms, restaurant, bar. A modest motel near the PEMEX station. After having driven so many miles even a modest establishment looks good.

SAN IGNACIO

HOTEL LA PINTA SAN IGNACIO — 28 rooms, restaurant, bar, pool. (800) 542-3283. My favorite of the original parador hotels, due in part to its setting in the palms and other vegetation at the edge of the charming town of San Ignacio.

LA POSADA MOTEL — 8 rooms. Write La Posada Motel, San Ignacio, B. C. S. Mexico. A small but pleasant motel on a San Ignacio back street 2 blocks from the civic plaza.

SANTA ROSALIA

HOTEL EL MORRO — 21 rooms, restaurant, cocktail lounge, pool. PO Box 76, Santa Rosalia, B.C.S. Mexico. (706) 852-0414. A modern motel with attractive stone buildings. Built on a bluff overlooking the Sea of Cortez. Some rooms have patios with water views. Adjacent to the Transpeninsular Highway at the southern edge of Santa Rosalia.

The old historic **HOTEL FRANCIS** was closed about 1990.

PUNTA CHIVATO

HOTEL PUNTA CHIVATO — About 30 rooms, restaurant, bar, pool, beachside camping. Write Apartado Postal 18, Mulege, B.C.S., Mexico (706) 853-0188. I would rate Punta Chivato as a destination resort except that it is a little difficult to reach, but for this reason it may be just the place you will love. A trailer court and subdivision are being developed. The secondary road leading to the hotel joins Highway 1 near **Km F-156**. Features windsurfing charters. See Chapter 5 for details.

MULEGE

HOTEL VISTA HERMOSA — About 20 rooms, restaurant, pool, bar. Located in an isolated setting above and on the north side of the Rio Santa Rosalia, a location that offers a good view over the mouth of the river and the Sea of Cortez. See Chapter 21 for directions.

HOTEL SERENIDAD — 32 rooms including 2-bedroom cottages, restaurant, bar, pool. Write PO Box 9, Mulege, B.C.S. Mexico. (706) 853-0111. This is one of Baja's longstanding fly-in hotels. The airstrip is directly adjacent to the hotel. An attractive facility readily accessible from Hwy 1 near **Km F-132** over 1/2 mi. of dirt road. Located at the mouth of the river with an adjoining boat launching ramp. Considering the ease of access and its overall attractiveness, it is probably Mulege's best hotel.

HOTEL TERRAZAS — 35 rooms. This is a clean but basic motel in the center of the Mulege business district.

HOTEL LAS CASITAS — 8 rooms, restaurant. Write Las Casitas, PO Box 3, Mulege, B.C.S. Mexico. (706) 853-0019. This is a small, older, inexpensive, and charming hotel near the center of town. It is the kind of place you would expect to find in a sleepy Mexican town. Mulege, of course, is no longer sleeply. The restaurant is a favorite with the local tourist community.

LORETO-NOPOLO AREA

HOTEL LA PINTA LORETO — 30 rooms, restaurant, bar, pool. (800) 542-3283. Still another of the original parador hotels. Large rooms with private patios or balconies. It is located on a good beach at the north edge of Loreto.

HOTEL MISION DE LORETO — 36 rooms, restaurant, bar, pool. Apartado Postal 49, Loreto, B.C.S. 011 (526) 833-0048. A very nice 3-story hotel but I feel it falls a little short of the destination resort list. It has no beach but fronts on an attractive waterfront street and breakwater facing the Sea of Cortez.

HOTEL OASIS — 35 rooms, restaurant, bar, tennis court, pool. Write Hotel Oasis, Loreto, B.C.S. 011 (526) 833 0211. This small attractive hotel has its 1 floor of rooms along the beach toward the south end of Loreto. I have left it off the destination resort list but it is very nice and may be just the kind of hideaway you are seeking.

HOTEL PRESIDENTE LORETO — 250 rooms, restaurant, coffee shop, bar, 2 pools, entertainment, convention facilities. PO Box 28, Loreto, B.C.S. Mexico. Toll free in Calif. (800) 542-6028. Other US states (800) 854-2026) This is the Loreto area's finest hotel, although it is not in Loreto but 6 mi. south at Nopolo. Located on the beach. Across the street is the international tennis center. A well-landscaped first-class destination resort.

Loreto's Hotel Oasis. This small modest hotel pleasantly blends desert landscaping and the use of native building materials with its beach side location.

The Hotel Presidente Loreto, the first, and up to now the only hotel to be constructed at the FONATUR resort community at Nopolo.

CIUDAD CONSTITUCION

HOTEL MARIBEL — 39 rooms, restaurant, bar. Write Maribel, Guadalupe Victoria 156, Ciudad Constitucion, B.C.S. Mexico. (706) 832-0155. A 3-story concrete building at the corner of the main street of town (Hwy 1) and Olachea St. This corner is 2 blocks south of the junction of Hwy 1 and Hwy 22. A clean spot for overnight, but nothing fancy.

HOTEL CASINO — 37 rooms, restaurant, bar. Write Casino, Ciudad Constitucion, B.C.S. Mexico (706) 832-0004. Located 2 blocks east of the Hotel Maribel on Olachea St. A basic motel, perhaps a bit more quiet than the Maribel, being 2 blocks from the traffic on the main highway.

LA PAZ

LA POSADA — 25 rooms, restaurant, bar, pool. PO Box 152, La Paz B.C.S. Mexico. 011 (526) 822-4021. This is the smallest and least expensive of the La Paz hotels that I have designated as a destination resort. It is a well-landscaped, and very pleasant spot on the beach. Its chief disadvantages are that it is located some distance from the downtown area and its access route leaves something to be desired. For those who are not concerned with doing the town, La Posada is a charming place to stay.

GRAN BAJA — 250 rooms, restaurant, bar, pool, tennis, disco. Write PO Box 223, La Paz, B.C.S. Mexico. 011 (526) 822-3988. The Gran Baja is a 13-story building, the only high-rise structure south of Ensenada. As a result, the well-landscaped, low-rise charm of most of Baja's hotels is missing. It is also some distance from the La Paz downtown area. Because of its height, it is easy to find.

HOTEL LOS ARCOS — 150 rooms, restaurant, coffee shop, bar, pool. Write Baja Hotel Reservations, 4332 Katella Ave, Los Alamites, CA 90720. (213) 583-3393 (800) 347-2252. The Los Arcos is the only La Paz destination resort located in the downtown area and within walking distance of stores and restaurants. It faces the beach but is separated from it by the city's main waterfront street. The 3-story structure is built around 2 inner courtyards containing the pool, fountain, and greenery. The downtown location, moderate prices, and excellent food make it a favorite. One often encounters guests who have moved from other hotels.

CABANAS DE LOS ARCOS — 55 rooms, pool. Other information is the same as for the Los Arcos. Located on an adjoining corner from the Los Arcos and operated by the same organization. A group of 16 Tahitian-style cabins in a tree-shaded area plus an adjoining 3-story building. It has its own pool but shares its other facilities with the Los Arcos.

HOTEL PERLA — 94 rooms, bar, sidewalk restaurant, pool. Write Hotel Perla, 1570 Obregon, La Paz, B.C.S. 011 (526) 822-0777 The best of those hotels that fall below the destination resort class with a top location on the main waterfront street near the heart of town. Greatly enlarged and upgraded in 1989. The adjoining sidewalk cafe La Terraza is a good place for breakfast or lunch.

PALMIRA — 120 rooms, restaurant, bar, pool, discotheque, meeting room for 600 people. 011 (526) 822-4000. A destination resort hotel located 2 mi. north of downtown La Paz on the highway to Pichilingue. It has a very nicely landscaped pool area, but the hotel is located on the side of the highway away from the beach.

LA CONCHA BEACH RESORT — 109 rooms, restaurant, bar, pool, meeting and banquet facilities. 011 (526) 822-6544. A destination resort hotel located 4 mi. north of downtown La Paz on the highway to Pichilingue and next door to the governor's mansion. This very pleasant hotel has what I believe is the best beach location of the La Paz hotels but it is also the farthest from the downtown area.

CLUB EL MORO — 22 apartments, restaurant, pool. P. O. Box 357, La Paz B.C.S. 011 (526) 822-4084. It is La Paz's best apartment complex with an attractively landscaped pool area. Units contain bedroom, sitting-room and cooking area.

HOTEL GARDENIAS — 56 rooms, restaurant, bar, pool. P.O. Box 197 La Paz B.C.S. Mexico. Corner of Aquiles Seroan and Querrero. Not as plush as some of the others, but nice and less than half the price. Located in a residential neighborhood about 8 blocks from downtown. Plenty of parking. If you are just passing through town and need to rest-up, this is the place.

TODOS SANTOS

HOTEL CALIFORNIA — 16 rooms, restaurant, bar, pool. A thick-walled, 2-story masonry building that looks like a hotel in a small Mexican town ought to look. Not built with today's fancy tourist needs in mind, but upgraded in 1988 to include a well landscaped pool area. A real charmer in a charming small town.

THE EAST CAPE

HOTEL LAS ARENAS — 40 rooms, restaurant, bar, pool, fishing fleet. PO Box 3766, Santa Fe Springs, CA 90670. In Calif. (800) 352-4334. Other US states (800) 423-4785. This is one of the several fly-in hotels that also rates as a destination resort. Rooms have balconies facing the ocean. It is a high-quality facility located on a remote section of the coast some 30 air miles southeast of La Paz and west of Punta Arena de la Ventana. It is also reachable by 40 mi. of highway and roads from La Paz. The route is described in Chapter 23 in relation to the side trip to Bahia de los Muertos. If you desire a luxury resort in a remote location, this is the place.

PUNTA PESCADERO — 21 rooms, with patios and ocean views, restaurant, bar, pool, tennis court, fishing fleet and paved airstrip. Write PO Box 1044, Los Altos, CA 94023 or PO Box 362, La Paz, B.C.S. Mexico. (415) 948-5505. One of the best fly-in hotels that also rates as a destination resort. A small hotel with adjoining homes. A remote location some 9.3 mi. by low-standard dirt road east from Hwy 1 at **Km J-111** near Los Barriles. See Chapter 23 for route description.

HOTEL PLAYA HERMOSA — 28 rooms, restaurant, bar, adjoining trailer court. PO Box 1827, Monterey, CA 93942. (408) 375-2251, (800) 347-6847. A pleasant spot on the beach at Los Barriles. I rate this as the most modest of the 4 hotels in the immediate Los Barriles-Buena Vista area but it could be just the one that suits you best. Popular with the younger set and is headquarters for windsurfing fans.

HOTEL PALMAS DE CORTEZ — 32 rooms and 10 suites, restaurant, bar, pool, fishing fleet. PO Box 9016, Calabasas, CA 91372. (800) 368-4334. One of the long-established fly-in hotels that now finds itself easily reached via the Transpeninsular Highway. This very nice destination resort has improved with age. It adjoins a fine, sand beach with its airstrip paralleling it on the inland side.

RANCHO BUENA VISTA — 57 rooms, restaurant, bar, pool, tennis courts, fishing fleet. PO Box 673, Monrovia, CA 91016. (818) 303-1517. Another fly-in destination resort that is now easily reached over a short side road from Highway 1 at Buena Vista. This is a very charming facility.

HOTEL SPA BUENA VISTA — 40 rooms, restaurant, bar, pool, tennis court, hot mineral bath, fishing fleet. PO Box 218, Placentia, CA 92607. (714) 524-6656, (800) 752-3555. The original building is a converted mansion near the beach at the south end of Buena Vista. Many new additional rooms have now been developed.

HOTEL PUNTA COLORADO — 29 rooms, restaurant, bar, fishing fleet. PO Box 9016, Calabasas, CA 91372. (800) 368-4334. A fly-in hotel located at an isolated spot overlooking the beach south of Buena Vista. Can be reached by road over the East Cape Loop (See Chapter 23). Not as fancy as some others, but very nice with a relaxing isolated location.

RANCHO LEONERO — 11 rooms, restaurant, bar. This is the areas newest fly-in hotel. P. O. Box 2573 Canoga Park, CA 91306, (818) 703-0930. Located on a rocky cliff overlooking the sea with dirt road access.

SAN JOSE DEL CABO

BRISA DEL MAR MOTEL — 10 rooms, restaurant, bar, pool. Apartado Postal 45, San Jose del Cabo, B.C.S. Mexico. A modest motel situated at the rear of the Brisa del Mar Trailer court. Both are on the outstanding beach at San Jose del Cabo.

STOUFFER PRESIDENTE — 250 rooms, 2 restaurants, coffee shop, bar, pool, tennis courts, discotheque, meeting and banquet facilities. 011 (526) 842-0582. A very good 3-story destination resort on the beach. Adjoins a pleasant coastal lagoon. I rate this as the best of the hotels along the beach at San Jose del Cabo.

HOTEL POSADA REAL — 150 rooms, restaurant, coffee shop, bar, pool, tennis court, meeting facilities. PO Box 51, San Jose del Cabo, B.C.S. Mexico. 011 (526) 842-0515, a Best Western affiliate. One of the destination resort hotels on the beach in San Jose del Cabo.

HOTEL AGUAMARINA — 100 rooms, restaurant, bar, pool. 011 (526) 842-0097. Another of the destination resorts on the beach in San Jose del Cabo.

FIESTA INN — 157 Rooms, restaurant, bar, pool. (800) FIESTA INN Another of the destination resorts on the beach in San Jose del Cabo.

CABO CORRIDOR

(Between San Jose del Cabo and Cabo San Lucas)

HOTEL PALMILLA — 70 rooms with verandas, restaurant, pool, fishing fleet, tennis courts, croquet. 4577 Viewridge Ave, San Diego, CA 92123. (800) 542-6082 in CA, (800) 542-6082 nationwide. Another of the fly-in hotels that is also a destination resort. Located on a point of land overlooking the sea 1/2 mi. south of Hwy 1 near **Km J-25**. This is one of the top hotel-resorts in Baja, if not the best.

HOTEL CABO SAN LUCAS — 125 rooms, multi-bedroom villas, restaurant, bar, pool, fishing fleet, tennis court, dive shop.

Lying on the find sandy beach at San Jose del Cabo is the Hotel Stouffer Presidente. There are other hotels in this same government developed resort area. A golf course is nearby.

PO Box 48088, Los Angeles, CA 90048. (800) 733-2226. Another outstanding fly-in destination resort. Built around a small picturesque cove with dense palm trees and other landscaping. One of Baja's top hotel-resorts. Located 1/4 mi. south of Hwy 1 near **Km J-15** between San Jose del Cabo and Cabo San Lucas.

HOTEL MELIA CABO REAL -- 302 rooms and everything else imaginable. This is the first of the mega-hotels at the major Cabo Real resort development between San Jose del Cabo and Cabo San Lucas. Golf course nearby. 011 (526) 843-0980. If you like your resort hotel done on a grand scale, this is the place.

Other hotels at Cabo Real were under construction in 1992.

HOTEL TWIN DOLPHIN — 50 rooms with terraces, restaurant, bar, putting green, pool, tennis court. Write 1625 W. Olympic Blvd, Suite 1005, Los Angeles, CA 90015. (213) 386-3940 (800) 421-8925. The twin Dolphins has made a special effort to use native desert plants in its landscaping. It is one of Baja's best hotels. Located a short distance south of Hwy 1 near **Km J-11** between San Jose del Cabo and Cabo San Lucas.

HOTEL CLARION CABO SAN LUCAS — 125 rooms with balconies, restaurant bar, 3 pools. 011 (526) 843-0044. The most westerly of the destination resorts along the highway between San Jose del Cabo and Cabo San Lucas. It is located south of **Km J-6.** This resort offers a fine view of the rocky tip of the peninsula with its famed arched rock. The 2 and 3-story buildings remind one of a SW Indian pueblo.

CABO SAN LUCAS

HACIENDA HOTEL — 114-plus rooms with private balconies or patios, restaurant, bar, pool, paddle tennis, variety of watersports. PO Box 48872, Los Angeles, CA 90048. Toll free in Calif. (800) SEE CABO. One of the very best destination resorts. It is located within the broad bay at Cabo San Lucas at a point where the beach is well protected from Pacific swells. It advertises the only safe beach in the area. The ocean-crusing fleet anchors directly in front of the hotel.

The logo of Mexico's tourism development agency.

? ?

WHAT ABOUT HOTEL RATES

? ?

In general, rates at Baja's hotels are considerable less than for equivalent accommodations in the United States, although the margin has narrowed recently. Rates will vary greatly from year to year and are thus not quoted in this book. Many hotels peg their prices to the U. S. dollar so that rapid decrease in the value of the peso does not result in lesser expense for the tourist. Grin and bear it, but rates charged to Mexican citizens often are much lower than those paid by the tourist.

HOTEL SOLMAR — 70 rooms with patios, restaurant, bar, pool. PO Box 383, Pacific Palisades, CA 90272. (800) 878-4115. The Solmar has the distinction of being the southernmost development in Baja. This destination resort is all but surrounded by the beach on the Pacific side of the peninsula's tip. The ocean surf is heavy at this point, but if you crave the beach, this is the place.

MAR DE CORTEZ HOTEL — 72 rooms, restaurant, bar, pool. PO Box 11, Cabo San Lucas, B.C.S. Mexico, (706) 843-0032, or PO Box 1827, Monterey, CA 93942, (408) 375-4755. This is the best of the moderately priced hotels at Cabo San Lucas. It is located on the main street (Lazaro Cardenas) of town about 1/2 mi. from the ocean. The rooms are built around a pleasant restaurant-bar-pool area. Should you wish to savor the charms of "Cabo" without the fancy prices of the fancy resorts the Mar de Cortez is an excellent choice.

HOTEL MELIA — 190 rooms, restaurants, bars, pool, Jacuzzi, tennis center. Three convention facilities for 100. (526) 843-1010 Cabo's newest hotel. On the beach of the Cabo San Lucas harbor which is well protected from Pacific swells. A first class hotel although not quite as large and fancy as the Melina in Cabo Real.

HOTEL FINISTERRA — 108 rooms (with a new wing under construction in 1992) with private balconies, restaurant, bar, pool, gym. Baja Hotel Reservations, 4332 Katella Ave, Los Alamitos, CA 90720. Toll free in Calif. (213) 583-3393, (800) 347-2252. What better place to end this tour of Baja's hotels than at the one called Finisterra, "Lands-end." But last is not least as the Finisterra is one of Baja's finest. Its stone architecture and ocean views are the best of any of its competitors. Don't miss the view from the hotel bar. (The men's room is also one-of-a-kind.)

CHAPTER 7
BORDER INFORMATION

In preparing this chapter it has been necessary to interview numerous government officials and visit many offices involved in entrance requirements. All too often it developed that there are differences between what the official regulations and the guidebooks say will happen and what, in fact, takes place. For this reason, be sure to read the WHAT ACTUALLY HAPPENS Section later in this chapter. The saving feature is that, in practice, traveling in Baja is an extremely simple process for most people.

One overall item of advice is appropriate. Do everything possible before entering Mexico, unless your previous experience tells you to do otherwise. This includes fulfilling the various entrance requirements and obtaining auto insurance, Mexican currency, foodstuffs, and other supplies. In doing this, you can minimize peak-period crowding at the border and the complications always inherent with unfamiliar surroundings.

IMPORTANT NOTICE

In considering the recommendations for entering Mexico offered in this book, please be aware that your choice of ports-of-entry and travel routes in and approaching Baja may be significantly altered when the surfacing of Highway 5 is completed south of San Felipe.

See the discussions presented in the "BAJA'S OTHER ROADS" section of Chapter 2, and at the beginning of Chapter 15.

ENTERING MEXICO

TRAVEL ZONES — The requirements for United States and Canadian citizens who travel to Baja California differ depending on the areas to be visited. There are three travel zones:

BAJA BORDER ZONE — In 1952, the United States and Mexico reached an agreement that citizens of its respective border cities could visit the other nations' border cities for up to 72 hours without permits. The Mexican regulations refer to such visitors as *visitante locales* (local visitors) and define the area in question as the *ciudades fronterizos* (city limits).

As tourism in Mexico increased, the regulations changed unofficially. A local visitor became anyone visiting the border area

regardless of place of residence. On the Pacific side, the city limits expanded to include Ensenada and the nearby towns of La Jolla and Maneadero. The tourist card checkpoint lay adjoining Highway 1 at Maneadero, about 60 miles south of the border. As a result, some travel books refer to a 60-mile-wide border zone. On the east coast, San Felipe is considered part of the border zone even though it is 120 miles south of the border.

Requirements in this elastic zone are the least restrictive of the three travel zones.

REMAINDER OF BAJA — Travel requirements for the remainder of the Baja peninsula are more restrictive than for the border area but are not as complex as those for the Mexican mainland.

MAINLAND MEXICO — Requirements for entering mainland Mexico are the most restrictive and must be anticipated by travelers (1) entering Baja by first passing through the mainland or (2) by those planning to transport their vehicles from Baja to the mainland on the ferry system or by driving them easterly on Highway 2.

ENTRANCE REQUIREMENTS — The requirements for entering Mexico will vary depending on how you travel, and on what vehicles and other equipment you take with you. I experimented with presenting this material in narrative form but found that something was always omitted or confusing. The end result resembled Mark Twain's incomprehensible description of how to harness a team of horses to a buggy, except that there was no humor in my product. Instead, I offer the ENTRANCE REQUIREMENTS Table. It summarizes the regulations for the three travel zones discussed above. The numbered text sections, below, provide additional material relating to the corresponding blocks in the table.

BLOCK #1 — Over 30 million people cross the border at Tijuana each year, making it the world's busiest international port-of-entry. Millions more use the other five border crossing points serving Baja. Requiring any type entrance permit for such large numbers of people would create a nightmare of paperwork. Tourists driving or walking across the border are normally waved through. No permits of any type are required for tourist visits of up to 72 hours within the Border Zone. A tourist card is needed when one stays over 72 hours.

BLOCK #2 — Mexican regulations define a tourist as "any foreigner who enters the country temporarily for up to six months for recreation, health, scientific or sports activities provided they are neither *remunerative* or *lucrative."* Every tourist who visits the Border Zone for more than 72 hours, or who travels beyond this zone into Baja or the Mexican mainland, must carry a validated tourist card. You need a tourist card even if you have a passport. If your trip is for business you must apply for a business visa at a Mexican Consulate. As with all visas, you must have a valid passport.

BLOCK #3 — Cars and recreational vehicles are waved across the border, and no vehicular permits are required for tourist travel within the Baja peninsula.

BLOCK #4 — A *Temporary Import Permit* must be obtained if you plan to take any motorized vehicle to mainland Mexico. This includes transporting such a vehicle to the mainland via the Mexican ferry system. There is no charge for these permits. To obtain one you are required to have:

1. Proof of citizenship (the same as for obtaining a tourist card).

2. The current registration certificate (original document, not a copy) or a notarized bill of sale for each vehicle. A notarized affidavit of authorization is also required if the vehicle is registered to a person or company other than the person applying for the permit. (See additional information on this subject in the box on page 66)

3. If you are purchasing your vehicle under a finance contract from a bank or other lending institution, you must obtain written notarized permission from the lien holder (the legal owner) authorizing you to take the vehicle into Mexico.

4. A valid driver's license.

There is a complication if you have more than one motor vehicle, such as a motorhome pulling a small car or carrying a motorcycle. One person may obtain a permit for only one vehicle. A second person in the party may obtain a permit for the second vehicle if it is registered in that person's name. Thus, a married

ENTRANCE REQUIREMENTS

ITEM	BAJA BORDER ZONE		REMAINDER OF BAJA	MAINLAND MEXICO	
PEOPLE	1	No permits required for tourist travel up to 72 hours. A passport and visa needed for business.	2 For tourist travel, obtain a TOURIST CARD and have it validated after entering Mexico. A passport and visa are required for business travel.		
MOTORIZED VEHICLES	3	No permits required for cars, campers, motor homes, motorcycles or other motorized vehicles.		4	Validated permits are required. Must obtain prior to boarding any mainland-bound ferry.
TRAILERS	5	No permits required for recreational or boat trailers unless they exceed 8 feet in width or 40 feet in length. Obtainable only in Tijuana.		6	Validated permits are required. Must obtain prior to boarding any mainland-bound ferry.
BOAT BY HIGHWAY	7	No permit is required to trailer or otherwise transport a boat into Baja by highway. A fishing license is required for the boat if it used for fishing.		8	Validated permits are required. Must obtain prior to boarding any mainland-bound ferry.
BOAT BY SEA	9	Obtain a validated CREW LIST at the Mexican Consulate in San Diego. Also obtain TOURIST CARDS for all persons aboard. Port Captain check-in required in Mexico. A fishing license is also required for the vessel.			
COMMER. AIRCRAFT	10	No special requirements. Obtain TOURIST CARDS in advance for airports beyond the border zone. Cards will be validated by officials at the international airports. This is the easiest way to enter Mexico as the validating officals are waiting at the airports and you do not have to search for them.			
PRIVATE AIRCRAFT	11	Must land and obtain a GENERAL DECLARATION at one of Mexico's international airports and file flight plans as required by both Mexican and American authorities. Also obtain TOURIST CARDS for all persons aboard.			

Entering Mexico at the San Ysidro-Tijuana port-of-entry. Notice the parking lot in the left rear of the photo. Wrong!! Those are lines of cars waiting to return to the United States. See the border crossing recommendations later in this chapter.

couple may obtain permits for two vehicles if they are registered in both their names. Also, another person in the party may obtain a permit for the second vehicle by using a notarized affidavit of authorization from the owner. In any case, all applicants must be qualified drivers. (Red tape is international.)

Early in 1992, the Mexican government announced new regulations concerning vehicles brought into Mexico from the United States. These regulations DO NOT apply to vehicles brought into Baja California. However, they will be enforced when vehicles are taken to mainland Mexico from Baja using the ferry system or when driving east on Highway 2. They are designed to deter the large numbers of vehicles that are stolen in the United States and illegally transported into Mexico.

The basic rule is that all imported vehicles must be covered by a current Mexican insurance policy or the driver must post a bond equal to the value of the vehicle. In addition, the driver must provide two photo copies of the following documents to customs inspectors: Title document, driver's license, vehicle registration, insurance policy, car rental contract in the case of rental cars.

It is the opinion of some people that this system will shortly collapse of its own weigh. In that my own crystal ball is at the repair shop, I can only advise that you ask your insurance agent for the current state of affairs when you are ready for your visit.

American and Canadian Automobile Association members can obtain their Temporary Import Permits through association offices. Otherwise the permit is obtained and validated at offices inside Mexico at the border crossings or at the ferry terminals. In Tijuana, permits are obtained at the office of the Registro Federal de Vehiculos, which is located next to the immigration office.

BLOCK #5 — Permits are required for trailers only if they, or their load, exceed 8 feet in width or 40 feet in length. These are obtainable only in Tijuana at the office of the federal highway police. Permits are issued at the discretion of the officials.

BLOCK #6 — The requirements for taking a trailer into mainland Mexico are the same as for a motor vehicle (see BLOCK #4). The trailer is included on the Temporary Import Permit of the towing motor vehicle and is obtained at the same time and place, as for a motor vehicle.

BLOCK #7 — See the FISHING LICENSES Section in Chapter 5.

BLOCK #8 — The Temporary Import Permit covers a boat along with the vehicle that brings it into Mexico.

BLOCK #9 — The crew list must be validated at all ports visited where there is a Mexican Capitan del Puerto (Port Captain). Check-in with the immigration office is also required. The paperwork needed from a yachtsman is considerably more complex than that required of other visitors.

BLOCK #10 — The table says it all.

BLOCK #11 — Private pilots must land at one of Mexico's international airports, fill out an application form, and receive an approved document known in aviation circles as a *General Declaration*. Tourist cards may be obtained at the same time and place. It is recommended that private pilots contact The Baja Bush Pilots for more detailed instructions concerning these and other procedures (See PRIVATE FLYING in Chapter 3).

TOURIST CARDS — Obtaining a tourist card is a simple matter, but do not be dismayed to find that the document in question is not a card, nor does it bear the title tourist card, although it is universally referred to by that name. It is in fact a 5 1/2" by 7", two-copy form that asks you in Spanish, English, and French to provide the answers to eleven easily answered questions.

The tourist card may be obtained north of the border at any Mexican Consulate, offices of the Mexican Government Department of Tourism, offices of Mexican airlines, car insurance companies, and at many travel agencies. It may also be obtained at the immigration offices at the ports-of-entry inside Mexico.

Cards are issued free upon showing proof of one's nationality. This requires that you have any of the following documents: birth certificate, passport, voter registration, naturalization letter, certificate of discharge from the armed forces, or a declaration sworn before a notary public. (Married women relying on a birth certificate also need a sworn declaration to support their change in names.) You are normally given a blank tourist card and asked to fill it out at leisure.

Children under 18 years of age who enter Mexico without <u>both</u> parents must obtain a notarized copy of the form *Permission For A Minor Child to Travel In Mexico* in order to obtain a tourist card. These forms are available at Mexican Government Tourism Offices and Consulates and must be signed by the absent parent or parents.

The regulations require that the tourist card be presented for validation to Mexican immigration authorities *upon entering the country.* The proof-of-citizenship papers will again be required for validation and should be carried with you during your stay in Mexico.

Obtaining your tourist card before entering Mexico gives you a head start, but obviously the entire process of acquiring the card, filling it out, and obtaining validation may be combined in one stop at the ports-of-entry offices.

WHAT ACTUALLY HAPPENS — Prior to 1980, obtaining and validating tourist cards took place at a roadside office at Maneadero on Highway 1. This station disappeared about 1980, reopened briefly a few years later, but appeared abandoned in 1992. As a result of this station being closed, few people entering Baja by highway have tourist cards. Currently there is no station on Highway 5 from Mexicali to San Felipe, and few people in San Felipe have tourist cards. I am also advised that the various complications noted above concerning tourist cards and car permits rarely cause a problem. In contrast to this relaxed attitude toward tourist cards for highway travel, cards are always checked and validated at international airports during both arrival and departure.

I should also note that Mexican authorities have become strict in their enforcement of the rules concerning foreigners doing work that could be preformed by a Mexican. I have heard of several persons being deported for doing home repairs and other simple tasks.

In writing this chapter I feel obligated to recommend that everyone obtain tourist cards and have them validated. Being prepared for the other complexities is also prudent, but there is no point in looking for trouble. Having performed this duty we will move on to more pressing matters.

CUSTOMS REGULATIONS — The Baja peninsula is classified as a *Free Zone,* and as a result your baggage or vehicle will be searched only under special circumstances. You are normally waved across the border at all points of entry. Should you plan to cross to the mainland by ferry you will be subject to inspection. At press time there were two agricultural check stations on Highway 1, one north of La Paz and the other at the line between Baja's two states. They stop north bound traffic looking for citrus fruit.

In any case, keep in mind that a tourist is one whose purpose of visit is neither remunerative nor lucrative. You should not sell items that you take to Mexico or carry supplies obviously in excess of your personal needs.

Possessing firearms is contrary to Mexican law, and they are serious about it. The requirements for taking in firearms for hunting is a cumbersome process that is described in Chapter 11. Possessing and using narcotics is also against the law. There is no quicker way to get into trouble in Mexico than by violating these statutes. Mexico welcomes tourists and they are very obliging in their enforcement of the various immigration and customs laws, but they draw the line with firearms and drugs.

PETS — My observation is that very few tourists take their pets to Baja. The potential for inconveniencing one's neighbors in the camping areas is considerable, and hotel operators may not permit them in their establishments. If you insist on taking your pet to Baja you will need (1) a rabies vaccination certificate from a veterinarian and (2) a validated *Official Interstate and International Health Certificate for Dogs and Cats* obtainable for a small fee at a Mexican Consulate north of the border.

CITIZENS BAND RADIOS — Citizens band radios may be used in Mexico but you must obtain a permit from a Mexican Consulate. These permits are not obtainable in Mexico. Three channels have been designated for tourist use: Channel 9 for emergencies, Channel 10 for communications between tourists, and Channel 11, which is reserved for directions and information.

MEXICAN INSURANCE — You need to give special consideration to insurance for vehicles, boats, and private airplanes.

<u>AUTO INSURANCE</u> — Mexican law does not recognize any insurance except that written by companies licensed in Mexico. A Mexican insurance policy guarantees that you are able to pay any potential damages and fines. If you are involved in an accident in Mexico and do not hold a policy issued by such a company, you may be held by authorities pending investigation and determination of fault. Spending time in a Mexican jail can ruin one's day.

Licensed companies are located on both sides of the border near the ports-of-entry. Watch for signs along the highways on the United States' side. Such companies also have offices in several of the larger cities in the United States. By far the least expensive insurance is obtainable through membership in one of the travel clubs listed on page 10 in Chapter 1.

Coverage may be purchased by the day, month, or on a annual basis. Daily rates are high by United States standards. You can hold down the amount of your premium by covering your vehicle only for the time when you will be traveling and excluding lengthy stays in trailer courts, etc. Obtaining annual insurance from one of the above noted clubs is usually the best course of action for any visit to Mexico for more than a few days.

TRAILERS AND BOATS — If you are towing a trailer, it must also be insured by a Mexican company or your vehicle insurance will be invalid. This coverage must also include your boat if one is being trailered.

Hull and liability insurance for seagoing yachts is a different matter. Some yacht policies issued in the United States include travel as far south as Ensenada as part of their regular coverage. Other companies will issue riders for longer trips at no additional charge. In other cases, riders may involve a considerable additional premium, and some companies simply will not provide coverage for Mexican waters. The skipper's cruising experience may play a considerable role in the insurance company's decision. No additional insurance is required from a Mexican company.

PRIVATE AIRCRAFT — Liability insurance for a private aircraft must be acquired from a Mexican-licensed company in the same manner as for a motor vehicle. In contrast to boat and auto insurance policies, many aircraft policies issued in the United States cover damage to the plane in Mexico. Aircraft insurance is issued by most Mexican insurance companies.

FISHING AND HUNTING LICENSES — Obtaining Mexican fishing licenses is discussed in Chapter 5 WATERSPORTS, while hunting licenses are included in Chapter 11 WILDLIFE.

RETURNING TO THE UNITED STATES

You will not be waved into the United States as you were when you entered Mexico. Instead, your vehicle will be required to stop at the United States Customs Service station located at the border. A uniformed officer is normally stationed curb-sid

If this officer believes that all is in order you will be allowed to proceed with little delay and without leaving your vehicle. If he/she should determine that checking your vehicle is required, you will be asked to proceed to a secondary parking area where another officer will perform the inspection. This process normally takes very little time, although you may experience considerable delay waiting your turn in line.

Mexico requires that tourist cards be surrendered when you leave the country. Pilots of private aircraft and the skippers of ocean-going vessels normally check out at their last point of landing in Mexico and return the cards. The United States customs inspectors may check for compliance and become suspicious if these requirements have been ignored. In sharp contrast, persons driving or walking home from Mexico normally retain their cards; there is no apparent effort made to enforce the rule by either government.

CUSTOMS REGULATIONS — The U. S. Customs Service enforces over 400 laws for some 40 different agencies, but they are particularly concerned with (1) preventing the importation of illicit drugs, (2) enforcing the immigration laws, (3) preventing the importation of plant and agricultural products that may harbor dangerous pests, and (4) collecting import duties on foreign goods imported for commercial use and over specified values.

To comply with these requirements, returning tourists should carry proof of citizenship. Also, wise travelers will have exhausted their supply of fresh food supplies, or they may have to be given up at the border. The most common prohibited items are (1) raw and cooked pork, (2) raw meat of both domesticated and game foul, (3) potatoes, and (4) many fruits, including all citrus fruits. The full list of specific items that may not be brought into the United States is extensive and beyond the scope of this book. Write "Quarantines," U.S. Department of Agriculture, Federal Building, Hyattsville, MD 20782 for full details.

Each returning resident of the United States may bring back up to $400 worth of personal and household goods obtained in Mexico. These goods may not be for business purposes or for someone else. Their value includes repairs or alterations to articles taken to Mexico and being returned. You are also limited to one liter of alcoholic beverage provided you are 21 years of age or older. The exemption from duty may be used only once every 30 days. For further information, obtain Publication # 512 "Know Before You Go" from U.S. Customs, P.O. Box 7407, Washington, DC 20229.

DRUG INTERDICTION — Preventing the transportation of drugs has become a priority objective for both the United States and Mexico. During a trip to Baja in 1989 I passed through no less than five drug checkpoints in Mexico. On my last trip in 1992 there were none. What the future holds is anyone's guess.

At the U. S. ports-of-entry checking for drugs has clearly become the priority concern. Recreation vehicles may be requested to stop at secondary checkpoints on a random basis and trained dogs used to sniff out violators. Customs officers also occasionally stop tourists prior to entering Mexico to inquire about guns, ammunition, and large sums of cash (over $10,000). All of these are related to the drug trade.

Possession of illicit substances is a minor crime (misdemeanor), but importing them into the United States is a felony. If your vehicle is found to contain "any measurable quantity" of illegal drugs, such as one marijuana cigarette, you risk the confiscation of your vehicle and its contents. If young Junior is back there on the weed, best eject him south of the border and air out your rig.

Should you be able to pass on any helpful information to the Customs Service concerning drug trafficking, please phone them at 1(800) BE ALERT.

CANADIAN CITIZENS — Canadians visiting Mexico must pass through both United States and Canadian customs on their way home. The $400 duty-free exemption made available to U.S. citizens is not available to Canadians. U. S. regulations permit Canadians to bring in $200.00 worth of goods purchased in Mexico duty-free. However, I am advised that U.S. officials will normally permit Canadians to import Mexican goods if they are to be transported promptly through the country to Canada. The Canadian's declaration comes at the Canadian border. At press time, the personal exemption was $300.00.

PRIVATE AIRCRAFT — The U. S. Customs Service has identified general aviation aircraft as the highest-risk vehicles for narcotics smuggling. Pilots of such planes are thus required to land at specified U. S. airports near the border for customs inspections. Brown Field SE of San Diego, Calexico International Airport, and Yuma International Airport are directly across the border from Baja. Customs officials must be notified at least one hour prior to the inbound crossing of the U. S. border. Pilots should obtain Customs Publication 513 *U. S. Customs Guide for Private Flyers* for full information.

RETURNING BY SEA — Skippers of yachts returning to the United States from Mexico must check in with U. S. Customs at the Harbor Police dock in San Diego.

PORTS-OF-ENTRY

There are six ports-of-entry serving Baja California. These are described in the PORTS-OF-ENTRY Table. One of these, at San Luis, is in the mainland state of Sonora, but tourists may pass in either direction from Baja California to San Luis without the extra paperwork normally required to visit the Mexican mainland.

Usually it takes little time going from the United States into Mexico; however, there can be lengthy delays returning north. Keep in mind that the vast majority of this traffic consists not of tourists but of people from the border area who live in one country and work, or shop, in the other. There is thus heavy border congestion from these *commuters* from 2:00 or 3:00 AM until mid-morning.

Aside from this commute period, U. S. customs officials at Tijuana and nearby Otay Mesa report that overall peak traffic periods are often unpredictable. However, on the average, Sunday traffic is the heaviest, followed in order by Saturday, Monday, and Friday. The lightest traffic occurs on Tuesday, Wednesday, and Thursday.

Peak traffic periods at Mexicali are also often unpredictable, but generally the busiest days are in descending order, Sunday, Saturday, Wednesday, Monday, Friday, Thursday, and Tuesday. The first and fifteenth days of each month are also generally busy regardless of the day of the week.

San Luis reports the heaviest traffic between 10:00 AM and 8:00 PM on Sundays when delays of from one-to-two hours may be encountered. November thru April are the busiest months, but even here non-Sunday traffic is light except from 2:00 AM until 7:00 AM when commute workers from Mexico cross to work in agricultural fields on the U. S. side. The busiest months at nearby Algodones are similar to those at San Luis with weekends bringing the most traffic.

At Tecate the busiest times occur on Sundays and holidays and on days with special events such as races and the August bull run. When traffic at Mexicali is especially heavy, Mexican authorities sometimes divert travelers to Tecate.

PORTS-OF-ENTRY

LOCATION	DESCRIPTION	HOURS
TIJUANA	This is the busiest port-of-entry. OK for entering Mexico but usually heavily congested when returning to the U.S.	24 HOURS
OTAY MESA	Built to relieve congestion at Tijuana. There are no adjacent communities so traffic is usually much lighter than at Tijuana.	6:00 AM to 10:00 PM
TECATE	A Mexican town of 35,000 people. No adjoining U.S. community. Traffic is usually light.	6:00 AM to Midnight
MEXICALI	A large Mexican city and a busy port-of-entry. OK for entering Mexico but often heavily congested when returning north.	24HOURS
ALGODONES	A small Mexican town with no adjoining U.S. community. Light traffic.	6:00 AM TO 8:00 PM
SAN LUIS	A Mexican town of 175,000 south of Yuma, Arizona. Moderate traffic.	24 HOURS

ITEM	POINT OF ORIGIN	
	U.S. & Canadian Pacific Coast	Other Parts of U.S. and Canada
ENTERING BAJA	1 Enter at Tijuana.	4 Enter at Tijuana, Tecate or San Luis.
MEXICAN TOURIST PAPERS	2 Acquire at Ensenada. Tijuana best for car permits.	5 Acquire at Ensenada, Tecate or San Luis
LEAVING BAJA	3 Leave at Otay Mesa or Tecate. Avoid Tijuana.	6 Tecate, San Luis, or Algodones. Avoid Tijuana and Mexicali.

The United States freeway system tends to funnel Baja-bound tourists living along the Pacific coast to the San Diego area. Persons living east of the coastal area more readily flow towards Yuma, Arizona. The POINT OF ORIGIN Table, provides border crossing recommendations for these two groups. In both cases, it is assumed that the traveler plans to visit the main portion of the peninsula south of Ensenada via Mexico Highway 1. (NOTE — Expect significant changes in traffic patterns when Mexico Highway 5 is completed from Mexicali to Laguna Chapala. See discussion at the start of Chapter 15.) The following numbered sections in the text refer to the corresponding blocks in the POINT OF ORIGIN Table.

BLOCK #1 — There is normally no delay in entering Mexico at Tijuana, and the total amount of traffic is so heavy that it is impracticable for Mexican officials to inspect incoming vehicles. Thus, should you have (heaven forbid!) alcoholic beverages in excess of the one-liter limit, this is a prudent place to enter. Should you stop to take care of your entrance papers here, you may find that your conveniently parked vehicle is chosen for inspection.

It is also very important to note that the Highway 1-D route around Tijuana avoids most of the city traffic. Thus considering all these factors, the busiest port-of-entry is a good place to enter Mexico.

BLOCK #2 — Car permits can be obtained, and tourist cards validated, on a 24-hour basis at Tijuana; however, there is less congestion and easier parking in Ensenada. The office hours there are 8:00 AM to 8:00 PM Monday through Friday; 8:00 AM to 3:00 PM Saturday. They are closed on Sunday.

BLOCK #3 — Avoid Tijuana at all costs. Crossing at Tecate is the best choice. There are several twists and turns on the way to the the San Diego freeway system north from Tecate so it is best to have a highway map of the San Diego area on hand.

A somewhat easier return to the United States freeway system is provided by returning home at Otay Mesa, but the port-of-entry is a bit hard to find from the Mexican side of the border. Directions are provided in Chapter 14.

BLOCK #4 — Many travelers will choose to take Interstate 8 from Yuma to San Diego and enter Baja at Tijuana along with their West Coast brethren. The distance from Yuma to Ensenada via San Diego is approximately 260 miles; however, one can see more of Baja and avoid the San Diego traffic by entering Mexico at San Luis and proceeding to Ensenada via Highways 2, 5, and 3. This route is only 30 miles longer, but does involve traveling over the winding mountain highway east of Ensenada on Highway 3, as noted in Chapter 16. As an intermediate alternative, enter at Tecate and reach Ensenada via Highway 3.

BLOCK #5 — Tecate and San Luis offer relatively congestion-free points to take care of the paperwork. Also see block #2 concerning Tijuana.

BLOCK #6 — It is really senseless not to return home via Tecate, Algodones, or San Luis and avoid Tijuana and Mexicali.

CHAPTER 8
TRAVELING IN BAJA

The pages to follow discuss a variety of subjects about which you need to know when traveling in the Magnificent Peninsula.

HEALTH CONSIDERATIONS

You will find that health conditions in Baja are good. It is widely reported, and it has been my experience, that tourists suffer considerably less from common intestinal disturbances (*turistas*) in Baja than on the Mexican mainland. Nevertheless, I shall pass on the standard fare offered to tourists everywhere in relation to this malady. Avoid overindulgence in food, beverage, and exercise, and get plenty of rest, at least until your system adjusts to its changed environment. In general, avoid tap water by obtaining your needed liquids from bottled water, carbonated beverages, beer, and wine. Avoid unpeeled fruits and uncooked vegetables that are the essential ingredients in salads. It is also advisable to inquire if the hotel swimming pool contains chlorinated water and avoid those that do not.

Having fulfilled this duty I report that I know that this advice is widely ignored in Baja with few ill effects. Travelers and retirees in Baja regularly drink the tap water from many of the towns, large and small, and produce acquired at the markets is treated no differently than it would be north of the border. My best advice is to ask current residents what they do and follow your own best judgements.

SPECIAL PROBLEMS — The requirement for having had a smallpox vaccination to enter Mexico and to return to the United States was discontinued many years ago. The Anopheles mosquito, which transmits malaria, has also been eradicated from the peninsula; Baja is classified as malaria free by the United States Public Health Service. This is not true for the mainland west coast from north of Mazatlan to the Guatamalan border. While there are no special medical requirements for visiting Baja, many doctors recommend vaccination for tetanus and hepatitis prior to visiting certain parts of the world. Contact your personal physician for advice.

MEDICAL FACILITIES — There are well-equipped hospitals in Baja's larger cities. In recent years government medical clinics have also been established in many of the smaller towns. These facilities prominently display the letters I.M.S.S. (Instituto Mexicano de Seguro Social) on the front of the building. All are equipped with radios so that air evacuation or other assistance can be summoned. In addition, two organizations in San Diego operate 24-hour, critical-care, air transportation service throughout Baja. These are Air-Evac International, Inc. (619) 278-3822, and Critical Air Medicine, Inc. (619) 571-8944. If you have special health problems it may be wise to make prior financial arrangements with one of these services so that there are no delays caused by credit considerations.

The Red Cross is much in evidence in Baja. It operates ambulances and provides emergency medical treatment throughout the peninsula. Roadside volunteers are often encountered soliciting funds for this work.

INSECT PESTS — Troublesome insects are not usually a problem in dry desert climates. I have found this to be the most common situation in Baja. However, there are some important exceptions.

Desert insects achieve enormous increases in numbers following rain. During these periods you may be plagued by large numbers of flies, mosquitos, gnats and no-see-ums. The latter are particularly painful and can make life miserable. Mosquitos can also be a problem year-round at hotels where landscape areas are kept continually moist. For these reasons it is advisable to take insect repellant and spray to Baja. A small section of mosquito netting used to throw over your head at night will help defeat that last buzzing pest that avoids your best efforts at extermination.

CURRENCY

The medium of exchange in Baja is the Mexican peso. A peso is divided into 100 centavos but its value is now so small that prices are rounded to the nearest peso. The same symbol ($) denotes the peso as is used for Canadian and U. S. dollars.

For decades the Mexican peso was an extremely stable currency, and from 1954 to 1976 the exchange rate was 12-1/2 pesos per United States dollar. In September 1976, the country's *spendful* economic policies forced a series of peso devaluations. In recent years the government has allowed the peso to devalue against the United States and Canadian dollars. Stop at any Mexican bank and a prominent sign will point out the current exchange rate which at press time was over 3,000 pesos per U. S. dollar.

The dramatic devaluation of the peso has flattened out in recent years. Also in spring 1992 there were reports that Mexico would adjust its monetary system to remove two or three zeros from the peso. Thus, you may find the exchange rate to be dramatically different from the 3,000 to one reported here.

I offer the following comments and suggestions that reflect my most recent experiences.

1. — Mexico needs United States and Canadian currency. You can exchange dollars into pesos at any Mexican bank for the going rate. If you try to change these same pesos back into dollars two minutes later the bank may be regrettably out of dollars. If you pay a bill in dollars, you will usually get your change in pesos. In other words, once you exchange your dollars for pesos it is often difficult to reverse the process. Prudent tourists plan ahead and spend all of their pesos before leaving Mexico. Stopping for fuel near the border, placing all your remaining pesos on top of the pump, and asking the attendant to dispense that much gasoline is one way to take care of the last centavo.

2. — There is no problem in exchanging or spending dollars or travelers checks in places that are practiced in dealing with tourists such as banks, hotels, and stores in the border towns. It is often harder to use these same dollars at gas stations, food stores, and other small businesses. For this reason, you should obtain a supply of pesos at a bank near your home, or at one of the border towns.

3. — There are often long lines at bank teller's windows. You can easily spend twenty minutes waiting only to find you are at the wrong window. Service is usually much quicker at an exchange dealer (Casa de Cambio). You will receive slightly fewer pesos for your dollars at these places so first check out the exchange rate at the bank and decide whether time or money is your current priority. In finding a bank, look for signs with the word *Banco* (bank) or such trade names as *Banamex*, or *Bancomer*.

4. — Canadians can exchange Canadian dollars for pesos at the major banks, however, this may not always be the case in the smaller towns. Canadian dollars also may not be as acceptable to business men and individuals. The U. S. dollar is the universal solvent in Mexico and will dissolve any problem. Wise Canadians will carry some of their resources in greenbacks.

5. — Always having pesos available will allow you to use them to purchase an item that is priced in pesos and to receive your change in pesos. Most of us can deal with the mathematics involved in such a transaction. Using dollars in the same situation may give rise to *creative change making* and awakens memories of grade school math tests where some of us received D-'s for not knowing how much change Johnny should receive in pesos when paying in dollars for a watermelon worth 4,855 pesos, when the exchange rate four days earlier was 3,060.75 pesos to the dollar and is increasing 13 pesos per day.

6. — It is always wise to carry a pocket calculator in case you find yourself at a gas pump where the peso gauge is broken or covered-over with tape and you are being told what to pay by a 12 year old kid who is probably playing hookey from school. I have had experiences where the presence of a calculator prevented mistakes in currency transactions. Have one in your hand and punch it even if you don't understand its use. Its mere presence makes everyone more careful.

7. — Many businesses and hotels will also exchange dollars into pesos. My experience is that the rate at stores will be a little better than the official rate. Their managers wish to attract your business. The rates at hotels are usually lower than bank rates as most often you are paying your bill and the hotel's proprietors have already enjoyed your trade.

SPANISH (ESPANOL)

Although most of us know that the language of Mexico is Spanish, it comes as a bit of a shock to find that all road and other signs immediately abandon the English language south of the border. There is no weaning area. However, even if you don't understand Spanish, you will have little trouble getting along in Baja. Almost all tourist-oriented stores in the border area employ someone who speaks English. English-speaking Mexicans rapidly diminish south of Ensenada, but there is rarely a

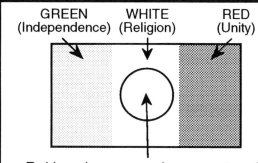

GREEN (Independence) WHITE (Religion) RED (Unity)

Emblem shows an eagle on a cactus with a snake in its beak. The cactus grows on an island in the middle of a lake.

MEXICO'S FLAG

The national emblem of Mexico is adapted from the Aztec symbol for their capital, now Mexico City, but originally TENOCHTITLAN, meaning Cactus Rock. Legend says that the wandering Aztecs could not settle until they found a place on an island in a lake upon which grew a cactus. On the cactus there would be an eagle holding a snake in its beak. This place they discovered about 1325. There they established the empire which was later to be conquered by Cortez in 1521. ------ The design has varied through the years. The present configuration was made official in 1968. Each state has an "ARMS' but no flag.

language problem at the hotels and other tourist facilities. Menus are frequently printed in both English and Spanish and will help you to become familiar with frequently used words. What better way to learn that eggs are *huevos* than when ordering breakfast *(desayuno)*.

One of the first things you learn upon entering the publishing business is that almost all books have a total number of pages that is divisible by 8, as the large sheets of paper used in printing presses are divided into 8 sections. If an author has nothing more to say, and is several pages short of the last 8, or if the book looks too thin to market well, the shortfall is frequently met with an appendix of ornaments *borrowed* from other sources. A list of foreign language words and phrases is one common appendix item.

There is no such section in *The Magnificent Peninsula*. Its appendix does present (1) a GLOSSARY of Spanish words, trade names, and acronyms and (2) a display of ROAD SIGNS. Both contain Spanish words that you will actually see in print in Baja. These two references, along with the bilingual restaurant menus, will meet your minimal language needs.

I suggest that you obtain a English-Spanish dictionary and a simple Spanish textbook. These items are not essential, but you can enjoy your trip more by becoming familiar with simple Spanish. Most Baja citizens are eager to help, and knowing even a little Spanish gives you common ground.

I also recommend a simple but highly effective little book on Spanish and Latin American customs entitled *Spanish Lingo for the Savvy Gringo* (See notice on page 72).

SHOPPING & PRICES

Baja's border cities owe much of their rapid growth to the allurements they have provided over the years to residents of southern California in the United States. In the past, gambling, prostitution, and alcohol (during prohibition) were the big sellers. Today, things have calmed down and just plain shopping has become a big money gainer. Each port-of-entry border town has clusters of shops and stores that cater to the shopping

tastes of the tourist. The same is true for Ensenada and San Felipe, farther south. The only other shopping center of significance is La Paz, although Cabo San Lucas is improving.

These cities offer a variety of goods ranging from inexpensive baskets, and similar tourist eye-catchers to more expensive silver, porcelain, perfumes, leather goods, and clothing. Much of this merchandise can be obtained at prices lower than in the United States. This is particularly true for products such as tooled belts, shoes, hand bags, and other items that involve considerable hand labor.

Prices are normally fixed, and marked on the merchandise, at the department stores and larger shops, but bargaining is the name of the game in many smaller establishments. This practice is a bit unfamiliar to many tourists, but you are simply paying too much if you don't participate. While there is money to be saved, bargaining often takes extra time as one needs to compare prices at different shops and engage in a sometimes protracted battle of wits with the proprietors. Having dollars rather than pesos will enhance your bargaining position. I normally despise shopping, but the sporting aspects of the bargaining process actually can make it enjoyable.

Liquor stores are plentiful. There is a wide selection of Mexican brands of beer (cerveza) as well as tequila, rum, brandy, gin, and vodka at prices near, or below, those in the U. S. Bourbon and Scotch are scarce and expensive. Santo Tomas and other brands of wine bottled in the Ensenada vicinity are also available at reasonable prices.

Now THE BAD NEWS. In early 1989 (after the election of President Carlos Salinas de Gortari), it was apparent that prices for many commodities had roughly doubled from one year ago. This was particularly true for food. The rates paid by businesses for various government services such as power and water also rose sharply. Finally, the sales tax rate in Baja rose from six to fifteen percent as it has long been on the Mexican mainland.

These price increases were the result of Mexico facing the reality that it could no longer subsidize much of what it provided for its people. Similar price escalations have occurred in other countries around the world as they back away from heavily socialized economies and move toward capitalism. And I believe there is a relationship between these policies and the recent decrease in inflation. But for what ever reason, living in Mexico is not nearly the bargain it once was. But keep in mind that this situation could change significantly for the tourist should there be another major devaluation of the peso against the U. S. dollar. And some items still cost very little. Tortillas and beer both come to mind. The essentials of life are still a bargain.

PROBLEMAS

One of the most common Spanish expressions that a tourist will hear in Mexico is "no problema," meaning that there is no problem, or that one's request will be complied with promptly. However, occasionally a traveler may in fact encounter a real problema and need assistance. Away from the larger towns, authority rests with the Delegado, an appointed official whose office will bear the name Delegacion Municipal, and there are uniformed police in all but the smallest communities. Consult these officials in case of need.

Should you encounter legal difficulties, including those with public officials, contact an office of the State Tourism Department. The State of Baja California also operates the *Procuraduria General de Protection al Turista* (Office of the Attorney General for the Protection of Tourists). Call in Tijuana (706) 684-2138 or the 24-hour hotline (706) 685-0302; in Ensenada (706) 676-3686; in Mexicali (706) 562-5744; and in San Felipe 7-11-55. They act as public defenders and render free legal service.

The laws of Mexico are based on the Napoleonic Code used in much of Europe and Latin America. In these countries, one is held to be guilty until proven innocent, a somewhat frightening prospect to those of us accustomed to the opposite foundation of English law. This legal difference is a key reason why you should carry Mexican insurance for your vehicles. Failure to do so could result in your being detained pending determination of responsibility in case of an accident.

Tourists may occasionally encounter the need to part with a small bribe or tip called *la mordida* (the death bite) to avoid a problem with a public official. The Mexican government has been making a considerable effort to eliminate this practice, but it still prevails on occasion. My personal familiarities with the practice all involve situations where tourists were in violation of Mexican regulations, or wished to avoid full compliance with such requirements. Conforming fully with Mexico's way of doing things would seem to be the simplest means of avoiding the need for la mordida.

TELEPHONING

Baja California has a modern telephone system but the number of individual telephones is relatively small. For example, there are less than sixty pages of phone numbers in the single phone book covering all of the state of Baja California Sur. Each phone book also has a yellow pages section which you may find useful in locating specific services. The phone systems for the various towns and cities are linked together by microwave radio; you will see the *microonadas* towers at many places along the main highways.

CALLING MEXICO — You may dial direct to telephones in Baja from many places in the United States and Canada. Consult the International Calling instructions in the front section of most phone books. The following examples utilize the phone number for the Estero Beach Hotel in Ensenada.

> (1) 011 + 52 + 667 + 6-6230
> (2)   (526) 676-6230

In areas served by International Direct Distance Dialing (IDDD) <u>011</u> is the *International Access Code*, <u>52</u> the *Country Code* for Mexico, and <u>667</u> the *City Code* for Ensenada. <u>6-6230</u> is the hotel's phone number as it appears in the Mexican phone book.

The second example lists the same series of numbers in the format familiar to U.S. and Canadian citizens. This is how the numbers are shown in most travel brochures and in this book. All of the *City Codes* in Baja start with <u>6</u>. Thus, for practical purposes, 52 + 6 or (526) is what we would call the *area code* for Baja.

CALLING HOME — It is possible to dial directly to the United States and Canada from Baja by using a private telephone. Most tourists do not have access to such a telephone, so the alternatives are to request one of the hotels to place the call or to utilize a long-distance calling service. Also, there are phone booths on the streets in the major cities.

In these northern towns calls go through quickly. When using a phone booth, place a coin in the slot at the top of the phone to activate the circuit. Follow the instructions in the phone booth to get the operator. I have always found that the operators speak sufficient English to complete a collect or credit card call.

Most hotels place calls for their patrons. If you are not a guest you may be refused assistance or charged a fee. In the larger towns you will find a long-distance office staffed with one or more operators who will place calls for a fee. In Mulege, the office is in the back of a store. In Ensenada, it is in a cubby-hole along the main tourist street, and you will find it at a counter in the Hotel Mar de Cortez at Cabo San Lucas. Because these offices tend to relocate from time to time you need to be alert for the *larga distancia* sign and ask other tourists for the latest location.

In the southern portions of the peninsula be prepared for lengthy delays in getting calls placed. The local office must dial the international operator; frequently this procedure takes considerable time. I have observed the local operator dialing scores of times before getting through. It is for this reason that some hotels will not help you with your calls.

PART II
HIGHER NEEDS

THE PAUPER PENINSULA

At an occasional oasis or in a sheltered bay
Small Spanish settlements managed to stay,
Loreto...Santiago...La Paz with the precious pearls,
San Ignacio...Todos Santos...Mulege...vital streams in this world;
Meanwhile Manila galleons with rich Philippine cargo
Which came to provision at San Jose del Cabo
Were often plundered by Cavendish and Drake
Who burned the ships and the treasures did take;
And although Mexico finally won freedom from Spain
Poor Baja California greatly neglected remains.

Ken Reimer

Ken's poem introduces us to a land which is perhaps poor in worldly goods but is rich in scenic beauty, vegetative variety, wildlife, and history. Viewing these features together with the people and culture of a land different from our own will provide enrichment for the visitor. PART II focuses on fulfilling these HIGHER NEEDS.

Adobe ruins of the Dominican mission at Santo Domingo. Here Baja's rich past lies next to the poor dwelling of a present-day Mexican farmer.

CHAPTER 9
GEOLOGY

PEASE READ THE FOLLOWING PARAGRAPH

Few people have training or knowledge concerning geology. Others may believe that they will have little interest in this subject. For these reasons, I am fearful that many readers may be inclined to pass over this chapter. *I implore you not to do so.* I make this pledge: everything presented in this chapter is essential background material concerning features which you may readily see from the peninsula's main highways. Excluded are lengthy descriptions of geologic history and the unnecessary use of technical terms which, for the average tourist, do little more than occupy space. If technical language is necessary, straightforward definitions are provided, enhanced where possible by sketches or tables.

SAN ANDREAS FAULT

The Baja peninsula split off from the Mexican mainland 25-30 million years ago. Along with adjoining portions of California in the United States, the peninsula has shifted several hundred miles northwest along the fault.

San Francisco

N

San Andreas Fault

Sea of Cortez Rift Zone

Puerto Vallarta

Baja's tip roughly conforms to the concave outline of the mainland coast.

I sincerely hope you have been persuaded to read on and savor Baja's geologic panorama. Making such a decision would be less important were you contemplating traveling through the vast plains and prairies of central and eastern United States and Canada where there is relatively little geologic story to be told. Even in areas such as the Appalachian Mountains in eastern United States, where there is much of geologic interest, the humid weather conditions and resultant dense forest vegetation tend to round over the landscape and mask the rocks and other structural features.

In contrast, geologic features are plentiful, varied, and easily seen in areas such as Baja that are both mountainous and arid. Perhaps the most outstanding such region in North America is the southwestern portion of the United States. I would rate this latter area as superior to Baja in both scenery and geologic interest, although the comparison may be unfair due to the tremendous size and diversity of southwestern United States. Regardless of its relative rank, the Baja peninsula is a place of fine, and at times outstanding scenery.

In presenting this picture, I will begin with the peninsula itself and then proceed through more specific elements. As in all the chapters of PART II, the material presented here will be further amplified as individual features are encountered in PART III.

THE PENINSULA IS BORN

Scientists estimate that the earth may be some 5 billion years old. In comparison to this incredible age, the geologic story of Baja California is a recent one, with reliable dating going back only some 150 million years. But even at this relatively recent time, there was yet to be a peninsula. The birth of the present jagged finger of land was not to begin until 25-30 million years ago as a byproduct of the formation of the famous San Andreas Fault and its undersea extensions both to the north and south. (See SAN ANDREAS FAULT Map.)

The San Andreas Fault is a deep, linear fracture extending from the floor of the Pacific Ocean some 25 miles north of San Francisco, south through Alta California to the mouth of the Rio Colorado, and then into the Sea of Cortez. On the floor of this body of water it continues southward as a zone of sea floor spreading called the Sea of Cortez Rift Zone.

Many geologists now ascribe to the theory of plate tectonics wherein the earth's crust is believed to be made up of a number

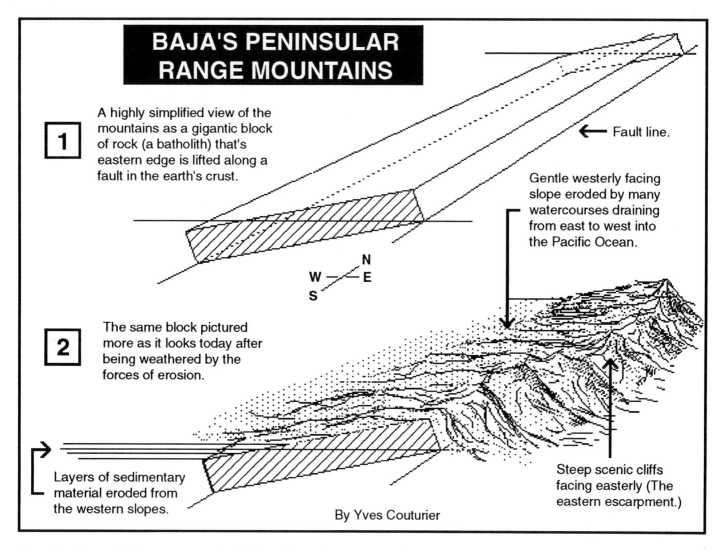

BAJA'S PENINSULAR RANGE MOUNTAINS

1 A highly simplified view of the mountains as a gigantic block of rock (a batholith) that's eastern edge is lifted along a fault in the earth's crust.

← Fault line.

Gentle westerly facing slope eroded by many watercourses draining from east to west into the Pacific Ocean.

N
W — E
S

2 The same block pictured more as it looks today after being weathered by the forces of erosion.

Layers of sedimentary material eroded from the western slopes.

Steep scenic cliffs facing easterly (The eastern escarpment.)

By Yves Couturier

of massive plates which move more or less independently from each other. The San Andreas Fault and the Sea of Cortez Rift Zone are part of the boundary between the two gigantic plates that form the North American Continent to the east and the Pacific Plate to the west.

Millenniums ago the Pacific Plate began to slide up the California coast in a northwesterly direction. The total displacement is estimated at approximately 450 miles and is still occurring at the rate of about one inch per year. The southern portion of the plate gradually separated from the continent to open up the area now occupied by the Sea of Cortez. There is a more westerly movement toward the southern portion of the sea which explains why it is wider there than to the north.

As a result, the Sea of Cortez one of the world's youngest seas and it, and the Red Sea to the west of Africa, serve geologists as classic examples of tectonic interaction. And because of all this, the American residents of southern Alta California are cast together with their Mexican neighbors in a slow and rocky boat to China. The former can take heart in knowing that the latter seem to get along quite well being separated from the mainland. It also appears that those northern California politicians who

yearn to separate California into two states may eventually get their way.

The splitting and northerly movement of the peninsula has been a slow and complex event. It would appear that the journey has not been uniform and that the peninsula has been stretched in the process. In particular, the mountains at the southern tip have lagged behind the northern portion. This situation may be clearly observed at the POINTS OF SPECIAL INTEREST Tour stop in the mountains north of La Paz. This vista point overlooks the low-lying Llano de La Paz, the gap which separates the lagging mountains of the Cape region from the Sierra Giganta to the north. It would take very little rise in sea level to convert the lethargic southern tip into an island.

BAJA'S BACKBONE MOUNTAINS

Perusing the topographic maps of the world will readily show that most of our planet's mountains occur in ranges or chains rather than as isolated peaks. In western North America, many of these ranges are the result of linear masses of molten minerals welling up from below the earth's crust and solidifying into gigantic structures called *batholiths*. The main backbone mountains of the Baja peninsula, the Peninsular Range, are formed from part of a chain of such batholiths which stretch along the west coast of the North American continent. It is thus a close cousin of similar ranges in British Columbia, Idaho, and the Sierra Nevada of Alta California.

The Sierra Nevada and Baja's Peninsular Range are similar in two basic respects. They are both formed from *fault block batholiths,* and in both cases the block has been tilted upward unevenly to create a steep face, or *escarpment*, along the eastern edge. Knowledge of these very basic circumstances will allow the traveler to observe and to understand the most prominent topographic features of the peninsula.

To comprehend the makeup of a fault block batholith, see the accompanying illustration and visualize the basic structure of these mountains as a gigantic piece of lumber sawn so that it is much wider than high. A 2" x 10" plank will do nicely. Then, because of tremendous forces developed within the crust of the earth, a fracture or fault occurred along the eastern edge of the plank.

Over millions of years this eastern edge was raised up along the line of the fault to form a steep cliff, or escarpment. What was formerly the top of the plank now becomes the gently sloping west face of a range of mountains. The forces of erosion carve the upper eastern edge into a linear series of peaks. These same processes of erosion also dissect the westerly face, sometimes creating quite rugged topography marked by scores of watercourses running from east to west.

In the United States, the situation just described is readily apparent in the Sierra Nevada to travelers crossing the range from east to west on Interstate 80. At Reno, Nevada, the steep eastern escarpment may be seen stretching majestically both north and south. A few miles west of the city the highway climbs steeply and in a short distance crosses over the crestline at Donner Summit. The descent over the more gentle western slope extends a much longer distance, and it involves several ups and downs resulting from the forces of erosion. The highly scenic eastern escarpment of the Sierra Nevada and its series of 12,000 - to-14,000 - foot peaks are in clear view for hundreds of miles to the south of Reno and east of Highway 395. This situation in the United States has been described because many visitors to Baja will have traveled in this area and will now be able to relate the two geologically similar circumstances.

The geologic story of the Peninsular Range has been complicated by the linear stretching previously described, by substantial volcanic activity, and by other factors; yet the dominant element is the fault-block mountain building just described. The traveler to Baja can see many evidences of this process and other related geologic events. Here is a list of the principal phenomena.

1. — In general, the highest mountain peaks lie along the main crestline divide in the eastern portion of the peninsula. In many places, this divide lies so close to the Sea of Cortez that the eastern escarpment falls directly into the ocean and there are no coastal roads. For this reason, some of the peninsula's most scenic areas are not readily accessible to the tourist. They may be viewed only by the boater sailing close to the rocky coast and by passengers of small private planes flying overhead.

2. — The scenic eastern escarpment of the Peninsular Range may be best seen by the land-based tourist in two places: (a) from the San Felipe area where Highways 2 and 5 traverse the flat desert lands east of the escarpment and (b) along the Sea of Cortez coast between Santa Rosalia and a point about 20 miles south of Loreto. This southerly portion of this section is the most scenic area along the Transpeninsular Highway.

Rugged mountainous areas may of course be visited in many other places by use of secondary and more primitive roads. Journeys to the National Parks in the Sierra de Juarez and Sierra San Pedro Martir are particularly rewarding. These side trips are described in Chapters 16 and 18.

3. — The Peninsular Range mountains are crossed by the main highway system in several places, thus affording the traveler the opportunity to experience the steep eastern escarpment. A classic example lies south of Loreto. After a steep climb of some 10 miles up the steep eastern slope, the traveler might well ask "where is the other side of the mountain?" For all practical purposes, there is none. The crestline of the mountain range falls gently to the west and eventually blends into the Llano de Magdalena and the Pacific Ocean.

4. — The lands lying to the west of the crestline divide are of fairly gentle overall topography. The large volumes of sediments caused by the erosion of this broad slope have been deposited to the west of the mountains resulting in the formation of some of the largest flat plains found along the west coast of the North American continent. The major areas are the Desierto de Vizcaino near the center of the peninsula, and the Llano de Magdalena in the south.

Much of the Transpeninsular Highway has been located in the western and central portion of the peninsula to take advantage of this relatively gentle topography. However, the highway must cross, at right angles, the hundreds of watercourses that have been cut in an east-west direction down the west facing slope of the mountains.

5. — While the eastern side of the peninsula has risen over time to form the steep eastern escarpment, the western side, south of the 28th parallel, has been subsiding for millions of years. This may be the result of the weight of erosion-deposited sediments that in places are 10 miles thick. Evidence that the land is sinking into the sea is provided by the large numbers of coastal lagoons lying between Scammon's Lagoon on the north and Bahia Magdalena on the south. Standing at the edge of any of these estuaries as the tide comes in makes even the hardiest of traveler consider the merits of retreating inland.

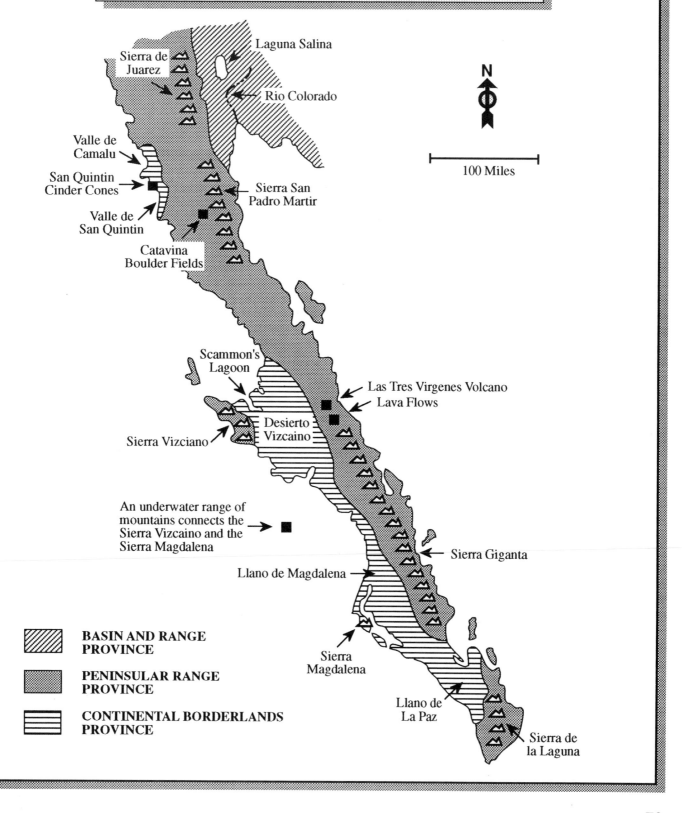

GEOLOGIC PROVINCES AND PROMINENT TOPOGRAPHIC FEATURES

N

100 Miles

Laguna Salina

Sierra de Juarez

Rio Colorado

Valle de Camalu

San Quintin Cinder Cones

Sierra San Padro Martir

Valle de San Quintin

Catavina Boulder Fields

Scammon's Lagoon

Las Tres Virgenes Volcano
Lava Flows

Desierto Vizcaino

Sierra Vizciano

An underwater range of mountains connects the Sierra Vizcaino and the Sierra Magdalena

Sierra Giganta

Llano de Magdalena

Sierra Magdalena

Llano de La Paz

Sierra de la Laguna

BASIN AND RANGE PROVINCE

PENINSULAR RANGE PROVINCE

CONTINENTAL BORDERLANDS PROVINCE

Las Tres Virgenes volcano north of Santa Rosalia. Note the organ pipe cactus on the left.

GEOLOGIC PROVINCES

Geologists have divided the North American continent into a large number of provinces. Each of these is an area of relatively homogeneous geologic features, and the dividing lines between the different provinces are in most places readily apparent to the traveler. Such geological provinces as the Sierra Nevada Mountains, the California Central Valley, the Cascade Mountains, the Willamette Valley, and the Colorado Plateau are well-known to the citizens of western United States.

For the Baja peninsula, the situation is relatively simple as there are only three provinces: the Basin and Range, the Peninsular Range Mountains and the Continental Borderlands. They are shown on the GEOLOGIC PROVINCES Map in this chapter. This map also shows the location of various other geologic and topographic features. Most of these features, and the dividing lines between the provinces, will be pointed out during the GRAND TOUR in PART III.

BASIN AND RANGE PROVINCE — The Basin and Range province is that vast area of the United States and Mexico which lies roughly between the Rocky Mountains on the east, and the Sierra Nevada and Cascade Mountains on the west. It is characterized by terrain which is quite flat overall although it is dissected by numerous, relatively short, ranges of mountains almost all running in a generally north-south direction. Highways through the province traverse flat terrain but usually curve to skirt the edges of the mountain ranges.

The southern extremity of this large province extends into the northeastern portion of the Baja peninsula, an area referred to as the San Felipe Desert. As in the province as a whole, the terrain is flat with a scattering of mountain ranges running north and south. While much of the floor of the province in the United States is thousands of feet above sea level, in Baja it is only a few hundred feet in elevation.

PENINSULAR RANGE PROVINCE — This province encompasses the Peninsula's backbone mountain range as previously discussed. Remember that the entire range is characterized by a precipitous east-facing escarpment and a much wider, overall gently sloping western portion. In the United State the Peninsular Range Province extends into northern San Diego and western Riverside counties in southern California. Its northern boundary roughly follows Interstate 10 through San Gorgonio pass east of San Bernardino.

The range has been divided into numerous sections, each with its own name. It is these names that are frequently shown on the maps available to travelers. The more important ones in Baja are shown on the GEOLOGIC PROVINCES Map.

One other point must be noted concerning the Peninsular Range Province. The mountains in Baja's northern half, and the Sierra de la Laguna at the southern tip, are composed primarily of *granite*, a plutonic rock. In contrast, the Sierra Giganta in the peninsula's southern half is made up of a volcanic rock named *basalt*. The differences between these two rock types will be readily apparent to the traveler. They are described in more detail in the final section of this chapter.

CONTINENTAL BORDERLANDS PROVINCE — While sailing along the Pacific coast of the United States and Canada, one is impressed by the fact that virtually the entire shoreline is steep and mountainous. This situation begins to change south of the United States-Mexican border where much of the western shoreline is backed by flat, or gently sloping, plains. These plains are located in four more or less separate areas. (See the GEOLOGIC PROVINCES Map.)

In the north, a relatively small area surrounds the towns of Camalu and San Quintin. To the south, the Desierto de Vizcaino, Llano de Magdalena, and the Llano de la Paz are names given to sections of what is actually one, continuous, largely level area. These lands are composed of deep layers of sediments eroded over geologic time from the Peninsular Range mountains to the east. The tremendous weight of these sediments is causing the western edge of the province to sink below sea level as evidenced by numerous saltwater lagoons along the Pacific shore.

Along the western edge of this province lie two relatively minor mountain ranges, the Sierra Vizcaino and the Sierra Magdalena. Oceanographic investigations have disclosed that the two are actually linked together by a ridge of mountains lying beneath the surface of the ocean. Taken together, this system comprises a rather significant range of mountains paralleling the main Peninsular Range.

ROCK TYPES

The discussion of the Peninsular Range Mountains introduced several geologic terms relating to different types of rocks. We now need to pause briefly to examine this subject. At the outset, it should be noted that the terminology being presented has worldwide application. Knowing these few facts can thus be used to enhance traveling experiences anywhere on earth.

Geologists have classified the world's rocks into three great classes, *igneous*, *sedimentary*, and *metamorphic*. The igneous class is further divided into two subgroups, *plutonic* and *volcanic*. Please refer to the ROCK CLASSIFICATION Chart to learn the basic elements common to these classes of rock. Each

of the classes will be encountered frequently while traveling through the peninsula and many will be pointed out in the course of the GRAND TOUR in PART III.

By now you know that you will be encountering igneous-plutonic rocks (granite) in the northern portions of Baja's Peninsular Range mountains and in the Sierra de la Laguna in the extreme south. One of the most interesting points will be the Catavina boulder fields south of El Rosario. Igneous-volcanic rocks (basalt) will dominate the scene in the Sierra Giganta. You will also see the massive Las Tres Virgenes volcano and nearby recent lava flows. Volcanic cinder cones will be in evidence near San Quintin. While traveling through the various sections of the Continental Borderlands, sedimentary rocks prevail and are easily seen in the highway cuts and other places.

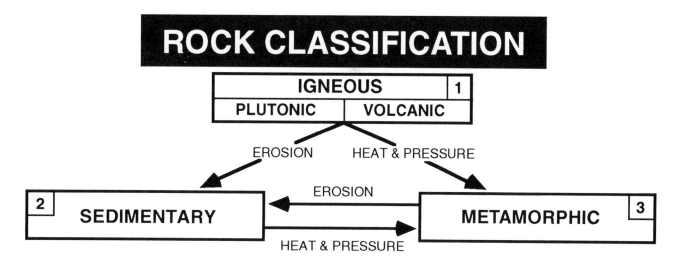

1 - IGNEOUS - All of the earth's rocks originate as igneous rocks formed by the cooling of molten material at, or near, the surface of the earth.

PLUTONIC - Intrusive rocks cooled slowly below the earth's surface, resulting in coarse grain, with identifiable crystals of various minerals. Light color. The most common rock is GRANITE.

VOLCANIC - Extrusive rocks cooled rapidly at the earth's surface, resulting in fine grain, with no identifiable crystals. Darker color. The most common rock is BASALT.

2 - SEDIMENTARY - Rocks made up of (1) fragments of preexisting igneous or metamorphic rocks worn down and deposited elsewhere by the forces of erosion (running water, wind, freezing temperatures, and gravity) or (2) by the accumulation of various organic materials. SHALE and CONGLOMERATE are common rock types.

3 - METAMORPHIC - Preexisting igneous or sedimentary rocks which have undergone change by being subjected to intense heat and pressure under the surface of the earth. Individual rocks are frequently banded or stratified.

Need another copy of THE MAGNIFICENT PENINSULA or other books about Baja? See the BAJA BOOKSHELF in the Appendix.

CHAPTER 10
VEGETATION

I have promised to be judicious in my use of superlatives, but it would be ignoring reality not to note that the desert vegetation of the Magnificent Peninsula is in itself magnificent. However, as in so many other fields, appreciation of vegetative beauty can be significantly improved by understanding something about what one is viewing. With this in mind Chapter 10 provides material concerning the desert itself, its various plant communities, and the common characteristics of desert plants. Photographs and descriptions of many of the more interesting species are also included.

VEGETATIVE REGIONS AND PLANT COMMUNITIES

Botanists have classified the world's vegetation into easily recognizable plant communities. The Douglas fir forests of the Pacific Northwest, various areas of grasses in the Great Plains, and the chaparral brushlands of southwestern United States are examples of such communities.

Norman Roberts discusses a total of eight plant communities in his *Baja California Plant Field Guide*. These are grouped into three broad regions: (1) The California Region, (2) The Sonoran Desert, and (3) The Cape Region.

The three regions may be easily distinguished from each other. They are shown on the VEGETATIVE REGIONS Map. Identifying all of the communities is a more difficult task. The map points out only the two communities that stand out best in the field.

Regional and community boundaries are distinct where there are sharp geographical changes but are more gradual where this is not the case. The map and an accompanying table point out places where boundary changes, or other regional distinctions, are easily detected.

The Sonoran Desert Region, lying in the central portion of the peninsula, is part of a far larger area classified as a true desert. The other two regions receive too much precipitation to rate this distinction. Delineating the three regions is thus basically a matter of knowing what is desert and what is not. Let us look briefly at the three regions, progressing from north to south.

CALIFORNIA REGION — This region is a continuation of the vegetational communities found to the north in Alta California. The principal plants are a number of densely growing species of shrubs, commonly referred to as chaparral. At the higher elevations the shrub community gives way rather sharply to forests of pinyon and Jeffrey pine and other conifers.

BAJA CALIFORNIA PLANT FIELD GUIDE

BY NORMAN ROBERTS

Norman Robert's book is THE definitive work on the plants of Baja California for the amateur plant enthusiast. The present edition is a heavily revised version of the original volume which has been out-of-print for many years. This 309 page guide describes 550 plant species with color photos of 275 of them.

BRILLIANT COLOR PHOTOS MAKE PLANT IDENTIFICATION EASY

Get your copy from the BAJA BOOKSHELF in the Appendix

The California Region will be passed over rather swiftly because it is not unique to Baja, and you may visit similar areas in the United States with relative ease. The coniferous forests in Baja are little different from those that clothe the higher lands in any of southern Alta California's four National Forests.

SONORAN DESERT REGION — There are a dozen or so major areas of desert and near-desert lands throughout the world. One is the North American Desert located in southwestern United States and northwestern Mexico. This area of over one-half million square miles is divided into four sections, one of which is the Sonoran Desert. Approximately two-thirds of the Baja peninsula falls within the Sonoran Desert, and this area constitutes the largest of the three vegetative regions.

Here, in the central portion of the peninsula, are located Baja's most intriguing plants. Included are a wide variety of cacti and other succulents along with the bizarre cirio, elephant tree, and a host of others. Many of the more prominent plant species have made special adaptations to arid conditions. Their physical characteristics are thus clearly different from plants living in the California Region and other moist areas. There is also a great deal of space between the individual plants in marked contrast to the dense brush fields to the north.

Botanists recognize four plant communities within this region. One of these, the San Felipe Desert, provides a sharp contrast to the glowing description I have just painted for the region as a whole. This community lies in the rain shadow east of the peninsula's tallest mountains along the shore of the Sea of Cortez. As a result, it is one of the driest areas in Baja and supports only low, sparse vegetation. It is easy to separate this region from its more entrancing neighbors.

THE CAPE REGION — The vegetation of the Cape Region is also far different from what we are accustomed to north of the border. Here, there are two plant communities. One of these, the *Oak-Pinyon Woodland,* is rarely seen by tourists as it is located at high elevations in the mountains where there are no roads. These peaks receive considerable rainfall as the result of high-intensity tropical storms, and they support stands of oaks, pinon pine, and other small trees.

The plant community through which the Cape Region highways pass is the *Arid Tropical Forest* . Because these highways are at relatively low elevations, you will still see many plants to which you have become accustomed in the Sonoran Desert. However, the hallmarks of this community are (1) vegetation that is far more densely spaced than in the Sonoran Desert and (2) the presence of a variety of low spreading trees. It has been referred to by one leading botanist as an impoverished tropical forest.

Elephant trees growing from the sterile lava flows east of San Ignacio along Highway 1. Part of PSI stop #11.

As our next step, let us take a closer look at the desert and near-desert lands of the Baja peninsula.

BAJA'S DESERT LANDS

CLIMATE — Deserts are characterized as areas receiving less than ten inches of annual rainfall and which have generally high temperatures. Their low humidity allows the sun's rays to penetrate the atmosphere easily and heat the ground far more than in moister areas. Ground temperatures 30-to-50 degrees warmer than the air are common. This same low humidity allows daytime heat to dissipate quickly; nighttime temperatures may decline as much as 50 degrees. The nighttime coolness is a key factor in the survival of both plants and animals and allows campers to enjoy cool, restful sleeping. The cheer and warmth of an evening campfire is always welcome in the desert.

It seems appropriate to ask why much of a long, narrow peninsula surrounded by water should be a desert. The answer lies in a combination of factors. At the broadest level, we find that Baja lies within a worldwide belt of high air pressure. Air is generally descending in such places, and because falling air increases in temperature it is able to absorb, rather than give up, moisture.

Perhaps of more importance is the continual presence of a cell of high pressure, called the Pacific High, off the west coast of the North American continent. It shields the peninsula from most of the moisture-laden air masses arriving from the Pacific Ocean. As this high shifts south during the winter months it allows considerable rain to fall along the west coasts of Canada and the United States; however, this air retains little moisture when, and if, it arrives over Mexico.

Finally, we find that the ocean off Baja's west coast is cold as the result of the upwelling of water from the depths of the sea. Air passing over these waters is chilled, and cool air can carry little moisture. As this air is warmed by contact with the land, it is able to retain, rather than dispose of, its moisture; therefore, there is little rain. These circumstances combine to make Baja a very dry part of the world.

The exception to these conditions occurs near the peninsula's tip due to tropical storms which are formed in the summer over the warm waters off the Mexican mainland to the south. Many of these storms dissipate in the Pacific Ocean, but others veer to the north and cross the southern tip of the Baja peninsula. Torrential downpours can occur, and scientists have reported witnessing continuous sheets of water one-half inch thick flowing over hundreds of acres of land.

Unfortunately, the desert's normally dry soils can absorb little water during such storms. As a result, areas in the Cape Region which receive considerable rainfall still support only semiarid types of vegetation. For deserts as a whole, it is estimated that only about three percent of their rainfall penetrates any distance into the soil.

HUMID VERSUS DRY ENVIRONMENTS — There are marked contrasts between the plant communities found in humid versus dry environments. In moist areas of the world, *space and light* are the key factors in competition between

POINTS OF VEGETATIVE SIGNIFICANCE
(See Vegetative Regions Map)

1 The segment of Highway 1 between the two arrows passes through the most impressive and picturesque vegetation in the Baja peninsula. The transition between the California Region and the Sonoran Desert is distinct near the upper arrow where Highway 1 rapidly gains elevation south of the Rio del Rosario.

2 The two squares indicate the location of Baja's two National Parks. Secondary roads may be driven to these parks which lie in the coniferous forest plant community. The boundaries between this plant community and the lower elevation chaparral are very evident as you enter both parks.

3 At this point on Highway 3 is the most dramatic elevation change in all of Baja's highways. At the base of the grade to the east is the sparsely vegetated San Felipe Desert. At the top of the grade lies the northern fringe of the pinyon pine and juniper portion of the coniferous forest community. To the west the chaparral brush fields dominate.

4 Highway 3 again crosses the eastern escarpment of the Peninsular Range Mountains as it did at point #3. This time the crossing is at a lower elevation so there is no coniferous forest. The boundary between the San Felipe Desert community and the chaparral of the California Region is very apparent. There is an outstanding area of barrel cactus at this point.

5 Here is another crossing of the mountain's eastern escarpment. At the base of the grade is, again, the sparse vegetation of the San Felipe Desert. To the west lies one of the most picturesque sections of the Sonoran Desert Region with an outstanding stand of Baja's most unique plant, the cirio tree. The boundary between the two is easily seen.

6 In this section of the Transpeninsular Highway lies another fine area of Sonoran Desert vegetation. The plant life is enhanced by the presence of the Tres Virgenes Volcano and the lava flows emanating from its southern flank. The elephant tree is the most interesting species here.

7 Look for dense growth of lichens and ball moss on the larger desert plants along Highway 22 and the secondary roads between Highway 1 and the Pacific coast. Also seen along Highway 1 in some places.

8 The section of Highway 1 in the mountains on either side of the town of El Triunfo provides the best view of Cape Region vegetation. Both the denseness and presence of several species of low, spreading trees characteristic of this region's vegetation are very apparent in this area.

9 The dense Cape Region vegetation is present along Highway 19 at the two places indicated by the arrows, although the stands are not as picturesque as those noted at point number 8.

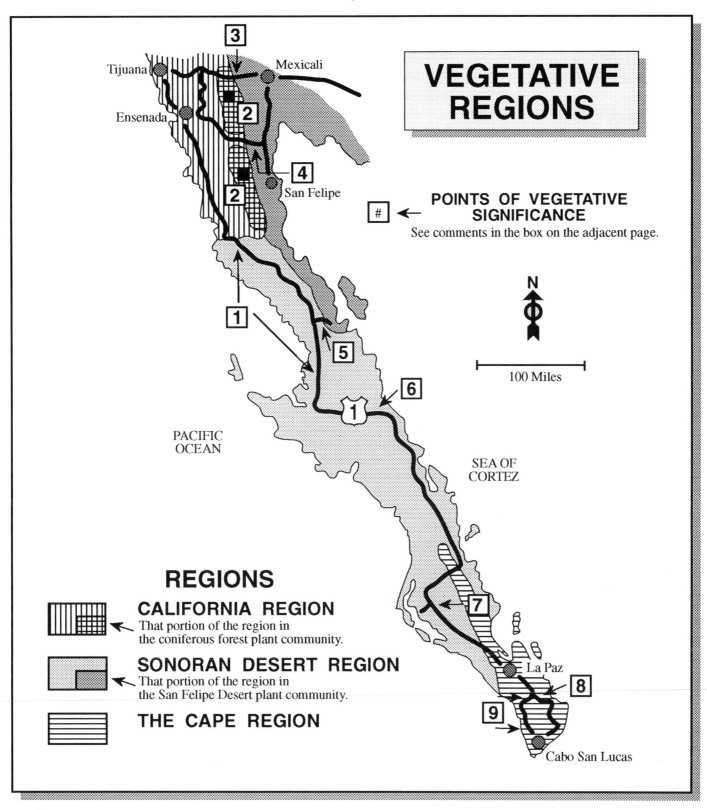

VEGETATIVE REGIONS

POINTS OF VEGETATIVE SIGNIFICANCE
See comments in the box on the adjacent page.

N

100 Miles

Tijuana
Mexicali
Ensenada
San Felipe

PACIFIC OCEAN

SEA OF CORTEZ

La Paz

Cabo San Lucas

REGIONS

CALIFORNIA REGION
That portion of the region in the coniferous forest plant community.

SONORAN DESERT REGION
That portion of the region in the San Felipe Desert plant community.

THE CAPE REGION

---

different species of plants and among individuals within a species. These communities are frequently *layered* with tall trees that form a canopy over smaller trees or shrubs. The lower layers are often of a different species. Below all this vegetation will be grasses and other ground-loving plants.

With the passage of time there is often a *succession* of plants. Shade-tolerant species will gradually grow through the canopy of the more light-requiring varieties that preceded them. In this manner, a stand of aspen trees will gradually be replaced by conifers, but should the latter stand be destroyed by fire or disease the succession will be repeated and aspen will return.

Finally, humid plant communities are frequently dominated by *one life form* such as coniferous or hardwood trees. All of these characteristics are different for desert plant communities.

85

Century plant in full bloom in the sparsely vegetated Sonoran Desert Region.

In desert areas, *water* becomes the critical element in plant competition. As little moisture penetrates more than a few inches into the soil, most plants have a broad network of roots near the surface to quickly collect what rain does fall. They cannot survive if other individuals are competing in their collection area. As a result, you will see that there is only one plant in a given spot and there is *no layering* as is common in moister areas. (You will see some degree of layering in the Cape Region due to its more humid environment.) If desert vegetation is destroyed it tends to be replaced with the same species of plants that were displaced and there is *no succession* of plants as in humid areas.

Finally, desert plant communities are made up of a wide *variety of species and life forms*, a factor that contributes significantly to the enjoyment that can be gained from studying desert vegetation.

SOILS — When you arrive in the desert area, look at the soil beneath your feet. There will be almost no organic material such as the deep layers of duff found in coniferous forests or the matting of dead grass in meadow areas. There are relatively few desert plants in a given area in comparison to plant communities in moister areas, and these individuals shed very little in the way of leaves and flower parts. Much of what little organic material is produced is washed away in the high intensity storms that are typical of desert areas. Desert soils tend to be high in salt content as there is little rainfall to dissolve and carry away these materials.

DESERT PLANT ADAPTATIONS

It is gratifying to be able to identify specific species of plants when you see them in your travels. Material to help you do this is presented further along in this chapter. However, in the desert, it is of equal, if not greater, interest to study and observe some of the common characteristics of all desert plants.

Most living things are segregated into either the plant or animal kingdom. Each kingdom is further subdivided by phylum, class, order, family, genus, and species. Individual species are named in the scientific world by combining the genus and species names. Thus, the galloping cactus must suffer through eternity being referred to as *Machaerocereus gummosus*, although you would perhaps call it something else should you be so unfortunate as to fall into one.

It would seem logical to suspect that most species of plants living in an environment as harsh as the desert would belong to a limited number of closely related genera and families. Reasoning in this way, one would assume that some particular characteristic of these select genera and families provided the key to dry-land survival. In many cases, it did not happen this way.

Ira Wiggion's classic *Flora of Baja California* notes that there are 2,705 species and 884 genera of plants in Baja California. The 179 most common species described in Norman Robert's original *Field Guide* belong in 64 different plant families. One can speculate that a wide variety of vegetative types were surviving contentedly in a moist environment, then, over time, they were confronted with drying climatic conditions. Those species that were to survive made certain physical and reproductive adaptations which permitted their living under desert conditions.

This process of change is termed *convergent evolution* and is defined as "the evolution of unrelated or distantly related groups of organisms along similar lines, resulting in the development of similar traits or features in the unrelated groups." The different types of adaptations which allow survival under dry conditions are amazingly few. As a result, many species of desert plants that look very much like each other are only distantly related.

All plants that live in the desert have to deal with surviving drought. Some species have solved the problem by simply avoiding it; they are called the *evaders*. Others have made the various adaptations mentioned above. These plants are the *resisters*. We will now examine these two groups.

EVADERS — These are the grasses, forbs and other annual plants. They quickly germinate from seed following a rain,

Ocotillo. Note the wide spacing of the other plants as is typical in the desert.

grow to maturity in a few weeks, produce a new crop of seed, and die. They survive in the form of millions of seeds cast on the desert floor to await the next cycle. This method of existence is little different from that of annual plants in more humid regions. Because desert annuals have not made any pronounced physical adaptation to resist drought, they resemble annual species in moister climates. Grass in Baja looks much like grass in Oregon, although it may not be as tall.

Desert annuals produce a seed crop far in excess of that needed for their own reproduction. This allows many desert animals to utilize seeds as a basic source of food.

How do seeds that survive the foragers know when to germinate and when to remain dormant? The survival of the species hangs in the balance. The answer is generally believed to be that seeds have a growth-inhibiting chemical in their coats which is dissolved away when exposed to sufficient quantities of rainfall. When they do germinate, the traveler is treated to the colorful spectacle of the desert in bloom.

RESISTERS — Perennial plants live continually from year to year and gradually grow larger. They are the trees, shrubs, cactus, and other species with woody superstructures which have made special adaptations to resist dry conditions. Look for evidence of these methods of adaptation in studying Baja's desert vegetation.

WATER STORAGE — Perhaps the desert's most interesting plants are the *succulents,* which have developed the ability to store water. The best known are the cacti, which use their stems as reservoirs. Species such as the century plant have adapted their leaves for this purpose. Others have underground containers as part of their roots. The wide-spreading and shallow root system of the commonly seen cardon cactus is capable of soaking up hundreds of gallons of water following a rain, after which four-fifths of its weight may consist of water.

ACCORDION STRUCTURE — A common characteristic of many species of cactus is the accordion-like structure of the stem. As the plant takes in water, the fleshy stem expands quickly. It subsequently contracts slowly as the supply is utilized. Note the stem condition of the cacti you examine.

If you are traveling south on Highway 1, following winter rains, you will observe that the water-filled cacti in the northern portion will display broad, U-shaped spacing between their ribs. Only a few days later, you may arrive near the peninsula's tip and see that the pleats are deeply indented and V-shaped. These southern plants normally receive their moisture as the result of summer, rather than, winter storms.

ARMAMENTS — A high proportion of the perennial plants in desert areas have developed thorns, leaves with sharpened points or toothed edges, and other similar armaments. Plants in other environments also contain thorns, but they are so prevalent in desert species that it is clear that they are an important adaptation for survival under arid conditions.

These armaments protect plants from browsing animals. They cannot afford to lose the food producing foliage that took up

Prickly Pear. Bright flowers grow on the ends of the pads after rain.

precious water to create. It is interesting to note that very few plants in the great desert in western Australia have thorns, and that this is the only one of the world's major arid areas that does not have, or has not once had, hooved, browsing animals. (Kangaroos do little browsing.) Also intriguing is the fact that some desert species that bear thorns in the wild produce no such protection when grown in the humid environment of a greenhouse.

LEAF CHARACTERISTICS — If you are fortunate enough to visit Baja's desert areas following significant rainfall, you will see that the ocotillo, cirio and similar plants are greenish in color, but you will have difficulty distinguishing any leaves from a distance. The leaves are there, but they are tiny affairs no more than an inch long. Small leaf size reduces the amount of water lost through transpiration. In addition to having leaves of such small size, these species quickly shed their foliage when the ground dries. The production of leaves is not a phenomenon one can count on at a particular time of the year but is clearly the result of recent rainfall, whenever it occurs.

The characteristic of having small, and even minute, leaves is typical of much of Baja's perennial vegetation. Even sizeable trees have small leaves. The most conservative of all are the cacti, which have no leaves except for a short period in youth. Their chlorophyll is located in the main stem of the plant as evidenced by their green color.

WIDE SPACING — As already noted, desert vegetation is widely spaced so that each individual plant has a water collecting area sufficient for its survival. Even in relatively dense areas of vegetation, it is possible to walk between the plants without being impaled by thorns. The open spaces are not filled with young plants, because they are unable to compete with their parents for moisture. Some species also seem to practice chemical warfare as their roots give off toxic substances which prevent the growth of other plants. Be particularly alert for the wide, uniform spacing of the creosote bush if you visit the San Felipe and Bahia de los Angeles areas.

VEGETATIVE REPRODUCTION — It is possible to reproduce many plants by placing cuttings from their stems in moist soil or water. Many desert plants routinely reproduce in this fashion without human assistance. Look at the several species of cholla cactus common in Baja. Their stems are made up of numerous segments. The terminal segments frequently fall to the ground and take root, often producing dense cholla thickets. Also, study the galloping cactus and other species of spreading plants; notice that they are able to produce new roots at places where their stems touch the ground.

These means of vegetative reproduction allow plants to avoid the costly water and energy-consumptive process of producing seeds and permit spreading of the species in years when seed production is not possible. If you visit the FONATUR nursery at Primer Agua, near Loreto, you will see a large number of species that are being propagated by vegetative means.

TRUNK FORM — Many species of low trees and shrubs in Baja have a trunk or main stem that is very thick in proportion to the size of the plant. The elephant tree is the most prominent example. There are in fact two different species of plants, both commonly called elephant trees. They are so similar that close inspection is required to distinguish one from the other, yet they are members of two distantly related families. (See POINTS OF SPECIAL INTEREST Tour stop No. 11.)

OTHER ADAPTATIONS — To resist drought conditions, desert plants have made a variety of other adaptations which are difficult to observe during a casual visit. Some species simply surrender and die back to ground level after each rain-enduced period of aboveground growth. Food and water are stored in a wide variety of underground structures related to the plant's roots. Other species have developed thick or waxy outer skins to reduce water loss, and they have fewer skin pores than their related wetland cousins. Still others are found to have developed poisonous or repulsive juices to ward off browsing animals.

ENDEMISM — An endemic species is one which is found in only one area of the world. Endemism is common in Baja because plant species have adapted to their harsh environment on an isolated peninsula. Almost 75 percent of the cactus species are endemic, as are many of the other easily observed plants. This uniqueness contributes to its aesthetic quality.

It can also be the cause of some frustration to those who are well versed in plant identification in other areas. For many years I referred to the abundant

Candelabra Cactus.

Galloping Cactus.

large cactus in Baja as a saguaro only to find that it was really the cardon. In a similar manner, the datilillo may be confused with the Joshua tree common in Alta California.

EPIPHYTES — Epiphytes are plants which gain physical support from other plants, poles, wires, and other objects. It is unusual to find epiphytes in deserts as they have no roots and must obtain their water from the air. But while the atmosphere in most deserts is extremely dry, fog and moist air overrun much of Baja's level Pacific coastal areas. Thus the larger desert plants growing here are often heavily festooned with such species.

The traveler may observe two basic types of epiphytes in Baja. Most common are lichens. These are associations of separate and distinct species of algae and fungi which live together in an intimate relationship called symbiosis. The algae provide the nourishment for the symbiotic pair, as they contain chlorophyll, and can make food using the sun's energy. The fungi, which have no chlorophyll, provide mechanical support and aid in the absorption of moisture.

While lichens are not a moss, they can best be described as looking like linear strands of moss. The Spanish moss which hangs from trees in SE United States is a lichen. Sometimes the lichens are so dense as to almost obscure the branches of the host plants, making them appear quite different than they would in dryer areas.

Ball moss also is not a moss, but a perennial herb. It forms spherical clumps about six inches in diameter. This rounded shape makes for easy identification.

Neither ball moss nor lichens harm the plants from which they gain support.

COMMON PLANTS

It is well beyond the scope of this book to present extensive material on the identification of individual species of plants. Included are photographs and brief descriptions of only sixteen. These are all in view from the highways and can be identified with reasonable certainty when they are called to your attention in the GRAND TOUR in PART III.

Should your interest in vegetation extend beyond this level, I highly recommend Norman Roberts' *Baja California Plant Field Guide*. This book has excellent color photos and amplifies the material on plant communities presented in this chapter. It is available from the BAJA BOOKSHELF in the Appendix (see notice on page 82). Also be sure to visit the botanical garden at **Km-57** on Highway 19 south of Todos Santos (See Chapter 24).

CIRIO Photo - 11
Idria columnaris — For once, a plant's scientific name imparts some information even to the amateur. In English, *columnar* means having the shape of a column; in Spanish, *cirio* means candle. So, in whatever language, the cirio is a plant shaped like a tapering column, although it often branches several times near the top. It can grow up to 60 feet high but is usually considerably shorter. Along the trunk are numerous branches smaller than the

Old Man Cactus. Note the clusters of spines at the tops of the stems which give the plant a bearded look. It is very easy to recognize.

diameter of a pencil and totally out of proportion to the plant as a whole. These bear the tiny leaves that clothe the cirio in green following rain.

If Baja California had a state plant, this would have to be it, as most people would concur that it is Baja's most unique species. It is endemic to Baja except for a small colony across the Sea of Cortez along the coast south of La Libertad. The cirio is present in groves along Highway 1 from immediately south of the Rio del Rosario to the northern edge of the Vizcaino Desert (Geographic Section No. 8). It also grows along the highway to Bahia de los Angeles.

CARDON   Photos 2 - 20

Pachycereus pringlei — While cirio may be Baja's most unique plant, the cardon, or giant cactus, is the most widespread of the peninsula's larger plants. Cardon is a very large cactus with one main trunk, which branches from one to numerous times as the plant grows older. The branches have from 11-to-17 vertical ribs. It is a good cactus in which to check the state of expansion of an accordion structure.

Don't confuse the cardon with the organ pipe which is also many branched but has no main trunk. It is also possible to confuse the cardon with the saguaro cactus of southwestern United States, but we amateurs are blessed by the fact that the saguaro does not grow in Baja. Like the cirio, the cardon is visible immediately south of the Rio del Rosario, but unlike the cirio, it is present all the way to the tip of the peninsula. Extensive stands of cardon are called *cardonals*. An outstanding cardonal covers many

Barrel cactus. The base of the cardon cactus to the right is growing straight up from the ground. Almost all barrels lean to the south as can be seen with this individual. This no doubt gives them minimum exposure to the sun.

square miles along the southern and eastern shores of Bahia Concepcion.

CENTURY PLANT   Photo - 86

Various species — Throughout the Sonoran Desert Region and in the southern portion of the California Region, you will begin seeing a variety of plants that are composed of a cluster of bayonet-like leaves. There are many species of such plants in Baja and throughout the world. Some species common to Baja bear the generic name Agave, while others are in the genus *Yucca*.

The specimen in the picture is *Agave Shawii* commonly called the century plant. This and similar species grow slowly for years, finally pouring forth all their reserves of energy in producing an amazingly luxuriant flower stalk. After blooming, the plant dies. You can see these stalks at many places in the desert; fine samples are present immediately south of the Rio del Rosario.

The century plant is a succulent because its leaves have become adapted for the storage of water. (Squeeze the leaves near their base to test the quantity of their water content.) A large number of distantly related species have developed leaves similar to the century plant, providing an excellent example of convergent evolution, and making species identification a difficult task for the amateur.

OCOTILLO   Photos - 87 - 156

Fouquieria splendens — The ocotillo is easily identified. It consists of numerous whip-like branches that spread out from its base. There is no

Cholla cactus. The most recent season's growth is lighter in color than the rest of the plant.

main trunk. Each branch is covered with thorns, thus providing an excellent example of the extreme protective armament which has been developed by many desert plants. Using ocotillo for firewood is a challenge.

The ocotillo is in the same family as the cirio and, like its cousin, produces a myriad of tiny leaves following rain. The plant is very sensitive to soil moisture and drops its leaves promptly at the first hint of drought. Several different crops of leaves may be produced in a given year in response to rainfall. The ocotillo is a good indicator of recent weather conditions and local soil moisture. Ocotillo is most common in the San Felipe Desert and along Highway 1 within Geographic Section No. 8. As one drives south, it comes into view shortly after crossing the Rio del Rosario.

Creosote bush. An uninspiring picture of this uninspiring but common plant.

PRICKLY PEAR Photo - 87

Opuntia Spp. — The plant in the photo is an example of the many species of cactus which bear the name prickly pear. They are probably the most familiar cactus to tourists as they also grow in many locations north of the border. The common feature of all species is their flat, thin, pad-like stem segments, which resemble a beaver's tail.

Prickly pears grow throughout Baja but are most common in the north. The flat stem, a popular food source, may be cut up and cooked as one would prepare green beans. You will find them fresh or canned in many Mexican food stores. The Spanish name for this cactus is Nopal, with the canned product bearing the name *Nopalitos*. Many excellent specimens of this cactus are located immediately south of the Rio del Rosario.

At one point in reviewing the literature for this chapter, I was seeking out what might be the common feature of all cacti. One author proudly announced, with no warning, that almost all species have no glochids in their areoles. Should you care, the areoles are the small depressions from which thorns project on the flat surface of the prickly pear stem (see photo). *Glochids*, tiny barbed hairs, are of course missing. Knowing all this will make you the hit of the evening at tonight's campfire.

CANDELABRA CACTUS Photo - 88

Myrtillocactus cochal — This is one of Baja's endemic species. There are many excellent specimens along Highway 1 south of the Rio del Rosario.

The candelabra's thick, woody branches are all nearly uniform in size and curve inward in graceful arcs toward the center of the plant. If hung upside down, it would resemble the outline of an enormous chandelier. There are six-to-eight ribs within each branch. Now that you are an expert in areoles (see the prickly pear cactus), note that they are spaced along the ridge lines as is the case with many other species of cactus.

This cactus blooms yearlong, often during the nighttime hours. So, if you and the love of your life just must go for an evening walk in the desert, here is the perfect excuse.

GALLOPING CACTUS Photo 89

Machaerocereus gummosus — The galloping cactus is one of the most widespread species seen throughout the Sonoran Desert and Cape Region and is often present along the highways. Its individual branches are essentially the same size as those of the candelabra cactus but look like mem-

Organ Pipe Cactus close to our campsite near Playa los Cerritos near Highway 19. Note that the vegetation is far more dense here in the Cape Region than it is in the Sonoran Desert Region.

A clump of Datilillo.

bers of the latter species who have been mixing growth hormones with their margaritas. The galloping cactus branches grow randomly in all directions, often touching the ground and taking root. They can form impenetrable thickets as large as 30 feet in diameter. The galloping cactus flowers in July and August and produces a fleshy edible fruit.

OLD MAN CACTUS   Photo - 89
Lophocereus schottii — Old man cactus branches near the base with each stem having five-to-seven ribs. The tip of each branch

is crested with large numbers of coarse, hairlike, gray spines giving it a whiskered look, and providing the basis for its name. It is common in the area south of the Rio del Rosario.

BARREL CACTUS   Photo - 90
Ferocactus Spp. — The barrel cactus is lower growing than many of the more prominent species, but it is easy to recognize, provided you are content with identifying only the genus. There are over a score of species in Baja.

Their common feature is one cylindrical stem that resembles a barrel or similar container. Occasionally they will branch. The spines are often flattened and hooked at the end, and the upper portion of the barrel is often reddened. Notice that most plants lean to the south.

CHOLLA CACTUS   Photo - 90
Opuntia Spp. — Here is another cactus genus represented by over a score of species. They are widespread throughout the Sonoran Desert and Cape Regions. The cholla stems are not flat like the prickly pear, or ribbed as in many other species. In contrast, the stem is made up of numerous linearly attached segments or joints. Each joint is further divided into many, small, rounded subsections called *tubercles.*

One of the most common species is the teddy bear cholla shown in the photo. Its silvery spines are so dense that they resemble fur at a distance, an illusion that can be promptly corrected by closer inspection. These spines are barbed at the ends and will catch on anything passing by. Joints readily break off, and if you are snared, a veritable pincushion of spines will attach themselves to your skin or clothing. Removing these with a bare hand is not recommended. You may see some of these joints lying about on the ground or rooted in vegetative reproduction.

CREOSOTE BUSH   Photo - 91 - 156
Creosote bush is one of the most common of Baja's desert shrubs. Most other shrubs are light green or grayish in color. The deep olive green of the creosote bush stands out in sharp contrast. Its small leaves are often coated with a shiny, sticky

---

A CONSERVATION ETHIC FOR BAJA CALIFORNIA

There are very few natural resource managers in Mexico, and most of the environmental constraints imposed on us north of the border are not readily apparent. Also, on occasion, we tourists will see Mexican citizens conducting their affairs in ways which are not in keeping with sound conservation practices. These conditions may influence us to forget our environmental manners in Baja.

To complicate matters, Baja California is largely a desert. Deserts are particularly sensitive to disruptive man-made change. Arid lands do not heal themselves nearly as rapidly as would be the case in areas with more moisture, as is the case where most of us live.

The conditions just noted place an added responsibility on visitors. If we are to preserve the features about Baja California which we find attractive, we must act responsibly, and do so on a voluntary basis. I recently heard a church sermon where the minister posed the question "How does one avoid doing what is wrong?" His answer was, "Just don't do it."

Avoiding environmental damage is largely a matter of using good common sense. It should be obvious that digging up sensitive plants, destroying tide-pool organisms, picking up artifacts, walking about in seabird nesting areas, and throwing trash in the sea will cause long-term damage. Something inside ought to say "Just don't do it."

substance. Small, five-petaled, yellow flowers are present throughout the year.

Creosote bush is one of the most drought-tolerant of desert plants. When the more interesting vegetation disappears, creosote bush often becomes dominant. Botanists believe its roots emit a toxic substance that prevents seedlings from growing too close to the parent plants. However, the intervening spaces are usually occupied by other species.

DATILILLO   Phptos - 92 - 180

Yucca valida — The datilillo is a yucca, but it becomes a small tree in contrast to other ground-hugging plants of the same genus. The leaves are bayonet-like, although they do not store water as does the succulent century plant. The species is similar to the Joshua tree of southwestern United States. Individual plants grow in clumps and branch along the trunk.

ELEPHANT TREE   Photo - 83

Pachycormus discolor — Elephant tree, endemic to Baja, is one of its most interesting species. Its principal characteristics are (1) the grayish-white to yellowish bark which peels off in papery layers and (2) the tree's overall shape with the trunk and main branches thick in proportion to the plant as a whole. Although found in many places along Highway 1, it is most prominent in the lava flow area east of San Ignacio.

The two principal characteristics noted above are also shared by other peninsular species, some of which are only distantly related. This appears to be an example of convergent evolution, discussed earlier in this chapter. *Bursera microphylla,* also called elephant tree, or torote, is a principal example. Its twigs and branch ends are reddish brown in contrast to the gray color of pachycormus discolor, and its leaves are also much smaller.

ORGAN PIPE CACTUS   Photos - 80 - 91

Lemaireocereus thurberi — The organ pipe is a large, erect cactus which at first glance may be confused with the cardon. Note, however, that the organ pipe branches near ground level and has no main trunk as does the cardon. It occurs only in the southern half of the peninsula.

This species produces a sweet globular fruit, about the size of a tennis ball, which was the prized food of the original Indian population. Apparently they were well fed only when it was

Palo Blanco. Note the light bark.

available. It is reported that once the supply was exhausted, the Indians would gather their own dried feces and collect the seeds that had passed through the intestinal tract. These were ground into meal.

PALO BLANCO   Photo - 93

Lysiloma candida — Palo, meaning stick or pole in Spanish, has become the first name of a large number of small trees. Many are quite common but the palo blanco (white) is the one most easily identified from the highway. The trunk is quite straight, with smooth, silvery-white bark which is its identifying feature. Except for one locality across the Sea of Cortez, this species is endemic to Baja.

PALMS   Photos - 190 - 205 - 234

There are over 1,100 species of palms worldwide in warm climates. The chart below will allow you to identify Baja's three basic types based on leaf and trunk characteristics.

PALMS		
TYPE	**LEAVES**	**TRUNK**
FAN	FAN SHAPED -- Individual leaflets radiate from the ends of the stems.	EXTREMELY ROUGH -- The bases of the dead stems remain attached to the trunk. This is true even if most of the stems have been pruned off.
DATE	PINNATE -- Individual leaflets project along both sides of the stem, similar to a birds feather.	
COCONUT		SMOOTH -- The entire dead stem falls from the trunk leaving a smooth surface.

CHAPTER 11
WILDLIFE

Accounts of wildlife frequently evolve around an array of animals that people rarely view. In this vein, I will present a few nonspecific introductory remarks about desert animals, but the major portion of this chapter relates to a relatively few animals which you should actually see in your travels in the Baja peninsula.

DESERT ANIMALS

As noted in the previous chapter, desert plants have made substantial physical adaptations as a means of surviving in the harsh living conditions of the desert. Such modifications are far less pronounced in the animal kingdom. Most desert birds and animals are quite similar to their cousins living in more humid areas. Also, the wildlife species found in Baja are essentially the same as those living in the Mexican mainland or farther north, in the United States. As is the case for many desert animals, they do tend to be smaller in size and paler in color.

Insect life in the desert is robust and peaks with the culmination of plant growth following rains. The immense supply of eggs and dormant pupae left behind by these creatures combine with the seeds of annual plants as the basic food for birds and animals. The majority of desert mammals are seed-eating rodents. (See discussion of Insect Pests in Chapter 8.)

The traveler will see relatively few land animals in Baja's deserts because most of them feed and move about only at night. Also, most species make their homes in burrows in the ground, or in large plants, where they can escape the rigorous environment.

For this reason, I suggest that you pay a visit to the zoological garden located in the small town of Santiago south of La Paz. It is stop No. 21 on the POINTS OF SPECIAL INTEREST TOUR. The unlikely location of this facility may lead the traveler to expect very little. Surprisingly, this very pleasant zoo, constructed in 1983, is well shaded and contains many different displays of living animals. Most are species of local Mexican mammals, birds, and reptiles. Here may be your only chance to see these animals. (Every cage had occupants in 1992.)

When you walk about in the desert you will see a variety of lizards darting about on the desert floor. Their scaled skin, which is highly resistant to drying, allows them to move about in the daytime. You will also see considerable bird life during the daylight hours, particularly near the coast. A discussion of several of the most common large birds is presented below. The concluding section describes the California gray whale and other marine mammals.

HUNTING

Hunting by tourists is permitted in Baja. Doves are taken throughout the peninsula. The Pacific coast chaparral region from Ensenada south to El Rosario produces some of the largest quail populations in North America. The Bahia San Quintin area is famous for Brant and other sea-duck hunting while the Valle de Mexicali SE from Mexicali produces a variety of waterfowl and pheasants.

Securing permission to hunt in Mexico is a complicated process due in part to the country's strict laws concerning gun possession. The hunter is required to obtain a multiple-entry tourist card and several other documents from different Mexican agencies including the military. A character reference also must be obtained from the hunter's local law enforcement agency.

The process is sufficiently complicated and so subject to change that I will not pass on further details but instead refer you to several organizations that are in the business of obtaining the necessary permits for a modest fee. These are (1) Mexican Hunting Association, 3302 Josie Avenue, Long Beach CA 90808, (310) 421-1619; (2) Wildlife Advisory Services, P.O. Box 76132, Los Angeles, CA 90076 (213) 385-9311; and (3) Romero's Mexico Service, 1600 West Coast Highway, Newport Beach CA 92663, (714) 548-8931. These organizations also provide a good source of information concerning seasons, bag limits, and other hunting information.

BIRDS

BIRD WATCHING — Baja is an excellent place to visit for those interested in observing and studying bird life. Desert vegetation supports little of the dense foliage common in humid climates. As a result, birds have relatively little cover and are easily viewed. You will often see hawks and other large birds perched on the top of giant cactus plants. The seashore and marsh areas are alive with bird life.

The serious observer should obtain Peterson's *A Field Guide to Mexican Birds*. Unfortunately, the illustrations of many of Baja's birds are omitted as they would duplicate those already included in previous Peterson volumes on Texas and eastern and western United States. As a minimum, the western guide is needed to augment the Mexico book. The National Geographic Society's *Field Guide to the Birds of North America* also describes much of the peninsula's bird life.

WATERBIRDS — Many North American waterbirds (ducks, coots and similar species) breed during the summer in Alaska, Canada, and northern United States. They then winter in southern United States and Mexico. These birds travel south in fairly well defined paths called *flyways*. Birds using the Pacific Flyway spend the winter in Alta and Baja California and along the west coast of the Mexican mainland. A few birds migrate to the delta of the Rio Colorado, but the majority of the marsh habitat here has been destroyed by the regulatory effects of upstream reservoirs.

An exception to this Rio Colorado situation can be found along Highway 5 where the main river is joined by the Rio Hardy. During wet years, bird life is abundant here and at the nearby southern end of Laguna Salada (See Chapter 15).

The principal waterbird wintering areas in Baja are along the Pacific coast from Ensenada south to Bahia Magdalena. If you are even remotely interested in bird life, I recommend that you drive the Puerto Venustiano Carranza side trip starting at the town of Guerrero Negro. It is described near the beginning of Chapter 20. The road to the abandoned port facilities passes through several miles of outstanding saltwater marsh which provides a home for thousands of egrets, pelicans, cranes, gulls, and many other species of marsh and seabirds. The roadbed is elevated some ten feet above the sea level so you may look down upon the many birds.

SEABIRDS — The Sea of Cortez area offers the most spectacular concentrations of nesting southern seabirds on the west coast of North America. The specific species involved are given in a table on this page. The majority of these birds nest primarily on the offshore islands. A few, the shoreline group (osprey, herons, and terns), are more frequently found along the peninsular shore. There are a variety of other seabird species that visit the Sea of Cortez but which do not breed in the area. Likewise, many of the breeding varieties migrate to both north

PRINCIPAL SEABIRDS THAT BREED IN THE SEA OF CORTEZ

black storm petrel	yellow-footed gull
least storm petrel	elegant tern
brown pelican	royal tern
double-crested cormorant	sooty tern
Brandt's cormorant	noddy tern
red-billed tropicbird	American oystercatcher
magnificent frigatebird	osprey
blue-footed booby	great blue heron
brown booby	reddish egret
Craveri's murrelet	black-crowned night heron
Heermann's gull	yellow-crowned night heron

List courtesy of Daniel W. Anderson

and south after the breeding season. These birds will be seen principally by those who participate in boating.

The interface of seabirds with the boating public presents a special problem in the Sea of Cortez. The adverse effect of human disturbance on nesting seabirds is well documented by the scientific fraternity. There is clear evidence that the brown pelican has abandoned its former nesting sites on Islas San Martin and Todos Santos along Baja's Pacific shore due to human disturbance. Visiting scientists have also observed damaging effects following such widely divergent visitations as; individual sightseers on their own, American tourists guided by Mexicans, curious Mexican fishermen, commercial egg collectors, and even American scientists and educational tours.

Regardless of who causes the disturbance, here are the destructive results when nesting seabirds are flushed from their nests.

1 — Eggs and chicks may be knocked from their nests by frightened adults.

2 — Unprotected chicks and eggs may die from excessive heat or cold.

3 — Predators, mainly gulls, may eat unguarded eggs and chicks.

The brown pelican is commonly seen on Baja's beaches and marinas. Frequently, as here, they are accompanied by sea gulls ever hopeful that one of the pelicans will drop a portion of its catch.

4 — Nests, and eventually entire nesting sites, may be abandoned.

If you should come upon nesting seabird colonies please observe them with binoculars from a distance. Stay at least 100 yards off when in a boat, and 300 yards away when onshore. Those desiring to seriously study seabirds should obtain a competent book on the subject. My recommendation is Peter Harrison's *A Field Guide to Seabirds of the World* which is available from the BAJA BOOKSHELF in the Appendix. Also see a brief advertisement in this chapter.

FIVE COMMON BIRDS — Following is a brief discussion of five of the common large birds seen in Baja.

BROWN PELICAN — There are pelicans north of the border, but only those who live near the sea coast will have seen them. In Baja the species is common along all coastal areas and if you don't see many of them, you simply aren't looking. The pelican is an unmistakable bird (see photo in this Chapter).

Breeding takes place locally on offshore islands. During the summer, many individuals migrate north into the United States, but their numbers greatly decreased in recent decades. Studies conducted during the 1970s in the breeding areas of Baja's Islas de los Coronados, south of San Diego, showed that the bird's egg shells contained concentrations of D.D.T. insecticide. The result was shell walls too thin to survive the reproductive process. Since D.D.T. has been banned there has been a dramatic increase in pelican birthrates.

FRIGATEBIRD — The frigatebird, or man-o-war bird, is unmistakable in flight. Their wingspan can exceed seven feet and is greater in proportion to the body than that of any other seabird. The wings are swept back like a WW II navy Corvair fighter plane. The tail is deeply notched. Those with white breasts are the female.

While the pelican is a master fisherman, the frigate is basically a thief. They cannot swim or dive but make a living largely by forcing other seabirds to disgorge or drop food that they have captured. You will see the frigate soaring over-head in coastal areas in the southern portion of the peninsula.

TURKEY VULTURE — The turkey vulture, or buzzard, is not unique to Mexico, but most people do not have the opportunity to study this bird near their homes. In Baja, you will sometimes have the opportunity of seeing groups of vultures at close range, particularly if your travels take you to a garbage dumping area. They are not pretty birds. The featherless head is small in proportion to the body and is red in color. The rest of the body is black. They will usually be observed feeding on a dead animal, which of course does not contribute to the artistic setting. You will also frequently see individuals sitting on the top of a cardon cactus.

Most commonly, the turkey vulture can be seen soaring over-head. Look for the small head, and two-toned wings which are held aloft clearly above the horizontal. The outer portions of the wings are lighter than the rest of the bird. It rocks unsteadily as it soars along.

ROADRUNNER — Bird guidebooks note that the roadrunner's call is a dove-like *coo*, but we all know they really go *beep beep*. Baja is a good place to observe this escapee from the movie cartoons. In the films, they seem to run up and down the roads, but in the wild they emulate the chicken and always seem to be crossing the road. They are more commonly seen on the secondary and dirt roads than on the main highways.

The roadrunner is 20-to-24 inches in length, heavily streaked, has a long, narrow tail and a shaggy, rooster-like crest on the head. If a large bird runs across the road, what else can it be?

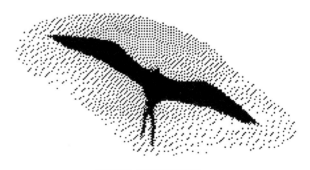

FRIGATEBIRD

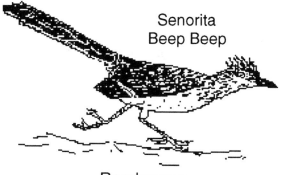

Senorita
Beep Beep

Roadrunner

CARACARA — The caracara is a large, long-legged, long-necked, dark bird who's white head is topped with a rooster-like crest. The bill is yellowish. In flight they display white markings on the wings and tail. They are a bird of prey like the turkey vulture. They are commonly seen in dry desert areas in the southern half of the peninsula.

MARINE MAMMALS

SEA LIONS AND DOLPHINS — My experience in cruising the Pacific coast clearly indicates that there are far more dolphins, and sea lions in Baja's waters than in those north of the border. Unfortunately, they are infrequently seen by the tourist unless one ventures out to sea. Seeing a dolphin is simply a matter of chance, but sea lions live in colonies well known to Mexican fishermen. You can arrange for sightseeing trips at Loreto, Cabo San Lucas, and other places. Ask to be shown the *lobos del mar*.

At press time the Mexican government was considering a new law that would set jail terms on the killing of dolphins and sea turtles. Both species are regularly taken by Mexican fishermen although it is against the law. I have seen pick-up truck loads of turtles on Baja's back roads. Environmental constraints are slow taking hold where many people live near the poverty line.

Baja's Pacific waters also provide a home for the elephant seal, but the known colonies are all on offshore islands. If you wish to see this fascinating marine mammal, the best place to do so is at the Ano Nuevo State Reserve north of Santa Cruz in Alta California. An excellent booklet on the elephant seal is available from the BAJA BOOKSHELF in the Appendix.

CALIFORNIA GRAY WHALE — In recent years, there has been wide public interest concerning whales in general and the

PELICAN RESEARCH PROJECT

Brown pelicans have been leg-tagged by University of California Davis researchers to study their movements, migrations, and interactions with man. Tags vary from plain aluminum bands to bands plus colored plastic markers. Each configuration has a meaning. If you see a tagged bird, please report the following information:

1 -- The configuration (what is on what leg).

2 -- The color (and number if possible).

3 -- Date and location of sighting.

4 -- The situation. How did you come to see the bird, was it sick or injured, was it being a nuisance, etc.

5 -- Your name and address so that you may be sent information on the bird's origin, age, etc.

6 -- Do not remove the tags or bands unless the bird is dead. In this instance please send the tags along with the other information.

Your help will be much appreciated.

BAND

TAG

REPORT FINDINGS TO:
Daniel W. Anderson
Pelican Research Project
Dept. of Wildlife and Fisheries
University of California
Davis, California, 95616

CALIFORNIA GRAY WHALE
CHARACTERISTICS

THE ANIMAL	A true mammal. Air breathing. Warm blooded. Nurse young on milk.
ADULTS	Length, 30 to 50 ft. Weight 20 to 40 tons. Avg. age 30 to 40 years, occasionally 60.
CALVES	Length 15 ft., weight 1.5 tons at birth. Consume 50 gal. of milk, gain 60 to 70 lb. daily.
MIGRATION	Travel 20 hours & 100 miles per day. Trip of 6,000 miles takes 6 to 8 weeks.
COLOR	Slate gray caused by natural pigments, barnacles, and barnacle scars.

California gray whale in particular. Whale-watching has become a popular pastime in many areas along the Pacific coast. The Baja peninsula plays a prominent part in this gigantic animal's life history as it is Baja's Pacific lagoons that are the primary destination of the whale's annual southern migration. The gray's basic characteristics are described in a insert above.

ANNUAL MIGRATION CYCLE — It was recently estimated that there are 17,000 gray whales. This population spends the summer months feeding in the Bering and Chukchi Seas off Alaska. Starting in October, they begin their annual southern migration to the subtropical waters of several coastal lagoons along Baja's south-central Pacific coast. Here the calves are born.

The whale's migration route is close to shore as the gray is a bottom feeder. As a result, whale spouts are easily seen from shore. Ocean cruisers sail in these same waters and are frequently in company with the migration.

Reference to the ANNUAL MIGRATION Chart will disclose that the several migration phases overlap each other. Some individuals are still arriving in Baja while others are already heading back north. Pregnant females, well into their 12-month gestation period, leave Alaska early with their mission clearly in mind. Others lag behind while males and in-season females court and mate on the way south.

By December, the whales begin arriving in the waters off northern Baja. By mid-January, most females have arrived at their destinations in the backwaters of the lagoons where most of the calving takes place. The return north occurs in somewhat reverse order. The newly pregnant females and other *single* whales begin north, starting in February, while the new mothers and their calves linger behind, occasionally as late as May and June. As a result, there are whales in Baja waters from December to June.

An excellent booklet concerning the California gray whale is available from the BAJA BOOKSHELF in the Appendix.

WHALE-WATCHING — The whale may be observed in a variety of ways. They are summarized as follows.

1. Viewing by Boat.
    a. Day Trips.
    b. Long-range Trips.
2. Viewing from the Air.
3. Viewing from Land.
    a. Coastal Observation Points.
    b. Baja Lagoons.

1. Viewing by boat — Many Pacific coast ports in the United States offer one-day whale-watching trips in the same type of vessels normally used for sportfishing. You can frequently get close-up views of the whales on these ventures. The various fishing charter organizations noted under fishing in Chapter 5 also provide whale-watching trips.

2. Viewing from the air — Passengers in small private aircraft can get fine views of whales both in the ocean and in the lagoons. The Baja Bush Pilots *Airports of Baja California* reports that landing at the dirt airstrip adjoining Laguna San Ignacio provides a ringside seat.

3. Viewing from land — Seaward views of Pacific waters are offered at numerous points along the southern portion of the highway between Tijuana and Ensenada. Take Highway 1, rather than 1-D, so you may easily pull off onto the side roads accessing the coastal bluffs. Also visit the MIRADOR vista point, which is stop No. 3 on the POINTS OF SPECIAL INTEREST Tour.

There are several good vantage points along the road to La Bufadora on the Punta Banda peninsula. Punta Banda projects well out into the ocean, and the road is a considerable distance above the water. See Chapter 18 for directions. Another point is Punta Baja, but its elevation is not nearly as high as at Punta Banda. See Chapter 19 for the side trip to this area.

During the winter of 1988-89 numbers of California gray whales migrated to the shallow waters immediately outside the harbor at La Paz. The spouts of these animals could easily be seen from many of the coastal areas described in Chapters 23 and 24.

Finally, the land-based traveler can drive to the edge of the calving lagoons at several places. In Bahia Magdalena, whales can be seen from the docks at San Carlos and boats may be rented to travel to the bay's opening into the Pacific where whales are more common. Today the easiest place in all of Baja to visit the whales at close range is at Puerto Lopez Mateos which can be reached by oiled highway. Boats may be rented to visit the calving grounds inside Boca de Solidad (see Chapter 22.)

There are two additional sites in the vicinity of Guerrero Negro. The first is the abandoned salt dock at Puerto Venustiano Carranza. In some years there are no whales here as the lagoon's entrance to the sea is blocked with sand. In others, they are present and may be seen from a tour boat advertised in the area's hotels (see Chapter 20). The most famous site is Scammon's Lagoon, which will now be discussed in more detail.

SCAMMON'S LAGOON — Scammon's Lagoon (Laguna Ojo de Liebre) is the largest lagoon in Baja. Its easternmost segment is called The Nursery. This area has been designated as the *Refugio Natural de la Ballena Gris* (Natural Refuge of the Gray Whale). You may camp on the shore of the lagoon in an area administered by one of the local Ejidos. See Chapter 20 for access details.

I recommend you visit this area not solely to see the whale, as obviously the great majority of the creatures' bodies will be below the water's surface. What you do absorb is an overall impression of a desolate area where nature is playing out the climax of a 6,000-mile journey. You will see and hear four signs of the whale:

1. The backs of the whales break the surface as they move about. From your vantage point on the six-foot-high sand bar at the edge of the lagoon, you see only a small portion of the whale.

2. Occasionally, the upper 8-10 feet of a whale's head projects vertically from the water. This behavior is called *skyhopping*. Apparently the animal is simply looking about.

The massive back of the gray whale.

3. Perhaps the most common sign of the whales are the spouts which rise up to 15 feet. What you see is largely condensation caused when a whale's warm breath cools in the sea air.

4. Accompanying the spout is an explosive "whoosh." The sounds of this breathing create an eerie feeling as evening falls at Scammon's.

If you make the trip to Scammon's, I recommend you spend the night at the lagoon's edge. Nothing that you will see is spectacular, and it takes some time to absorb what is occurring. Be sure to take your field glasses.

THE WHALE'S FUTURE — Because populations of whales hunted by European and Yankee whalers became depleted during the early years of the 19th century, it became necessary for them to turn to the gray whale to fill their holds. By 1845, the migration route and the Baja calving lagoons had been discovered, and in 1857 Captain Charles M. Scammon first entered Laguna Ojo de Liebre. Fifteen whaling stations were eventually established along the Alta and Baja California coasts. Hunting continued until 1890, when it was abandoned because the population had been reduced to only a few thousand.

Today, the gray is protected under the auspices of the International Whaling Commission. In 1972, the Mexican government established sanctuaries at Scammon's Lagoon and the other principal breeding areas. As a result, the gray whale has experienced a remarkable recovery.

In the past, the animal's predictable migration pattern made it an easy mark for the hunter. These same habits have now worked to save the species because mates are easily found. As a result, breeding has flourished. By 1991, the total population was estimated to be 21,000, a number probably higher than prior to commercial whaling activities. Late in that year the U. S. National Oceanic and Atmospheric Administration proposed removing the whale from the U. S. Endangered Species list. If this occurs, it would still be off-limits to hunting and would be protected by a variety of other statutes. The whales recovery represents a remarkable environmental success story.

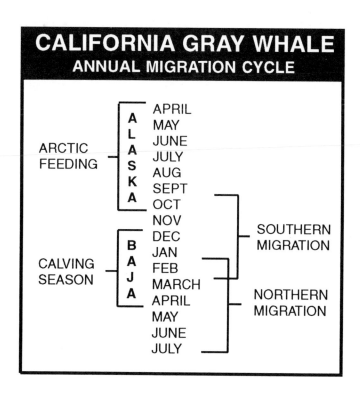

CALIFORNIA GRAY WHALE
ANNUAL MIGRATION CYCLE

ARCTIC FEEDING	A L A S K A	APRIL MAY JUNE JULY AUG SEPT OCT
		NOV
CALVING SEASON	B A J A	DEC JAN FEB MARCH APRIL MAY JUNE JULY

SOUTHERN MIGRATION

NORTHERN MIGRATION

CHAPTER 12
HISTORY

Remote, isolated, arid, and little known. This is Baja California. One might expect to find little of historic interest in such a place. It is just the opposite. Our Magnificent Peninsula boasts an amazingly rich and fascinating history beginning a scant 42 years after Columbus's first voyage to the new world in 1492 and almost a full century before the pilgrims landed at Plymouth Rock in Massachusetts. It employs a cast of characters no novelist could have devised: Hernan Cortez, Juan Cabrillo, Francis Drake, Thomas Cavendish, Padres Francisco Kino and Junipero Serra, and the notorious filibuster, William Walker.

In addition to many persons of Spanish origin, Baja's soil has witnessed the coming and going of Jesuit missionaries from Italy, English adventurers, Dutch pirates, French miners, war with the United States, internal revolution, and incredible land fraud. The broad aspects of this enticing drama are presented in this chapter. Details will be interwoven as the many easily visited sites are encountered along the GRAND TOUR in PART III.

But first this historic stage must be set with a brief review of Baja's pre-Hispanic inhabitants. I must also note that much of the material presented in this chapter is based on an English Translation of *A History of Lower California* by Pablo L. Martinez.

THE PREHISTORIC CALIFORNIANS

A sharp contrast existed between the Indian inhabitants of the Baja peninsula and the native populations that the Spanish conquistadors encountered in mainland Mexico and much of South America. In these latter areas, the Aztecs, Mayas, and Incas had developed highly advanced civilizations with large cities and complex religious and cultural institutions. The Indians of southwestern United States also had well developed, although somewhat less advanced, civilizations. As a result of their isolated location on the Baja peninsula, the Baja California Indians were found to be among the most primitive in the Americas. This situation was to have important impacts on their interrelationships with Spanish conquerors in the centuries to come.

The early Spanish encountered three well defined tribal groups. The most southerly were the *Pericues*. They inhabited the peninsula's tip north to a line drawn south of present-day Todos Santos and San Bartolo. They were to interface with the Spanish during the important early day events at San Jose del Cabo.

North of the Pericues were the *Guaycuras*. Their domain stretched from the line mentioned above north to Loreto. From a historic standpoint, these people were the most important as it was they who were destined to greet the early Spanish landings in the La Paz and Loreto areas, and they were to be the objects of the earliest missionary activities.

The balance of the peninsula was the home of the *Cochimies*. The three tribal areas are shown on the SPANISH EXPLORATIONS Map.

In keeping with their primitive nature, the peninsula's Indians had no written language and only the most elementary of religious beliefs. They lived in communal groups in the vicinity of fresh water and slept on the bare ground. Shelter was provided by holes dug in the earth, crude arrangements of branches, and occasionally by a cave. More commonly, the Indians slept within a low circle of stones without any roof. A fire would be kept burning during the night in the winter. They cultivated nothing and lived from their native environment by hunting, fishing, and gathering.

In spite of stone age conditions, these Indians were described by the early Spaniards as strong, tall, and healthy. They were good runners and swimmers. The men went totally nude, if one discounts their habit of painting the body in various grotesque patterns. The women normally wore some form of garment made from native materials.

Their possessions were limited to a few crude cups, bowls, baskets, and simple implements for fishing, hunting, and warfare. For these latter activities they had mastered the use of the bow and arrow, boomerang, and wooden lances. This mention of warfare leads to a discussion of several attributes of the Indians which were of particular importance in their future relationships with the Spanish.

TRIBAL WARFARE — There appears to have been a more or less continuous state of warfare between the tribes; the males were practiced in this art. On the whole, the Indians did not transfer their hostilities toward the Spaniards. There were few organized attempts to eject the intruders. The Spaniards did not have to conquer California with force of arms as was necessary on the mainland. Nevertheless, there were armed encounters between the two parties, and the Spanish possession of firearms was all important. In addition, the Indians' warlike behavior toward each other frequently cast the Spaniards in the role of referee. It also led in part to the next point of importance.

BAJA CALIFORNIA HISTORY

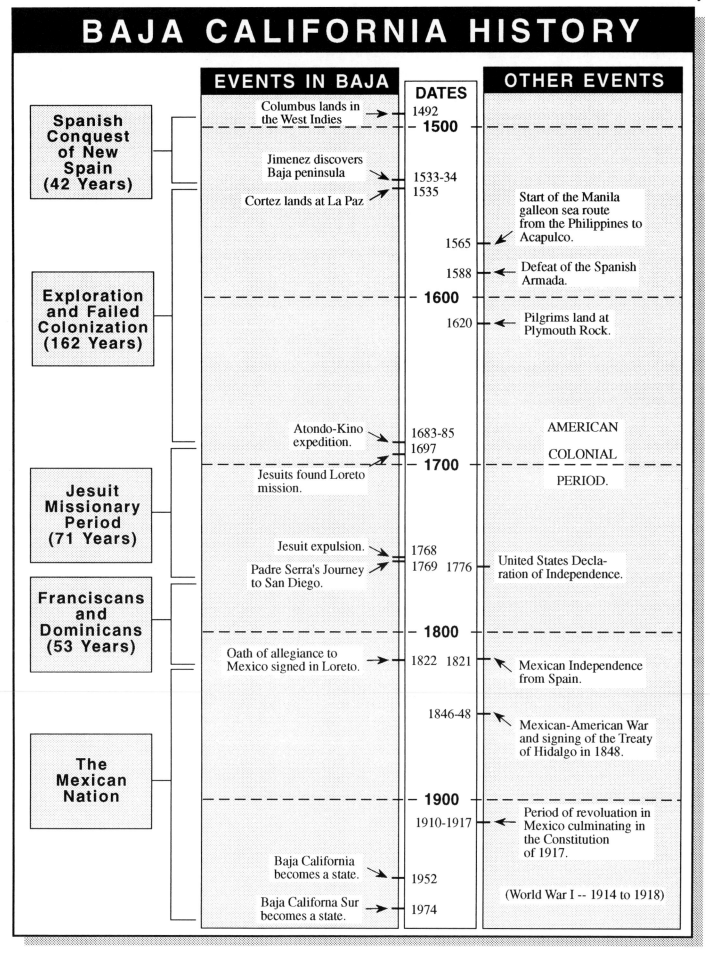

EVENTS IN BAJA | **DATES** | **OTHER EVENTS**

Spanish Conquest of New Spain (42 Years)

Columbus lands in the West Indies → 1492
1500

Jimenez discovers Baja peninsula → 1533-34
Cortez lands at La Paz → 1535

Start of the Manila galleon sea route from the Philippines to Acapulco.

1565

Defeat of the Spanish Armada. 1588

Exploration and Failed Colonization (162 Years)

1600

Pilgrims land at Plymouth Rock. 1620

Atondo-Kino expedition. → 1683-85
1697

AMERICAN

COLONIAL

1700

Jesuit Missionary Period (71 Years)

Jesuits found Loreto mission.

PERIOD.

Jesuit expulsion. → 1768
Padre Serra's Journey to San Diego. → 1769 1776

United States Declaration of Independence.

Franciscans and Dominicans (53 Years)

1800

Oath of allegiance to Mexico signed in Loreto. → 1822 1821

Mexican Independence from Spain.

1846-48

Mexican-American War and signing of the Treaty of Hidalgo in 1848.

The Mexican Nation

1900

1910-1917

Period of revoluation in Mexico culminating in the Constitution of 1917.

Baja California becomes a state. → 1952

(World War I -- 1914 to 1918)

Baja Californa Sur becomes a state. → 1974

POLYGAMY — As a result of battlefield mortality, there were considerably more women than men. The natural outcome was that the surviving males acquired more than one wife. Multiple wives also contributed considerably to the husband's standard of living in a culture requiring the constant gathering of food. This polygamous lifestyle was to lead to considerable conflict with the missionaries, who endeavored to enforce Christian morality.

SHAMANS — The California Indian had little in the way of a tribal hierarchy, except during periods of warfare. However, there was the universal presence of the *shaman*, or witch doctor. These individuals, usually elderly men, had considerable influence over the Indian. They functioned as healers and exercised their authority during the frequent public dances and at funeral ceremonies. The coming of the Spanish missionary was to threaten their authority. As a result, the shaman became the principal obstacle to the work of the missionaries.

LANGUAGE — The missionaries found the Indian languages inadequate to use for instructing their charges in Christianity and the arts of civilization. The native tongues were very basic, and there were significant dialect differences between the tribes and subtribes. The Indians were thus taught Spanish, a process which was duplicated in many other areas and had far-reaching consequences for the Americas. It explains, in part, why Spanish is the native tongue in most of Mexico and South America.

HISTORIC OVERVIEW

The historic pageant of Baja California is summarized in a full-page chart. It commences with Columbus's landing in the West Indies in 1492 and ends with the achievement of statehood by Baja California Sur in 1974. It is divided into five historic periods that correspond to the five remaining sections in this chapter. Each section begins with a small chart summarizing additional dates and events. The full-page chart also indicates the chronological relationship of Baja's history to several other well-known world events.

SPANISH CONQUEST OF NEW SPAIN

1492--1502-------	COLUMBUS's 4 voyages to the West Indies.
1519 --------------	CORTEZ lands at Vera Cruz to conquer New Spain (Mexico).
1522 --------------	CORTEZ conquers the Aztecs and founds Mexico City.
1532 --------------	Failed MENDOZA expedition.
1533--34 ---------	Baja peninsula discovered by mutineer FORTUN JIMENEZ.

It is perhaps a natural tendency for those of us who live in the highly developed areas of the United States and Canadian Pacific coast to surmise that the historic events in these areas must surely have preceded those in a land as remote as Baja California. As can be seen, it was just the reverse. Civilization on the Pacific coast was to flow from south to north. The founding of the Loreto mission on the east coast of the Baja peninsula preceded the first Alta California mission by 72 years.

SPANISH CONQUEST OF NEW SPAIN (42 YEARS)

Columbus's discovery of the islands of the Caribbean Sea promptly engendered Spanish colonization. The first colony was on the island of Haiti, then called Espanola. By 1511, there were settlements on the islands of Jamaica, Cuba, and Puerto Rico. Among the earliest settlers was the nineteen-year-old Hernan Cortez, who arrived in 1505. He proceeded to earn his living from ranching and mining.

In time, reports of golden cities in the interior of Mexico reached the islands, and Cortez resolved to lead an expedition of conquest. After many intrigues, he boldly sailed for the mainland in 1519 leading a force of 11 ships, more than 800 Spaniards and Cuban Indians, 16 horses, and 14 cannons. Upon landing, he founded the first Spanish city in Mexico at Vera Cruz. He promptly scuttled his ships to prevent the desertion of his forces. In a series of adventures that would fill a novel, he brutally captured the Aztec capital of Tenochtitlan in 1522, with the estimated loss of 100,000 of its inhabitants.

In the decade to follow, Cortez and his men ravaged the land in all directions, accumulating great wealth and enslaving the native populations. Mexico City was constructed on the site of Tenochtitlan. During this period, Cortez operated largely on his own initiative, with his own resources, and only marginally within the auspices of the Spanish government.

This same methodology was also employed by Cortez's bitter rival Nuno de Guzman, a fellow Spaniard who had amassed great wealth by illegal slave trading in the Caribbean Islands. During 1530-31, Guzman conquered vast areas of land northwest of Mexico City and established a personal empire. This action established Guzman as the master of the lands on the Mexican coast opposite the southern tip of the Baja peninsula.

During this same period, the King of Spain gradually moved to gain control of the actions of his freewheeling conquistadors.

The world was aware that Magellan had circled the globe in 1522, passing through a strait at the southerly tip of the South American continent. Cortez longed to explore to the northwest along the recently discovered Pacific Ocean in order to discover a similar passage above the North American continent. However, he was blocked from doing this by land by the presence of Guzman.

Cortez thus reached agreement with the Spanish crown that he would, at his own expense, undertake seaborne explorations of the Pacific coast. To this end, Cortez established a ship building station on the Pacific coast near the mouth of the Rio Balsas about 100 miles north of present day Acapulco. Native porters endlessly transported all of the rigging, iron work, and similar materials needed for the ships across the mountains of Mexico from Vera Cruz.

The stage was thus set for the discovery of the Baja peninsula. In 1532, Cortez dispatched the first of four expeditions into the Pacific. The first was under the command of Diego Hurtado de Mendoza, Cortez's cousin. Mendoza sailed north and penetrated the Sea of Cortez; however, the expedition was never to return. It met its end at the hands of Indians, Guzman, or both.

Undaunted, Cortez sent forth a second group of two ships which departed from present-day Manzanillo on October 29, 1533. The two ships soon parted company. The first discovered the Revilla Gigedo Islands, which lie some 400 miles off the Mexican coast, and then returned to the mainland at Acapulco.

The second vessel was placed under the command of Diego de Becerra, a captain of tyrannical nature. As a result, Becerra was soon set upon and killed by many of his crew under the

leadership of the pilot Fortun Jimenez. After depositing the non-mutinous crew members on the Mexican mainland, Jimenez and the others fled to the north and stumbled upon the Baja peninsula. They became the first Europeans known to have set foot on this land.

The Magnificent Peninsula was thus discovered through accident by a group of mutineers. The date of the discovery is unknown as journals are rarely kept on such adventures. It was either late 1533 or early 1534. The spot of the landing was subsequently determined to be Bahia de La Paz.

It is reported that Jimenez and most of his crew were killed by the Indians as a result of their attempts to violate the Indian women. The survivors sailed across the gulf to the mainland, where they fell into the hands of Guzman. There they passed on stories of their discovery of what was then believed to be an island. Of equal importance was their report of the abundance of pearls. This news would increase Cortez's desire to continue with his exploratory efforts.

EXPLORATION AND FAILED COLONIZATION (162 YEARS)

Angered at the interference of Guzman and by the failure of the two expeditions he had dispatched, Cortez chose to lead the next effort himself. This expedition differed from the previous two in that Cortez was aware of his destination, the Island of California. It was to be the only serious effort to actually conquer and colonize the new land until 162 years later.

Three new ships were constructed and loaded with 300 men and 130 horses. Many of the men took along their families, among them 37 women. In May 1535, Cortez landed at Bahia de La Paz and named it Santa Cruz. There he was to find evidences of the Jimenez mutineers and the pearls that they had reported. It is now believed that the actual location of Santa Cruz was at Pichilingue, 14 miles north of present day La Paz.

Cortez's colonization efforts were to prove unproductive. He did build a church and houses for the colonists. It has also been reported that he made exploratory trips into the interior of the peninsula. However, there were apparently no efforts made to raise crops, and the colony had to be supplied by ship from across the gulf. After a year of failure and the death by starvation of many of the colonists, Cortez returned to Mexico and shortly ordered the others to follow.

Upon his return to Mexico, Cortez encountered Antonio de Mendoza, the first of a long line of Viceroys of New Spain appointed by the King. From this time forward, adventurers like Cortez and Guzman were to have far less

ORIGIN OF THE NAME
CALIFORNIA

The name "California" was first encountered in the diary of one of the people who accompanied Francisco de Ulloa on his exploratory voyage. For centuries its origin was a mystery. It was surmised that it had been derived from the Latin words "calida formax" meaning hot furnace. Then in 1862 a New England clergyman, Edward Hall, came upon a Spanish novel "The Adventures of Explandian," which was known to be popular during the years of the conquest of Mexico. It describes a fantastic island inhabited by Amazons: "It is known that to the right of the Indies there exists an island called California very near the side of the Terrestrial Paradise... and was peopled by black women, among whom there was not a single man.... Their weapons were all of gold... because in all the island there was no metal except gold."

This story flourished along with other legends of golden cities in the unknown lands beyond New Spain. It is now the opinion of most historians that the seafarers of the day came to mix these prevailing legends with the tale of California from the "Adventures" and applied the name to the newly discovered "island" to the west. In any event, from then on, the land from the tip of the peninsula north was to be known as California.

EXPLORATION AND FAILED COLONIZATION

1535	CORTEZ lands at La Paz.
1539--40	ULLOA expedition.
1542--43	CABRILLO expedition.
1565	Start of the galleon sea route from Manila to Acapulco.
1578	DRAKE circles the world.
1586	CAVENDISH in Baja.
1596-1602	VISCAINO expeditions.
1615	PICHILINGUE pirates.
1644	GONZALEZ expedition.
1663	BERNAL expedition.
1683-85	ATONDO-KINO expedition.

of a free hand, and decisions affecting the Baja peninsula would emanate largely from the Viceroys at Mexico City.

FRANCISCO DE ULLOA — For his part, Cortez remained obsessed with the desire to press forward by sea to the northwest. Without the approval of the Viceroy, he dispatched his fourth and final expedition under the command of Francisco de Ulloa. Ulloa's orders were to press as far north as possible. He left Acapulco in July 1539, and accomplished an amazing feat of navigation. (See the SPANISH EXPLORATIONS Map in this chapter.)

Ulloa sailed the full length of the Sea of Cortez exploring both coasts, stopping at La Paz going and coming. He anchored at the mouth of the Rio Colorado and established that the Baja peninsula was not an island, although the island myth was to persist for centuries. Finally, the expedition rounded the peninsula's southern tip, and explored the Pacific coast to north of Isla Cedros. From there Ulloa sent one of his ships south to report to Cortez concerning his findings, a most fortunate decision, as nothing further was ever heard from this intrepid explorer.

At this point it may be well to reflect that the humble California peninsula was discovered, explored, and first colonized under the auspices of one of the most renowned men in the history of the new world. But although Cortez was the conqueror of Mexico, he was, in turn, largely conquered by the Magnificent Peninsula. He secured little of the riches he sought and spent a significant part of his personal fortune in the process.

While other explorers were to push even farther north, up the Pacific coast, the route they discovered was not to be the one

used in the northern expansion of New Spain. In the years after Cortez, great land expeditions under Coronado and others pressed north along the mainland Sea of Cortez coast and up the Rio Colorado into what is today southwestern United States.

By the year 1600, over 160,000 Spaniards had migrated to the New World. There were over 200 chartered towns in New Spain. The path of this movement was on the mainland, not along Baja's Pacific coast. The Baja peninsula was not to be settled by Europeans for more than 150 years after the era of Cortez.

It is apparent that the peninsula acted as a massive barrier in the path of the northerly march of European civilization. With the help of a margarita or two, it would be interesting to speculate on what would have occurred along the west coast of the United States if the *Baja barrier* had not existed. Certainly Alta California would have been heavily colonized by the Spanish at a far earlier date, and the course of history would have been greatly altered.

RODRIGUEZ CABRILLO — After the Ulloa expedition, Cortez returned to Spain and faded from the new world scene. In New Spain, Viceroy Mendoza was faced with the reality of the California coast and not our margarita-induced speculation. As a result, he dispatched a new expedition under the command of Juan Rodriguez Cabrillo. It was to prove to be one of the most remarkable in the history of navigation.

Cabrillo left the Mexican mainland on June 27, 1542, from the well-protected harbor at Navidad. He arrived at the tip of the Baja peninsula in early July and took on water at San Jose del Cabo. His ships were to join the hundreds that were to make this open roadstead a key stopping point along the Pacific coast. Today, the hotel Stouffer Presidente has been constructed adjacent to the stream-fed estuary that provided water to these mariners.

After this brief stop, Cabrillo rounded Cabo San Lucas and on the 13th of July sailed by the magnificent harbor at Bahia Magdalena. In August, he arrived at Isla Cedros, the farthest point north known to have been reached by Ulloa two years earlier. From here, Cabrillo inched his way north, anchoring each night. He reached the broad, protected bay at present-day Ensenada in September; a few days later he stepped ashore near what is now San Diego. On September 28, 1542, he claimed this land in the name of Spain and became the first European known to have set foot on the west coast of what was to become the United States.

In the months to come, Cabrillo beat his way through the notoriously bad weather off Point Conception and reached as far north as Fort Ross on the California coast. After retreating south, Cabrillo met his death on San Miguel Island as the result of an accident. His second-in-command took charge, fought his way north again during winter weather, and eventually reached latitude 42 off the Oregon coast.

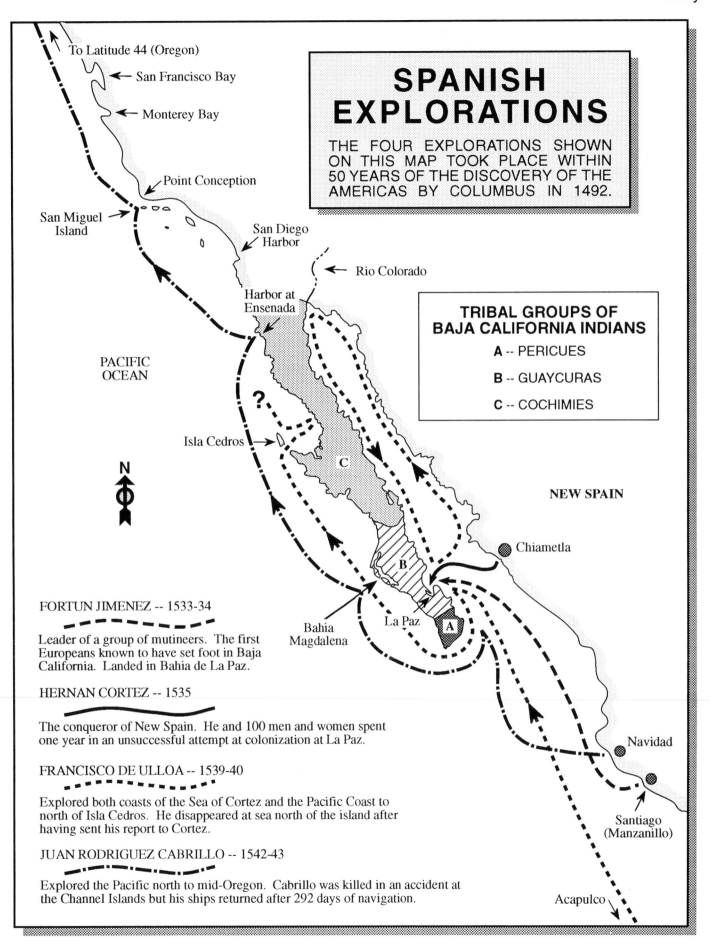

SPANISH EXPLORATIONS

THE FOUR EXPLORATIONS SHOWN ON THIS MAP TOOK PLACE WITHIN 50 YEARS OF THE DISCOVERY OF THE AMERICAS BY COLUMBUS IN 1492.

To Latitude 44 (Oregon)

San Francisco Bay

Monterey Bay

Point Conception

San Miguel Island

San Diego Harbor

Rio Colorado

Harbor at Ensenada

PACIFIC OCEAN

TRIBAL GROUPS OF BAJA CALIFORNIA INDIANS

A -- PERICUES

B -- GUAYCURAS

C -- COCHIMIES

Isla Cedros

C

N

NEW SPAIN

Chiametla

B

La Paz

A

Bahia Magdalena

Navidad

Santiago (Manzanillo)

Acapulco

FORTUN JIMENEZ -- 1533-34

Leader of a group of mutineers. The first Europeans known to have set foot in Baja California. Landed in Bahia de La Paz.

HERNAN CORTEZ -- 1535

The conqueror of New Spain. He and 100 men and women spent one year in an unsuccessful attempt at colonization at La Paz.

FRANCISCO DE ULLOA -- 1539-40

Explored both coasts of the Sea of Cortez and the Pacific Coast to north of Isla Cedros. He disappeared at sea north of the island after having sent his report to Cortez.

JUAN RODRIGUEZ CABRILLO -- 1542-43

Explored the Pacific north to mid-Oregon. Cabrillo was killed in an accident at the Channel Islands but his ships returned after 292 days of navigation.

From there, the expedition returned to the point of origin, in Navidad, after an absence of nine and one-half months. Tragically, the results of Cabrillo's voyage were considered of little importance by the Spanish officials and no further formal efforts at exploring the peninsula were undertaken for more than 50 years.

PIRATES AND THE MANILA GALLEONS — The Viceroy of New Spain was ordered to shift his efforts to the Philippine Islands, which had been discovered by Magellan during his circumnavigation of the globe. Ships sent from the coast of Mexico sailed west to the islands and developed trade with the countries of the Far East. Starting in the spring of 1565, Spanish ships voyaged northeasterly from the Philippines almost to Japan to reach the prevailing westerly winds. These winds blew them west to the California coast along the northern part of the Baja peninsula and then south to Acapulco. The following winter, the galleons would return to the islands with the aid of the southeast trade winds. The ships making these circuits became known as the *Manila Galleons,* and their annual trips were to continue for an incredible 250 years.

The development of this important trade route was to be of special importance to the California peninsula. The long voyage east from the Philippines was a difficult undertaking requiring six to eight months (twice the time of the westerly leg). By the time the galleons reached the waters off California their food and water supplies were nearly exhausted, and the crews often suffered from scurvy. There was obviously a pressing need for a coastal supply point. While this need was to go unmet for many decades, it did strongly influence future activities on the Baja peninsula.

The presence of the Manila Galleons also resulted in the Baja California cape region becoming the hiding place of pirates who would lay in wait for the annual passage of the richly laden ships. In 1578, Francis Drake entered the Pacific through the Straits of Magellan and became the first to prey on the Spanish galleons. Drake's prizes were seized in waters to the south of Baja, but he and the *Golden Hind* touched at San Jose Del Cabo to take on water, joining the illustrious ranks of those who would visit the peninsula at this point.

Drake was followed eight years later by his fellow Englishman, Thomas Cavendish. After ravaging the South American coast, Cavendish arrived in the protective shelter of the harbor of Cabo San Lucas to lie in wait for the annual trip of the Manila Galleons. On November 4, 1587, he attacked the 700-ton *Santa Ana,* which was so heavily laden that her guns had been left behind. After a fierce defense with small arms, the *Santa Ana* was captured and taken to the anchorage off San Jose del Cabo and the Spanish survivors were cast ashore.

On the 17th of November, Cavendish hosted the Spanish on board his vessel to celebrate the seventeenth anniversary of the coronation of Queen Elizabeth. Two days later, he set fire to the *Santa Ana* , promptly weighed anchor, and arrived in England after circling the globe.

Remarkably, the stranded Spaniards, headed by Sebastian Vizcaino, were able to extinguish the fire. After performing makeshift repairs, they sailed her to the Mexican mainland.

Today, the site of the burning of the *Santa Ana* is in plain view from the swimming pools of the hotels that line the beach at San

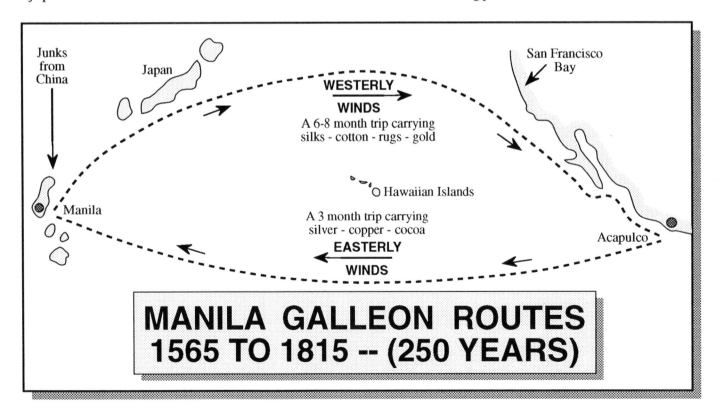

Junks from China

Japan

San Francisco Bay

WESTERLY WINDS

A 6-8 month trip carrying silks - cotton - rugs - gold

Hawaiian Islands

Manila

A 3 month trip carrying silver - copper - cocoa

EASTERLY WINDS

Acapulco

MANILA GALLEON ROUTES
1565 TO 1815 -- (250 YEARS)

Jose del Cabo. From the balconies of the Hotel Finisterra, on the cliffs at Cabo San Lucas, one may look over the harbor where Cavendish lay in wait for his prey.

The lure of the Manila Galleons and Spanish shipping along the South American coast also attracted Dutch pirates in the years after the adventures of Drake and Cavendish. Sizeable fleets of these raiders entered the Pacific through the Straits of Magellan starting in 1598. The year 1615 was to witness the coming of a Dutch armada of eight well-armed ships commanded by Boris van Spilbergen. Following a victorious battle with a Spanish fleet to the south, the Dutch fleet infested the waters of the Baja peninsula in hope of capturing ships from Manila.

The men of these ships came to be known as the *Pichilingues*. This name was left behind on the excellent natural harbor north of La Paz, which today is the terminal for the La Paz-to-Mazatlan ferries. This obviously non-hispanic name has become a tongue twister for today's tourists.

Spanish authorities became concerned with the losses incurred at the hands of these adventurers. The need for reliable supply points on the peninsula became clearly apparent. However, these distant events were overshadowed by the defeat of the Spanish Armada in European waters the year following the sacking of the *Santa Ana*. It was thus several years before the Viceroy of New Spain obtained authority to press forward with exploration and colonization in Baja, and it was stipulated that few public funds were to be expended.

SEBASTIAN VIZCAINO — Further authorization for exploration was then awarded to Sebastian Vizcaino. This intrepid seaman made two expeditions. The first, in 1596, resulted in an effort of several months to colonize La Paz. The second, in 1602, was to see Vizcaino sail as far north as Cape Mendocino in Alta California. He visited the sites of present-day San Diego and Monterey and described the latter port as an excellent possibility for establishing a supply station for the Manila Galleons. Plans were actually made to put these recommendations into action but they were not carried out.

Vizcaino had essentially duplicated the path that Cabrillo had taken 60 years earlier, and with similar results. Little occurred as the result of either voyage. Monterey and San Diego faded from memory. They were not colonized for more than 160 years, but many of Vizcaino's geographic place names have survived. The extensive Vizcaino Desert surrounding present-day Guerrero Negro is named in his honor.

Following the expedition of Sebastian Vizcaino, more than 80 years were to pass with only an occasional attempt at colonizing California. Brief efforts were made in 1644, under the command of Alonzo Gonzalez, and again, in 1663, under Bernardo Bernal. While these ventures seem to have been in response to various royal decrees, they do not appear to have been vigorously pursued. As in the past, little in the way of public funds was allocated to these projects; in reality they were little more than pearl fishing ventures.

It was not until 1683 that an expedition was mounted that was to have lasting effect on the colonizing of the Baja peninsula. The Spanish authorities came to realize that public funding was going to be required if colonization was to be achieved. They thus provisioned a small fleet of three ships and gave command to Isidro de Atondo y Antillon.

ATONDO AND KINO — In January 1683, Atondo crossed the Sea of Cortez in four days and arrived at La Paz with some 200 men. With him was the Jesuit padre Francisco Kino. In Kino's hands was to lie the future of the peninsula.

The first event of importance occurred within a short time. The Indians in the La Paz area had grown accustomed to the temporary presence of ships engaged in pearl fishing. In contrast, Atondo and his party obviously intended to stay. The Indians became restive. In due course, Atondo invited the native leaders to a feast and used the occasion to fall upon, and kill, ten of their number.

This event made matters worse. Atondo was forced to abandon La Paz and return to the mainland. As a result of this tragic but important event, the center of colonization efforts on the peninsula was to shift to the north.

After refitting their ship, Atondo and Kino set out again and in October 1683 landed at a place far to the north of La Paz which they named San Bruno. This site is 12 miles north of present-day Loreto. At San Bruno they erected a small triangular fortification surrounding a church and other buildings. Some ten miles inland they found better water and established a livestock farm at a site they named San Isidro. From these bases of operations Atondo and Kino mounted four expeditions into the interior. On one, Padre Kino reached the Pacific coast and became the first European known to have crossed the peninsula on foot.

The San Bruno colony was to last for 19 months. In May 1685, supplies were exhausted and the colonists returned to the mainland. However, the aborted San Bruno colony was to give rise to the permanent settlement of the Magnificent Peninsula within a few years.

JESUIT MISSIONARY PERIOD (71 YEARS)

THE JESUITS — The driving force behind the permanent colonization of the Baja peninsula was the Company of Jesus, the Jesuits. (They are also known today as the Society of Jesus.) Because of the importance of the missionary system in general, and the Jesuits in particular, it is necessary to examine them both briefly.

As the result of the Catholic Counter Reformation in Europe, members of several religious orders accompanied the conquerors of new lands to many parts of the world. Use of the missionary system became a hallmark of Spanish colonization.

It was to become an effective and economical tool for accomplishing the purposes of the kings, for the orders had their own internal administrative systems and access to sources of revenue other than the royal treasury.

Ignatius Loyola founded the Company of Jesus in 1534. Members of the order came to Mexico in 1572 and soon established extensive missions in the northwestern region. Their members were university-trained men of good family from many European countries. By the time of the Atondo colonizing effort at San Bruno, the Jesuits had over 100 years of missionary experience in Mexico.

The *mision* was to become an institution under Spanish law along with the *pueblo* and the *presidio*. Each mission was planned to last only ten years. It was then to be replaced by the pueblo, with the mission lands divided between communal acreage, town site areas, and individual plots for each Indian. As we shall see, this transfer process was a long time coming in Baja. The presidio was the headquarters of the military establishment that accompanied the missionaries.

In Baja, each mission consisted of a central village where the missionary and any accompanying soldiers lived. Each had a number of outlying *visiting stations* which are sometimes mistakenly referred to as missions.

Establishment of a mission was not done at the whim of the local priest but required following well-established rules and sequences. After securing approval for a new mission, the padre would bless the chosen site and erect the necessary buildings. Indians were attracted through gifts of food and other items. Children and any dying adults were baptized. The receptive Indian was required to give up his wandering ways and settle down in the vicinity of the mission. The teaching of Spanish and the tenets of Christianity were to follow.

Each mission aimed at becoming self-supporting through farming and grazing, but this was difficult because of Baja's arid conditions. Heavy reliance had to be placed on supplies shipped from the mainland.

Padre Francisco Kino was of Italian birth and had been educated in mathematics at German universities, a strange background for his assignments in spreading Christianity in remote areas of the world. Upon returning to the mainland from the failed effort at San Bruno, Kino and Atondo found the Viceroy unwilling to expend additional funds in colonizing the arid lands across the Sea of Cortez.

As a result, the Jesuits assigned Padre Kino to missionary efforts in the mainland northwest, where he was to become one of the most successful and famous figures in the history of Mexico and the American southwest. But before moving to these tasks, he was to transfer his enthusiasm for missionary work in California to a visiting Jesuit, Padre Juan Maria de Salvatierra. The two made a mutual promise to work toward establishing missions on the distant peninsula.

The burden of pursuing this effort was to fall to Salvatierra, but he was to meet with continual frustration. Neither the Spanish authorities or the leader of the Jesuits in Mexico would undertake the project. Finally, help came from none other than Father Santaella, the General of the Jesuit order, who visited Mexico in 1696. His support resulted in the order giving Salvatierra permission to enter California.

But frustration was to continue because the Viceroy would not provide financial support for such an enterprise. It became necessary for Salvatierra to solicit contributions from private sources. Accomplishing this, he finally secured a license to proceed on February 6, 1697. Because they were to provide the funding, this document gave the Jesuits almost complete control over the peninsula. After additional delays, Salvatierra and his followers finally arrived on the California shore in October of that year. The Baja peninsula was never again without settlers from the old world.

FOUNDING OF LORETO — San Bruno was the site of the Jesuit landing. Little remained of the fortifications that had been constructed fourteen years earlier. Salvatierra decided to search for a better location for his mission because San Bruno was situated more than a mile from the coast and the water supply was brackish. In a few days a suitable place was found to the south.

On October 19, 1697, supplies from the ship began to be unloaded on the beach at the present location of Loreto. This was to be one of the most momentous events in the history of the Californias as Loreto was to become the mother mission for all those to follow in Baja and Alta California.

The settlers were able to converse with the Indians because the elements of their language had been documented by one of the padres who had accompanied the Atondo expedition. A porridge of corn meal was shared with those who had helped in the work as was the missionaries' practice. This act of charity was soon to cause the Indians to covet the limited food supplies.

After more than three weeks of tension, the Indians attacked the meager fortification, which consisted of a wall made up

JESUIT MISSIONARY PERIOD

1697 -----------	Founding of Loreto mission by Salvatierra.
1717 -----------	Salvatierra dies -- succeeded by Ugarte.
1734 -----------	Pericue Indian revolt.
1742-48 --------	Epidemics kill many Indians.
1768 -----------	Jesuits expelled from Baja.

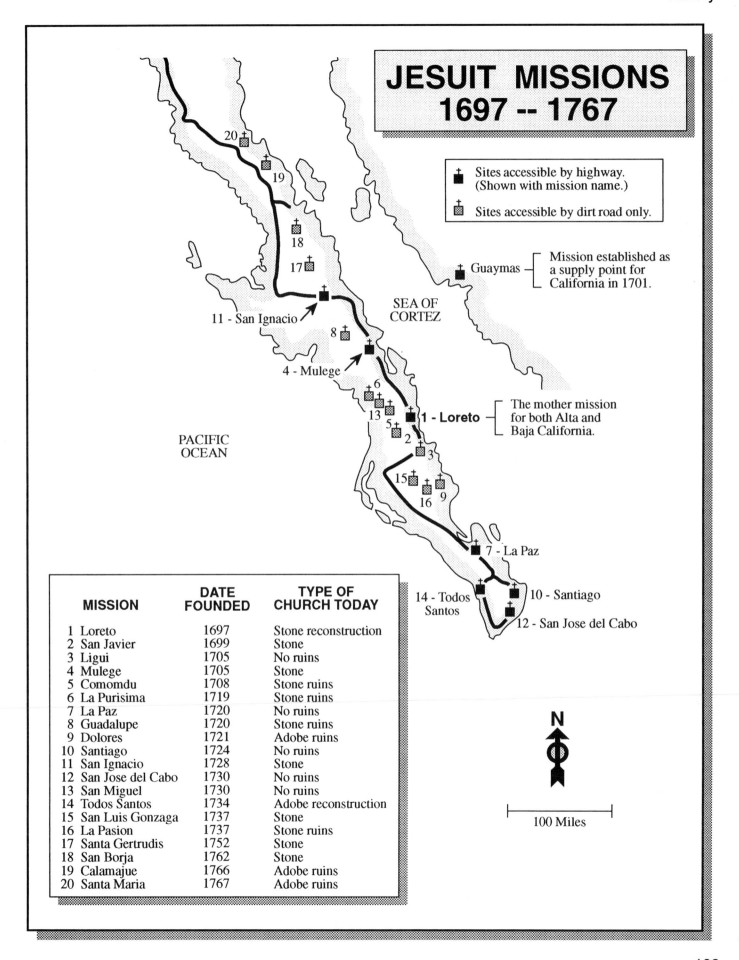

JESUIT MISSIONS 1697 -- 1767

†■ Sites accessible by highway. (Shown with mission name.)

†▨ Sites accessible by dirt road only.

Guaymas — [Mission established as a supply point for California in 1701.

SEA OF CORTEZ

11 - San Ignacio

8

4 - Mulege

6

13

5

1 - Loreto — [The mother mission for both Alta and Baja California.

2

3

PACIFIC OCEAN

15

16   9

7 - La Paz

14 - Todos Santos

10 - Santiago

12 - San Jose del Cabo

MISSION	DATE FOUNDED	TYPE OF CHURCH TODAY
1 Loreto	1697	Stone reconstruction
2 San Javier	1699	Stone
3 Ligui	1705	No ruins
4 Mulege	1705	Stone
5 Comomdu	1708	Stone ruins
6 La Purisima	1719	Stone ruins
7 La Paz	1720	No ruins
8 Guadalupe	1720	Stone ruins
9 Dolores	1721	Adobe ruins
10 Santiago	1724	No ruins
11 San Ignacio	1728	Stone
12 San Jose del Cabo	1730	No ruins
13 San Miguel	1730	No ruins
14 Todos Santos	1734	Adobe reconstruction
15 San Luis Gonzaga	1737	Stone
16 La Pasion	1737	Stone ruins
17 Santa Gertrudis	1752	Stone
18 San Borja	1762	Stone
19 Calamajue	1766	Adobe ruins
20 Santa Maria	1767	Adobe ruins

N

100 Miles

of the expedition's supplies. It was finally necessary to resort to firearms and the death of several Indians to save the day. One cannot help but compare the Loreto Indians' reaction to the missionaries' generosity with the feelings of outrage often encountered in today's world when the accustomed benevolences of church and state are threatened with reduction.

During the next seventy years, the Jesuits established twenty missions (see JESUIT MISSIONS Map) and many more visiting stations from the tip of the peninsula north to the vicinity of Catavina. Certain missions were to be used as bases from which new ones were founded. This stepping stone sequence was eventually to lead to the establishment of a chain of missions with its northern limit at Sonoma, north of San Francisco, in Alta California.

ADDITIONAL JESUIT MISSIONS — By the end of the first year, there were twenty-two Spaniards at Loreto, and the situation with the Indians had quieted to the point where Padre Salvatierra set forth in search of new mission sites. The initial efforts at expansion were located in the mountains to the west of Loreto and north along the coast to Mulege. Father Salvatierra was also called to cross to the mainland and establish a mission at Guaymas for use as a supply point for the peninsula. By the time of Salvatierra's death in 1717, a total of five peninsula missions were in operation.

NO MAN'S LAND

When Cortez and the conquistadores
To Baja California came,
They discovered a poor land
That they could not tame;

Then the missionaries tried
With the same short success,
They found very little
And they left even less;

The "civilization" they brought
For the Indians' release
Killed most of the natives
With the white man's disease.

No treasures were gained
When Spain's flag was unfurled
And the souls converted
Soon departed this world.

So Baja was abandoned,
Like a poor bastard child,
To shift for itself
and revert to the wild.

Ken Reimer

Salvatierra's successor was Padre Juan Ugarte. Considerable progress was made under his leadership; eleven new missions were established during the next twenty years. But while there was continual progress, there was also the never-ending need for additional financial support. Arid conditions on the peninsula resulted in very little food being raised, and the missions did not become self-supporting as was usually the case in better agricultural areas. It was continually necessary to bring supplies across the Sea of Cortez by ship.

Over the years, the peninsula's leaders wrote letters and even made trips to the mainland to plead their case with government authorities. The response was always negative. The padres' only alternative was to continue to seek out contributions from wealthy citizens on the mainland.

In the long run, they were very successful in this effort. The money and lands that were acquired were to become known as the Pious Fund. It was this fund that later became the financial basis for the founding of the future chain of missions in the United States.

The founding of the mission at San Jose del Cabo in 1730 was to be an important, although tragic, event. Within a short time of its establishment, one of the great ships inbound from Manila dropped anchor nearby. Fearing hostile Indians, the captain sent armed men ashore in search of water. To their astonishment, they were met by the padre and his charges and were provided with fresh supplies. At long last, after 165 years, the Manila Galleons had a supply point on the California coast. This good news was carried to Mexico City and Manila, and the order was given for all future sailings from the Philippines to stop at San Jose del Cabo. Sadly, this state of affairs was to be short-lived.

INDIAN UPRISING — As previously noted, the peninsula Indians were polygamists. It was with the Pericue Indians at the southern missions that the padres' efforts to change this system was most resented. Many came to conspire against the missionaries under the leadership of the shamans. By 1733, the rebellious individuals felt they had sufficient strength and plotted to eliminate the few soldiers who guarded the missions - only one at La Paz, two at Santiago, and three at Todos Santos. There were no soldiers at San Jose del Cabo.

The Indians made their move the following year by killing the soldier stationed at La Paz. Within a short time they killed the padre, two soldiers, and an Indian at Santiago, and the padre at San Jose del Cabo. The padre and other surviving mission personnel from Todos Santos fled first to La Paz and then to the mission at Dolores.

Upon receiving news of the uprising, soldiers from the presidio at Loreto moved south to La Paz. They were joined by Indian soldiers from the mainland. Military action was taken against the peninsula Indians with little success. In January 1735, a ship from Manila arrived at Cabo San Lucas in search of the padre and the warm reception they were told to expect. Instead, they were greeted with violence at the hands of some 600 natives who almost succeeded in taking over the vessel.

Upon arrival in Acapulco, the galleon captain traveled to Mexico City and advised the Viceroy of the situation on the peninsula. As a result, the authorities were finally moved to provide greater assistance to the struggling missionaries. As is so often the case, it was economically related events that were to be the motivating factor. None other than the governor of mainland Sinaloa was ordered to the peninsula. Although his initial efforts were ineffective, the rebellious Indians were finally crushed by the end of 1736.

In response to all this unrest, a new presidio was established at San Jose del Cabo with a complement of thirty soldiers. Little by little, modest buildings rose to replace those destroyed in the rebellion, but conditions would never be the same. While the Manila galleons brought silks and jewelry to the mainland, they left smallpox, measles, and venereal disease in California.

During the years 1742 to 1748, epidemics spread throughout the peninsula, particularly in the south. Almost the entire Pericue tribe was wiped out. Some missions were abandoned, and the few remaining Indians concentrated at other points. The port of La Paz was abandoned and bore no sign of life for many years.

With the curtailment of activities in the south, the Jesuits began to push toward the north. In the final fifteen years of their reign they were to establish four new missions in the mountains north of San Ignacio. The previous missions were located where concentrations of Indians and the best sites for agriculture and grazing were found. The majority were in places which today support substantial communities. To the north, such favorable conditions were located near the crest of the peninsular divide, which lies to the east of the Transpeninsular Highway and far from the path of today's activities.

In founding these new missions, the padres were endeavoring to establish stepping stones linking the peninsula missions with those on the Mexican mainland. Although this was never to occur, the new outposts were eventually to serve as the supply route for the founding of a new empire of missions in Alta California.

These final years for the Jesuits were to be restless ones in other ways. The increase in support from Mexico City brought with it conflict between civil and Jesuit authorities. The Indians began to petition the government authorities to grant them the lands they were cultivating. Diseases continued to cause many deaths particularly among the women, who suffered disproportionately from venereal disease. Men who had only recently ceased the practice of polygamy were now unable to find even one wife.

The stone church at San Javier. It is the best preserved of the missions established by the Jesuits in Baja.

JESUIT EXPULSION — While the Jesuit situation on the peninsula was in a deteriorating condition, the ultimate blow was to be delivered from the outside. The military-like Company of Jesus had attracted many enemies throughout the years, and there was world-wide resentment of their power and wealth. Even in Baja, it was believed that the Jesuits had accumulated and concealed a sizeable treasure.

These resentments peaked in Europe where the Company was expelled from Portugal in 1759, France in 1764, and finally from Spain in 1767. The Viceroy of New Spain was to receive a double-sealed package from Charles III to be opened June 24, 1767. In this message, the king ordered all Jesuits to be arrested and sent to the port of Vera Cruz for deportation to Spain.

On the peninsula, the unhappy task of carrying out this order fell to Captain Gaspar de Portola. He and fifty soldiers arrived in San Jose del Cabo that same year and proceeded to arrest sixteen padres from the fourteen remaining missions. On February 3, 1768, the missionaries met in front of the church in Loreto, where the image of the virgin was draped in black. There the weeping inhabitants watched as the Jesuits departed for the mainland with only a few personal possessions. By July, they were imprisoned in Spain in company with Jesuits from other regions.

To the Jesuits goes the credit for bringing civilization to California. Each mission had a school. Primitive roads were constructed which were to ultimately connect Baja and Alta California. There was even a regular postal service linking the missions. The first garden plants were introduced at Loreto, and in 1730 date palms were brought to San Ignacio, Loreto, Mulege, and other locations.

Most of the buildings were constructed of adobe and have not survived. The principle exception is the stone church at San

Javier built between 1744 and 1758. It is located some twenty-four miles from Highway 1 by secondary road. Tourists staying in the Loreto-Puerto Escondido area will be well rewarded with a visit to this historic spot.

Tragically, through no fault of the padres, contact with the outside world during this period brought the diseases that were soon to almost exterminate the Indian. Estimates of the pre-Hispanic population range from 40,000 to 50,000 persons. By the end of the Jesuit period, only some 7,000 remained.

FRANCISCANS AND DOMINICANS (53 YEARS)

THE FRANCISCANS — Prior to the expulsion of the Jesuits, the Franciscan order had been responsible for missionary activity in northwestern Mexico. Now they were pressed to also take over the area vacated by the Company of Jesus on both the mainland and the Baja peninsula. There was to be little lapse in authority because the Franciscan padres sailed for California on the same ship which had just delivered their expelled predecessors to the mainland.

Fifteen priests landed at Loreto on April 1, 1768, under the leadership of Padre Junipero Serra. Each of Serra's charges was assigned to one of the fourteen missions remaining in service at the time of the expulsion.

During the Jesuit period, the missionaries had been the virtual masters of life on the peninsula, which included authority over military personnel. They had discouraged the settlement of lands by immigrants from the mainland, so there was little activity outside the missions. All of this was to change dramatically. Captain Portola, who had expelled the Jesuits, had been appointed governor. He met the Franciscans and advised them that he and his soldiers would dispense justice and administer farming, grazing, and other economic activities.

The missionary system had remained in effect for over seventy years rather than the ten-year period that had been anticipated. The change to civil authority was now to come, even though conditions on the peninsula had not advanced to the point where the transformation was fully justified.

Shortly after the arrival of the Franciscans, there came to the peninsula one Jose de Galvez, a personal agent of the King of Spain. He established himself at Santa Ana, a silver mining center near the present towns of San Antonio and El Triunfo south of La Paz. Mining, here, was one of the few economic activities carried out on the peninsula outside the administration of the missionaries. It is a very interesting area to visit, and El Triunfo is included in the POINTS OF SPECIAL INTEREST Tour.

FRANCISCANS & DOMINICANS

1768 ------------	Franciscans arrive in Baja.
1769 ------------	Expedition to San Diego.
1772 ------------	Dominicans take over Baja missions.
1780-82 --------	Severe Indian epidemics.
1810--22 -------	Revolution against Spanish rule.
1822------------	Baja swears allegiance to Mexico.

Galvez carried royal orders to organize an expedition aimed at colonizing Alta California and to make changes in operations on the peninsula. From Santa Ana, he issued numerous decrees to which little attention was paid once he departed the region. However, he was successful in giving birth to the new missionary venture.

The padres had been pressing for the establishment of settlements in San Diego and Monterey for over 150 years since these sites were discovered by Cabrillo and Vizcaino. However, the Spanish authorities showed no interest in expending effort in this direction until it became known that Czarist Russian fur trappers and explorers were working their way down the northwestern Pacific coast. They had set up outposts as far south as the Farallon Islands off San Francisco.

From his headquarters at Santa Ana, Galvez summoned Padre Serra and Captain Fernando Javier de Rivera y Moncada, commander of the Presidio at Loreto. There, in this obscure hideaway in the mountains south of La Paz, the plans were drawn up for the settlement of what was to become the homes of millions of people in today's southern and central California in the United States.

Governor Portola was placed in command of the venture. He was delighted to be relieved of the political obscurity of his post in Loreto. Padre Serra was also eager to join and quickly secured release from his peninsular duties. The expedition was to be divided into four units, two by land and two by sea. In January 1769, the packet *San Carlos* weighed anchor at La Paz and sailed for San Diego. (Six years later, this same *San Carlos* became the first European ship to sail into the harbor at San Francisco.) A second vessel, the *San Antonio,* followed a month later. Both arrived at San Diego in April.

The first land party was led by Captain Rivera y Moncada. It was his assignment to visit the missions north of La Paz and collect everything that he could in the way of livestock, food, and other supplies and to proceed with these to the northernmost mission at Santa Maria. This task was successfully accomplished, although he was forced to move northwest from Santa Maria to obtain better pasturage. This was found at a place to be named Velicata. After recouping there, Rivera y Moncada set out for

San Diego where he arrived on May 14, 1769, after a journey of fifty days.

Portola and Serra led the last party and proceeded to Velicata where Rivera y Moncada had rested. Here, Padre Serra founded Mission San Fernando, the only mission to be established on the peninsula by the Franciscans. It was to stay in operation for forty-nine years providing one more link in the chain of missions stretching north from Loreto.

The ruins of this mission lie three miles west of the Transpeninsular Highway midway between El Rosario and Catavina in what is a very remote area even today. Its location will be noted during the GRAND TOUR in PART III. It is hoped the traveler will pause briefly to honor the passage of Portola and Serra on their historic journey.

The two leaders arrived in San Diego on July 1, 1769. While both land parties had suffered great hardships, the crews of the ships which had arrived earlier in April were in worse condition. Scurvy had claimed the lives of over one-third of the crew on each vessel.

From this base in San Diego, Father Serra and his successors were to found twenty-one missions and to give birth to western civilization in what has become California in the United States. It is clear that the success of what has taken place in the north was predicated on events preceding it in the Baja peninsula. It is certainly ironic that the mighty giant of the north owes such an enormous debt to a place that most of its citizens know virtually nothing about.

THE DOMINICANS — While Padre Serra labored to advance the cause of Christianity in Alta California, the reign of the Franciscans to the south was to be brief. Following the Jesuits' expulsion from the Spanish domain, the Dominican order petitioned the King of Spain to obtain missionary territory in California. This request was soon granted, and the King ordered

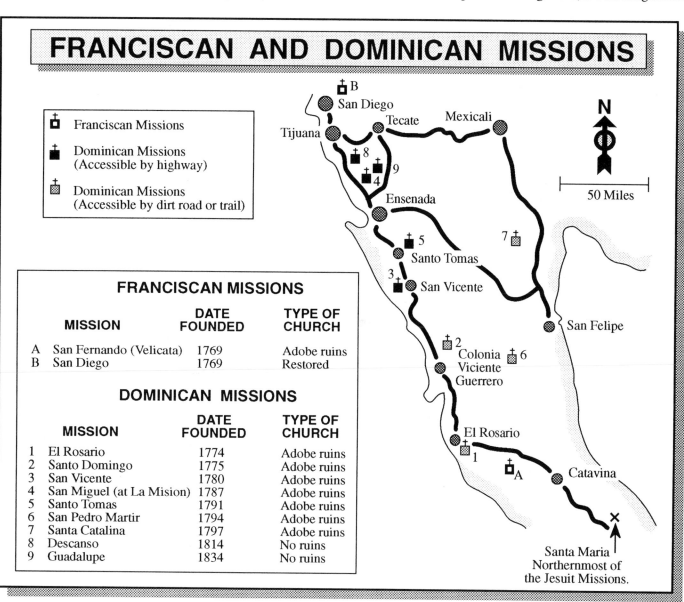

FRANCISCAN AND DOMINICAN MISSIONS

| ✠ Franciscan Missions |
| ■ Dominican Missions (Accessible by highway) |
| ▨ Dominican Missions (Accessible by dirt road or trail) |

FRANCISCAN MISSIONS

	MISSION	DATE FOUNDED	TYPE OF CHURCH
A	San Fernando (Velicata)	1769	Adobe ruins
B	San Diego	1769	Restored

DOMINICAN MISSIONS

	MISSION	DATE FOUNDED	TYPE OF CHURCH
1	El Rosario	1774	Adobe ruins
2	Santo Domingo	1775	Adobe ruins
3	San Vicente	1780	Adobe ruins
4	San Miguel (at La Mision)	1787	Adobe ruins
5	Santo Tomas	1791	Adobe ruins
6	San Pedro Martir	1794	Adobe ruins
7	Santa Catalina	1797	Adobe ruins
8	Descanso	1814	No ruins
9	Guadalupe	1834	No ruins

Santa Maria
Northernmost of
the Jesuit Missions.

the peninsula to be divided equally between the Dominicans and the Franciscans.

The Franciscans, who had originally resisted their assignment to California, soon found that they were in continual disagreement with the peninsula's civil authorities. Various epidemics caused the death of some 2,000 Indians in only three years, and the missions in the south were in a state of complete deterioration. Thus, it is not surprising, that after some initial disagreement, the issue was resolved by providing the Dominicans with the entire peninsula, while the Franciscans received Alta California. We prideful U. S. citizens would no doubt maintain that the latter order negotiated a very favorable settlement. Avoid playing poker with a Franciscan.

Dominican friars arrived in Loreto on October 14, 1772. There had been only four and one-half years of administration by the Franciscans. Inspection of the existing missions and their Indian charges made it clear to the Dominicans that their future lay to the north. Within two years, they established a new mission on the banks of the Rio del Rosario at the present town of El Rosario. The site of the buildings was to be moved down river some twenty-eight years later. The crumbling ruins may be easily visited in a short side trip from the Transpeninsular Highway. They are included in the POINTS OF SPECIAL INTEREST Tour.

Within twenty years of their arrival on the peninsula, the Dominicans responded to royal order by establishing a total of five new missions between Velicata and San Diego. These served as stepping stones along the road pioneered by Junipero Serra. The linkage with Alta California was complete. In the years to follow, four additional missions were founded in the northern portion of the peninsula.

It should be noted that the churches which may be visited by today's travelers were built some years after the original missions were founded. Several stone buildings were built by the Dominicans, but the only one still standing is the beautiful church at San Ignacio. More recently, reconstruction at other sites has been sponsored by the Mexican government and private groups.

Epidemics also followed the northward march of the Dominicans. Smallpox struck the northern missions in 1780 to 1782. Indians who were moved from the north to populate the decimated southern missions often met prompt death from disease.

A report prepared in 1786 paints this horrible picture. "The missions of San Jose, Santiago, Todos Santos, San Javier, Loreto, Comondu, Cadegomo, Guadalupe, and Mulege are on the way to total extinction. The reason is so evident that it leaves no doubt. Syphilis has taken possession of both sexes to such a degree that mothers do not conceive, and if they do conceive, the fetus is born with little hope of living. There are three times as many adults who die as there are babies born." By 1800, there

were no more than 4,000 to 5,000 Indians still living in the entire peninsula, only ten percent of the original population.

Changes in the peninsula's civil administration under Governor Portola also led to the decay of the entire missionary system. These same adjustments did bring about small increases in the number of Spaniards and *Mestizos,* and in their hands rested the future of Baja and all of Mexico. In 1800, the estimate of their number was 700 to 800. They gained a living from cattle raising and farming. Historic accounts also frequently refer to the mining of silver at Santa Ana (near present-day San Antonio and El Triunfo) as well as the salt deposits on Isla Carmen. These salt mines had been worked from the early days of the Jesuits and may be visited today by boat from Loreto or Puerto Escondido.

There were also important administrative changes made during the reign of the Dominicans. Shortly after their arrival, a 1776 royal order separated the provinces of Texas, New Mexico, New Viscays, Coahuila, Sinaloa, Sonora, and the Californias into a new *Internal Province* to be governed from Arizpe rather than Mexico City. The capital of the Californias was also to be changed from Loreto to Monterey. Under this arrangement, peninsular business matters had to travel from Loreto to Monterey and then to Arizpe.

It is a matter of considerable wonder that the great state of California in the United States was once governed from what is now a small Mexican town (Arizpe) located on a side road northeast of present-day Hermosillo on the Mexican mainland. Twenty-eight years after the capital was moved to Monterey, the seat of peninsula government was to return to Loreto as the result of Baja and Alta California being separated into two provinces.

Of far more importance to Mexico were the events which took place from 1810 to 1822. Mexico was to rise in revolution against the authority of Spain, as were peoples throughout the Americas. Action began September 16, 1810, now Mexico's Independence Day. Independence was finally achieved in 1821; however, there remained some hesitancy by the peninsular people to accept the rule of the new Mexican nation. As a result, they were to come under attack from a amazingly unlikely source.

Almost two and one-half centuries after Francis Drake and Thomas Cavendish had left Baja's waters, another English adventurer appeared in the Sea of Cortez. Lord Thomas de Cochrane arrived off San Jose del Cabo with two ships on February 17, 1822. This seaman was the archenemy of Spain and had arrived after pillaging along the South American coast wherever any vestiges of Spanish authority were to be found.

A ship in the roadstead off San Jose del Cabo still flew the Spanish flag, and Cochrane used this as an excuse to sack the town. From there he turned to Loreto where fifteen days later he made a similar attack. The governor and other citizens fled, but

Cochrane was repulsed by fifteen men led by Ensign Jose Maria Mata. Mata took command and felt that the time had come to swear allegiance to Mexico. An official ceremony took place in July of that year at Loreto; the peninsula formally took its place in the Mexican nation.

The dominance of the mission system and the authority of Spain had come to an end. In the years ahead, events on the peninsula would reflect the political aftermath of the revolution. Civil rather than religious matters would dominate, and war would come with the United States.

THE MEXICAN NATION

Many aspects of life were to change on the Baja California peninsula and throughout Mexico following independence from Spain. Mexican officials arrived from the mainland to rule in Loreto. In time, all the missions were converted to pueblos, many lands distributed to those who worked them, and religious affairs turned over to the secular clergy. The peninsula was divided into four municipalities, each under the authority of a mayor. In 1828, the town of Loreto was largely destroyed by heavy rains and flooding. The capital was transferred briefly to the silver mining town of San Antonio and then, in 1830, to La Paz. Loreto was to languish in obscurity for many years.

Political passions rose in the peninsula. There were Indian uprisings in the north. Uprising of citizens and soldiers occurred at La Paz, and small battles were fought. Clearly, economic factors and the press for land ownership were becoming important issues to the peninsula's people as the influence of the clergy dissipated. Finally, as the midpoint of the 19th century approached, the peninsula was to be caught up in the fringes of war between Mexico and the United States.

THE MEXICAN-AMERICAN WAR — Momentous events were occurring in the outlying Mexican lands that are today a part of southwestern United States. Texas had declared itself a separate republic in the 1830s, and Mexico's General Santa Ana was defeated by the forces of Sam Houston. In Alta California, there were only scattered Mexican forces and settlers along the coast. English-speaking peoples from the east were migrating west and taking up lands.

It became clear that both England and France coveted possession of Alta California and its fabulous harbor at San Francisco. By 1837, the United States was making proposals to Mexico for the purchase of Mexican lands in the west. A mood of expansionism, *manifest destiny* prevailed in the United States. In 1845, James Polk was elected president, standing on a political platform advocating the annexation of Texas and the purchase of Alta California from Mexico.

As a result of the election mandate, the United States issued, and received acceptance of, an invitation for Texas to join the Federal Union. This *annexation* infuriated Mexican authorities and resulted in armed conflict along the border. In addition to the issue of Texas, the United States had various grievances against Mexico and also feared the potential takeover of California by England or France. As a result, the United States declared war on May 11, 1846.

Prior to the outbreak of hostilities, the United States had been prepared to pay approximately $25 million for California, depending on the inclusion or exclusion of Baja California. This *either/or* proviso would seem to indicate that obtaining possession of Baja California was not a primary goal of the United States government. However, once war started, specific military steps were taken to bring the peninsula under United States authority.

The decisive battles of the Mexican-American War took place in mainland Mexico. Invading United States forces under the command of Zachary Taylor and Winfield Scott conducted successful campaigns. The latter general captured Mexico City on September 14, 1847. Lesser actions took place in New Mexico and Alta California. Perhaps the least known of all were the battles that took place in the Baja peninsula, where the fighting was actually heavier than it was to the north. These peninsular events are depicted on a map and are amplified below. The item numbers in the text correspond to similar numbers on the map.

1. — A squadron of eight United States navy ships and their marine contingents had been stationed in Pacific waters for some time. They were commanded by Commodore John D. Sloat, who was under instructions to occupy San Francisco and other Alta California ports in the event of war with Mexico.

Ruins of the Dominican mission at Santo Domingo. Several sites similar to this one may be visited within a few miles of the Transpeninsular Highway.

THE MEXICAN NATION

1822 -------------	Baja swears allegiance to Mexico.
1830 -------------	Capital moved --Loreto to La Paz.
1846 -- 48 ------	Mexican -- American was in Baja.
1853 -------------	William Walker invades Baja.
1864 -------------	Baja leased to the Americans.
1883 -------------	Law to Colonization passed.
1885 -------------	Copper mining at Santa Rosalia.
1901 -------------	Founding of Mexicali.
1911 -------------	Revolutionary activity in the north.
1933 -------------	End of the Law of Colonization.
1952 -------------	Baja California becomes a state.
1974 -------------	Baja California Sur becomes a state.

Sloat stationed his fleet at Mazatlan, where there was a United States consul; it was apparently the best site along the entire Pacific coast for him to receive instruction from Washington.

On May 16, 1846, he received word that fighting had begun along the Rio Grande. While he did not know that war had been declared several days earlier, he moved his ships north along the California coast and during July took possession of Monterey, San Francisco, and San Diego - without resistance.

2. — After completing this assignment, some of the American ships returned south to blockade the Mexican coast and take possession of additional ports. In September 1846, these ships arrived in La Paz. The United States commander told local authorities they were under American control and secured an agreement that they would remain neutral. The United States forces were under orders to utilize this *neutrality* approach to pacify the Mexicans and to make them more receptive to a change in authority.

3. — On March 29, 1847, the United States sloop *Portsmouth* sailed to San Jose del Cabo and imposed the same arrangement.

4. — Prior to the declaration of war, the United States Congress had authorized the formation of battalions of volunteers as backup forces to the regular army. The first was to be the First Battalion of Volunteers from the State of New York. It was composed mostly of young boys eager for adventure and was referred to in New York newspapers as the Baby Regiment.

The battalion was placed on ships and transported around Cape Horn to Alta California, where it arrived in spring 1847. The boys were assigned to guard the various towns in the region. Subsequently, two companies were ordered to La Paz, where they went ashore without incident on July 20, 1847.

5. — Word reached the Mexican government of the neutral position taken by their small military force that was stationed at La Paz. In anger, they dispatched Captain Manual Pinada and a small group of officers and arms to take over military matters in the peninsula. Pinada had previous knowledge of the terrain and people of Baja. He crossed the Sea of Cortez from Guaymas and arrived at Mulege in September 1847. Here, he organized the local people into a force to defend the peninsula from the Americans.

6. — Hearing of Pinada's arrival, the Americans dispatched the sloop *Dale* to Mulege, where it arrived in October. The sloop's commander sent a message ashore demanding that the inhabitants preserve neutrality. Pinada responded with a prideful message that he and his soldiers would defend their country until the last drop of blood was shed.

Hearing this, the United States commander sent boats ashore with some 60 men and a small artillery piece. This force was fired upon by Pinada and his small group of men. There followed a considerable exchange of gun fire, including some 135 canister shots from the *Dale* lying offshore. The proud Mexicans held fast, and by afternoon the Americans returned to their ship.

Having met with resistance, the *Dale* left Mulege leaving a smaller ship behind to provide a blockade. All this action took place at the mouth of the Rio Santa Rosalia near El Sombrerito, a small but conspicuous peak that now bears the Mulege lighthouse. It is in plain view from Highway 1 and is within a few yards of the Serenidad Hotel.

7. — The heroic defense of Mulege gave rise to considerable public spirit. Pinada was able to recruit a force that Mexican historians say numbered about 300 men. They came from the pueblos of San Ignacio, Mulege, and Comondu, and later from San Antonio and Todos Santos.

8. — Pinada marched his soldiers south. Part of the force was detached and sent to San Jose del Cabo. On November 16, 1847, the main body of some 180 men under Pinada attacked the New York Volunteers who had fortified themselves in buildings within La Paz. There was to follow 12 days of fierce fighting, with the Americans defending themselves with cannon fire and by tearing down buildings which were providing the Mexicans with cover. At one point these forces penetrated to within 100 feet of the fortified Americans, but Pinada finally had to withdraw due to lack of ammunition. After the fighting was over, American reinforcements arrived by sea.

9. — After hearing of the Mexican successes at Mulege, the citizens of San Jose del Cabo tore down the American flag and declared an end to American rule. As a result, American ships arrived and left a detachment of twenty-four men. As at La Paz, this force was required to fortify itself in the town buildings when they were attacked by the Mexicans from Pinada's forces that had marched south from La Paz. The assault failed, and the Mexican leader, Naval Lieutenant Jose Antonio Mijares, was

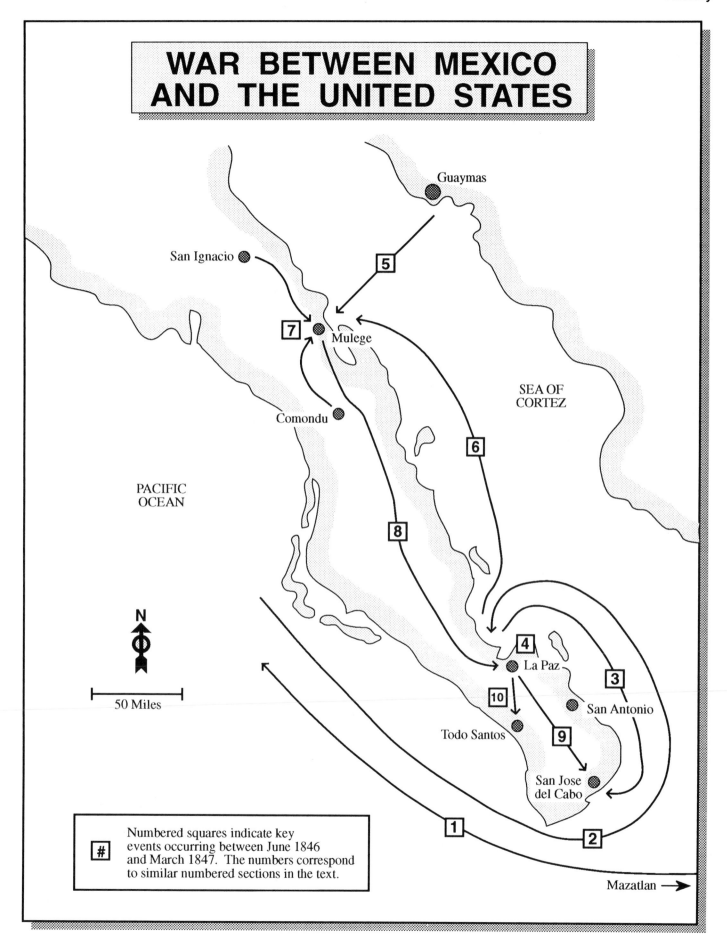

WAR BETWEEN MEXICO AND THE UNITED STATES

Guaymas

San Ignacio

5

7 Mulege

Comondu

SEA OF CORTEZ

6

PACIFIC OCEAN

8

N

50 Miles

4

La Paz

3

10

San Antonio

Todo Santos

9

San Jose del Cabo

1

2

Numbered squares indicate key events occurring between June 1846 and March 1847. The numbers correspond to similar numbered sections in the text.

#

Mazatlan →

mortally wounded. A monument to this fallen hero may be seen in the town plaza at San Jose del Cabo.

As at La Paz, American ships arrived, and the garrison was reinforced with 46 additional men. The Mexican forces were also reinforced by Pinada's soldiers from the north. When the American ships left, the Mexicans renewed the attack in mid-January 1848. They surrounded the American position and cut off all sources of water and supplies.

By mid-February, surrender seemed inevitable; but reinforcements again arrived by sea. The Mexicans attacked these newcomers. Fierce fighting and artillery fire was to occur on the way from the sea to the pueblo. In the end, the arrival of these reinforcements required the Mexicans to retire to the north.

10. — During March, the American forces from La Paz conducted several campaigns to put an end to the Mexican resistance. On March 27, 1848, they captured Captain Pinada in San Antonio. A few days later, a force of more than 200 Americans surrounded and captured the remaining Mexican defenders north of Todos Santos. The fighting thus came to an end.

Much of the fighting at San Jose del Cabo and the final actions at San Antonio and Todos Santos were to take place after the signing of the peace treaty on February 2, 1848, but this information had not been received in the peninsula.

Having been victorious in the major land battles on the Mexican mainland, the United States was in a position to demand a harsh settlement. However, their proposal was not to differ greatly from that made prior to the war. Under its terms, Mexico ceded Alta California and New Mexico. In return, they received $15 million, and the United States agreed to pay various claims held by its citizens against Mexico.

The original draft of the treaty presented by the United States included the Baja peninsula within the lands to be ceded by Mexico. In its counter-proposal, Mexico asserted "The cession of Lower California ... offers great embarrassment to Mexico, considering the position of that peninsula, facing our coast of Sonora, which is separated from it by the narrow Gulf of Cortez." The United States negotiator bowed to the Mexican position. As a result, the peninsula together with sufficient land to tie it to the mainland was left in the Mexican republic.

One can readily draw the conclusion that the principal objective of the United States occupation of the peninsula was that of obtaining a bargaining chip. If so, this posture was apparently not conveyed to the American military commanders, who assured the Mexican citizens in the south that United States administration was there to stay. With these assurances, many Mexicans placed themselves openly on the side of the invading forces. After the peace treaty, these people were branded as traitors. When the American military left the peninsula in September 1848, more than 300 of these people were taken to Monterey in Alta California to prevent their being killed by their outraged fellow Mexicans.

While they were not to prevail in the military actions on the peninsula, the Mexican forces obviously conducted themselves with valor. This is particularly impressive when one considers that most of them were not professional soldiers but only citizens gathered from far-flung towns where there was little knowledge of the overall motivations of the war. Hopefully,

Aerial view of the estuary forming the mouth of the Rio Santa Rosalia at Mulege This area was the site of the Mexican-American War battle between the U. S. sloop Dale and Mexican patriots.

today's tourists will stop at the sites and monuments relating to this conflict and pay homage to the combatants.

FILIBUSTERS AND FRAUDS — Turbulent years lay ahead for Baja. The decade following the war was to give rise to a period of filibustering. Filibusters were lawless military adventurers who entered Mexico and Central American countries with the intent of overthrowing the national authorities. Americans involved in these activities in Mexico had as their objective the annexing of the *conquered* areas into the United States, as had occurred with Texas.

The most notorious of these individuals was William Walker. He gathered forty-eight armed followers in San Francisco and sailed for Mexico. On November 3, 1853, he landed at La Paz, seized control from the local authorities, and declared the establishment of the Republic of Sonora. Within a few days, he was attacked by Mexican forces and lost six men. He retreated to Cabo San Lucas and eventually to Ensenada.

Near Ensenada there were several armed conflicts and deaths. During the weeks to follow, Walker's men were to assert their authority at San Vicente, San Quintin, and El Rosario, all towns visited by today's traveler along the Transpeninsular Highway. From this area, Walker moved east to conquer mainland Sonora but in turn was defeated by the rigors of the Sonoran desert. He was forced to return to the United States, where he was captured and tried.

In the years to come, William Walker was to move his operations to several Central American countries. He was put to death in 1860 by Honduran authorities, bringing to an end the era of filibustering.

These same years were to see civil war within Mexico between groups with opposing liberal and conservative political views. Baja California was firmly on the liberal side. There was some fighting in the peninsula. The year 1857 was to see the establishment of a new constitution for Mexico and Benito Juarez became president in 1861. Statues and other references to Juarez may be seen throughout Mexico.

In 1862, new silver mines were discovered in the historic mining district of San Antonio in the mountains south of La Paz. The area became a bonanza, and many miners came from the United States. The ruins of the smelters and other facilities may be seen at the town of El Triunfo and San Antonio and are included in the POINTS OF SPECIAL INTEREST Tour in PART III.

In the years to follow, some twenty-five to thirty mining and colonizing land frauds were known to have been perpetrated on North Americans using the claimed resources of the Baja peninsula as bait. The most outrageous of them all was instigated by none other than President Juarez himself.

As a means of obtaining badly needed funds, Juarez actually leased some two-thirds of the entire peninsula to a United States citizen named Jacob P. Leese. In 1864, Leese sold out to a group of New York capitalists whose object was to raise $25 million, through fraud, on a massive scale. Announcements in California newspapers read "Free lands, free commerce, homes for the poor, riches for the wealthy. For the first 1,000 colonists who acquire land in Lower California a lot of 160 acres is offered absolutely free." Colonists were actually transported to the Bahia Magdalena region to till the "pure black humus soil where the grass was higher than the shoulders of a horse." The lease was cancelled within a few years because the company was unable to meet some of its near-impossible terms.

Twenty years after issuance of the lease to Jacob Leese, Mexico passed a Law of Colonization as a means of raising foreign capital. Under this 1883 law, some thirty land concessions covering vast areas of the peninsula were granted to foreigners. Few were aggressively pursued, but as a result Mexican citizens were prohibited from developing the land of their own country and economic growth was impeded. This era of concessions was not to end until 1933. Because of its unsuccessful background in foreign concessions, the Mexican government today, understandably, maintains stringent control on private ownership of businesses and foreign ownership of land.

At least one of the Law of Colonization concessions was to be aggressively pursued. This concession was issued on July 17, 1885, for the mining of the large copper deposits found some years earlier at Santa Rosalia. It came into the hands of a French syndicate that operated the mine and smelter until 1954. Coal and coke were shipped from northern Europe in square-rigged ships to the smelter at Santa Rosalia, one of the last world ports used in the age of sail. The smelter, French buildings, port facilities, and machinery provide a must stop for the traveler along the Transpeninsular Highway.

Santa Rosalia's copper operation was also to be of importance to the peninsula's history in another way. Labor conditions there have been described by one Mexican historian as nauseating. This situation was to contribute to labor unrest and revolutionary uprisings in the future.

ACTIVITIES IN THE NORTH — As can be seen, historic events were concentrated in the southern portion of the peninsula up to this point. At the time of passage of the Law of Colonization in 1883, there were some 30,000 people in the entire peninsula. Only a few hundred lived in the northern portion. In this region, all of the missions had been abandoned. Ensenada was little more than a ranch, and Mexicali did not exist. But conditions were to change rapidly as the result of the land concessions issued by the federal government.

In 1884, large acreages of land in the north came under the control of New York capitalists who organized the International Company of Mexico. The usual land-promotion schemes were soon to follow, with the objective of selling land to gullible persons north of the border. However, the developers were required to make some investment in Mexico.

The town site of Ensenada was laid out, and various business enterprises sprang up. Within four years it had a population of approximately 1,400 people. Government inspectors issued such a glowing report that in 1887 the peninsula was formerly divided into two parts; and the *District of the North* was to have its own government, independent of La Paz.

In 1899 gold was discovered at El Alamo southeast of Ensenada. Thousands of miners poured in from north of the border. In the United States an irrigation project was undertaken to bring water from the Rio Colorado to the Imperial Valley. Small communities sprang up along the border as an indirect result of activities in the United States. One of these was Mexicali, which was founded in 1901 and was destined to become the capital city of the state of Baja California. Within a few years after the turn of the century, it became apparent that few projects of the International Company of Mexico were to flourish, but life in the north had taken root.

POLITICAL TURMOIL — In the minds of some North Americans, Mexico is a land of revolution and political unrest. Actually, the country has had a remarkably stable government for many decades, but its reputation in this regard suffers from its inaccurate association with revolutionary activities in countries in Central and South America, and from its own previous political turmoil in the years surrounding the turn of the century. This period will now be briefly reviewed.

There were small armed conflicts in the south in 1865, 1875, and again, in 1880. More serious unrest was to follow in both the north and south after the turn of the century. These activities reflected political turmoil in the nation as a whole, arising from the thirty-year dictatorial reign of President Porfirio Diaz and from various socialist and labor-oriented movements that were present in many parts of the world. Revolution was to force Diaz to resign in 1911, and his successor also was overthrown, and assassinated.

Also in 1911, revolution broke out in the newly populated areas in Baja California along the United States-Mexican border. This conflict was led by Mexican citizens based in the United States. Small armies of Mexicans were organized, and battles were waged with Mexican federal troops in the general area around Mexicali, Ensenada, and Tijuana. For a time, the latter town was controlled by the revolutionary forces. Additional federal troops from the Mexican mainland were sent to quell the uprisings. As a result of this unrest, some 30,000 United States troops were sent to the international border to protect their country's interests.

The revolutionary forces may be labeled *socialist*, although historians also utilize the terms *liberal* and *anarchist*. Their leaders clearly associated themselves with labor movements in the United States that advocated strikes, boycotts, and sabotage.

There was also added intrigue spawned by the political activities of foreigners who owned or controlled most of the land in the peninsula. There were always the threats, some real and some invented, that a popular uprising would be used as the rationale for the purchasing, or otherwise annexing, of the peninsula by the United States as had occurred with Texas some sixty-five years prior. Such an event would of course have been favored by the U.S. landowners.

Revolutionary action in the south was to follow that in the north by two years. It was to be more purely Mexican without the overtones of involvement by foreigners. The leader of this "Constitutionalist Revolution" was Felix Ortega, who organized a band of armed men who fought with federal troops in many battles at La Paz and in the mountains and towns to the south. During these campaigns, in 1913 to 1915, Ortega's forces frequently took refuge in the cape region mountains. Today's tourists drive through this same terrain on the Transpeninsular Highway between La Paz and San Jose del Cabo.

The size of the forces engaged in these battles was often considerably larger than those involved in the war with the United States sixty-five years earlier and thus represents the largest military operation ever to take place on the Baja peninsula. While the federal forces were to prevail, as in the north, Baja's citizens are proud that their efforts contributed to the civil liberties and land reforms gained on a national level from these revolutionary activities. The Constitution of 1917 was to be the result.

Steam engine monument at Santa Rosalia. A remnant of this historic town's heyday as a copper mining center. Other old mining machinery is also on display nearby.

A very brief review of historic events that took place in the north and south, following the revolutionary period, will now be presented.

SUMMARY OF ACTIVITIES IN THE SOUTH -- There were to be continuing revolutionary activities on the mainland, but a relative calm prevailed in the southern peninsula. Various public works projects were undertaken starting in 1920, including the beginning of construction of the Transpeninsular Highway between La Paz and Bahia Magdalena.

One of the most important events in the history of the peninsula took place in 1933, when the national government recovered the lands that had been encumbered for fifty years in various foreign-dominated concessions. It is from this very late date that the citizens of the peninsula were able to take up the colonization and development of their own land.

Agricultural settlement was started at Santo Domingo north of the highway junction at Ciudad Insurgentes. The extensive farming activities resulting from this early effort are clearly evident to the traveler. A second agricultural effort was started at San Juan de Los Planes in 1946 and may be visited on Highway 286.

During this period of agricultural development, the peninsula was to suffer the tragic loss of its pearl and oyster fishing industry. Between 1936 and 1949, the oysters in the Sea of Cortez were attacked by an unknown disease. The pearl, which had lured the original explorers and which had been a source of wealth for 400 years, was to disappear.

In its place, as a source of revenue, hotel and other tourist facilities came into being in the 1940s and tourism is now the region's principal industry. The population gradually increased, and in 1974 the southern territory proudly entered the Union. It, and Quintana Roo in the Yucatan peninsula were the last two Mexican states.

SUMMARY OF ACTIVITIES IN THE NORTH -- Following the revolutionary activities of the early 1900s, the northern territory was to see a period of spectacular development. Two progressive and skilled administrators were to govern during most years between 1915 and 1929. The second of these, Abelardo Rodriguez, was later to become President of the Mexican Republic. Roads, schools, and extensive other public works were developed.

Much of this activity was financed by astute taxation on gambling houses, prostitution, and drug traffic centering largely in Tijuana. In 1920, the Mexicans struck it rich with the coming of prohibition in the United States. The saloons and restaurants of Tijuana contributed on a massive scale to the prosperity of the territory. Its greatest natural resource was its location adjacent to the international boundary. As in the south, the inefficient land concessions were recaptured in the 1930s, but here the process was not as simple.

Most land in the fertile Valle de Mexicali west of the Rio Colorado was owned by foreign interests under the name of the Colorado River Land Company. These lands were not farmed, as existing irrigation systems served only the Imperial Valley to the north in the United States. Company lands were used only for grazing, with the labor performed by imported Chinese and other Asians.

It required protests by local Mexicans and action by the progressive President Lazaro Gardenas to bring about removal of the foreign interests and placement of the lands in the hands of Mexican farmers. This action was completed in 1937. New villages promptly sprung up, and the population rapidly increased.

Large-scale irrigation of the valley lands was to follow as the result of a water treaty with the United States in 1945, and the construction of the Morelos Dam on the Rio Colorado three years later. During these same years, construction work on Baja's only railroad was to take place. After its completion in 1948, for the first time in history there was a land transportation link between the Baja peninsula and the Mexican mainland that did not pass through the United States.

The Mexican constitution requires that a territory must have a population of 80,000 to merit admission into the national union. By 1950 there were actually more than 225,000 people. For this and other reasons, the northern territory became Mexico's twenty-ninth state on January 16, 1952.

The towering eagle statue at the 28th parallel.

CHAPTER 13
OUR DEVELOPING COUNTRY NEIGHBOR

This chapter is concerned with Baja's people and her political, economic, and social systems. Much of what is presented is of a positive nature and should provide encouragement to those interested in beneficial social change. And, I hope you might concur that acquiring an understanding of a country's people may, in the final analysis, be the most important benefit derived from travel to a foreign land. It is the objective of this chapter to assist in bringing this about.

In recent years there has been much reference in the news to the *third world* and to *developing countries*. Many of us may have a vague conception as to where these countries are located. We are perhaps most likely to think of nations in Africa, South America, and Southeast Asia. We may overlook the fact that the United States has such a country on its southern doorstep, and in visiting the rural areas of Baja California we are viewing some of the last sections of Mexico to experience modernization. The states of Baja California Sur, along with Quintana Roo in southeast Mexico, were the last to receive statehood in Mexico.

Mexico and Baja California are considerably more advanced than the average third world country. They nevertheless share many characteristics and problems in common with these nations. As a result, there is much to learn about the developing world through a trip not very far from home.

In other portions of this book, the material presented is founded on some degree of my personal experience or training. In the present chapter, I clearly tread beyond my fields of expertise. A friend once told me that I know just enough to be dangerous. Perhaps that will be the result here.

It will also be difficult to discuss the subjects of sociology, economics, and politics with complete objectivity. I apologize in advance for the almost certain bias of my personal convictions. Conversely, one rarely finds two economists or politicians who agree with each other, so perhaps I am after all on sound ground. I believe that the worst course of action I could take would be to omit discussion of these subjects.

MEXICO'S PEOPLE

Some seven-to-nine million Indians lived in what is present day Mexico when Cortez arrived in 1519.

(A century later, their numbers were reduced to only 1 million by disease and warfare.) These various Indian nations had developed some of the most brilliant civilizations in the world. Today's Mexican is the end product of the intermarriage of these people with Europeans, almost all of Spanish origin. The result has been the emergence of a new race, the *Mestizos*. These are the people you will meet in Baja. There are millions of Indians still living in Mexico, but very few of them reside in Baja.

POPULATION GROWTH — Although Mexico begat a new race of people, a case can now be made that they have made too much of a good thing. Mexico's exploding population is a serious national problem which tends to cancel out the country's significant economic advances.

The population of Mexico was 13.5 million in 1900. It grew slowly during the revolutionary period and was only 15 million in 1920. Continued slow growth brought the population to 19.6 million in 1940. Then after World War II the explosion began. There were 35 million in 1960, 46 million in 1970, 67 million in 1980 and 76 million by 1884. During these latter years, Mexico's population growth rate was 3.4 percent, one of the highest in the world.

Statues of three of Mexico's famous men in the civic plaza in Ensenada. On the left is Benito Juarez the symbol of Mexico's nationhood and a full-blooded Zapotec Indian. He was a leader in the reform movement that resulted in the Constitution of 1857.

During most of this period, the law, public policy, individual inclination and the influence of the Roman Catholic Church favored population growth. Perhaps influenced by the results of the 1970 census, the government came to realize that Mexico had a population problem. 1973 saw passage of the General Population Law which began a series of steps aimed at *Integrated Family Planning*. The result has been one of the most successful state-coordinated programs of family planning in the world.

Today, free contraceptives are supplied at government clinics; population and sex education are included in the public education system, and there is dissemination of material on these subjects on radio and television. Although abortion is prohibited by law, one in six pregnancies ends in this manner, often resulting in serious harm to the woman. The overall result of these actions has been a reduction of the population growth rate to 2.4 percent by 1984, and the national goal is to reduce it to *1.0 percent* by the year 2000.

The United Nations reports that many developing countries have achieved substantial reductions in birth rates and that the most important factors involved relate to improvements in (1) family planning, (2) health, and (3) education. (We will examine Mexico's progress in the last two areas in the pages to come.) Ironically, a byproduct of improvements in these areas is a marked increase in life expectancy, a factor that counteracts lowering of the birth rate. This has occurred in Mexico and accounts for much of the population explosion.

In Baja, my personal observations can attest to substantial population increases in nearly all population centers, both large and small, although there has been no detectable increase in the number of communities themselves. Baja is still largely a thinly populated land although the traveler on Highway 1 must pass south of El Rosario to realize that this is true.

IMMIGRATION — Mexico's population growth is also of concern to the United States. Prior to World War II, the vast majority of immigrants into the United States came from western Europe. A quota system established by U.S. law had the effect of maintaining this European ethnic composition while minimizing the influx of peoples from other countries. Since the war, the law has changed and the country again is experiencing a wave of immigration, but this time consisting largely of peoples from Asia and Latin America. Approximately 40 percent of the total inflow comes from Mexico.

In the past a great majority of this immigration from Mexico entered the United States without permission. This situation aroused national concern and the U.S. Immigration Reform Act was passed in 1988. It is perhaps to early to fully assess the impact of this legislation on Mexican immigration. However, U.S. port-of-entry officials report a significant increase in Mexican citizens passing properly through their stations. In the past these people entered illegally and stayed for a full work season. They now return home to Mexico on a daily or weekly basis.

Current birth rates in the United States have declined in recent years, and immigration now accounts for almost half of the country's population growth. If the present trends continue, a time will come in the next century when all population growth will come from immigration. I make no judgements as to whether this situation is good or bad, but it does raise questions about the future size and ethnic proportions of the United States.

GOVERNMENT AND POLITICS

Although Mexico freed herself from Spanish rule in 1821, the new nation continued to be dominated by the institutions of the past. The country was ruled by authoritarian leaders. The Catholic Church controlled from one-third to one-half of the national wealth and owned nearly one-half of the land. All but 3 percent of the remaining land was vested in the hands of a mere 830, mostly absentee owners.

The *Mestizos* gradually grew to dominate the racial com-position of the country and became the core of various liberal movements which culminated in the revolution of 1910. The Constitution of February 5, 1917 resulted from this struggle. Almost all of Mexico's current political and economic institutions and progress stem from this date and constitution. The Mexican citizen's civil rights guarantees are contained in the first 29 articles. Mexico's Indian, rather than her Spanish, heritage predominate after 1917.

The new constitution also severely limits the position of the Catholic Church. Today the church may not own property and priests are not permitted to vote or wear clerical garb in public. (NOTE - Press reports in early 1992 indicate that the Mexican congress has given preliminary approval to a series of constitutional reforms that would give the Church formal recognition by the government.)

The ninety-six years between Mexico's independence from Spain (1821) and enactment of her present constitution (1917) were filled with upheaval. There were wars with other nations, civil war, the loss of one-half the nation's territory to the United States, and political, economic, and social degeneration. It can be seen that while western civilization was well established in Mexico far earlier than in Canada and the United States, Mexico's modern era was to get a very late and tumultuous start. Its underdeveloped status is a product of its history.

THE GOVERNMENT — Although the Constitution of 1917 establishes a tripartite division of power between the executive, legislative, and judicial branches of the government, the authority of the executive far exceeds that of the latter two. The President is elected by universal suffrage for a six-year term. (Minimum voting age is 18.) An individual may serve only one term. The most recent presidential election was held in July 1988. The President appoints a cabinet to oversee more than twenty ministries, or *Sectetarias*. You will see this word and the names of the various ministries in numerous places in your travels in Baja California.

There are two houses of the national legislature. The Senate is composed of two individuals elected for six-year terms from each of the thirty-one states and the Federal District. The Chamber of Deputies is made-up of over 200 members elected for three-year terms. Each member represents a specific number of citizens. The members of both houses are barred from reelection, so there is an often disruptive turnover in both the legislature and the ministries following elections.

The state governments consist of an elected Governor and a Chamber of Deputies, but the autonomy of the states is limited. The federal system is not the result of a merging compact between independent states as in the United States. In Mexico, the states have been created by the national government. Federal financing and administration of programs dominate at all levels, and the states are expected to enforce federal law. While traveling in Baja, you will see the names and acronyms of federal agencies on signs and government construction projects throughout the peninsula.

Each of Baja's two states is divided into municipalities similar to those of counties in the United States. The cities do not incorporate and establish separate governments. Thus, the official that tourists may refer to as the Mayor of Ensenada is in fact the *Presidente Municipal* of an area of hundreds of square miles which includes many communities other than Ensenada. The municipalities of the peninsula are shown in an accompanying table. Look for the *Palacio Municipal* (municipal palace) when you visit the towns which are the *Cabacera Municipal* (the seat of government).

In other towns, the government building will bear the name *Delegado Municipal*. The *Delegado* (delegate) is an official

The PRI symbol of Mexico's dominant political party, the Partido Revolucionario Institucion.

appointed by the *Presidente Municipal* to represent him in the area in question. In the smallest communities, there are *subdelegados*. Thus, the citizens of a small town find themselves governed by a Subdelegado, Delegado, Presidente Municipal, Gobernador, and finally, El Presidente.

POLITICS — A common characteristic of developing countries throughout the world is the presence of one dominant political party. Mexico has been no exception. Since 1929, the country's government has been dominated at all levels by the *Partido Revolucionario Institucion* (Institutional Revolutionary Party). You will see the PRI symbol on fences, the sides of buildings, signs and in endless other places throughout Baja.

In reading of the immense powers of the Mexican president, and the domination of the PRI, one could easily come to the conclusion that the country's government should be classified as a dictatorship. Certainly, one party dominance has resulted in substantial government corruption. Nevertheless, the PRI has provided Mexico with a stable administration for decades. There is a minimum of domination by the military, and social programs aimed at providing a better life for the masses are in evidence everywhere.

In the past the PRI party's nominees for president, governors, and other officials was tantamount to their being elected. They often received some 90 percent of the vote although it has been alleged that vote fraud was widespread. In any case, PRI's dominance was severely tested in the July 1988 elections.

The principal opposition party has been the *Partido de Accion Nacional* (National Action Party). Its acronym is PAN. PAN's agenda can best be described as "conservative" and it is supported by the business community and the Catholic Church. However, emerging in 1988 was a coalition of several liberal-leaning parties, who along with the PAN, mounted a serious challenge to PRI. Vote counting fraud was again charged by the opposition parties, and the PRI candidate was eventually announced to have won by a narrow 50.5 percent. It is widely alleged that PRI actually lost the election.

It would appear that Mexico is now on the threshold a multiparty political system and three state's governors are now from op-

MUNICIPALITIES	
MUNICIPIO*	**CABACERA* MUNICIPAL**
BAJA CALIFORNIA	
Tijuana	Tijuana
Tecate	Tecate
Mexicali	Mexicali
Ensenada	Ensenada
BAJA CALIFORNIA SUR	
Mulege	Santa Rosalia
Comondu	Ciudad Constitucion
La Paz	La Paz
Los Cabos	San Jose del Cabo

* MUNICIPIO ------ Municipality.
* CABACERA MUNICIPAL -- Seat of government.

position parties. Events in 1994 presidential election will be most interesting to watch. Some may conclude that traveling in Mexico is unwise because of this political situation. I firmly believe this to be untrue. In my view the political changes occurring in Mexico are positive and will have no direct effects on foreign visitors. My travels in Baja after the 1988 election have been no different than they were in past years.

THE MILITARY — Those who keep abreast of current events in developing countries are well aware that many nations' military establishments dominate and often overthrow the civilian authority. This was true in Mexico in the distant past, but it is generally conceded today that the military has only modest influence on the government. The last president who was also a general left office in 1942.

The Mexican army, air force, and navy are assigned the responsibility of defending the independence of the country, but from a practical standpoint, their most significant mission is the preservation of internal order. The navy patrols the coastline and in general assumes the duties assigned to the Coast Guard in the United States. Over the years, the army has been called on to suppress riots and other forms of civil unrest, to control illicit drug traffic, to register firearms, and to undertake similar activities. In effect, the army is assigned duties that citizens of Canada and the United States would normally associate with the civil police.

Because of their policing responsibilities, the army and navy are much in evidence to the tourist in Baja, which, from a public relations standpoint, is unfortunate. These people normally carry automatic rifles and those of us from north of the border tend to associate such weapons with trouble. A blue-uniformed policeman with a sidearm in the United States is one thing; a soldier in brown combat fatigues and helmet carrying a machine gun, in a country where the traveler is a bit squeamish to begin with, is quite another.

My messages here are that you will frequently see the *militar*, that their role is keeping the peace, and that you should not be concerned. However, the Mexican government would be well advised to prevail upon the military to put their automatic weapons out of sight in the vicinity of tourists and to provide them with public relations training. They should save their machismo for the senoritas. (My personal observations are that they have heeded this advice in recent years).

You will see the military at their encampments in many peninsula communities. There are also small detachments at recreation spots such as Puerto Escondido and Santispac. Usually there is an enlisted man on guard duty who speaks no English and who has an exaggerated view of the importance of his assignment. I have found them almost universally brusque, quick to wave their rifle about, and obviously wanting me to depart. I have also found that if you can arrange to see an officer, only courtesy and helpfulness prevail. My counsel is to avoid the military unless you have a particular need, and then ask for the brass.

MEXICO'S ECONOMY

A DEVELOPING COUNTRY — A majority of the countries in the world are considered developing countries. They are endeavoring to improve the quality of life of their people through industrialization and other means. From an economic standpoint, such a country is defined as "one that has not yet reached a stage of economic development characterized by the growth of industrialization, and a level of national income sufficient to yield the domestic savings required to finance the investment necessary for further growth." This complex definition simply means that a developing country must rely on foreign investment and international borrowing to fuel its economic growth.

During the 1970s and 80s, Mexico, along with Brazil, led the world in such borrowing. Mexico made rapid industrial growth and is now classified by the World Bank as a *Newly Industrialized Country* and as a *Middle Income Developing Country*. By the mid-1980s, however, the cure (borrowing) became the disease, and the country's payments on its immense national debt threatened to collapse its economy. The situation was known as *La Crisis* (the crisis).

Traveling in Baja during the mid-1980s, the signs of La Crisis were readily apparent. Construction at the FONATUR developments at Loreto and San Jose del Cabo had ceased and other projects were held in abeyance. More recently, however, progress on many government undertakings has moved ahead. There is no economic stagnation in evidence in Baja although the number of projects discernible to the traveler was less from 1988 to 1992 than it was the previous three years..

FOREIGN INVESTMENT — In 1973, Mexico enacted the Foreign Investment Law. It was designed to *promote foreign investment*, while at the same time ensuring the *government's autonomy and control over the country's economy*. Under this law, a foreign investor's interest in a commercial enterprise is limited to 49 percent. A Mexican national must own the controlling 51 percent. Mexico coveted foreign assistance, but on its own terms.

In addition, a foreigner may not own real estate within 100 kilometers of the border or 50 kilometers of the coastline. That very well blankets the desirable locations in the Baja peninsula. Foreign interest in land is secured through a trust arrangement which requires that after thirty years the trust must be sold to *persons or entities capable of acquiring legal title*. It is understandable why Mexico would not wish to engender a recurrence of the land frauds and other negative aspects of past foreign control of its assets, but many feel that these rules inhibit, rather than encourage, investment.

As of 1991 some of Mexico's landownership laws have been changed or are in the process of change. It appears that the realities of La Crisis and Mexico's own economic self-interest are forcing modification in the country's position toward foreign investment and business. What little I know about these matters leads me to suggest caution to potential investors and to advise that they seek the counsel of a competent attorney not connected with persons offering land for sale or lease.

A unique form of foreign investment, the *maquiladora* program, occurs at Baja's border cities. It started two decades ago when the Mexican government permitted these cities merchants to import U. S. goods duty free so that local citizens would not do their shopping north of the border. In due course, U. S. manufacturers established hundreds of assembly plants across the border where finished products are produced by cheap, nonunionized Mexican labor from U. S. raw materials imported duty free. When shipped back north, the U. S. tariff is paid only on the value added. The two chief maquiladora cities in Baja are Tijuana and Mexicali, with rapid expansion occurring in Tecate.

SOCIALISM — A great majority of the world's developing nations look on their economies as *socialistic*. Mexico has fit this mold. Certainly, they have not been *communistic* as there is much private land and thousands of small private businesses, but major enterprises have been government owned or controlled. During La Crisis the banks were nationalized as was one of the countries airlines.

However, the winds of change have been blowing. During the last several years hundreds of government businesses have been moved into the private sector. President Salenas's economic training as an economist appears to be in evidence. Mexico, along with the countries of Eastern Europe, the former Soviet Union and much of Latin America that experimented with socialism are finding it prudent to move rapidly toward a capitalistic economic system. These changes appear to be meeting with success. The Inter-American Bank recently re-

ported that Mexico and other Latin American countries had made impressive economic gains in 1991 after the "lost decade" of the 1980.

But while change is occurring, much of socialism remains. The CONASUPO stores are government owned as is much of the land with tourism potential brokered by FONATUR. The entire fishing industry is based on government-controlled and financed cooperatives, and its modern fishing fleet has been constructed with federal funds. Government planning and control is evident to the traveler in most aspects of Mexico's social and economic systems.

It is my understanding that Canada can be classified as somewhat more socialistic than the United States, but Mexico is clearly far more socialistic than either. Travel to Baja thus gives citizens of these two countries an opportunity to view a nation different from their own. Talk to the Mexicans; see how they view their socialist country and how they view the changes that are taking place. How would you change Mexico if, suddenly, you were president? After all, you have to think about something while lying there in the sun.

LAND REFORM — Since the 1910 revolution, much of Mexico's land has been distributed to the people. In Baja, one principal method of accomplishing this has been the *ejido*. You will see this word on maps and on countless road signs along the highways, and it is easy to arrive at the conclusion that it means village or town. This is not the case. An ejido is a landholding institution established under Mexican law. There were over 28,000 of them in Mexico in 1990.

It is the ejido rather than the individual that has been made the legal proprietor of the land. Land may be worked on a cooperative basis or may be distributed to individuals who acquire what are called usufructuary rights. Land may be passed on through inheritance, but it is lost if not worked for two consecutive years. The ejido is administered by elected officials. Here, again, is another Mexican institution which has skirted the private land and capitalist systems we are accustomed to in Canada and the United States.

But the edido system is also in the process of change. Ejido farmers have been unable to secure credit for seed and machinery because they do not own the land they farm. And as farmers divided their plots among their children, the average acreage of an ejido holding dwindled to an unprofitable size. In Baja, there is clear evidence of areas that have been cultivated that are submarginal for such purposes.

Under the new order, ejido lands can be sold or rented. This situation will have an impact on lands made available to tourists for recreation homes along the Baja coasts.

A modern flood control and water conservation dam upstream from the agricultural lands at Todos Santos. One of scores of government projects readily seen by the traveler in Baja.

Ejidos engage in enterprises other than farming. Members of ejidos work in the CONASUPO stores; there is a mining ejido in the town of El Triunfo on Highway 1, south of La Paz; and ejidos run camping areas on the highway to La Bufadora, near Ensenada, and at the whale-watching site at Scammon's lagoon.

DEVELOPMENTAL ACTIVITIES

Publications by the United Nations and the World Bank discuss common problems which must be addressed by all developing countries. Of these, family planning, the need for industrialization, and land reform have already been discussed. This section briefly reviews several others. An effort has been made to emphasize items that will be of interest to the tourist and can be seen while traveling in the Baja peninsula.

In reading about Mexico and other developing countries, it is often noted that progress has been made but that its benefits have not spread to the rural areas. While I am sure this is true to some extent in Mexico, I can attest that there are clear evidences of government-sponsored improvements in even the smallest and most remote of Baja's villages. Even at isolated fish camps the fishermen's boats are modern fiberglass pangas provided by government-sponsored cooperatives, and access may be over a newly modernized road.

The distribution of income in Mexico is amongst the most inequitable in the world, but it is also evident, at least to this observer, that some degree of social improvement is being shared by most of Baja's citizens.

AGRICULTURAL PRODUCTION — The development of Baja's agricultural lands was almost totally prevented until 1933 due to the presence of various foreign land leases. (See Chapter 12 HISTORY.) Today you will see substantial farming areas in (1) the Valle de Mexicali near the mouth of the Rio Colorado, (2) along the Pacific coast from Ensenada to south of San Quintin, (3) in the desert surrounding Ciudad Constitucion and Ciudad Insurgentes, and (4) in the plains near San Juan de los Planes southeast of La Paz. Irrigation is from deep wells.

EDUCATION — You will see recently constructed school buildings in many locations. Often they are clearly the newest buildings in town. Sometimes there is even a school building and no community. Look for one-room school houses at crossroads along the highways.

Be alert for the *Jardin de Ninos* (kindergarten) where attendance is optional for three years for children from ages four to six. Most of the *escuelas* (schools) will bear the name *Primaria* (primary). Here, attendance is mandatory from ages six to fourteen, or until six grades are completed. Middle schools, *Secundaria* (secondary), *Secundaria-Tecnico* (secondary-technical), and *Tecnico* (technical) are less in evidence to the traveler but are frequently seen if you drive off the main roads.

The number of new schools is impressive, as is the fact that the children are frequently well dressed. There is an obvious pride taken in the children. Sadly, you must keep in mind that many of the people you will meet have no more than a sixth-grade education, but progress is clearly evident.

MEDICAL SERVICES — There are private doctors in Mexico, but most people receive medical attention at clinics and hospitals operated by the *Instituto Mexicano de Seguro Social* (Mexican Social Security Institute). Look for the large letters IMSS on the front of the buildings. Most of them are new facilities in the smaller towns. Social security refers to health services in Mexico rather than to retirement pensions as in the United States.

WATER AND SEWAGE — A major water pipeline was constructed early in the 1970s from water sources in the mountains north of San Jose del Cabo, all along Highway 1 to Cabo San Lucas. FONATUR has developed a new water system from wells for Loreto and the tourist facilities at Nopolo. On a recent visit to Mulege, I saw roads being torn up for new pipelines. In 1986, a large water line was constructed to serve the coastal towns south of Guerrero Negro. This line will replace salt water conversion plants which are themselves only a few years old. The ocean cruisers always fill their tanks from city water lines

A CONSERVATION ETHIC FOR BAJA CALIFORNIA

There are very few natural resource managers in Mexico, and most of the environmental constraints imposed on us north of the border are not readily apparent. Also, on occasion, we tourists will see Mexican citizens conducting their affairs in ways which are not in keeping with sound conservation practices. These conditions may influence us to forget our environmental manners in Baja.

To complicate matters, Baja California is largely a desert. Deserts are particularly sensitive to disruptive man-made change. Arid lands do not heal themselves nearly as rapidly as would be the case in areas with more moisture, as is the case where most of us live.

The conditions just noted place an added responsibility on visitors. If we are to preserve the features about Baja California which we find attractive, we must <u>act responsibly</u>, and do so <u>on a voluntary basis</u>. I recently heard a church sermon where the minister posed the question "How does one avoid doing what is wrong?" His answer was, "Just don't do it."

Avoiding environmental damage is largely a matter of using good common sense. It should be obvious that digging up sensitive plants, destroying tide-pool organisms, picking up artifacts, walking about in seabird nesting areas, and throwing trash in the sea will cause long-term damage. Something inside ought to say "<u>Just don't do it</u>."

DISTANT NEIGHBORS

By ALAN RIDING

Probably nowhere in the world do two neighbors (The USA & Mexico) under stand each other so little. The purpose of Alan Riding's book is to bridge this gap and make Mexico more accessible to non-Mexicans. Great coverage on: the Mexicans; a concise historical summary; the political system; economic, social, and population problems; Mexico City; foreign policy; and much more.

Author Alan Riding was born in Brazil and educated in England. He has spent 12 years as a journalist in Mexico for various publications including 6 years as the The New York Times bureau chief. I learned more about Mexico in a few hours with this book than I had in years of travel in the country. Its simply

the best book I have ever read about Mexico.

Jack Williams

NO MAPS, NO PHOTOS. JUST 385 PAGES OF THE MEATIEST TEXT YOU WILL EVER READ. ---------------- ---------------- A FOREIGN AFFAIRS BEST SELLER

at La Paz and with no ill effect. These and other signs of safe water and sewer systems are in clear evidence throughout the peninsula.

ELECTRIC POWER — There are three major diesel-fueled electric power plants in Baja, all in clear view to the traveler. The northern plant is located between Highway 1-D and the coast near Rosarito, south of Tijuana. The southern plant is adjacent to the highway between La Paz and Pichilingue. The most recent plant lies a few miles inland from San Carlos near Bahia Magdalena.

Look for the power lines extending from these facilities. They serve the entire peninsula except for the central portion between El Rosario and Guerrero Negro where there are no power lines. While not served by the two main generating facilities, almost all the remote towns have small, diesel-fueled, electric generating facilities.

COMMUNICATIONS — Baja's telephone system has been described in some detail in Chapter 8 (TRAVELING IN BAJA). Making international calls involves some inconveniences for the traveler. In spite of this shortcoming, the system is founded on modern microwave radio techniques. Watch for the numerous microwave radio towers along the main highways.

TRANSPORTATION — Hundreds of miles of new roads were constructed in Baja during the 1980s. (See Chapter 3 TRANSPORTATION.) From 1989 to 1992 road building has been largely limited to the southern part of the peninsula where it will serve income producing tourist facilities.

Although the standards of Baja's roads are considerably lower than those encountered north of the border, they meet the needs of the Mexican people and are an immense improvement over what was available only a few years ago. In addition, the past two decades have seen the construction of several international

airports, numerous smaller airfields, and port facilities at Ensenada, San Carlos, La Paz and several other places.

DISTANT NEIGHBORS

Since producing *The Magnificent Peninsula* I have had to guard against the tendency of being overly critical of the works of other writers, particularly when their subject is Mexico. Professional jealousy strikes us all. I note this shortcoming to add extra weight to my uncompromising praise for Alan Riding's 1986 best-selling *Distant Neighbors*. It is must reading for anyone seriously interested in understanding Mexico and Mexicans.

Here in *The Magnificent Peninsula* I have endeavored to enhance your ability to interpret and enjoy what you see in Baja California. *Distant Neighbors* presents a remarkable account about the things in Mexico that you can't see. If this chapter on OUR DEVELOPING COUNTRY NEIGHBOR has aroused your interest, you need to know that it has merely scratched the surface. *Distant Neighbors* plows far deeper.

Distant Neighbors is available from the BAJA BOOKSHELF in the Appendix. But trust me, I am not making this endorsement to make money. Alan's book sells for so little that my profit is not worth the promotional effort. It is offered for sale because I believe it is the best book I have ever read on Mexico, that you will enjoy it, and that it will help in achieving mutual understanding between those of us who have been cast together on the North American continent.

SUMMARY

What I now set down are my own personal views about my observations concerning social and economic progress in Baja.

First, it is evident that there has in fact been substantial progress. Much has been accomplished between my first visit and my most recent, but perhaps progress has been a bit too swift. The leaders of developing countries are under tremendous pressures to produce progress rapidly. If they don't, they face political upheaval. In Mexico, as in other nations, much of this progress has been financed through the borrowing of foreign capital and with the vehicle of deficit federal spending. The result in the early 1980s was a near collapse of the Mexican economy.

The hand of the federal government is everywhere. It has built hotels and airfields that simple observation indicates are financial liabilities. The creation of jobs, not profitability, seems to be the objective. I have observed dozens of government projects, ranging from the ferry terminal at Puerto Escondido to the buildings in the center of the highway at the state line, that lie unused and unrepaired. The major recent airport between Santa Rosalia and Mulege lies without use.

The Mexican people must come to grips with the question of how many non-income-producing government services they can afford to provide for themselves. We, in Canada and the U. S., also face this same question, but I believe it is more aggravated in Mexico. Perhaps what we observe while traveling in Baja can offer an insight into addressing such problems in our own countries.

It is my personal view that the current administration of President Salinas has recognized the shortcomings that have been noted above. I have seen far fewer governmental white elephants in recent years and the president moved very early in his administration to make major economic changes as noted earlier in this chapter. He has also moved rapidly to develop an international trade agreement with the United States and Canada.

Unfortunately, many recent changes designed to produce long-term benifit have more immediate negative impacts on working people. This is occuring all over the world as countries move away from socialism to market-oriented economies. The crucial test for Mexico will come in the presidential election in 1994. If PRI, the ruling political party, allows truely free elections it could fall from power to those promising a return to the failed policies of the past. Time will tell.

A final observation. I have come to the conclusion that one of Mexico's most pressing problems involves the construction and maintenance standards of almost everything one sees. Often the traveler can observe partially completed buildings and other structures lying unused. Concrete is often mixed by a shovel in a small depression in the sand pile with little concern for the proportions of its ingredients. The use of reinforced concrete construction in multi-storied buildings, and the total lack of structural steel, is frightening, as the country found to its sorrow in the 1985 Mexico City earthquake. Fortunately, there are few such buildings in Baja.

Much of what is completed appears to receive little maintenance. The doors of public buildings hang from their hinges, windows are broken and not repaired, letters fall from signs and are not replaced. It is as if no one in the community possesses a screwdriver, wrench, or other simple hand tools, and that the most common repair items from a hardware store are unavailable. Alan Riding's *Distant Neighbors* notes that Mexican's have little desire to contribute to the upkeep of such public improvements. This lies in sharp contrast to the obvious pride they take in their persons and their own homes. Perhaps their lack of concern for public property lies in the "cradle to the grave" philosophy inherent in socialism. (Again I should note that I have seen improvement in this area in recent years. The move from government to private ownership of businesses may be having its effect.)

These comments have not been presented to be critical of a country that I very greatly admire. Rather, they are intended as a foundation for my reader's own observations and contemplations concerning Mexico as a developing country.

The port city of Ensenada and its extensive port facilities built by the Mexican government.

PART III
THE GRAND TOUR

The pages ahead will guide the reader along more than 3,100 miles of the Magnificent Peninsula's roadways. Road log information is tied to kilometer post signs which adjoin all the principal highways.

BAJA DISTANCE TABLE

Top line is distance in miles.
Bottom line is distance in kilometers.
Figures based on use of Highway 1-D between Tijuana and Ensenada.

All distances are over Highway 1 except for the last line which utilizes the Highway 1 and Highway 19 route between La Paz and Cabo San Lucas.

Distances shown as miles / kilometers.

To ↓ \ From →	Tijuana	Ensenada	Colonet	San Quintin	El Rosario	Catavina	Bahia de los Angeles Junction.	State Line	San Ignacio	Santa Rosalia	Mulege	Loreto	Ciudad Insurgentes	La Paz
Ensenada	68 / 109													
Colonet	145 / 234	77 / 125												
San Quintin	185 / 299	118 / 190	39 / 61											
El Rosario	223 / 360	156 / 251	78 / 126	38 / 61										
Catavina	297 / 479	239 / 370	157 / 245	112 / 180	74 / 119									
Bahia de los Angeles Junction.	363 / 585	295 / 476	218 / 351	177 / 286	140 / 225	66 / 106								
State Line	442 / 713	374 / 604	297 / 479	257 / 414	219 / 353	145 / 234	79 / 128							
San Ignacio	533 / 860	466 / 751	388 / 626	348 / 561	310 / 500	236 / 381	171 / 275	91 / 147						
Santa Rosalia	579 / 934	512 / 825	434 / 700	394 / 635	356 / 574	282 / 455	216 / 349	137 / 221	46 / 74					
Mulege	617 / 995	549 / 886	472 / 761	432 / 696	394 / 635	320 / 516	254 / 410	175 / 282	84 / 135	38 / 61				
Loreto	701 / 1131	634 / 1022	556 / 897	516 / 832	478 / 771	404 / 652	339 / 546	259 / 418	168 / 271	122 / 197	84 / 136			
Ciudad Insurgentes	776 / 1251	708 / 1142	631 / 1017	590 / 952	552 / 891	479 / 772	413 / 666	334 / 538	242 / 391	197 / 317	159 / 256	74 / 120		
La Paz	924 / 1490	856 / 1381	778 / 1256	738 / 1191	701 / 1130	627 / 1011	561 / 905	482 / 777	391 / 630	345 / 556	307 / 495	223 / 359	148 / 239	
Cabo San Lucas Via Highway 1	1059 / 1711	993 / 1604	916 / 1477	875 / 1412	838 / 1351	764 / 1232	698 / 1126	619 / 998	528 / 851	482 / 777	444 / 716	360 / 580	285 / 460	137 / 221
Cabo San Lucas Via Highway 1 & 19	1003 / 1618	936 / 1509	858 / 1384	818 / 1319	777 / 1254	706 / 1139	604 / 1033	561 / 905	470 / 758	424 / 684	386 / 629	302 / 487	228 / 367	79 / 128

GASOLINE STATIONS (PEMEX) ALONG HIGHWAY 1 (North to South)

CHAPTER 17
Tijuana	Km A-1
Rosarito	Km A-34
El Descanso	Km A-53
El Mirador ***	Km A-84
El Sauzal	Km A-100
Ensenada	Km A-109

CHAPTER 18
Maneadero	Km B-21
Santo Tomas	Km B-51
San Vicente	Km B-90
Colonet	Km B-127
Camalu	Km B-157
C. Vicente Guerrero	Km B-172
San Quintin	Km B-190

C. Lazaro Cardenas	Km B-193

CHAPTER 19
El Rosario	Km C-55
Catavina	Km C-174
Bahia de L. A. Junct.	Km C-280
Villa Jesus Maria	Km D-96

CHAPTER 20
Guerrero Negro	Km E-217
Vizcaino Junction	Km E 208
San Ignacio	Km E-74
Santa Rosalia	Km E-0

CHAPTER 21
Mulege	Km F-136
Loreto	Km F-0

CHAPTER 22
Puerto Escondido ***	Km G-94
Fed. Water Project #1	Km G-17
Ciudad Insurgentes	Km G-0
Ciudad Constitucion	Km H-211
El Cien	Km H-100
El Centenario	Km H-12
La Paz	Km H-0

CHAPTER 23
San Antonio	Km J-156
Los Barriles	Km J-110
Santiago	Km J-85
Miraflores	Km J-71
San Jose del Cabo	Km J-33
Cabo San Lucas	Km J-0

*** Under construction 1992.

LITERS TO GALLONS

Liters	Gallons	Liters	Gallons
1	0.26	40	10.57
2	0.53	50	13.21
3	0.79	60	15.85
4	1.06	70	18.49
5	1.32	80	21.14
10	2.64	90	23.78
20	5.28	100	26.42
30	7.93	150	39.63

1 gallon = 3.78 liters.

KILOMETERS TO MILES

Kilometers	Miles	Kilometers	Miles
1	0.62	30	18.6
2	1.24	40	24.8
3	1.86	50	31.0
4	2.48	60	37.2
5	3.10	70	43.4
10	6.20	80	49.6
15	9.30	90	55.8
20	12.40	100	62.0

1 mile = 1.61 kilometers. To convert kilometers into miles divide by 2 and add 25%.

Geology THE BAJA HIGHWAY Biology

BY John Minch and Thomas Leslie

Here is a great companion piece to Chapters 9,10 and 11 of *The Magnificent Peninsula* for those with an interest in geology and biology. The BAJA HIGHWAY is subtitled **"a geology and biology field guide for the Baja Traveler."** Its 233 pages contains hundreds of descriptions concerning plants, animals and geologic formations along Baja's main highways. References are keyed to roadside kilometer posts just as in *The Magnificent Peninsula*.

THE BAJA HIGHWAY is authored by two college professors who have spent much of their time working in Baja for some 30 years. Nature lovers should not miss their informative book.

Get your copy from the BAJA BOOKSHELF in the Appendix

INTRODUCTION TO PART III

Now that you have completed the background and introductory materials in PARTS I and II, you are ready to begin your PART III - GRAND TOUR - of the Magnificent Peninsula.

What is the GRAND TOUR? It has three basic objectives. These are to provide:

1. Essential travel directions needed for use of the main highways and secondary roads. The maps found in each chapter will be principal tools. The material presented has been kept from becoming an all-inclusive road log of everything one encounters. This has been done because such an exhaustive treatment simply is not necessary. It is possible for the first-time traveler to become temporarily disoriented within the larger cities, but on the open road it would really take special effort to become lost. There are very few paved side roads, and I submit that most people could find their way from Tijuana to Cabo San Lucas by adhering to only one instruction, "Stay on the blacktop and follow your nose."

2. Travel directions on recommended side trips off the main highways. The symbol SIDE TRIP will alert you to this information. The text will frequently be supplemented by large-scale local maps.

3. Special information concerning local history, vegetation, geology, etc., which builds upon the background material presented in PART II - HIGHER NEEDS. In this regard, don't forget to consult the **GLOSSARY** found in the appendix. Many of the words and acronyms it presents are seen along Baja's highways, and in the towns you will visit. It can be a substantial help in increasing your understanding of the Spanish language.

The GRAND TOUR is presented in eleven chapters. The first three cover the border towns along Highway 2, Mexicali to Highway 1, and Highway 3. The seven that follow relate to the Transpeninsular Highway. The concluding chapter describes the region accessible by Highway 19, the Pacific coast highway to Cabo San Lucas via Todos Santos.

Several other techniques are also used throughout the GRAND TOUR. These are as follows:

KILOMETER POSTS AND HIGHWAY SECTIONS — To many of us, *milepost* is a common word. Unfortunately few roads in the United States have them. Most U.S. highways are marked with long numbers that give the distance to the one-hundredth of a foot from the initial point of the construction survey, a place known only to God and the highway department.

In Baja, the road engineers have shared their secret with travelers. Along all main highways are numbered white signs every kilometer.

The Mexican highway department has divided the Transpeninsular Highway into nine sections. For the purposes of this book, these sections have been designated by the letters **A** through **J**. The kilometer post numbers begin with zero in each section. The location of each section, along with its

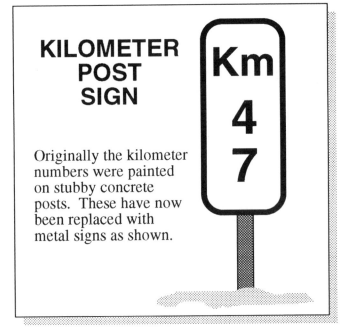

KILOMETER POST SIGN

Km 4 7

Originally the kilometer numbers were painted on stubby concrete posts. These have now been replaced with metal signs as shown.

distances in kilometers and miles, is shown in an accompanying map. In the northern state of Baja California, the numbers run consecutively from north to south. To add zest to your travels, they proceed from south to north in Baja California Sur. In this state, the south-bound traveler encounters the numbers in reverse order.

The seven chapters of this book that cover the Transpeninsular Highway begin and end at the same places as the highway sections, except that in two cases, two sections are combined in one chapter. (See the Kilometer Post Sections map.)

If you need to be alerted to look for some particular point of interest, the GRAND TOUR will reference it to the *nearest* kilometer post. All you need to do is watch for the proper kilometer post without the necessity of keeping track of your odometer readings from some obscure reference point. Canadian drivers should be particularly pleased with this system as their highways and odometers utilize the metric system.

Knowledge of sectional breakpoint locations also allows you to use the posts to assess your progress all along the way. Kilometer post numbers will be printed in **BOLD TYPE**. Thus **Km D-14** refers to the 14th kilometer in section **D**. Travel distances for many of the **SIDE TRIPS** are given in miles as there are no kilometer posts.

TRANSPENINSULAR HIGHWAY GEOGRAPHIC SECTIONS

— This book segregates the Transpeninsular Highway into nineteen geographic sections based on geologic and topographic aspects of the land through which it travels. There are ten odd-numbered sections of gentle terrain, and nine even-numbered ones with steeper topography. These gentle and steeper areas alternate.

The ten gentle sections gross 956 Km (595 miles) or 56 percent of the total length of the highway. The nine steeper areas account for the remaining 748 Km (464 miles) or 44 percent. These figures demonstrate that the highway is basically level and straight for over onehalf of its length, even though Baja as a whole is a mountainous land. Also, large portions of the steeper sections follow valleys or cross gently rolling plateaus which provide relatively easy driving conditions.

The nineteen geographic sections are shown on a map and described in a table in this Introduction. Kilometer post starting and ending points and the length of each section also are included. By using these aids you can look ahead to the kind of terrain through which you will be driving and also will be more aware of the peninsula's geological story. The symbol of the mountain, shown above, will alert you to textual material relating to these geographic sections.

POINTS OF SPECIAL INTEREST TOUR

— As noted earlier, I sincerely hope that you will decide to savor your trip through the Magnificent Peninsula and will not choose to drive through it in the shortest possible time. With this in mind, a thirty-stop POINTS OF SPECIAL INTEREST Tour has been prepared to guide you along the Transpeninsular Highway. These stops are listed in a table and are described in more detail in the text.

Look over the brief comments presented in the table to obtain an overall impression of the attractions included and the time involved in paying them a visit. Some of the points are adjacent to the highway. A majority require stopping and visiting a town or other feature just off the highway. A few require a more lengthy side trip, the longest being 16 miles to visit the whales at Scammon's Lagoon. Many stops on this POINTS OF SPECIAL INTEREST Tour also are logical places to spend the night. Thus, paying them a visit may not significantly increase your travel time.

In both text and maps, the POINTS OF SPECIAL INTEREST Tour will be identified by the **PSI** symbol shown above. The text will alert you to a few of the stops that provide special problems for the larger R.V.'s. And finally, to add a bit of sporting challenge, a specific number of points have been assigned to each of the POINTS OF SPECIAL INTEREST. The more time and effort involved in visiting a site, the more points allotted. The top score is 100 points. Rate yourself as follows:

90	to	100	— Grande Baja Buff
70	to	89	— Baja Buffito
50	to	69	— Baja Amigo
30	to	49	— Posiblemente Manana
0	to	29	— Speed Merchant

No fair saying "There it is!" and roaring by. You have to stop and at least stretch your legs. There is no prize for scoring 100 points, but you know I will want to shake your hand, and should we chance to meet, the cerveza is on me. We have received a letter from one couple who made it from Portland, Oregon, to Cabo San Lucas and back in two weeks and scored 100 points on the tour. They are Grande Baja Buffs who also qualify as Speed Merchants. Hopefully you can proceed at a more leisurely rate.

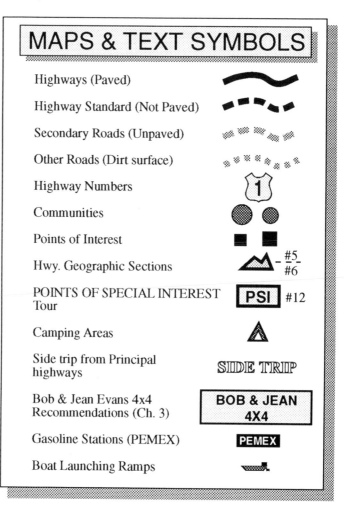

MAPS & TEXT SYMBOLS

Highways (Paved)	
Highway Standard (Not Paved)	
Secondary Roads (Unpaved)	
Other Roads (Dirt surface)	
Highway Numbers	1
Communities	
Points of Interest	
Hwy. Geographic Sections	#5 / #6
POINTS OF SPECIAL INTEREST Tour	PSI #12
Camping Areas	
Side trip from Principal highways	SIDE TRIP
Bob & Jean Evans 4x4 Recommendations (Ch. 3)	BOB & JEAN 4X4
Gasoline Stations (PEMEX)	PEMEX
Boat Launching Ramps	

TRANSPENINSULAR HIGHWAY KILOMETER POST SECTIONS

Total Length of Highway is 1,704 Km (1,059 Miles)

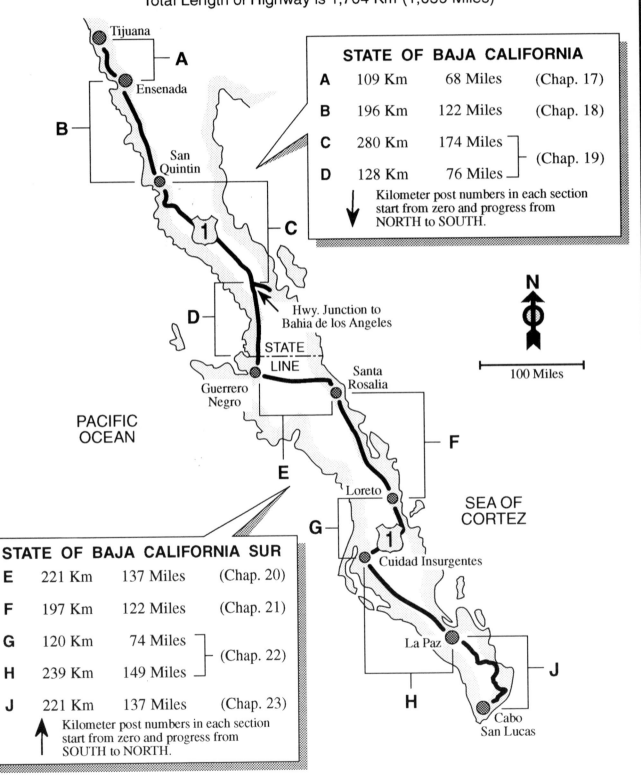

STATE OF BAJA CALIFORNIA

A	109 Km	68 Miles	(Chap. 17)
B	196 Km	122 Miles	(Chap. 18)
C	280 Km	174 Miles	(Chap. 19)
D	128 Km	76 Miles	(Chap. 19)

Kilometer post numbers in each section start from zero and progress from NORTH to SOUTH.

STATE OF BAJA CALIFORNIA SUR

E	221 Km	137 Miles	(Chap. 20)
F	197 Km	122 Miles	(Chap. 21)
G	120 Km	74 Miles	(Chap. 22)
H	239 Km	149 Miles	(Chap. 22)
J	221 Km	137 Miles	(Chap. 23)

Kilometer post numbers in each section start from zero and progress from SOUTH to NORTH.

Tijuana
Ensenada
San Quintin
Hwy. Junction to Bahia de los Angeles
STATE LINE
Guerrero Negro
Santa Rosalia
PACIFIC OCEAN
Loreto
SEA OF CORTEZ
Cuidad Insurgentes
La Paz
Cabo San Lucas

N

100 Miles

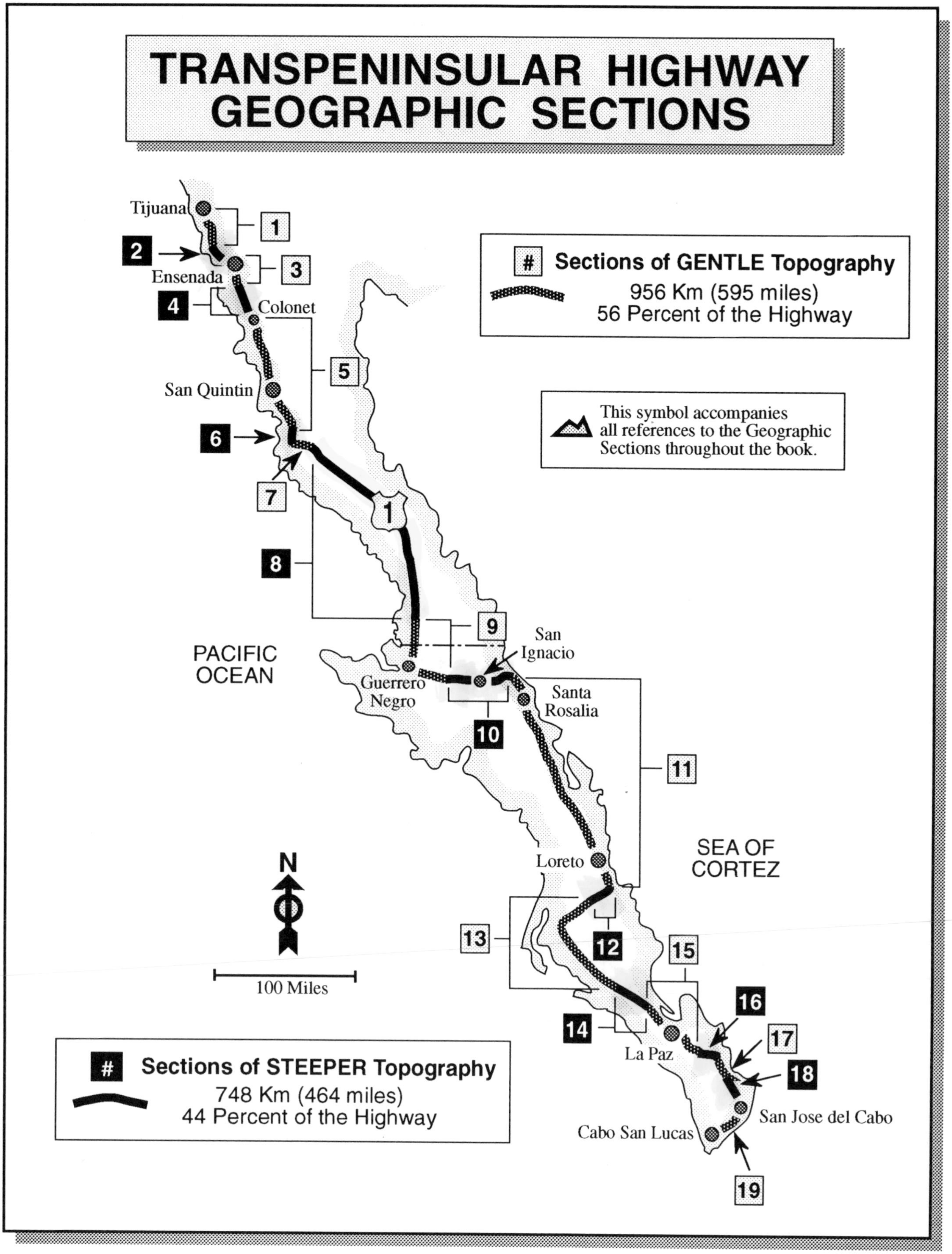

TRANSPENINSULAR HIGHWAY GEOGRAPHIC SECTIONS

Tijuana

1

2

3

Ensenada

4

Colonet

5

San Quintin

6

7

8

**Sections of GENTLE Topography**
956 Km (595 miles)
56 Percent of the Highway

This symbol accompanies all references to the Geographic Sections throughout the book.

1

9

San Ignacio

Guerrero Negro

Santa Rosalia

10

11

PACIFIC OCEAN

SEA OF CORTEZ

Loreto

N

100 Miles

13

12

15

14

16

17

18

La Paz

**Sections of STEEPER Topography**
748 Km (464 miles)
44 Percent of the Highway

San Jose del Cabo

Cabo San Lucas

19

GEOGRAPHIC SECTIONS ALONG THE TRANSPENINSULAR HIGHWAY

NO.	FROM	TO	DESCRIPTION	GENTLE		STEEPER	
				Km	Mi	Km	Mi
1	International Border at Tijuana.	Km (A-75) 21 mi. N of Ensenada.	Limited access freeway (Hwy.1-D) near sea level. Traverses flat areas and gentle hills along the coast.	75	47	--	--
2	Km (A-75) 21 miles N. of Ensenada.	Km (A-99) Tollgate 6 mi. N of Ensenada.	Limited access freeway (Hwy.1-D) Low mountinous section. Good views of the Pacific Ocean along southern portion.	--	--	24	15
3	Km (A -99) Tollgate 6 mi. N of Ensenada.	Km (B-25) 16 mi. S of Ensenada.	Flat lands around Ensenada. Some agriculture in southern portion. Narrow 4-lane hwy. from Ensenada to Maneadero. 2 lanes to south.	35	22	--	--
4	Km (B-25) 16 mi. S of Ensenada.	Km (B-125) at the town of Colonet.	Moderately steep mountains with numerous intermountain valleys.	--	--	100	62
5	Km (B-125) at the town of Colonet.	Km (C-41) 28 mi. S of San Quintin.	Mtns. move inland at Colonet. Hwy. passes over wide coastal plain. Southerly 17 Km. (11 mi.) is within 1/4 to 1/2 mi. of the ocean.	112	70	--	--
6	Km (C-41) 28 mi. S of San Quintin.	Km (C-55) at the town of El Rosario.	A short mountainous section involving a moderate climb to a plateau, and then a steep descent into El Rosario.	--	--	14	9
7	Km (C-55) at the town of El Rosario.	Km (C-63) at the Rio del Rosario bridge.	A short flat section along the north edge of a valley through which flows the Rio del Rosario.	8	5	--	--
8	Km (C-63) at the Rio del Rosario bridge.	Km (D-70) North edge of the Desierto de Vizcaino.	A section of high dissected plateaus, ridges and mtns. The gentle west slope of the Peninsular Range Mtns. The longest mtn. section of Hwy. 1.	--	--	287	178
9	Km (D-70) North edge of the Desierto de Vizcaino.	Km (E-84) SE edge of the Desierto de Vizcaino.	Hwy. straight & level, but narrow. The most dangerous section of hwy. E of Guerrero Negro, hwy. climbs slowly to a pass through the mtns.	192	119	--	--

NO.	FROM	TO	DESCRIPTION	GENTLE		STEEP	
				Km	Mi	Km	Mi
10	Km (E-82) SE edge of the Desierto de Vizcaino.	Km (E-8) Highway 1 meets the Sea of Cortez.	Hwy.1 passes over the Peninsular Range Mtns. through a gentle pass. Eastern 27 Kms. (17 miles) has steep descent to the sea.	--	--	74	46
11	Km (E-8) Highway 1 meets the Sea of Cortez.	Km (G-83) Highway 1 leaves the Sea of Cortez.	Coastal benches and low hills between the coast and the Sierra Giganta. Near sea level in most places. S portion very scenic.	241	150	--	--
12	Km (G-83) Highway 1 leaves the Sea of Cortez.	Km (G-45) Mtns. blend with Llano de Magdalena.	Highway 1 again passes over the main Peninsular Range Mountains. Eastern 10 Km fairly steep with many curves. A scenic section.	--	--	38	24
13	Km (G-45) Mtns. blend with Llano de Magdalena.	Km (H-120) Llano de Mag. blends with plateau lands.	Highway 1 is straight and level through the Llano de Magdalena. Passes through agricultural lands near Ciudad Constitucion.	164	102	--	--
14	Km (H-120) Llano de Mag. blends with plateau lands.	Km (H-31) Plateau lands end. Start Ll. de La Paz.	A section of relatively level plateau lands formed by the gentle western slopes of the Peninsular Range Mountains.	--	--	89	55
15	Km (H-31) Plateau lands end. Start Ll. de La Paz.	Km (J-170) End Ll. de La Paz. Start Sr. de la Laguna.	Highway 1 passes over the level Llano de La Paz. This is the peninsula's lowest and narrowest section.	82	51	--	--
16	Km (J-170) End Ll. de La Paz. Start Sr. de la Laguna.	Km (J-112) Hwy. 1 meets the sea near Los Barriles.	Section through the granitic Sierra de la Laguna and its "arid tropical forest" plant community.	--	--	58	36
17	Km (J-112) Hwy. 1 meets the sea near Los Barriles.	Km (J-93) Junction with the road to La Ribera.	Section along coastal flat lands. Northern portion adjoins the Sea of Cortez coast near the resort towns of Los Barriles and Buena Vista.	19	12	--	--
18	Km (J-93) Junction with the road to La Ribera.	Km (J-35) Hwy.1 meets the sea at San Jose del Cabo.	Highway 1 passes over low hills and plateaus lying between the Sierra de la Laguna to the west and a lesser range to the east.	--	--	60	37
19	Km (J-35) Hwy.1 meets the sea at San Jose del Cabo.	Km (J-0) Highway 1 ends at Cabo San Lucas.	A section of coastal benches and low hills at the peninsula's southern tip.	33	21	--	--

TRANSPENINSULAR HIGHWAY
POINTS OF SPECIAL INTEREST TOUR
Points 29 and 30 are along Highway 19.

NO.	POINT OF INTEREST	HRS	PTS	KM	COMMENTS
1	International boundary monument.	0:20	3	A-9	Historic monument near Bullring by-the-Sea at Tijuana. Photo Ch. 17.
2	Rosarito Beach Hotel.	0:20	2	A-34	Historic hotel, wall decorations, etc. Former 1930s gambling casino.
3	El Mirador (the vista point).	0:10	1	A-84	Fine views of coast and Islas Todos Santos. Adjoins Hwy 1-D.
4	Ensenada -- Tourist Row.	1:00	4	A-109	One of Baja's best shopping areas, plus a taste of a large Mexican city.
5	La Bufadora.	1:00	5	B-14	Intriguing ocean blowhole and fine coastal views. 14-mile side trip.
6	Adobe ruins of mission at El Rosario.	0:30	4	C-55	1.6-mile side trip to ruins overlooking Rio del Rosario. Photo Ch. 19.
7	Excellent desert vegetation.	0:30	3	C-63	Northern edge of Sonoran Desert vegetation region. First cirios.
8	Catavina Boulder Fields.	0:15	2	C-157	Geologically interesting boulder fields and fine desert vegetation.
9	Scammon's Lagoon -- Whale-watching. **	3:00	8	E-208	Major whale calving area. 16-mile side trip. Consider overnight stay.
10	San Ignacio.	0:45	3	E-74	One of Baja's most charming towns. Historic church, square, and palms.
11	Tres Virgenes Volcano and lava flows.	0:15	2	E-42	Lava flows adjoining hwy. Excellent specimens of elephant trees.
12	Santa Rosalia.	2:00	6	E-0	Historic church, copper smelter, French buildings, and harbor.
13	Mulege.	2:00	6	F-136	Savor the town and visit the historic prision and restored mission church.
14	Microwave radio tower and fine scenic view.	0:30	4	F-124	Excellent views of the Sea of Cortez. A 3/4-mile side trip.
15	Loreto	1:00	5	F-197	Historic town -- Site of the mother mission. Visit church and museum.

** A drive, and boat trip at Puerto Lopez Mateos (Chapter 22) may be substituted.

TRANSPENINSULAR HIGHWAY
POINTS OF SPECIAL INTEREST TOUR
Points 29 and 30 are along Highway 19.

NO.	POINT OF INTEREST	HRS	PTS	KM	COMMENTS
16	Nopolo.	0:30	2	G-111	Visit the hotel and tennis courts in this developing resort area.
17	Puerto Escondido.	0:30	2	G-94	Baja's best natural harbor. Trailer court and developing resort area.
18	Vista point north of La Paz.	0:10	1	H-35	Views of La Paz, Llano de La Paz, Sea of Cortez, and islands.
19	La Paz.	4:00	6	H-0	Tour the downtown area and waterfront. Good shopping and hotels.
20	El Triunfo.	1:00	4	J-162	Historic silver mining town. Visit old smelter and cemetery.
21	Santiago.	1:30	5	J-85	Pleasant town and site of a Jesuit mission. Visit the zoological garden.
22	Tropic of Cancer monument.	0:05	1	J-82	Stop and stretch your legs as you enter the tropics. Photo Ch. 23.
23	San Jose del Cabo.	2:00	4	J-33	Tour the town square, church, and developing resort area.
24	Hotel Palmilla	0:30	2	J-26	One of Baja's finest hotels. Walk in if driving large R.V. or trailer.
25	Hotel Twin Dolphin.	0:30	2	J-11	Another of Baja's fine hotels.
26	Cabo San Lucas Vista.	0:10	1	J-5	Stop and celebrate arrival at "Cabo" at this roadside vista of the cape.
27	Hotel Finisterra.	0:20	2	J-0	A fine hotel plus excellent views of the Pacific and inner harbor.
28	Boat trip to the tip of Cabo San Lucas.	2:00	5	J-0	Hire a glass-bottomed boat to visit the Cabo arch and view tropical fish.
29	Todos Santos. (On Hwy 19.)	1:00	3	Hwy 19	A charming historic town and farming area. Jesuit mission site.
30	Botanical Garden.	0:30	2	Hwy 19	Excellent garden of labeled desert plants. Adjacent to the highway.

CHAPTER 14
THE BORDER AREA
AND HIGHWAY 2

This initial chapter of your GRAND TOUR of the Magnificent Peninsula begins with an examination of Highway 2 and the Mexican communities lying along the international border. It is divided into eight sections:

    1 — Tijuana
    2 — Highway 2, Tijuana to Tecate
    3 — Tecate
    4 — Highway 2, Tecate to Mexicali
    5 — Mexicali
    6 — Highway 2, Mexicali to San Luis
    7 — San Luis
    8 — Algodones

Large numbers of tourists enter Mexico at the Tijuana-San Ysidro port-of-entry and simply wish to pass through Tijuana as quickly as possible to head south on Highway 1. If you are one of these, I suggest you read the first two items in the Tijuana section and then proceed to Chapter 17. The two items in question concern entering and leaving Mexico in the Tijuana area.

TIJUANA

We North Americans mispronounce the name of many Mexican communities, but our reference to the city of Tijuana as Tia Juana heads the list. I thought the blame could be laid at the door of the Tijuana Brass, but reference to their music labels shows the name spelled correctly, and travel books of the 1950s note that the problem already existed for many years. In deference to our long suffering Mexican friends, let us proceed to the blackboard with chalk in hand and try to get it right.

The town of Tijuana did not come into existence until the 1870s, almost three and one-half centuries after the Baja peninsula was discovered, and 175 years after the founding of the first Jesuit mission at Loreto in 1697. Today, it has a population of well over one million, is the fourth largest city in Mexico, and is reportedly the fastest growing city in North America.

The portion of Chapter 12 HISTORY concerning the years after the Mexican-American War will provide the community's background. Its rapid rise to prominence came in the 1920s as

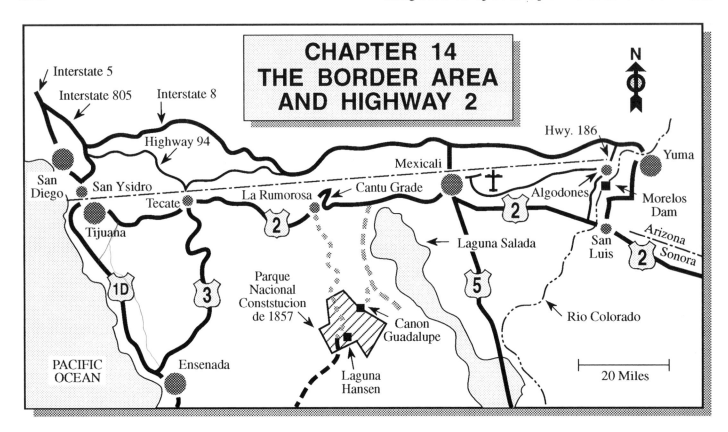

CHAPTER 14
THE BORDER AREA
AND HIGHWAY 2

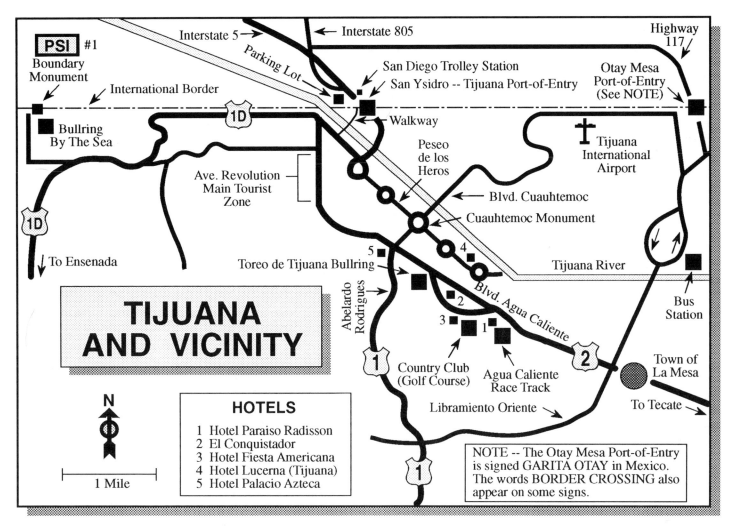

TIJUANA AND VICINITY

PSI #1
Boundary Monument
International Border
Bullring By The Sea
To Ensenada
Ave. Revolution Main Tourist Zone
Interstate 5
Interstate 805
Parking Lot
San Diego Trolley Station
San Ysidro -- Tijuana Port-of-Entry
Walkway
Peseo de los Heros
Blvd. Cuauhtemoc
Cuauhtemoc Monument
Highway 117
Otay Mesa Port-of-Entry (See NOTE)
Tijuana International Airport
Toreo de Tijuana Bullring
Abelardo Rodrigues
Blvd. Agua Caliente
Tijuana River
Bus Station
Town of La Mesa
To Tecate
Country Club (Golf Course)
Agua Caliente Race Track
Libramiento Oriente

N
1 Mile

HOTELS
1 Hotel Paraiso Radisson
2 El Conquistador
3 Hotel Fiesta Americana
4 Hotel Lucerna (Tijuana)
5 Hotel Palacio Azteca

NOTE -- The Otay Mesa Port-of-Entry is signed GARITA OTAY in Mexico. The words BORDER CROSSING also appear on some signs.

the result of prohibition in the United States. Tijuana led the way in attracting visitors from the north interested in gambling, prostitution, and the drowning of sorrows in unnumbered saloons. This *wicked* past is now largely replaced by a modern metropolis with much business activity and more conventional tourist attractions.

Please refer to the TIJUANA AND VICINITY Map. Depicted are the main points of interest and principal travel routes of concern to the first-time visitor. Hundreds of lesser streets are omitted. This *highlight approach* will be used for the community maps throughout this book. Detailed maps are available in a variety of publications obtainable at the border and in almost every hotel and other places frequented by tourists.

ENTERING TIJUANA FROM THE NORTH — In approaching Tijuana from the north, you will be led directly into the port-of-entry from either Interstate 5 or 805. A canopy over the Mexican entry station bears directional signs. (See photo in Chapter 7.)

The directional signs will guide recreation vehicles to the center lanes on the assumption that their drivers will wish to proceed south immediately on Highway 1-D. The offramp for this route

bears sharply to the left a short distance after the border, circles over the entrance road, and heads west directly adjoining the border fence. Follow the signs for *Rosarito* and *Ensenada*. This route skirts Tijuana and most of its traffic, and in a few miles delivers its users to the Pacific coast in the vicinity of the *Bullring by the Sea* . (Follow the Rio Tijuana signs if you wish access Paseo de los Heros and Tijuana's better hotels.)

If you are heading south on Highway 1-D in this manner, you will now wish to move to Chapter 17; but first read the following item if you plan to return to the United States in the Tijuana area.

RETURNING TO THE U.S.A. — In returning north on Highway 1-D, you may enter the United States at San Ysidro or Otay Mesa. The decision on which crossing point to use must be made at the Highway 1-D offramp at the north end of the town of Rosarito. (See the map in Chapter 17.) Here are the advantages and disadvantages of these two alternatives.

SAN YSIDRO — Returning home this way is essentially a retracement of the south-bound Highway 1-D route described above and in Chapter 17. It is largely a sea level route with few hills. Traffic is modest, as most of the route is on a limited access toll road. Then brace yourself for lengthy delays while waiting your turn in line at United States customs. (See comments concerning the ports-of-entry in Chapter 7.)

OTAY MESA — This station was opened in 1985 to help alleviate the lengthy delays experienced at San Ysidro. This route to the border is steeper and a bit more complex than that to San Ysidro, but the crossing delays are usually less. I recommend it for everyone unless you are pulling a trailer. The complications relating to the possibility of taking a wrong turn put the trailerite at a disadvantage. Proceed as follows from Highway 1-D to Otay Mesa.

1. — Exit Highway 1-D at the north end of Rosarito. The exit sign reads "Tijuana Libre." Drive north on the old two-lane Highway 1 through largely undeveloped country. The route is hilly, so some delay may result if slow moving trucks are encountered.

2. — Exit Highway 1 at the top of the grade onto Libramiento Oriente, a four-lane freeway. The exit sign reads "Garita Otay Mesa/Border Crossing." From this exit, it is 3.8 miles to Boulevard Agua Caliente (Highway 2) and an additional 1.7 miles to the bus station turnoff. The freeway ends about one-half mile south of Boulevard Agua Caliente, and heavy city traffic may be encountered from here north to the vicinity of the bus station. Follow signs for the "Aeropuerto" along the way.

3. — From the bus station, climb up the mesa on a one-way highway to an intersection. Turn right here. The sign reads "GARITA DE OTAY." After 0.6 miles turn left at a similar sign. From this last turn it is 1.2 miles on a six-lane divided boulevard to the border. This all sounds a bit difficult, but try it, you'll like it, and once you have it down, you will never use San Ysidro again.

VISITING TIJUANA — If you plan to visit Tijuana for only a short period, why not leave the car behind? There is a 500-car commercial parking lot immediately adjoining the border west of the port-of-entry on the United States side. From the lot, it is about one-half mile over a pleasant walkway to the north end of the Avenida Revolution tourist zone.

As at all the ports-of-entry, the walking circulation is counter-clockwise, so you will return to the United States on the east side of highway. There are elevated pedestrian walkways over the highway on both sides of the border. Customs delays are usually minimal.

Better yet, take the San Diego Trolley to the border and walk into Mexico. The trolley station is adjacent to United States customs on the east side of the highway. By leaving the car at home you escape the need for Mexican insurance, greatly diminish U.S. Customs delays, and avoid traffic and parking problems. There are plenty of taxis, and the distances to most of the tourist attractions are minimal. Consult the map to locate the following places.

AVENIDA REVOLUTION — A seven-block stretch of Ave. Revolution is the main tourist zone. There are many shops, restaurants, and nightclubs. Its northern end is easily reached by the walkway from the border. A few blocks to the west is the principal shopping and business district.

BOULEVARD AGUA CALIENTE — The Tijuana Bullring, Country Club, and Agua Caliente Race Track are all located on the south side of Blvd. Agua Caliente. This same segment of the boulevard also is the location of most of the city's better hotels and motels.

PASEO DE LOS HEROES — This broad boulevard and several other similar thoroughfares lie south of the Rio Tijuana and are centered around the statue of Cuauhtemoc (the last king of the Aztecs, defender of Tenochtitlan, and for many Mexicans, the original patriot). This is the newest section of the downtown area. There are many businesses, government offices, and grassy open areas.

HIGHWAY 2
TIJUANA TO TECATE

All of Baja's highways are constructed to approximately the same engineering standards. Thus, Highway 2 differs little from the Transpeninsular Highway in this regard.

Tijuana's principal east-west street is Agua Caliente. It is also Highway 2. The route crosses Presa Rodriquez (Rodriquez Dam) 14 miles east of downtown Tijuana. Between these two points there is considerable traffic as the highway is also the main four-lane artery for this city and the communities of La Mesa and La Presa. In La Presa, the highway becomes two-lane. East of the dam, traffic is light.

Km-166 PRESA RODRIQUEZ — Here the highway crosses the narrow crest of the concrete Rodriquez Dam. Natural runoff captured by this structure was Tijuana's principal source of water prior to 1960. The reservoir ran dry in 1961 as the result of rapid population growth and a series of dry years. Runoff is now supplemented by water piped in from La Mision, south of Tijuana on the Pacific coast, and from the Rio Colorado to the east.

From Presa Rodriquez to Tecate, Highway 2 passes through pleasant rolling hills. There are scattered rural homes, with the flatter lands utilized for farming, grazing, and olive orchards. The underlying rock is granite. Note the many hills that are being fractured and eroded into large, light-colored, granite boulders. When these boulders occur adjacent to the highway, they create natural billboards used to advertise political parties and their candidates.

Km-163 BYPASS HIGHWAY — Highway 2 is joined at this point by an expressway that bypasses the towns of La Mesa and La Presa. Its western terminus is a short distance south of the

Tijuana bus station. (I am advised that this highway has now been completed easterly to Tecate but the deadline for producing this 4th edition has not permitted me to investigate its exact location.)

Km-133 TECATE — Between Tijuana and Tecate, Highway 2 has slowly climbed the western slopes of the Peninsular Range Mountains. A sign at the western edge of Tecate marks the 500-meter (1,650 feet) elevation point.

TECATE

Tecate's population of 85,000 is supported by agriculture and growing numbers of assembly plants operating under the maquiladora program. It is also the home of the Tecate Brewery. As with other communities in Mexico, it is amazing how a town with this many people is compressed into such a relatively small area.

The community contains several tourist-oriented stores, the largest being the FONART (Centro Artesanal), but its chief attributes for the traveler are the port-of-entry and the town's location at the junction of Highways 2 and 3. Highway 3 is described in Chapter 16, but it should to be noted here that it is a very pleasant way to travel south and is the recommended route for tourists returning to the United States from Ensenada.

There is no adjoining community on the United States side of the border; thus, there is little commuter traffic and usually little time is spent waiting in line. Mexican customs and immigration offices are found immediately on the right when entering Mexico. There are also several auto insurance offices within one block of the crossing. Parking is usually available on the city streets. The Motel El Dorado lies 0.8 miles west of the Highway 2 and 3 junction on the north side of Highway 2. The Hotel Hacienda is found 0.7 miles further along, in the same direction. Tecate has no trailer courts.

I am advised by a reliable source that Tecate is the only Baja border town that does not support prostitution, a notable distinction. It may be the only one in the world. I must hasten to add that this bit of information does not reflect my own personal observations. On to Mexicali.

HIGHWAY 2 TECATE TO MEXICALI

East of Tecate, Highway 2 continues to climb gradually upward. Most of the agricultural land has been left behind, to the west. The land becomes steeper and is vegetated largely with chaparral.

Km-109 — At approximately this point the steeper lands are left behind, to the west, and the highway enters

a broad plateau with views of the main peaks of the Peninsular Range Mountains to the east.

Km-80 VEGETATIONAL CHANGE — Starting near this point and continuing for the next 20 Km (13 miles), you will see a scattering of Parry pinon pine trees and low-growing California junipers. This is the best location for observing these species from Baja's highway system. More extensive stands may be viewed by taking the side trip noted below at **Km 72**. Pinon pine produces cones containing large nut-like seeds which are easily gathered when they mature in May. They make good eating and may be found marketed as *Indian Nuts* .

SIDE TRIP
Km-72 ROAD TO NATIONAL PARK - A secondary road leaves Highway 2 to the right (south) 0.1 miles east of this point. Immediately east of this junction is a CONASUPO store. This road provides the backdoor route to the Parque Nacional Constitucion de 1857, one of Baja's two National Parks. It passes through excellent stands of Parry pinon pine and numerous unimproved places to camp. Be extremely careful with fire in this area. Pinon pine burns with great intensity and is very slow to regenerate as its heavy seeds cannot be spread by the wind.

It is 38 miles to Laguna Hanson, the park's principal attraction. This route is recommended only for pickup and van-type vehicles. See full description and map of the park in Chapter 16.

End **SIDE TRIP**.

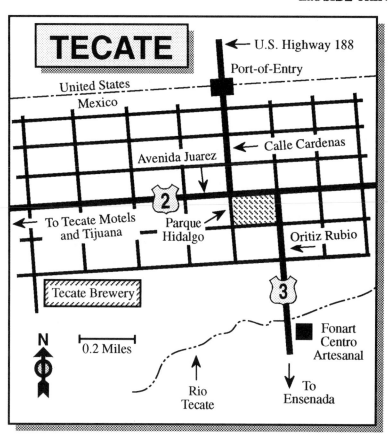

Km-68 LA RUMOROSA — Here, at over 4,000 feet in elevation, lies the small town of La Rumorosa. It contains a modest restaurant and a PEMEX station but is of little other interest to the tourist. Its chief claim to fame is that it lies at the top of the grade. What grade? You will shortly discover:

THE CANTU GRADE — East of La Rumorosa you will be making a 15-mile-long descent of the eastern escarpment of the Peninsular Range Mountains. It is the most dramatic segment of highway in the Baja peninsula. This steep and rapid drop, combined with the lengthy and gradual grade to the east, is the peninsula's best demonstration of its fault block mountain structure. (See Chapter 9 GEOLOGY.)

Although the highway is well constructed, careful driving is required. Slow moving vehicles and high winds can be a problem, and snow may be encountered during winter storms. On the positive side are the excellent views to be had of the United States, to the north, and Laguna Salada and the San Felipe Desert, to the east. Also, note the light blue pipeline north of the highway. It brings water from the Rio Colorado to Tijuana. Pumping stations are in view at the base of the grade and near the conduit's midpoint.

SIDE TRIP
Km-27 CANYON GUADALUPE — A secondary road leaves Highway 2 to the south a short distance west of **Km-27**. It provides access to one of Baja's hidden hot spring oasis, Canyon Guadalupe. Nestled at the foot of the magestic Sierra de Juarez's eastern escarpment, it has long been a favoite of offroad vehicle fans. In 1987 most of the route into the spring was upgaded to seconday road standards.

The road roughly parallels the western edge of Laguna Salada for 26.7 miles. At this point take a branch road to the left an

Daughter Barbara poses with the Green Angels at La Rumorosa at the western edge of the Cantu Grade. Note the pinyon pine trees behind the building.

additional 7.7 miles to the campground. The last 1.5 miles crosses the arroyo several times among granite bolders. This final section of road is clearly not suited for larger R.V.'s.

Hot spring waters are piped to rock tubs at each campsite among native fan palms and other desert vegetation. The per night fee in 1989 was $6.00 per night. A delightful spot. Indian petroglyphs may be visited further into the mountains. End **SIDE TRIP**.

SIDE TRIP
Km-25 LAGUNA SALADA — A sign for Playa Laguna Salada marks the junction of a secondary road which leads south for 0.5 miles. to the north end of Laguna Salada. Here are located a modest cafe and camping area on the beach. It is also the base for fishing boats that work the lake. This is one of the few places in Baja where one may camp at the edge of a lake and this feature, combined with the dramatic mountains to the west and lower ranges to the east, make it a pleasant spot. End **SIDE TRIP**.

VALLE DE MEXICALI — Approximately halfway between Laguna Salada and the city of Mexicali on Highway 2 lies the agricultural community of Colonia Progreso. This town marks the western edge of the vast Valle de Mexicali agricultural area which stretches east to the Rio Colorado. It is Baja's largest farming area. The history of its development is contained in the closing section of Chapter 12 HISTORY.

HIGHWAY 5 JUNCTION — Highway 2 joins Highway 5 near the southern edge of the city of Mexicali. (See MEXICALI Map)

MEXICALI

Tourism statistics indicate that Mexicali is the final destination point for 15 percent of the foreign visitors who enter the state of Baja California. The comparable figure for Tijuana is 34 percent and 23 percent for Ensenada. In spite of Mexicali's reasonably high share of total visits, the city has a definite non-tourist flavor. One can only speculate that most of her visitors are from farming communities in the nearby Imperial Valley and are bent on activities not usually associated with tourism. The economic well-being of Mexicali's 600,000 people rests on industry, agricultural activities in the Valle de Mexicali, and on its being the capital of the state of Baja California.

Mexicali's principal business district adjoins the international border generally SE from the port-of-entry. Most of its newer development is taking place in the Centro Civico-Comercial some two miles south of the border. Here are located state and federal office buildings, bus station, bullring, and the pink zone (shops, theaters, restaurants, etc). The city's hotels and motels cluster around the intersection of Boulevard Benito Juarez and Boulevard Justo Sierra.

The Cantu Grade. Baja's most dramatic segment of highway. Its eastern end lies in the desert while there are high elevation pinyon pines at its western terminus.

Tourists entering Mexico at Mexicali and heading south to San Felipe need merely follow Calzada Lopez Mateos (a multilaned boulevard) SE through town. The railroad lies in the median strip for the first two miles and will serve to keep you on *track*. Follow the signs for San Felipe. See Chapter 15 for a full description of the Highway 5 route from Mexicali to the San Felipe area.

Motorists waiting their turn to enter the United States line up east of the port-of-entry on Avenida Cristobal Colon. This street directly adjoins the border fence and carries one-way, west-bound traffic. Travelers returning north might best enter Cristobal Colon at its eastern end (via Benito Juarez and Justo Sierra) to most judiciously assume their place in line.

HWY. 2 MEXICALI TO SAN LUIS

The junction of Highways 2 and 5 is near the southern outskirts of Mexicali. The nature of the intersection is shown on the MEXICALI Map. This is a busy industrial area so drive with care.

It is 65 km (40 miles) from the above referenced junction to the Rio Colorado and an additional 3 km (2 miles) to San Luis. From the junction to the river, the entire highway is four-laned, straight, and level. In terms of roadside activity it may be divided into three sections:

1. — The westerly 6 miles is adjoined by numerous industrial buildings. The railroad paralleling much of this section serves these facilities.

2. — East of the industrial area, Highway 2 passes through the heart of the Valle de Mexicali agricultural area but, initially, the highway is lined with scores of farm dwellings and garden plots reflecting the nearness of the city.

3. — Approximately halfway between Mexicali and the Rio Colorado the city's influence ceases. The highway then passes through pleasant, well-ordered farms watered by an extensive irrigation ditches.

Highway 2 crosses the Rio Colorado on a two-lane toll bridge and enters the state of Sonora.

SAN LUIS

San Luis is a town of 135,000 people in the Mexican state of Sonora. Tourists may enter or leave Mexico here, as at any of Baja's ports-of-entry. No Mexican car permit is required to pass through this small section of the Mexican mainland en route to the peninsula.

The main street of San Luis is also Highway 2. At the most westerly traffic light a turn to the north will lead to the port-of-entry only one block away. Cars returning to the United States line up east of the port-of-entry on the street that directly parallels the border fence. Drivers should access this street several blocks to the east of the above referenced light to most conveniently locate the end of the line.

San Luis is visited by many tourists from the large city of Yuma, Arizona, 23 miles to the NW. It thus contains many shops and other tourist-oriented activities. Mexican immigration offices and insurance outlets are present near the crossing.

ALGODONES

Algodones is a small farm community located on the international border directly west of the Rio Colorado. It has the most lightly used of Baja's ports-of-entry. The station is open from 6:00 AM to 8:00 PM. Immigration and insurance offices are adjacent to the crossing.

Algodones may be reached from Highway 2 over a level, paved highway that parallels the Rio Colorado. Travel distance is 18.1 miles through pleasant agricultural country. The junction of the two highways is 2.0 miles west of the Rio Colorado near **Km-3**. Travelers may stop and look at the Morelos Dam a short distance south of the community. It diverts all of the water used to irrigate the Valle de Mexicali.

The Morelos Dam on the Rio Colorado near the town of Algodones.

BAJA CALIFORNIA

WHERE THE DESERT MEETS THE SEA

CHAPTER 15
HIGHWAY 5

Chapter 15 describes the Highway 5 route from the international border at Mexicali to its junction with Highway 1 at Laguna Chapala 267.5 miles to the south . All of this road is constructed to highway standard, but at press time the oiled surface terminated at the community of Puertecitos 180.1 miles south of the border. The southerly 87.4 miles remains to be paved.

In the previous edition of this book I noted that it was reported that this highway would be completed by 1989. In the 3-years that have transpired since, nothing new has occurred. For now, the unpaved section is heavily washboarded and should be traveled only by pickups, vans and other vehicles designed to take rough treatment.

Once the new highway is completed, it will provide a major alternative to Highway 1 for accessing the southern half of Baja California. People approaching the peninsula from Arizona, Nevada, and other states to the north and east will no longer have to travel to, and through, the Tijuana-Ensenada area to head south. The new highway joins Highway 1 near **Km C-229** a point approximately 324 miles south of Tijuana. Almost 1/3 of the Transpeninsular Highway, and the congestion of the two metropolitan areas can thus be bypassed.

And travelers heading south to Baja from northern California, Oregon, Washington, and Canada along U. S. Interstate 5 might choose to route themselves from Bakersfield, California to Mexicali through the Mojave Desert and, believe it or not, bypass *The Jungle*, and those delightful monuments to man's insanity, the Los Angeles-San Diego Freeway systems. It is approximately 580 miles from Bakersfield to Lake Chapala via Tijuana and Highway 1, and 607 miles using Highway 5 when entering Mexico at Mexicali. The small additional mileage of only 27 miles should be more than compensated for by safer, easier, faster, and more scenic driving conditions.

Even travelers from the Los Angeles area may choose the Highway 5 alternative by traveling east on Interstate 10 toward Mexicali. Those from San Diego can also easily reach Mexicali over Interstate 8. The completion of Highway 5 should thus bring about a dramatic reduction in the use of the Transpeninsular Highway as a route to southern Baja. Tourism in the towns along Highway 5 will increase accordingly.

HIGHWAY 5 OVERVIEW — Reference to the GEOLOGIC PROVINCES Map in Chapter 9 GEOLOGY will show that the portion of Highway 5 between Mexicali and Puertecitos is within the *Basin and Range* Geologic Province. The western edge of this province is the escarpment of the Peninsular Range Mountains. This steep-faced cliff rises dramatically from near sea level to over 10,000 feet in elevation. The escarpment is in view from this section of the highway, although in most places its base is obscured by lower intervening ranges of mountains. The latter are typical of the north-south ranges found throughout the Basin and Range Province.

From Puertecitos to Laguna Chapala the highway passes through the edge of the Peninsular Range Mountains and moderately steep terrain is encountered in many places. Much of this section of road is within sight of the Sea of Cortez. Scenic qualities are thus considerably better than along Highway 1 far to the west.

Most of the area traversed by Highway 5 lies in the rain shadow of Baja's highest segment of the Peninsular Range Mountains and is thus its driest area. Reference to the VEGETATIVE REGIONS Map in Chapter 10 shows that the area's vegetation has been classified as the San Felipe Desert portion of the Sonoran Desert Region. Few of Baja's large and attractive species of desert plants are present here. The area's vegetation is thus rather drab. Plant variety improves west of the Highway 5 junction with the secondary road to Calamajue and is comparable with the better plant areas seen along Highway 1.

MEXICALI — It is approximately 6 miles from the Mexicali port-of-entry to the junction of Highways 2 and 5 over the multilaned Calzada (wide avenue) Lopez Mateos. See the MEXICALI Map in Chapter 14. The accompanying text provides suggestions for approaching the port-of-entry when returning to the United States and other information about Mexicali.

VALLE DE MEXICALI — Highway 5 is fringed by urban activity for a short distance south of its junction with Highway 2; however, this is soon replaced by agricultural fields. This farming region in the Basin and Range Province is called the Valle de Mexicali. It is irrigated by an extensive series of canals emanating from the *Presa Morelos* (Morelos Dam). This facility extends across the Rio Colorado just south of the international border near the town of Algodones. (See map and photo in Chapter 14.)

The history of the valley's development is indicated in the final section (SUMMARY OF ACTIVITIES IN THE NORTH) in Chapter 12 HISTORY. The agricultural area extends south to approximately **Km-46**.

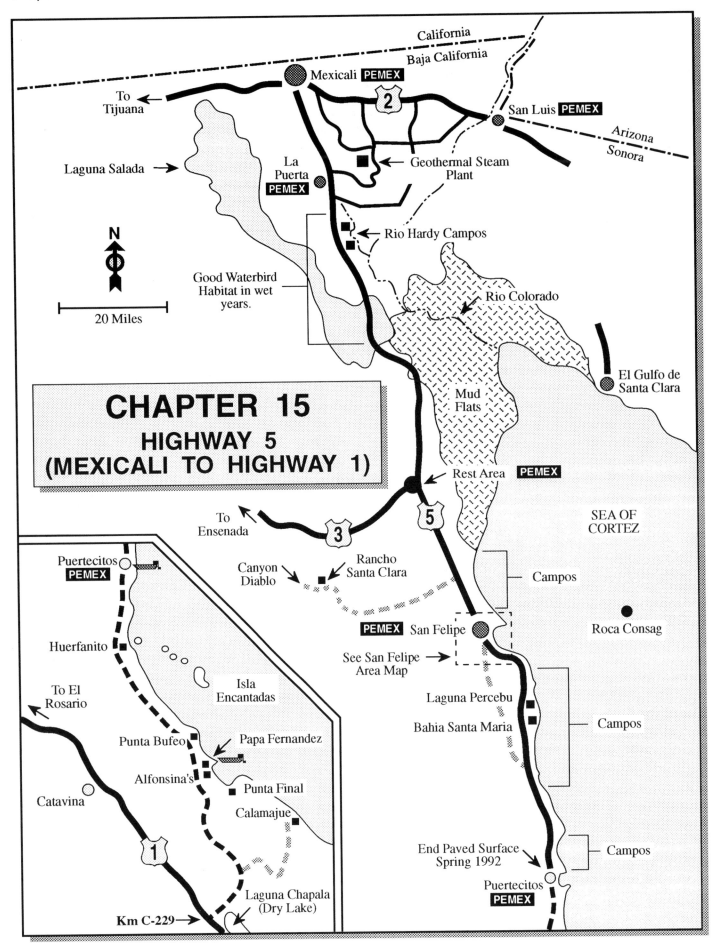

California
Baja California

To Tijuana

Mexicali **PEMEX**

2

San Luis **PEMEX**

Arizona
Sonora

Laguna Salada

La Puerta **PEMEX**

Geothermal Steam Plant

N

20 Miles

Rio Hardy Campos

Good Waterbird Habitat in wet years.

Rio Colorado

El Gulfo de Santa Clara

Mud Flats

CHAPTER 15
HIGHWAY 5
(MEXICALI TO HIGHWAY 1)

Rest Area **PEMEX**

To Ensenada

3

5

SEA OF CORTEZ

Canyon Diablo

Rancho Santa Clara

Campos

PEMEX San Felipe

Roca Consag

See San Felipe Area Map

Puertecitos **PEMEX**

Huerfanito

Laguna Percebu

Bahia Santa Maria

Campos

To El Rosario

Isla Encantadas

Punta Bufeo

Papa Fernandez

Alfonsina's

Punta Final

Catavina

Calamajue

End Paved Surface Spring 1992

Campos

1

Puertecitos **PEMEX**

Laguna Chapala (Dry Lake)

Km C-229

(Km-20) GEOTHERMAL STEAM — Approximately five miles east of the highway at this point lies the Cerro Prieto geothermal steam wells and its related electric generating plant. The facility produces 620 megawatts of electricity, making it the second largest producer of geothermal steam energy in the world. It is exceeded only by the Geysers development north of San Francisco in the United States.

If the air is cool, extensive clouds of water vapor may be seen rising into the air above the wells. These may be visible during the morning hours but often are absent in the afternoon.

(Km-30) LA PUERTA — A small, Valle de Mexicali farming community with a cafe, store, and PEMEX Station.

RIO HARDY AND RIO COLORADO — The Rio Colorado and its short tributary, the Rio Hardy, roughly parallel Highway 5 on the east from approximately **Km-50** to **Km-72**. During most years there is no water in the Rio Colorado as it is all diverted for domestic and agricultural purposes. During the early 1980s, SW United States experienced heavy rainfall, and water flowed down the Rio Colorado in excess of the storage capacity of its reservoirs. As a result, most of the older Campo communities along the Rio Hardy were flooded. In spring 1992 a new campo (Campo Mayor) had been developed on the river at **Km 55**. There are also other campos located easterly from the highway which I have not investigated. These campos advertise bird hunting and fishing.

(Km 72) LAGUNA SALADA — At this point, Highway 5 lies on top of a 9-mile-long levee constructed across the southern end of Laguna Salada. The lake was filled during the flood years referred to above, but at press time there was no water in sight. During wet years, there are many waterbirds and some limited marsh lands along the northern shore. The San Felipe desert vegetation starts south of the lake.

(Km-104) MUD FLATS — In this vicinity, the desert vegetation is interrupted and the highway passes over the edge of the extensive mud flats that make up the delta area of the Rio Colorado. They are also closely approached near **Km-111**. These mud areas are up to 15 miles in width and extend easterly from the highway from Laguna Salada to near **Km-174**, a distance of almost 60 miles.

Wildlife experts report that the Rio Colorado delta once consisted of extensive marsh lands that made excellent waterbird habitat. The Auto Club map of Baja California still identifies these areas with the symbol for marsh lands. Moisture-loving vegetation has now disappeared as a result of the water-regulating effects of the reservoirs along the river. This situation provides another example of mankind's environmental compromises.

A section of the Rio Hardy in the level agricultural plain between Mexicali and San Felipe.

SIDE TRIP
(Km-141) JUNCTION OF HIGHWAYS 3 AND 5 — It is 210 km (130 miles) to Ensenada via Highway 3. See Chapter 16 for a full description. The easterly portion of this route provides an interesting side trip from Highway 5. It is 28-miles to the base of the majestic escarpment of the Peninsular Range Mountains, through terrain typical of the Basin and Range Geological Province. A further 5-mile climb reaches the top of the grade.

The vegetation of this Highway 3 segment of the San Felipe Desert is considerably more interesting than that in view from most of Highway 5. This is particularly true of the 5-mile section which climbs up the escarpment. An outstanding stand of barrel cactus is present at the top of the grade.

A fancy picnic area, restaurant, and PEMEX were under construction at this Highway 3 and 5 junction in early 1992. I can't conceive of why a picnic area is needed at such a place and will make book that it will shortly be in ruins.

A roadside residence and cafe lie about 0.7 miles south of the Highway 3 and 5 junction. Of particular interest are the antique gas pumps that require pumping fuel into their glass containers by hand. They are still in use. The new PEMEX at the junction will no doubt put it out of business. End **SIDE TRIP**.

ROCA CONSAG — After proceeding south of the Highway 3 and 5 junction, start looking to the SE, over the Sea of Cortez, for a view of *Roca Consag* (Consag Rock). It is a steep-sided, isolated pinnacle rising sharply from the sea to a height of 286 feet. It lies approximately due east from San Felipe at a distance of 18 miles offshore. Fishing boats from the town use it as a destination point.

The rock is named in honor of Padre Fernando Consag, one of the most prominent of Baja's Jesuit priests. In 1746 he conducted a maritime exploration of the northern reaches of the Sea of Cortez and the mouth of the Rio Colorado.

Also look ahead for several isolated peaks along the coast of the Sea of Cortez. They lie only a few degrees to the east of the line of the highway. These peaks are situated immediately north of San Felipe. They can be used to judge one's progress in the journey to this community.

(Km-172) SAN PEDRO MARTIR MOUNTAINS —At this location, high points on the main ridge of the Sierra San Pedro Martir are approximately due west from the highway. The principal peak is 10,126-foot Picacho del Diablo, Baja's highest point. As at other places along Highway 5, the base of the mountain's eastern escarpment is obscured from view by intervening lower ranges.

Picacho del Diablo (the Devil's Pike) lies near the center of the Parque Nacional Sierra San Pedro Martir. The park and its pine and fir forests may best be reached from Highway 1 south of Colonet. It is described in Chapter 18.

(Km-174) CAMPOS — Near this point is the southern end of the Rio Colorado mud flats. The desert vegetation now directly adjoins the sea. As a result, the coast between here and San Felipe is lined with a series of campos. (See comments under San Felipe below.) Each campo is reached over a short dirt road extending easterly from Highway 5.

> **BOB & JEAN 4X4**

(Km-180) CANON DIABLO — Leaving Highway 5 to the right (west) is the most direct route to Canon Diablo and Canon Diablito. It is trip #1 of the "Bob and Jean 4x4" Recommendations presented in Chapter 3. The two canyons are cut into the steep eastern escarpment of the Sierra San Pedro Martir. They offer year-round streams, pools and waterfalls along with a shady camping spot. The road into the canyons is west from Rancho Santa Clara as shown on the AAA map. This a trip of about 32 miles.

(Km-191) SAN FELIPE ARCH — A large, white, double-arch monument is constructed within a traffic circle at this point. It marks the entrance to the community of San Felipe.

SAN FELIPE — One mile east of the entrance arch on Highway 5 lies another traffic circle. Highway 5 turns southward at this point. Continue straight ahead for the town's downtown area. Also located at the traffic circle is one of the town's PEMEX Stations. Diesel fuel has not been available. It can be obtained at the diesel storage area at the southern end of the harbor south of town.

The community's main shopping area is located on Calzada Chetumal and Mar de Cortez within a few blocks of the junction of these two streets. See the SAN FELIPE AREA Map for the location of the principal hotels and trailer courts. The trailer courts in San Felipe and the El Faro court located south of town are good-to-excellent facilities and are in sharp contrast to most of the campos described below.

The San Felipe-Puertecitos area is one of Baja's six principal tourist areas. This is due in large measure to its location only a few miles from the United States. It can thus be reached on weekend trips and is particularly busy on holiday weekends. Tourism statistics show that more tourists visit the San Felipe area than the entire peninsula served by Highway 1 south of Ensenada.

Perhaps because of this ease of access, some of the area's visitors fall into the category of what one source describes as an *unruly brand of tourist*, particularly on three-day weekends. There are long, sandy beaches both north and south of town. These are an inviting environment for the owners of motorcycles, dune buggies, and other types of off-road vehicles.

Adjoining the beaches are dozens of campos. They vary in size but generally consist of a group of modest residences and trailers owned by Norte Americanos. The mandatory decoration for these dwellings appear to be signs appropriated from the highways and other public places north of the border.

It would also appear that ownership of some form of open-air, specially crafted dune buggy is required equipment. Although I am sure that the great majority of the campo people do not fall in the unruly category, the San Felipe-Puertecitos area, without question, has an atmosphere quite different from that found in other parts of the peninsula.

The double-arch monument at the entrance to San Felipe.

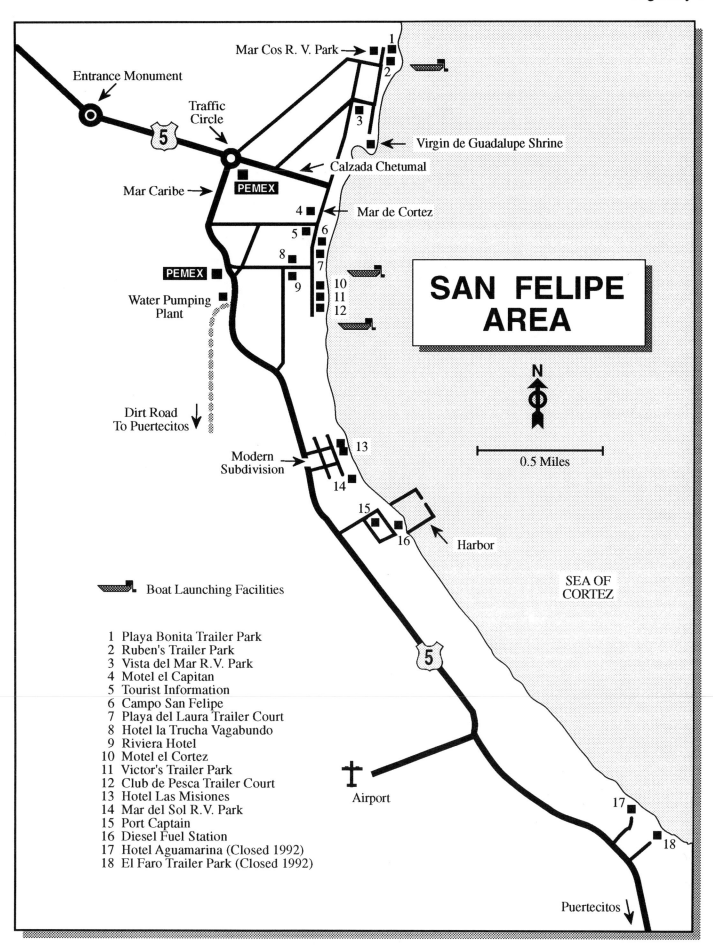

Entrance Monument

Traffic Circle

Mar Cos R. V. Park →

Virgin de Guadalupe Shrine

Calzada Chetumal

Mar Caribe →

PEMEX

Mar de Cortez

PEMEX

Water Pumping Plant

Dirt Road To Puertecitos

Modern Subdivision →

SAN FELIPE AREA

N

0.5 Miles

Harbor

SEA OF CORTEZ

Airport

Boat Launching Facilities

1 Playa Bonita Trailer Park
2 Ruben's Trailer Park
3 Vista del Mar R.V. Park
4 Motel el Capitan
5 Tourist Information
6 Campo San Felipe
7 Playa del Laura Trailer Court
8 Hotel la Trucha Vagabundo
9 Riviera Hotel
10 Motel el Cortez
11 Victor's Trailer Park
12 Club de Pesca Trailer Court
13 Hotel Las Misiones
14 Mar del Sol R.V. Park
15 Port Captain
16 Diesel Fuel Station
17 Hotel Aguamarina (Closed 1992)
18 El Faro Trailer Park (Closed 1992)

Puertecitos ↓

The dark hill in the photo's left sector is Punta San Felipe. San Felipe and its harbor are to the right of the point.

Lying south of San Felipe is a breakwater-lined harbor. It is the home port for many of the shrimp boats that ply the shallow waters of the northern Sea of Cortez. Conventional fishing is good in the area, but launching small boats is complicated by the high tides associated with the constricted upper end of the Sea of Cortez. These may exceed twenty feet. Thus, there are no marinas, and launching ramps are usable only at high tide.

San Felipe is home for Tony Reyes Fishing Tours. This firm charters a large sportfishing vessel that travels to the Midriff Islands 200 miles south in the Sea of Cortez. For information contact The Long Fin, 4010 E. Chapman Ave. Suite D, Orange CA 92669 (714) 538 8010.

SAN FELIPE TO PUERTECITOS — Puertecitos is the approximate dividing point between the Basin and Range Geological Province to the north and the Peninsular Range Province to the south. With few exceptions, the coastline between San Felipe and Puertecitos is formed by level terrain with almost continuous sandy beaches and shallow offshore depths. Mountains start south of Puertecitos and a majority of the coast consists of rocky bluffs or shingle beaches with deep water close to shore. Thus, both swimming and the launching of small boats at high tide is far more easily accomplished north of Puertecitos.

It is 56.1 miles (paved) from San Felipe to Puertecitos and an additional 87.4 miles (unpaved) from Puertecitos to Highway 1 at Laguna Chapala (total 143.5 miles). The mileage figures below start at San Felipe. There were no kilometer posts in place when this account was prepared.

1.1 Miles — The San Felipe sea water pumping plant adjoins the north side of the highway. An old dirt surface road toward Puertecitos leaves the highway directly in front of this facility. After 35 miles, it joins Highway 5.

2.7 Miles — A blacktop road leads to the San Felipe harbor and its adjoining industrial park. Note that most vessels are moored along the outer breakwater. This is because there is no water in the inshore portions of the basin at low tide.

6.5 Miles — Highway junction. An oiled surface highway to the airport runs straight ahead (west). Highway 5 veers to the left (SE).

9.4 Miles — A branch oiled road leads left (east) to the Hotel Aguamarina (Closed in 1992).

10.8 Miles — A concrete road leads in a short distance to the El Faro Beach Trailer Park. Its sign boasts that it is the finest resort in Baja, and it does appear to be an excellent facility although closed in 1992. Between here and Puertecitos you will encounter dozens of side roads leading to beach-side campos.

56.1 Miles — Arrive at Puertecitos. The paved road ended here in spring 1992. The road to the south is built to highway standards except for a short segment through the community of Puertecitos. The eventual paved highway will no doubt pass a short distance inland.

PUERTECITOS — This community surrounds a well protected but very shallow natural harbor. There is a boat launching ramp on the north side of the entrance to the cove. Near the head of the cove is the Posada de Orozco, a cafe and PEMEX station. Camping has been permitted nearby on the beach. There is a nearby airstrip.

Puertecitos consists of several hundred homes owned mostly by Norte Americanos. The quality of these structures is generally well above that found in the campos, but the community clearly bears the special flavor of the San Felipe-Puertecitos area. It is no doubt the world's leading depository for stolen road signs. No house is complete without one or more. Dune buggies are also in plentiful supply. Perhaps the highpoint is a very small but prominent outhouse bearing the delightful label "Hoppy's El Stinko House."

PUERTECITOS SOUTH TO HIGHWAY 1 — There are a few small resorts between Puertecitos and Highway 1. Signs announcing lots for rent and new campos are also appearing. There are many good places to drive to camp sites on the seacoast over dirt roads from 1/4-to-1/2 miles in length. Some of these will no doubt be taken over by campos but for now this section of coast has little development. Perhaps the extreme shortage of fresh water in the area will keep it that way. Also there are few good sand beaches. Most coastal areas are rocky making boat launching and swimming access a bit difficult.

<u>74.6 Miles</u> — Side road to the Huerfanito fish camp and camping area. Fishing boats are for rent.

<u>82.1 Miles</u> — A small store "Camp of the Five Islands" lies west of the road. Its beer and soft drink cooler is a welcome oasis when the temperatures start rising.

<u>96.6 Miles</u> — A dirt road leads to the east and in <u>0.7 miles</u> arrives at the small Punta Bufeo Resort. Most of its buildings are made of stone. Those along the beach are private residences. Inland a short distance is a small but attractive restaurant and three rental cabins.

<u>102.3 Miles</u> — A <u>0.6 mile</u> long side road leads to the Papa Fernandez Resort and its dirt air strip. It offers several modest cabins, concrete boat ramp, and fishing pangas for rent. A dirt road leads westerly a short distance to a good camping area at Punta Willard. Papa Fernandez founded his resort many years ago and in spring 1989 was still greeting visitors at the age of 94. Stop by and say hello.

<u>106.1 Miles</u> — A <u>0.8 mile</u> long secondary road leads to Bahia San Luis Gonzaga and the southern end of a long row of vacation homes with an outstanding sand beach on their eastern flank. A dirt airstrip is on the other side. At the north end of the residential area is Alfonsina's, a modest hotel offering four cot-filled rooms and a restaurant.

Highway 5 moves inland at this point and leaves the Sea of Cortez behind. The road passes over relatively level terrain southward to the <u>120.3 mile</u> point noted below.

<u>116.5 Miles</u> — A low standard dirt road branches to the east and arrives at the Punta Final development in <u>9.1 miles</u>. (I have not driven this road.) When visited by sea in 1984 there were a group of about 30 houses and trailers owned by Norte Americanos most of whom arrive by private aircraft

on a nearby dirt strip. There was no resort facility. Small boats can be launched at low tide from a sand spit connecting the peninsular shore with a small nearby island.

<u>120.3 Miles</u> — At this point the highway enters more mountainous terrain. The desert vegetation ahead improves in aesthetic appeal and many granite boulders begin to appear. It is similar, but not of as high a quality, as the Catavina Boulder Fields area along Highway 1.

SIDE TRIP
<u>129.9 Miles</u> — A good quality secondary road branches to the left (north) and arrives at the fish camp of Calamajue in <u>23.0 miles</u>. The camp houses the single male fishermen while families live at a village some 1/2 mile inland. A few camp spots are available on the shingle beach north of the camp.

My trip into Calamajue provided one of the most pleasurable experiences I have had in Baja California. The area's metamorphosed rock provides road building material that permits a relatively smooth ride with minimal washboarding. In my view, it is the best secondary road in the peninsula. The surrounding mountains are also very scenic and the soil supports a far greater growth of annual plants than most other places. I hope you might arrive as similar conclusions. End **SIDE TRIP**.

<u>143.5 Miles</u> — Junction with Highway 1 near **Km C-229**. The dry lake bed of Laguna Chapala lies south of the junction point. There is a small cafe and residence west of Highway 1 near the junction point.

The Hotel Las Misiones. Punta San Felipe lies in the background.

CHAPTER 16
HIGHWAY 3

This chapter describes the two separate sections of Highway 3. They are Baja's most lightly used highways; yet road construction standards are as good as anywhere in the peninsula. Both sections traverse hilly-to-mountainous terrain and offer good scenery.

HIGHWAY 3 OVERVIEW

TECATE TO HIGHWAY 1 NEAR ENSENADA — This 106 km (66 mile) segment of Highway 3 passes through rolling hills covered with chaparral. Also present are several flat valleys devoted to agricultural. There are no large communities, and in the spring the green countryside is very pleasant. It resembles the area surrounding the cities of southern California in the United States but is without the massive intrusion of urbanization. It has the type of highway scenery one would like to admire on a Sunday drive.

This section of Highway 3 also provides tourists northbound on Highway 1 with the opportunity to cross into the United States at the lightly used port-of-entry at Tecate. I do not understand why anyone who has been to Ensenada would return home any other way. (See the port-of-entry discussion in Chapter 7.)

ENSENADA TO HIGHWAY 5 — Containing 196 km (122 miles), this section of Highway 3 is almost exactly twice the length of the first segment. It also passes through hilly, and in some places, quite steep terrain. However, most of the route is over relatively gentle plateaus and valleys. There are few communities.

This section of highway offers travelers from the Yuma, Arizona area a means of reaching Ensenada and the area to the south without passing through San Diego and Tijuana. If your purpose is to see Mexico, why not drive through it, and leave the United States freeway system to the less fortunate. (This Highway 3 alternative will become unneccessary when oiling of the new highway from San Felipe south to Lake Chapala is completed. See Chapter 15).

TECATE — This community and the route to the Tecate port-of-entry are described in Chapter 14. Only about one mile of Highway 3 lies within the community. Traffic is moderate to light. Northbound travelers should have little trouble finding the crossing point.

The hills between Tecate and Valle de las Palmas are made-up of granite rock. The surface areas have been fractured and eroded into thousands of light-colored boulders. This coloration and erosion pattern is typical of granitic rock areas.

(Km-29) VALLE DE LAS PALMAS — Here is a beautiful valley surrounded by hills. It is planted with grain, grapes, and olive and citrus orchards. To the south, the highway passes through a series of similar valleys.

(Km-76) VALLE DE LA CALAFIA — This broad, flat valley is planted exclusively with vineyards and is home to the DOMECO Winery. It is a modern facility and produces *Pedro Domeco* wine. The overall setting is the match for anything available in the wine country north of San Francisco in Alta California. There are no public tasting rooms or organized tours. However, a trip through the plant can be arranged upon request.

(Km-79) GUADALUPE — The community of Guadalupe lies a short distance to the right (west) of the highway in another valley devoted largely to vineyards. This pleasant spot is the site of the last mission (no ruins) founded in Baja California. It saw service for only seven years (1834-1840).

The Valle de la Calafia framed in the archways of the DOMECO winery.

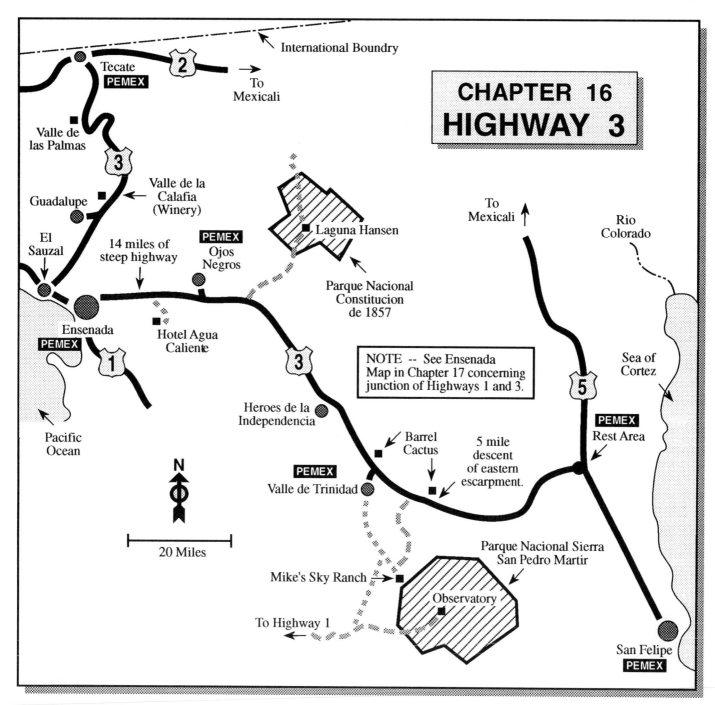

International Boundry

Tecate
PEMEX

2

To
Mexicali

Valle de
las Palmas

3

Guadalupe

Valle de la
Calafia
(Winery)

El
Sauzal

14 miles of
steep highway

PEMEX
Ojos
Negros

Laguna Hansen

To
Mexicali

Rio
Colorado

Parque Nacional
Constitucion
de 1857

Ensenada

PEMEX

1

Hotel Agua
Caliente

3

Pacific
Ocean

Heroes de la
Independencia

NOTE -- See Ensenada
Map in Chapter 17 concerning
junction of Highways 1 and 3.

Sea of
Cortez

5

Barrel
Cactus

5 mile
descent
of eastern
escarpment.

PEMEX
Rest Area

PEMEX
Valle de Trinidad

N

20 Miles

Mike's Sky Ranch

Parque Nacional Sierra
San Pedro Martir

To Highway 1

Observatory

San Felipe
PEMEX

(Km-101) SCENIC VIEW — The journey from Tecate to the Pacific coast is almost over, and Highway 3 begins its final descent to the sea. In view, ahead, are the Islas Todos Santos. These two rocky islands lie ten miles offshore, SW from Ensenada.

(Km-105) JUNCTION WITH HIGHWAY 1-D — Highway 3 joins the Highway 1-D freeway at the coastal town of El Sauzal. Highway 1-D is a toll road north to Tijuana but is toll-free from this junction point south into Ensenada. See Chapter 17 for details of Highway 1 and Ensenada.

JUNCTION OF HIGHWAYS 3 AND 1 IN ENSENADA — The second section of Highway 3 starts in the heart of Ensenada

at a junction point with old Highway 1. See the Ensenada Map in Chapter 17. The initial 4 km of the route proceeds easterly over four-lane Calzada Cortez, one of Ensenada's main business streets. There are several PEMEX stations along the way.

(Km-4) ENTER MOUNTAINS — The flat lands on which much of Ensenada is built terminate near **Km-4,** and Highway 3 begins the longest sustained climb found anywhere on the peninsula's highways. The grade winds upward to near **Km-20,** after a brief respite it continues to **Km-26.** This steep and curving area can be taxing for vehicles pulling large recreation trailers. This could preclude their owners from using this otherwise fine highway as a route from the Yuma, Arizona, area to Ensenada.

This steep grade near the Pacific coast provides the exception to all other highway crossings of the peninsula. In other cases the steep section of highway is encountered near the Sea of Cortez coast where the highway crosses the eastern escarpment of the Peninsular Range Mountains. In all these other cases the climb from west to east is a very gradual one.

SIDE TRIP
(Km-26) AGUA CALIENTE — A short distance east of **Km 26** the highway reaches the top of the grade and descends into the Valle de Ojos Negros. Exactly at this high point a dirt road leaves to the right (south) and descends steeply for <u>5.4 miles</u> to the Hotel Agua Caliente. (See HOTEL DESCRIPTIONS Section in Chapter 6.) The descent is steep but suitable, if recently graded, for most large R.V.'s (other than trailers) .

The hotel has large swimming pools fed by hot springs. Camping is permitted in a area of giant live oak trees adjoining the hotel and the Rio San Carlos. End **SIDE TRIP.**

(Km-36) VALLE DE OJOS NEGROS — Highway 3 enters the western edge of the broad Valle de Ojos Negros (Black Eyes Valley). A short oiled access road heads left (north) at **Km-39** to the farming community of Ojos Negros. It has a PEMEX station. (Nova only.) The flat valley continues to near **Km-50.**

SIDE TRIP
(Km-55) PARQUE NACIONAL CONSTITUCION DE 1857 (LAGUNA HANSON) — A secondary road leaves the highway 200 yards east of **Km-55.** It is signed for Laguna

Ocotillo and creosote bush thinly vegetate the San Felipe desert as seen from Highway 3 west of its junction with Highway 5.

Hanson 35 Km. This shallow lake (and the extensive stands of Jeffrey pine surrounding it) are the park's main attractions. It is <u>22.0 miles</u> to Laguna Hanson from Highway 3. Although constructed to secondary road standards, the road has some rough spots. The entire route lies in decomposed granite soils and thus is subject to erosion following rain. It is marginal for larger R.V.'s. (See the accompanying map for additional details.)

One may also drive to Laguna Hanson from the north. See Chapter 14, **Km-72.** This northern road is of lower standard than the route from Highway 3, with the most difficult <u>2.5 mile</u> segment lying in a granite, boulder area just inside the park's northern boundary.

Laguna Hanson contains water following rains; when it is full it provides a very pleasant environment. The area surrounding the lake is heavily forested and of gentle terrain. There are minimum facility campsites at the water's edge along the western shore. End **SIDE TRIP.**

VEGETATION — The vegetation east of Ensenada is chaparral typical of the California Vegetative Region. (See Chapter 10 VEGETATION.) East of Valle de Ojos Negros the highway slowly climbs over plateau lands. Near **Km-76** the traveler begins to see low juniper trees and an occasional pinyon pine. This is the lower fringe of the coniferous forest that covers the land in the national park to the NW.

(Km-91) HEROS DE LA INDEPENDENCIA - A small community lies at this point. A PEMEX station (Nova only) is on the east side of the highway.

Laguna Hansen is framed in Jeffrey pine foliage in the Parque Nacional Constitucion de 1857.

(Km-119) DESCENT INTO VALLE DE TRINIDAD
The highway starts a steep descent into the Valle de Trinidad. This is the start of a two-part drop from the mountains into the desert. The second segment takes place east of the valley near **Km-149**. During this first portion notice the numerous barrel cacti growing on the steep slopes. They are a sign that the highway is rapidly approaching a change in vegetational types.

Near **Km-123** a secondary road bears right (south) to the farming community of Valle de Trinidad. It reaches the town's main street in a short distance. At this junction turn left for 0.5 miles to the PEMEX station. The road to the right leads to one of the backdoor entrance to the Parque Nacional Sierra San Pedro Martir. The preferred access route to this park leaves Highway 1 at **Km B-140** south of Colonet. (See Chapter 18.)

The valley is long and wide. Its land has orchards and irrigated pastures.

(Km 138) ROAD TO MIKE'S SKY RANCH — A secondary road to the right leads to Mike's Sky Ranch, a resort catering to private flyers. I have not been over this route.

(Km-149) HIGHWAY DESCENT — Highway 3 now starts the 4.9 mile second leg of its descent of the eastern escarpment of the Peninsular Range Mountains. As at the first segment, notice the dense stand of barrel cactus. Nowhere else in Baja are such large numbers of these plants in view from the highway. Also present are ocotillo, agave, cardon, and other species which are common in Baja's desert areas. The descent represents a vegetational transition from the California Region vegetation, to the west, and the San Felipe Desert, to the east.

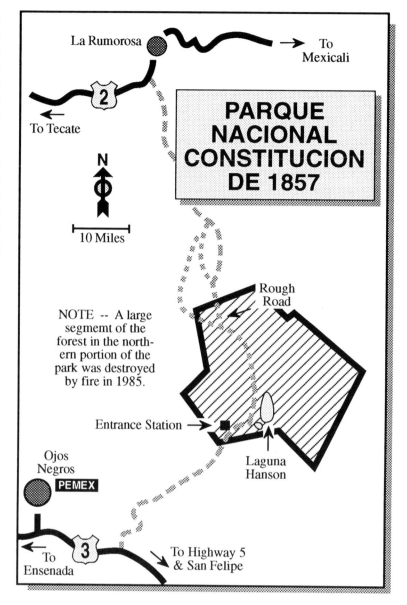

PARQUE NACIONAL CONSTITUCION DE 1857

NOTE -- A large segmemt of the forest in the northern portion of the park was destroyed by fire in 1985.

(Km-157) VEGETATION AND GEOGRAPHIC CHANGE — Here, at the base of the mountains, are encountered two major changes. The chaparral vegetation of the Peninsular Range Mountains is left behind, to the west, and is replaced with the widely spaced species of the San Felipe Desert. Between here and the Highway 5 junction the presence of numerous ocotillo plants gives some degree of character to the landscape; yet overall this San Felipe Desert has relatively drab vegetation due to the extreme dryness caused by its location in the rainshadow of the mountains.

The highway has also entered a typical portion of the Basin and Range Geologic Province. (See Chapter 9 GEOLOGY.) Note that the highway will traverse relatively flat land but that several north-south ranges of mountains project from the plain. Also note the majestic cliffs extending south from the foot of the grade. This is one of the best places in Baja to view the dramatic eastern escarpment of the Peninsular Range Mountains.

Km-196 JUNCTION WITH HIGHWAY 5 — Highways 3 and 5 meet at this uninspiring point in the desert. Fortunately, the inviting Sea of Cortez has been in view from Highway 3 en route to the junction for several miles to the east. While I feel the place is uninspiring, the Mexican Highway Department was inspired in 1992 to build a picnic area, restaurant and PEMEX station at the spot. If anyone ever decides to have a picnic here please let me know.

CHAPTER 17 TIJUANA TO ENSENADA

Thousands of Baja Buffs find that the Magnificent Peninsula provides a welcome relief from, shall we say benevolently, the hectic conditions of the Los Angeles-San Diego metropolitan areas. Many buffs would also agree that decompression takes place in three stages: (1) Tijuana to Ensenada, (2) Ensenada to San Quintin, and (3) south of San Quintin. Described below is the first stage of relief. It may be undertaken without a doctor's perscription.

Highway 1-D between Tijuana and Ensenada is Baja's best highway. It and the older, more or less parallel Highway 1 are described in this chapter.

OVERVIEW OF HIGHWAY 1-D — Highway 1-D is a four-lane, limited access toll road. It is signed "Cuota" meaning fare. A toll is collected to use all but short sections at either end. It may be paid in either pesos or U.S. dollars. (There are three tollgates.) This route is the fastest, safest, and most scenic way to travel between Tijuana to Ensenada.

There are approximately twenty interchanges along Highway 1-D. I say "approximately" in that several of the original interchanges are currently closed but may be reopened in the future. In all cases, it is possible to leave the highway and then to reenter at or near the same point to travel in the same direction. In most places, one may also reenter to travel in the opposite direction.

A teaming residential area in hilly Tijuana.

OVERVIEW OF HIGHWAY 1 — There are four distinct sections of Highway 1. All are built to good two-lane standards. There is no toll on this road so it is signed "Libre" meaning free.

TIJUANA TO ROSARITO — This is the quickest way to travel south for those starting their journey from the vicinity of the bullring on Boulevard Agua Caliente in Tijuana. However, it offers no advantages for the southbound traveler starting at the Tijuana-San Ysidro port-of-entry who should use Highway 1-D. In contrast, it is my recommended route for returning north as it provides access to the Otay Mesa port-of-entry. It is described in the RETURNING TO THE U.S.A. Section in Chapter 14.

ROSARITO TO CANTAMAR — This section of highway passes along the edge of a continuous series of communities made-up largely of homes, condominium developments, restaurants, and other facilities serving people from north of the border. I estimated that 75-percent of this area was committed to some form of development during my 1992 survey. Unless you are headed for one of these destinations, taking this route offers no advantages to the southbound traveler.

CANTAMAR TO LA MISION — The urbanization noted above decreases south of the Cantamar interchange. There are several short dirt roads leading from the highway to camping spots along the edges of the coastal bluffs overlooking the Pacific Ocean. These places are used for camping mostly during peak three-day weekend periods and many are being displaced by residential development. These high points are also good places to watch for the California gray whale, which travels only a short distance offshore.

LA MISION TO EL SAUZAL — This is an inland road through the mountains. It provides a pleasant drive through undeveloped countryside but does not offer the excellent scenic vistas of the ocean and coast which are available from Highway 1-D.

The balance of this chapter describes the Highway 1-D route from Tijuana to Ensenada.

(Km A-0) TIJUANA — After entering Mexico at the San Ysidro port-of-entry one must drive a circle route bearing left. Follow the signs for Rosarito and Ensenada. After the circle, Highway 1-D proceeds west along the international boundary fence toward

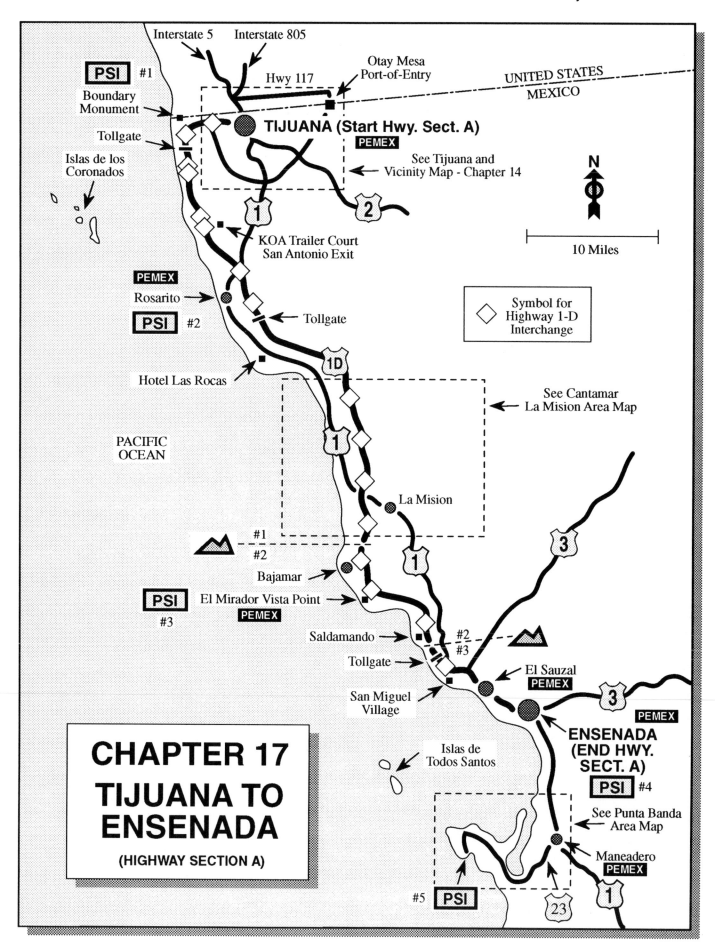

Interstate 5   Interstate 805

Otay Mesa
Port-of-Entry

Hwy 117

UNITED STATES
MEXICO

PSI #1

Boundary
Monument

Tollgate

Islas de los
Coronados

TIJUANA (Start Hwy. Sect. A)
PEMEX

See Tijuana and
Vicinity Map - Chapter 14

N

10 Miles

1

2

KOA Trailer Court
San Antonio Exit

PEMEX
Rosarito

Symbol for
Highway 1-D
Interchange

PSI #2

Tollgate

Hotel Las Rocas

1D

See Cantamar
La Mision Area Map

PACIFIC
OCEAN

1

La Mision

3

#1
#2

Bajamar

PSI

El Mirador Vista Point
PEMEX

1

#3

Saldamando

#2
#3

Tollgate

El Sauzal
PEMEX

San Miguel
Village

3

PEMEX

Islas de
Todos Santos

**ENSENADA
(END HWY.
SECT. A)**

PSI #4

See Punta Banda
Area Map

CHAPTER 17
TIJUANA TO
ENSENADA

(HIGHWAY SECTION A)

Maneadero
PEMEX

#5 PSI

23

1

the Pacific. See the TIJUANA AND VICINITY Map and the ENTERING TIJUANA FROM THE NORTH Section of Chapter 14 for more details.

PSI #1

(Km A-9) BOUNDARY MONUMENT — Just prior to Km A-9 one encounters an interchange signed "Playas de Tijuana" as Highway 1-D begins a broad curve from westbound to southbound. The Bullring by-the-Sea is in view near the coast, and its access road is easy to find by taking this offramp.

Immediately north of the bullring and adjacent to the Tijuana lighthouse is the international boundary fence and a twelve-foot obelisk commemorating the establishment of the United States-Mexican boundary which resulted from the Mexican-American War and the February 2, 1848, Treaty of Guadalupe Hidalgo. While the monument itself is not overly impressive, it has been included as stop No. 1 on the POINTS OF SPECIAL INTEREST Tour. It is a good place to pause and reflect on the history of the two countries and also to relax a moment and celebrate your safe arrival in Mexico's Magnificent Peninsula.

The northerly tollgate is located just south of the "Playas de Tijuana" interchange.

(Km A-11) ISLAS CORONADOS — Islas Coronados (Coronados Islands) lie about 6 miles offshore. These islands are in view for many miles along Highway 1-D but all four of the two large and two smaller islands can be seen from here, near **Km A-11**.

Also note the large pipeline constructed parallel to the highway. It carries water to Ensenada from the Rio Guadulupe, which the highway will cross near **Km A-68** to the south.

The international boundary monument a few yards from the Pacific Ocean at Tijuana. Sadly, there has to be a chain-link fence between the two countries.

(Km A-22) SAN ANTONIO DEL MAR — The Rosarito KOA trailer court lies on the side of a nicely landscaped hill 0.2 miles east of the highway after taking the San Antonio interchange. It is the closest trailer court to the international border and offers overnight rates substantially below those encountered in the San Diego area. Most of its sites are rented on a year-round basis but there is always room for overnighters.

(Km A-34) ROSARITO — Rosarito is a major center of tourist-orientated shops, motels, and restaurants. Government statistics indicate that 11 percent of the tourists entering Baja have Rosarito as their destination point. The most visible facilities are the eight-story Quinta del Mar Resort and other highrise buildings.

PSI #2

I have difficulty recommending the community of Rosarito as a place to stop for other than those who are limiting their Baja visit to the border area. The historic Rosarito Beach Hotel provides an exception. This low-rise building is one of three casinos that operated in the border area during the late 1920s and early 1930s. Many of the rooms have recently been remodeled and a new wing has been added. It is stop No. 2 on the POINTS OF SPECIAL INTEREST Tour. The hotel is directly opposite the interchange at the southern end of Rosarito at **Km A-34**. It is thus easy to find. The middle of the three tollgates straddles the highway south of this interchange.

There are many smaller motels, restaurants, and condominiums from Rosarito south to Cantamar. One must travel on non-toll Highway 1 to access this area. This is also the route to use to reach the Hotel Las Rocas and the Hotel New Port Baja.

(Km A-53) CANTAMAR AND EL DESCANSO — The Cantamar interchange is the place to exit Highway 1-D to drive on old Highway 1 if you wish to take advantage of the undeveloped camping sites mentioned in the description of this section of highway at the beginning of this chapter. A short distance south of the interchange on Highway 1 is the community of El Descanso. At its southern edge are situated large coastal sand dunes that provide an excellent dune buggy area.

South of the sand dunes, Highway 1-D crosses the Rio Descanso at **Km A-55**. Just south of this kilometer post look for a large complex of glass greenhouses inland from the highway. Behind the greenhouses can be seen a small church. This church stands on the site of the Descanso mission established here in 1814 by the Dominican Order. It was the next to last of the peninsular missions.

(Km A-66) LA MISION — The La Mision-Alistos interchange is the place to exit Highway 1-D to visit the La Fonda Hotel, the Plaza Del Mar Hotel Spa and to take the side trip noted below.

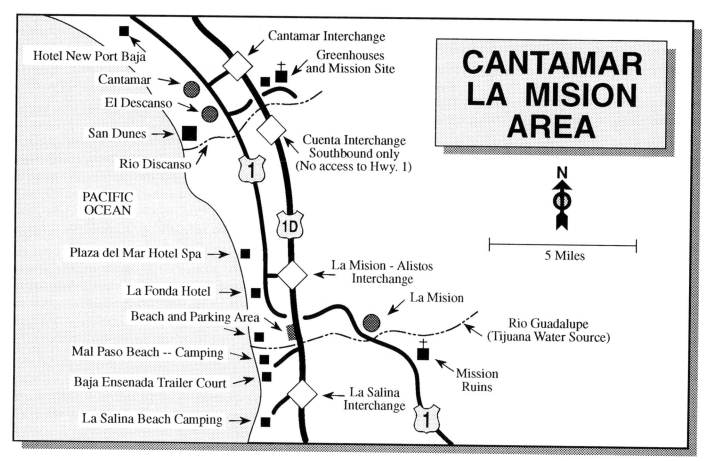

Map labels:
Hotel New Port Baja
Cantamar
El Descanso
San Dunes
Rio Discanso
PACIFIC OCEAN
Plaza del Mar Hotel Spa
La Fonda Hotel
Beach and Parking Area
Mal Paso Beach -- Camping
Baja Ensenada Trailer Court
La Salina Beach Camping
Cantamar Interchange
Greenhouses and Mission Site
Cuenta Interchange Southbound only (No access to Hwy. 1)
La Mision - Alistos Interchange
La Mision
Rio Guadalupe (Tijuana Water Source)
Mission Ruins
La Salina Interchange

CANTAMAR LA MISION AREA

N

5 Miles

Eat at La Fonda

SIDE TRIP — It is <u>3.8 miles</u> south and then east on Highway 1 from the La Mision-Alistos interchange to the ruins of the San Miguel de la Frontera mission. These adobe remains lie within a chain-link fence in the yard of the La Mision community school. They are directly adjacent to the highway <u>0.8 miles</u> east from the Rio Guadalupe bridge. You may also continue south on this old Highway 1 toward Ensenada. This drive is through pleasant, undeveloped hill-country but lacks the ocean views afforded by staying on Highway 1-D. End **SIDE TRIP**.

(Km A-69) PARKING AREA AND BEACH — Just north of the Highway 1-D crossing of the Rio Guadalupe estuary is a 50-car parking lot and fine sandy beach directly adjoining the highway. It gets heavy use on holiday weekends.

(Km A-71) PLAYA MAL PASO — Immediately north of **Km A-71** a dirt road leaves the highway and shortly arrives at the residence of the operators of the beach camping area at Playa Mal Paso. This beach can be reached only from the southbound lanes of the highway. Extra care is needed in reentering the highway as this is not a regular interchange.

(Km A-72) BAJA ENSENADA — Located here is one of the finest trailer courts in Baja operated by Outdoor Resorts of Baja (800) 356-2252. It has 137

units, tennis courts, pool, clubhouse, and related facilities. Rates are expensive. The court is directly on the beach but Pacific waters are cold this far north. Plans call for expanding the court or building a hotel on nearby vacant land.

(Km A-73) LA SALINA — A short drive south from the La Salina interchange brings one to the Playa La Salina beach, restaurant and small hotel.

The northernmost of the three tollgates on Highway 1-D.

#1 ▲ #2

(Km A-75) GEOGRAPHIC CHANGE — You have now reached the most northerly breakpoint between the nineteen geographic sections encountered along the Transpeninsular Highway. The relatively flat coastal beaches (Section 1) will be left behind as the highway starts a climb into steeper terrain (Section 2). In a few miles, this increase in elevation will reward the traveler with excellent vistas of the coastline.

(Km A-78) BAJAMAR — Immediately west of this interchange lies the Bajamar golf course and surrounding residences. There is a pro-shop, restaurant, and bar. Bajamar is one of the finest residential developments in the Baja peninsula. There is little development between Bajamar and the southernmost tollgate at Km A-99.

`PSI` #3

(Km A-84) EL MIRADOR VISTA POINT — An interchange a short distance north of **Km A-84** provides direct access to a parking lot near the cliffs overlooking the Pacific Ocean. A PEMEX station, restaurant and improved overlook facilities were under construction here in early 1992. They should be completed by the time this edition of *The Magnificent Peninsula* is in print.

From here, you will be rewarded with the best views of the Pacific coast that are available from the entire Transpeninsular Highway. Also in view are the Islas Todos Santos which lie 12 miles to the SW. These two ismall slands guard the outer limits of the broad bay on whose shore is built the city of Ensenada. Because of the excellent view, El Mirador is included as stop No. 3 in the POINTS OF SPECIAL INTEREST Tour.

Ensenada's annual Carnaval celebration. Small circuses and carnaval shows are frequently seen in Baja's larger communities.

(Km A-92 to A-94) SEDIMENTARY ROCKS — The majority of the rocks visible in the mountainous areas of the peninsula will be granitic or volcanic. Both of these are igneous rocks. Here, north of Ensenada, the highway cuts clearly display the layering which is the most common characteristic of sedimentary rocks. (See the ROCK TYPE Chart in Chapter 9 GEOLOGY.)

(Km A-94) SALDAMANDO — Just past **Km A-94** a dirt road to the west descends steeply to the residence of the operator of a camping area on the bluffs above a rocky shoreline. Several camping spots have been carved out along the road for about 1/2 mile south from the residence. They provide excellent views of the ocean but are not well-suited for larger R.V.s.

#2 ▲ #3

(Km A-99) TOLLGATE AND GEOGRAPHIC CHANGE — Near **Km A-99** is situated the southernmost of Highway 1-D's three tollgates. The remainder of the trip into Ensenada is toll-free. The toll station also marks the end of mountainous Geographic Section No. 2. For the next 22 miles the highway passes over flatlands (Section No. 3) surrounding the city of Ensenada.

Immediately south of the tollgate is San Miguel Village. A minimum facility camping area is present on a level bench near the rocky shoreline.

EL SAUZAL AREA — Approximately 1.5 miles south of the tollgate is the junction of Highway 1-D and Highway 3 and the community of El Sauzal. El Sauzal is one of the largest fishing ports on the Baja peninsula. Note the breakwater-lined harbor that is usually filled with numerous fishing vessels. Adjoining the harbor are a packing plant and related buildings. We tourists can rejoice that most of the fishing business has been established away from the tourist areas in Ensenada.

Between El Sauzal and Ensenada there are several motels and trailer courts. The latter cater mostly to year-round tenants.

`PSI` #4

(Km A-109) ENSENADA — Ensenada is Baja California's third largest city. Twenty-three percent of the tourists entering the peninsula have Ensenada as their destination point. It is thus second only to Tijuana as a tourist attraction.

To classify Ensenada as a beautiful city would be inaccurate in my view. There are no major beaches and the tourist section of the city is fronted with a busy breakwater-lined harbor. But certainly it is a pleasant place, with a climate similar to San Diego. It gives the one-day or weekend tourist the feeling of having really been to Mexico that somehow does not result from a visit to Tijuana.

ENSENADA

N

0.5 Miles

Collinas Chapultepec

Quarry

Ave. Ruis

Ave. Juarez

See Large-scale Map

Benito Juarez Monument

Ave. Lopez Mateos

Civic Plaza

Campo Playa Trailer Court

Blvd. Lazaro Cardenas

Bahia Todos Santos

Ensenada Harbor

Cruise Ship Dock

Calle General Agustin

Ave. Reforma

Ave. Gastelum

Arroyo de Ensenada

Ave. Juarez

Ave. Ruis

Blvd. Lazaro Cardenas

Ave. Lopez Mateos

POINTS OF INTEREST

1 Bank
2 Hussong's Cantina
3 PESCA (Fishing Licenses)
4 Inmigracion (Immigration)
5 Capitan de Puerto (Port Captain)
6 PEMEX

7 Food Market
8 Sportfishing Docks
9 Plaza Civica (Civic Plaza)
10 Naval Base
11 El Cid Hotel

12 Ensenada Travelodge
13 Casa del Sol Motel
14 Hotel Villa Marina
15 Mision Santa Isabel
16 Tourist Information

17 Riviera del Pacifico
18 Hotel Corona
19 Hotel La Pinta
20 San Nicolas Resort Hotel
21 Post Office

INMIGRACION -- The Mexican immigration office is located on the right side of the street as you enter Ensenada from the north. There are about six parking spots in front of the building. Here is the place to obtain, or validate tourists cards if you are heading south of the city where they are required. A tourist information office is located within walking distance a short distance away. (See the ENSENADA MAP.)

TOURIST ROW — The city's main tourist area centers in and around the section of Avenida Lopez Mateos shown on the inset map of the ENSENADA Map. Traffic is usually heavy on this street, so the wise visitor will park along Boulevard Lazaro

Cardenas or the streets surrounding the civic plaza. An aerial photo of Ensenada's waterfront area is presented on page 129 in Chapter 13.

This section of the city is stop No. 4 on the POINTS OF SPECIAL INTEREST Tour. At first glance it may appear to be just another long array of tourist traps. Typical souvenir items are of course in plentiful supply, but there is also much quality merchandise I have found the selection to be much better than in La Paz. If you are a budget-minded person it is simply foolish not to stock up on Christmas and birthday presents, etc., while in Ensenada. The savings can be substantial.

Also consider visiting the Riviera del Pacifico (former gambling casino), the Santo Tomas winery at 666 Avenida Miramar, and, of course, Hussong's Cantina. You may find the latter establishment a bit lowbrow, but thousands of we less discerning beer drinkers like the place, and the mariachi music is free (unless you are so unwise as to request your favorite song). It was established in 1892 and is still operated by the same family.

DRIVING THROUGH ENSENADA — It is recommended that the Highway 1-D, Lazaro Cardenas, General Agustin route is the best way to travel through the city. These streets are multilaned all the way and traffic is usually moderate. I see no advantages for the average tourists in taking the old Highway 1 route unless they are interested in increasing the chances of the culturally rewarding experience of becoming lost.

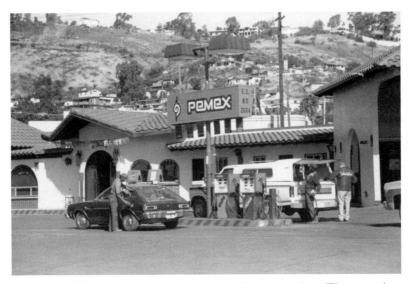

The PEMEX station in downtown Ensenada. The station logo shown on the sign is the same on every gas station in Mexico.

THIS 'NO MAN'S LAND'

The conquistadores came with their greed
But Baja California would not concede,
Cortez...Mendosa...Cabrillo...Vizcaino...and more
The riches they sought were not on her shores;
Not even enough food could be found
To feed men and beasts on this arid ground,
Native Pericues and Guaycuras barely survived
and with white man's diseases too many died.
Then missionaries tried but despite their valiant struggle
Many missions remain only as heaps of old rubble,
Padres Kino...Salvatierra...Serra...Ugarte...
Like the conquistadore bands,
Left only their names on this inhospitable land.

KEN REIMER

CHAPTER 18
ENSENADA TO SAN QUINTIN

The GRAND TOUR now proceeds from Ensenada south to the town of San Quintin and nearby Bahia San Quintin. This 196 km (122 mile) section of the Transpeninsular Highway is the second decompression step from the Southern California Pressure Cooker. There are far fewer tourist accommodations and travelers than there were north of Ensenada. However, you will still encounter a series of sizeable towns, much agricultural development, many people, and vegetation that still looks much like it does north of the border. You will have to wait until the next chapter to get into the *real* Magnificent Peninsula.

PASSING THROUGH ENSENADA — There is considerable traffic in Ensenada. I recommend that you enter from the north on Highway 1-D and follow the Lazaro Cardenas-General Agustin route to Highway 1 south of the downtown area. See the Ensenada Map in Chapter 17.

ENSENADA TO MANEADERO — It is 14 km (9 miles) from Ensenada to Maneadero over a four-lane highway. This section of Highway 1 provides a transition from the freeway to the north and the two-lane road which starts south of Maneadero. The terrain is flat. There is much urbanization from Ensenada to the Estero Beach road. Farther south, the highway passes through farms and olive orchards. As in other metropolitan sections, the kilometer posts are often missing. Watch for the Estero Beach turnoff along the way.

SIDE TRIP
(Km B-15) ESTERO BEACH — At the 15-km point a paved road leaves Highway 1 to the right. (See PUNTA BANDA AREA Map.) A 0.8 mile drive brings one to an intersection. The road to the right leads to El Faro Beach, a residential subdivision. Take the left fork a short distance to the very fine Estero Beach Resort Hotel, trailer court, shops, and boat launching ramp. They lie on the shore of Estero de Punta Banda. The trailer court here is one of the best in the Baja peninsula and is often used as the first nights stop for large R. V. caravans heading south.

Estero means estuary. Estero Beach is the northern shore of a sizeable saltwater estuary (Estero de Punta Banda). The western side is a wide, 4-mile-long coastal sand spit which protects the estuary from the swells of the Pacific Ocean. Launching small boats is thus an easy matter, but the breaking bar at the mouth of the estero must be negotiated to reach the open ocean. The hotel and its grounds are very pleasant and they are worth a visit even if you don't plan to stay. There is ample parking and turnaround area for the large R.V.'s. End **SIDE TRIP**.

PSI #5

SIDE TRIP — (Km B-21) HIGHWAY 23 AND LA BUFADORA — Highway 23 branches to the west from Highway 1 in the town of Maneadero about 200 yards south of a pedestrian overpass. (See PUNTA BANDA AREA Map.) It is a good standard blacktopped highway of some 20 km's (14 miles). Its first 8 miles cross flat terrain, some of which supports olive orchards and other agricultural fields. The last 6 miles traverse the sides of precipitous Punta Banda, a narrow, rocky peninsula that projects into the Pacific Ocean.

As the road gains elevation, one is afforded excellent views of the ocean and Ensenada to the northeast. The spouts of the California gray whale also may be seen during the months of its migration from Alaska to Baja's Pacific lagoons. (See Chapter 11 WILDLIFE.)

There are several places of interest served by Highway 23 including the La Bufadora blowhole. The commanding views and intriguing blowhole demand that this side trip be placed on the POINTS OF SPECIAL INTEREST Tour.

Numerous souvenir stands have been built along the road near the blowhole so there is no lack of things to buy. There is parking at La Bufadora, although trailers should not proceed past the restaurant (0.2 miles from La Bufadora) due to the steepness of the parking lot.

PUNTA BANDA BARRIER BEACH — Barrier Beaches are low-lying, narrow, spits of sand built by wave action along shallow sections of ocean coastline. They are separated from the mainland by saltwater estuaries. Here at about 8-miles from Highway 1 is such a formation. An oiled road leads north out the barrier to the Baja Beach & Tennis Club and numerous private residences. A major new marina is planned for construction a short distance out along this road.

LA JOLLA — La Jolla is a community made up of several older recreation home subdivisions 14 km (9 miles) from Highway 1. Lots are very small and many contain trailer houses. There are several R. V. parking areas for short-term visitors, along with a boat launching ramp. The ramp, which provides access to the open Pacific, will pose problems at low tide and would be unusable in heavy swells.

CAMPGROUNDS — There are several gently sloping areas adjacent to the highway near the point where it starts descending

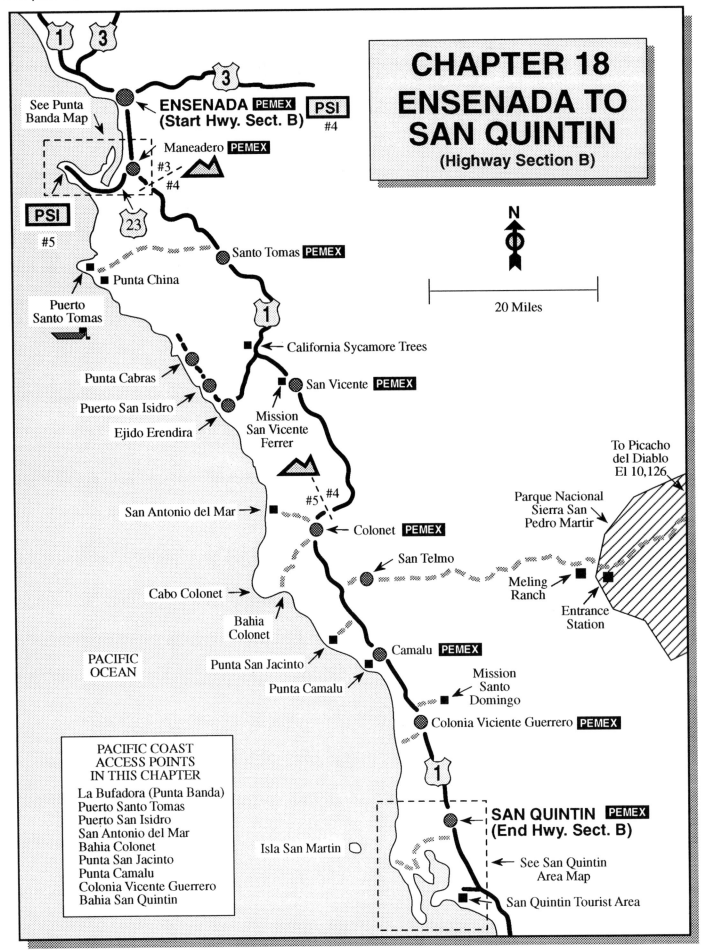

CHAPTER 18 ENSENADA TO SAN QUINTIN
(Highway Section B)

ENSENADA PEMEX (Start Hwy. Sect. B)

PSI #4

See Punta Banda Map

Maneadero PEMEX #3 #4

PSI #5

23

Santo Tomas PEMEX

Punta China

Puerto Santo Tomas

N

20 Miles

California Sycamore Trees

Punta Cabras

San Vicente PEMEX

Puerto San Isidro

Ejido Erendira

Mission San Vicente Ferrer

To Picacho del Diablo El 10,126

Parque Nacional Sierra San Pedro Martir

#5 #4

San Antonio del Mar

Colonet PEMEX

San Telmo

Meling Ranch

Cabo Colonet

Entrance Station

Bahia Colonet

Camalu PEMEX

Punta San Jacinto

PACIFIC OCEAN

Mission Santo Domingo

Punta Camalu

Colonia Viciente Guerrero PEMEX

1

PACIFIC COAST ACCESS POINTS IN THIS CHAPTER
La Bufadora (Punta Banda)
Puerto Santo Tomas
Puerto San Isidro
San Antonio del Mar
Bahia Colonet
Punta San Jacinto
Punta Camalu
Colonia Vicente Guerrero
Bahia San Quintin

Isla San Martin

SAN QUINTIN PEMEX (End Hwy. Sect. B)

See San Quintin Area Map

San Quintin Tourist Area

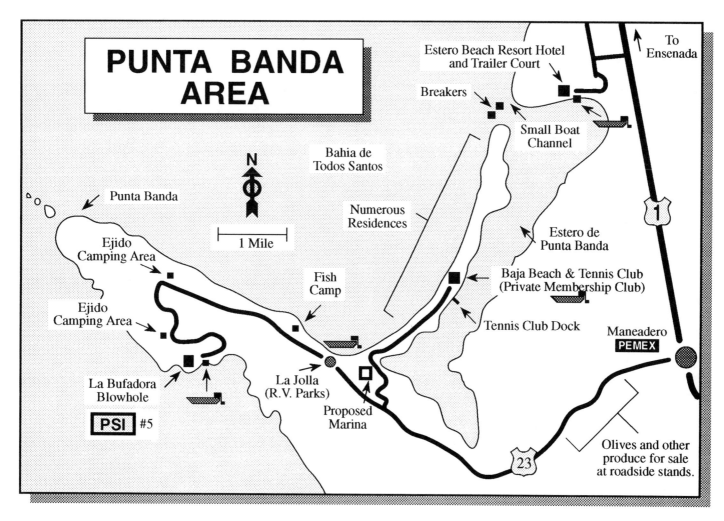

PUNTA BANDA AREA

To Ensenada

Estero Beach Resort Hotel and Trailer Court

Breakers

Small Boat Channel

Bahia de Todos Santos

N

1 Mile

Punta Banda

Numerous Residences

Estero de Punta Banda

Ejido Camping Area

Baja Beach & Tennis Club (Private Membership Club)

Fish Camp

Ejido Camping Area

Tennis Club Dock

Maneadero
PEMEX

La Bufadora Blowhole

La Jolla (R.V. Parks)

PSI #5

Proposed Marina

23

Olives and other produce for sale at roadside stands.

---

to La Bufadora. They provide the sites for minimum facility campgrounds operated by the members of a local ejido (See GLOSSARY). What you receive for your modest fee in these places is little more than a place to park, but there are excellent views of the ocean. Some of these camps may give way to subdivisions which are making their appearance.

LA BUFADORA BLOWHOLE — Highway 23 passes over the top of the Punta Banda ridge and descends to the rocky coast on the slope facing SE. Here you will find a scattering of homes, restaurants, open-air shops, parking areas, and a masonry viewing structure adjoining the blowhole. There are several R. V. camping areas on flat benches above the shoreline cliffs. The area is a popular weekend recreation spot for people of the Ensenada area.

There are occasional points along the Pacific Coast where rock formations cause the incoming ocean swells to cast up a spout of water; but La Bufadora (The Roarer) is a blowhole without rival. It consists of a substantial sea-level cave. After observing it for some time, one can readily imagine that it is a living creature. The rhythmic ocean swells impart a breathing cycle to the cave. Water is first taken in. Then, following a pause, it is sprayed back outside by internally compressed air to the accompaniment of a deep roar. Heavy swells cause a large vertical

geyser, but La Bufadora puts on a good performance even in calm seas. End **SIDE TRIP**.

(Km B 23) INMIGRACION — *Inmigracion* is the Mexican equivalent of the Immigration Service in the United States. Here at the town of Maneadero was the immigration checkpoint where officials issued and validated tourist cards. Their building is 1 mile south of the Highway 1 junction with Highway 23. During the past eight years it has been open on an intermittent basis. It appeared abandoned in spring 1992. See comments concerning this station under the WHAT ACTUALLY HAPPENS Section in Chapter 7.

The Transpeninsular Highway has two lanes from here to the tip of the peninsula except within some of the larger communities.

#3 #4

(Km B-25) GEOGRAPHIC CHANGE — Here the highway enters Geographic Section No. 4 and initiates a 100 km (62 mile) journey through moderately steep mountains with numerous intermountain valleys. The area and its chaparral vegetation are similar to those in the mountainous areas in southern Alta California. The brush here in Baja is not as dense as that found north of the border due to the occurrence of frequent uncontrolled wildfires.

Although the Transpeninsular Highway begins to curve, its grades are moderate and there are many straight, level sections. Its course through this area is reasonably typical of what lies ahead for hundreds of miles, so if what you see here is acceptable you can relax and enjoy the remainder of your trip.

SIDE TRIP
(Km B-48) PUERTO SANTO TOMAS — A secondary road signed "La Bocana 26 km, and Punta China 28 km" leaves Highway 1 to the right (west). This road is constructed along the foot of the mountains bordering the northern side of the Rio Santo Tomas. It is well constructed but it is not recommended for use by larger R.V.'s.

16.1 Miles — The road to Punta China forks to the left and crosses the Rio Santo Tomas. A 2.9 mile drive brings one to the workers camp at the Punta China limestone mining operation. A short distance to the south, rock is loaded by conveyor belt into barges for shipment to the cement plant in Ensenada. There are nice ocean views along the way.

17.6 Miles — The road arrives at the small village of La Boca (The Mouth), appropriately located at the mouth of the Rio Santo Tomas. There is a small store and a camping spot with a good view of the ocean. Another nearby campground is operated on a treelined meadow adjoining the beach and a marshy lagoon. If the croaking of frogs will keep you awake consider camping elsewhere.

20.3 Miles — This point brings you to Puerto Santo Tomas, presently the site of a modest fish camp. The small cove provides protection from the ocean swells that crash on the shore only a few yards to the south. Surprisingly, this insignificant cove was a principal port during the missionary period. It served the inland settlement of Santo Tomas. In viewing its waters, picture it containing the ship of Juan Rodriguez Cabrillo, who anchored here during his historic exploratory voyage in 1542.

Within the fish camp is a small cantina and camping is permitted nearby. There is also a narrow, concrete boat ramp facing the open Pacific. Launching boats in heavy swell would not be possible. End **SIDE TRIP**.

HISTORIC NOTE — THE MISSIONARY TRAIL Since leaving Ensenada, you have been following the approximate route used by Gaspar de Portola and Padre Junipero Serra on their history-making 1769 expedition north from Loreto to found the first Alta California mission at San Diego. In the ensuing twenty-two years, Dominican missionaries were to establish three new missions along that portion of the route described in this chapter. These were at the present-day towns of Santo Tomas, San Vicente, and Santo Domingo. Directions for visiting these sites are given later in this chapter. The ruin of an additional mission near El Rosario is described in the following chapter.

(Km B-51) SANTO TOMAS — Santo Tomas is a small town located in a broad, fertile section of the Rio Santo Tomas. It is the site of a Dominican mission founded in 1791. To view the mission ruins, proceed to the roadside rest directly across the highway from the PEMEX Station. Walk several hundred feet north along the east side of the highway. The fifty-foot-square ruins may be seen in a pasture near several tall fan palms and 250 feet north of the olive orchard which contains the El Palomar Trailer Court.

Grapes were cultivated by the missionaries to produce altar wine. Santo Tomas came to lend its name to one of Mexico's most popular brand of wines, although the winery itself has long been located in Ensenada. In the past, much of the valley was planted to grapes. Today, there are relatively few vineyards and most of the land contains olive orchards or is used for grazing. Grape production has been moved to the Guadalupe area along Highway 3 NE of Ensenada and the the region south of San Vicente ahead along Highway 1.

Today, Santo Tomas offers the tourist a PEMEX station, and the El Palomar motel, restaurant and gift shop. Across the highway is the El Palomar Trailer Court. It is a pleasant, shady spot surrounded by olive trees. It provides full hookups, swimming pool and toilet facilities.

(Km B-72 to B-77) CALIFORNIA SYCAMORE — Highway 1 passes along the stream channel of a moderately steep canyon. Here you can observe numerous California sycamore trees (*Platanus racemosa*), a species commonly found in similar moist locations in Alta California and northern Baja. Note the mottled exfoliating brown and white bark. The broad, sharply lobbed leaves fall in the

All that remains of the Dominican mission founded in Santo Tomas in 1791. The ruins are visible from the Transpeninsular Highway.

winter months, but many spherical fruiting bodies can be seen dangling from the branches. See the outline of the leaf below on this page.

Many of the canyon walls in this area are composed of granite rocks. They can be identified by their light color. Review the ROCK TYPE Table in Chapter 9 GEOLOGY.

Outline of the leaf of the California sycamore. (1/3 actual size.)

SIDE TRIP
(Km B-78) PUERTO SAN ISIDRO AREA — Midway between **Km B-78** and **Km B-79** a blacktop highway leaves Highway 1 to the right (west). It is signed for E.J. Erendira. This is one of the few places where you can drive to within a few hundred yards of the Pacific shore on a oiled highway.

The hard surface highway proceeds along the Rio San Isidro and ends in 12.0 miles at the farming community of Erendira. A secondary road continuing NW up the coast provides access to the small fishing port of San Isidro. It is 13.3 miles to the port from Highway 1. A reef of rock that projects from the coast provides protection for a fleet of small fishing boats. Small class 4 boats can be launched with some difficulty from the steep road leading to the water's edge.

Nearby there is a group of small rental cabins bearing the name Castro's. Boats are available for rent. Across the road is a R. V. park which in spring 1992 was little more than a place to park. There is a small cafe in Erendira.

I have driven 9.0 miles north of Puerto San Isidro on a good secondary road. Starting at 1.6 miles north of the port are a series of very nice camping sites on the bluffs overlooking the ocean. At places there are good beaches. At 5.5 miles north of the port is the growing village of Punta Cabras which is made up largely of Americans. At 5.9 miles is a turnoff to the beach-lined cove at Punta Cabras. The road is a bit rough but large R. V.s make it to many of these camping spots. End **SIDE TRIP**.

SIDE TRIP
(Km B-88) MISSION SAN VICENTE FERRER — It is a 0.4 mile drive over a low standard (but passable) dirt road to the ruins of the San Vicente Ferrer mission. This road leaves Highway 1 to the right (west) 0.2 miles south of **Km B-88**. Shortly after leaving the highway take the left fork which leads to a parking area adjoining the ruins. A flimsy thatched shelter has been constructed over the crumbling walls of the buildings, but it is falling down and provides pitifully little protection.

Dominican padres founded the mission in 1780, on a low rise a few yards from the Rio San Isidro. It was to become the administrative center for the northern *Frontera* mission district and headquarters for a garrison of troops. End **SIDE TRIP**.

(Km B-90) SAN VICENTE — At this point is the town of San Vicente. The only things of interest to the tourist are several stores and a PEMEX station.

(Km B-90 to B-107) LLANO COLORADO — There was little agricultural development on the Baja peninsula prior to the 1940s as the land was controlled by unproductive foreign concessions. Previous travel guides reported only a few families around San Vicente.

Today's traveler will see extensive vineyards, olive orchards, and grain fields in the level valley south of San Vicente. This is the Llano Colorado (the Colorado Plain). You will see other rapidly expanding agricultural developments on many of the flat lands in the section of the peninsula covered in this chapter. It is interesting to note that while these Mexican lands are only now being developed for agriculture, tracts used for similar purposes in southern California in the United States have long since given way to urbanization.

#4 ⛰ #5
(Km B-125) GEOGRAPHIC CHANGE — Just before entering the town of Colonet, the highway leaves the mountains that started 100 km (62 miles) to the north. You will now be entering Geographic Section No. 5, the northernmost segment of the Continental Borderlands Province. As you can see, this dividing line between provinces is easy to identify and is typical of others you will encounter to the south.

Highway 1 will now traverse 112 km (70 miles) of rolling coastal plain with the mountains always in view to the east. The northern portion of the plain is called the Llano (plain) de Camalu, and the southern portion the Valle (valley) de San Quintin. Many of these lands are used for agriculture. The highway is constructed near the inland portion of the plain, so the ocean is mostly out of sight.

ROAD CONDITION NOTE Several secondary road side trips to the Pacific shore are described over the level lands of the Continental Borderlands in this and the following chapter. Soils in this area are fine-grained and become muddy following rain. Local traffic continues during such periods and many ruts and

The largest of the three telescope buildings in the Parque Nacional Sierra San Pedro Martir. Note the gnarled Jeffrey pine tree and the snow remaining from a late March storm.

short detours are created. Be very cautious about using these roads for up to ten days following heavy rain and expect occasional rough spots long afterwards.

SIDE TRIP
(Km B-126) SAN ANTONIO DEL MAR — North of the town of Colonet a secondary road bears west to the Pacific shore. It leaves Highway 1 about 100 yards NE of the Rio San Rafael bridge and between the bridge and a white church. A small group of residences, San Antonio del Mar is reached in 7.0 miles. There is limited camping area here but extensive sand beaches and dunes lie in both directions. A great area for those with vehicles capable of traveling over such terrain. End **SIDE TRIP**.

(Km B-127) COLONET — South of the Rio San Rafael bridge lies the small farming community of Colonet and its PEMEX station. A considerable agriculture area can be seen on the lands bordering the river.

After passing through Colonet, look south near the western edge of the inland mountains. Here, on clear days, you will see Isla San Martin and a group of volcanic cinder cones lying west of the town of San Quintin. At other times, these peaks may be shrouded in fog or low clouds.

SIDE TRIP
(Km B-129) BAHIA COLONET — Near **Km B-129** a secondary road leaves Highway 1 to the right (west) and in 8.1 miles arrives at the southern end of Bahia Colonet on the Pacific coast. The junction is signed for E.J. Villa Morelos.

The road is constructed along the base of low hills bordering the broad valley of the Rio San Rafael. A lesser standard road continues south, along the coast, accessing numerous places to camp on the bluffs overlooking the Pacific. End **SIDE TRIP**.

SIDE TRIP
(Km B-141) PARQUE NACIONAL SIERRA SAN PEDRO MARTIR — Leading to the left (east) is the main access road to the largest of Baja's two national parks (Parque Nacional Sierra San Pedro Martir) and the highest mountains in the peninsula. The road is signed "Observatorio and San Telmo." The park features extensive Jeffrey pine forests mixed with several other coniferous species. There are many undeveloped places to camp. At the end of the road is an observatory with one large and two smaller telescope buildings. The clearness of the air makes this an excellent point for astronomical observations.

Much of the access road passes over mountainous terrain making a total climb of approximately 10,000 feet. Its construction standards are better than those of most of Baja's secondary roads, but the entire route is through decomposed granite soils that are subject to severe erosion. I have seen this road recommended for use by large R.V.'s and believe that it is suitable for such vehicles (no trailers) if it has been recently maintained. Following heavy storms, this is not the case.

6.0 Miles — Here lies the pleasant farming community of San Telmo.

22.0 Miles — To this point the road has passed along the edge of a broad valley used for agricultural purposes. The route has been level, with few hills. Now it begins to climb the mountains in earnest.

32.1 Miles — A 0.5 mile dirt road to the right brings one to the Meling Ranch. This is an operating cattle ranch, which also provides very pleasant accommodations for overnight guests. It has a nearby airstrip and has long been a favorite hideout for private flyers. An excellent place to get away from it all

50.7 Miles — Here are located the park's gate, entrance station, and small campground. A modest entrance fee is charged.

65.0 Miles — The living quarters and administrative buildings for the observatory are located here. It is possible to camp at this point, although there are no facilities and little flat ground. Visitors are required to walk the remaining 1.5 miles up to the telescopes. End **SIDE TRIP**.

(Km B-150) PUNTA SAN JACINTO — A secondary road branches to the right (west) north of **Km B-150**. After about 1-

mile the road standard decreases but arrives with no difficulty in 4.1 miles at Punta San Jacinto on the coast. There are endless numbers of places to camp on the low bluffs overlooking the sea in both directions.

(Km B-157) CAMALU — Camalu is a town of little interest to the tourist except as a source of supplies and for its PEMEX station. In addition, Red Cross volunteers are usually present in the middle of the highway soliciting donations. A contribution will net you a Red Cross sticker for your window which will save you from a repeat performance on the return trip. Pay-up.

SIDE TRIP
PUNTA CAMALU — Immediately north of the Camalu PEMEX station a dirt road leads in 2.3 miles to Punta Camalu. At 1.7 miles along the way, a side road bears left to a fish camp. Keeping right at this point will provide access to numerous good camping spots along the coast. End **SIDE TRIP**.

SIDE TRIP
(Km B-169) MISSION SANTO DOMINGO — About 200 yards north of the bridge over the Rio Santo Domingo a side road leaves Highway 1 to the left (east). It leads to the ruins of a mission founded by the Dominicans in 1775. Its photo appears on the first page of PART II. The road is poorly constructed but passes over flat terrain. It is not recommended for larger R.V.'s

The trip to the mission site and small village of Santo Domingo is 4.9 miles. The ruins lie immediately west of the town's primary school. The full outline of the mission quadrangle is still in evidence, along with several three-foot-thick adobe walls. As with the other missions, the remains lie fully exposed to the elements. End **SIDE TRIP**.

(Km B-172) COLONIA VICIENTE GUERRERO — Colonia Viciente Guerrero is another small agricultural town. It supports a PEMEX station and two R. V. parks. The road to these parks leaves Highway 1 to the right (west) 0.2 miles north of **Km B-173**. A sizeable electrical substation lies opposite the junction point. The first park (Don Pepes) is close to the highway. The second (Posada Don Diego) is 0.3 miles to the west in a pleasant orchard setting. Both have restaurants and full hookups.

SIDE TRIP
From the Posada Don Diego park drive west 2.7 miles to an excellent sand beach backed by dunes. Camping behind the dunes will cut the wind. The road is low standard with many twists and turns; but no problema, keep heading west and stop short of the water. End **SIDE TRIP**.

(Km B-175) ISLA SAN MARTIN AND SAN QUINTIN CINDER CONES — Isla San Martin and the San Quintin cinder cones should now be clearly in view to the right. The island lies some 5 miles offshore. It is the furthest peak to the right (NW). It provides a home for several species of marine mammals and is the site of a Mexican fisherman's camp. An

anchorage on its SE shore is a frequently used stopover point for yachts making the passage from San Diego to Cabo San Lucas.

CULTURAL NOTE (FISH CAMPS) — The *fish camp* on Isla San Martin is one of scores of such camps to be found on islands and isolated stretches of coast throughout the Baja peninsula. They consist of one or more shacks made of sheet metal, tar paper, poles, and scraps of other building material. There is little, if any, furniture. These crude dwellings provide permanent or seasonal sites for fishing and lobstering operations which are usually outposts for a headquarters cooperative in the larger towns.

Fishing and transportation to and from supply points is done in open, outboard-motor-powered pangas (See photo in Chapter 5.) I have visited dozens of such camps and always found their residents to be friendly, hard working, and usually eager to sell a portion of their catch. The location of other fish camps is noted at many other places. Hopefully, you might take the opportunity to pay some of them a visit and gain an understanding of a way of life quite foreign and primitive to most North Americans.

(Km B-190) SAN QUINTIN — San Quintin and adjoining Colonia Lazaro Cardenas are the southernmost of the towns that dot the coastal plain through which you have been traveling. The area's principal tourist facilities lie some 14 km (9 miles) to the south, but you need to make an important decision here in town concerning your vehicle's fuel supply.

The objective is to be able to pass through the remote mountains and desert between El Rosario and Guerrero Negro to the south without exhausting your fuel supply. In past years it was often difficult to obtain fuel within this section (about 400 km or 250 miles in length). Now it is usually available but you should not count on it. This fueling situation has improved somewhat with the installation of a gas station (extra only) at the hotel at Catavina. However, in the event of low supplies, this station will serve only its hotel customers, and may refuse service to caravans at all times.

Ideally, you would obtain fuel at El Rosario. However, should the stations there be closed or out of fuel you may have a problem. The prudent plan is to fuel at San Quintin, and top off at El Rosario if it is available.

SIDE TRIP
(Km B-193) COLONIA LAZARO CARDENAS & BAHIA SAN QUINTIN — To the highway traveler, the town of Lazaro Cardenas will appear only as a southerly extension of San Quintin. It is, however, the gateway to Bahia San Quintin.

Bahia San Quintin is a large, shallow, almost totally landlocked estuary. (See the SAN QUINTIN AREA Map.) Its northern section is served by a highway standard, but badly washboarded road. If you are heading south toward the peninsula's tip there is no particular reason to pay a visit here. However, it is a good

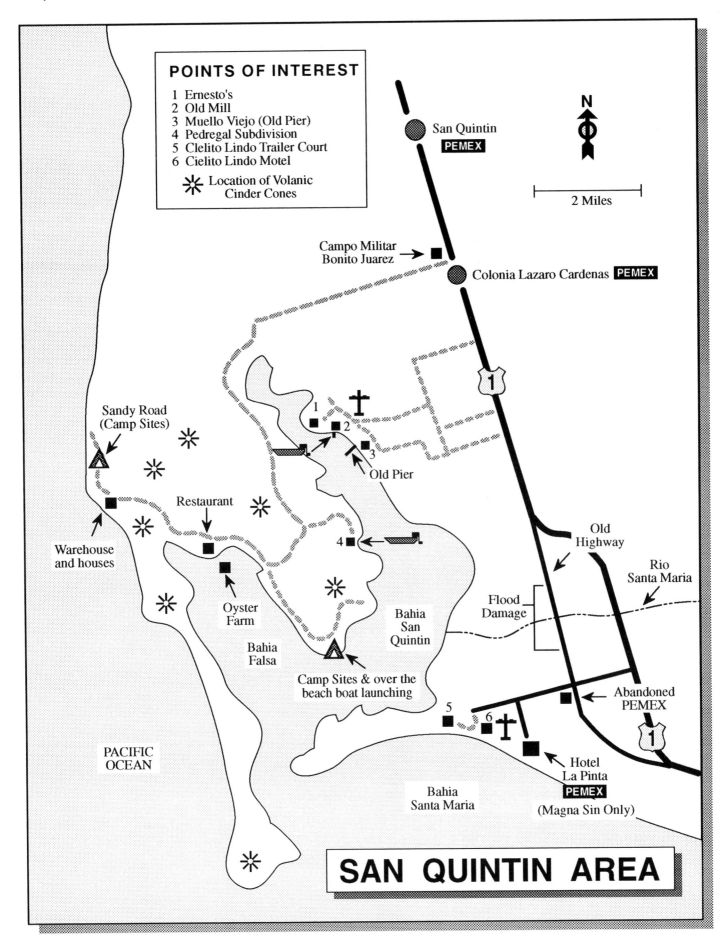

POINTS OF INTEREST
1 Ernesto's
2 Old Mill
3 Muello Viejo (Old Pier)
4 Pedregal Subdivision
5 Clelito Lindo Trailer Court
6 Cielito Lindo Motel

✳ Location of Volanic Cinder Cones

N

2 Miles

San Quintin PEMEX

Campo Militar Bonito Juarez →

Colonia Lazaro Cardenas PEMEX

1

Sandy Road (Camp Sites)

1

2

3 Old Pier

Restaurant

4

Warehouse and houses

Oyster Farm

Bahia Falsa

Bahia San Quintin

Old Highway

Rio Santa Maria

Flood Damage

Camp Sites & over the beach boat launching

Abandoned PEMEX

PACIFIC OCEAN

5

6

Hotel La Pinta PEMEX

Bahia Santa Maria

(Magna Sin Only)

SAN QUINTIN AREA

place to reach the water's edge if the San Quintin area is the destination point of your trip.

The road to the bay leaves Highway 1 to the right (west) near the center of Colonia Lazaro Cardenas at a point about 0.1 miles north of the PEMEX station. There is a military base on the NW corner and a CONASUPO store on the SW corner. A road sign reads "Bahia Falsa." Bahia Falsa is the westerly arm of the Bahia San Quintin estuary.

A trip of 14 km (9 miles) over this road will bring you to the shores of the bay. Taking the left fork at this point will bring you in about 2 miles to bay-side camp spots and places to launch small boats over the rocky beach.

The main road continues to the right for 2 more miles and terminates at a fishing village and warehouse facility on the Pacific shore. En route, you pass by an oyster farm (Campo Ostionero) and small restaurant and drive very close to the bases of the cinder cones you have been seeing from Highway 1. Note the reddish color of these volcanic rocks compared with the light-colored granite you have seen in other areas.

There are places to camp at various places along the bay shore but they are difficult to access with larger R.V.'s. Lightweight class 4 boats can be launched over the beach near the fish camp or at boat ramps at the Old Mill Motel (see Chapter 19) and the Pedregal subdivision. You will have to negotiate the shallow bars at the entrance of the bay to reach the open ocean. This entrance is protected from the prevailing NW swells, but careful attention should be given to the state of the tides and weather. End **SIDE TRIP**.

(KM B-196 AND C-0) END OF HIGHWAY SECTION B — The breakpoint between Highway Sections **B** and **C** lies six kilometers south of the center of the town of San Quintin.

CONGRATULATIONS — YOU HAVE ARRIVED AT THE POINT WHERE THE REAL BAJA PENINSULA BEGINS

EL MALO Y EL BUENO
(The Bad and the Good)

This arid land, so hot and so dry,
   Where the sun always shines in a bright azure sky
On rough ragged rocks and on scorching sand,
   Offering to humans a most desolate land
Covered with cacti and thickets of thorn,
   A prickly jungle, dense and forlorn;

Where the coarse cardon commands and at its feet
   The pin-cushion cholla and the ocotillo meet;
The ridiculous roadrunner hurries about
   Pursuing a lizard that skitters in rout;
The merry mockingbird sings in his bower,
   The promiscuous hummingbird kisses each bright cactus flower
And along the shores within easy reach
   The snowy white surf caresses a golden beach.

Ken Reimer

CHAPTER 19
SAN QUINTIN TO THE STATE LINE

Most North Americans who have traveled the Transpeninsular Highway will agree that you really haven't visited the Baja peninsula until you progress south of San Quintin. Once this is done, most of the larger towns will have been left behind, there are substantial areas of open space, and after a few miles the peninsula's fascinating desert vegetation will begin to dominate the landscape. A new world will emerge. You will have entered the final decompression stage in the escape from the land of the freeways to the north.

Roll down the window of your vehicle and take in the fresh air. To hell with the air conditioner. Wave hello to the Mexicans and stop looking like you expect to be attacked by bandits. This is the Magnificent Peninsula. Enjoy.

(Km C-1 AND C-4) BAY-SIDE MOTELS — A short distance to the west there are three modest motels located on the low bluffs overlooking the eastern shores of Bahia San Quintin. These are Ernesto's, the Old Mill and the Muelle Viejo. Each has an accompanying restaurant. The Old Mill was being extensively refurbished in 1992 and includes a boat launching ramp, boat rental, and R.V. park.

These facilities provide pleasant spots at the water's edge, but the access roads which leave Highway 1 between Kms C-1 and C-4 are low standard affairs running between agricultural fields (See the SAN QUINTIN AREA Map in Chapter 18). They are not well suited for larger R.V.'s, particularly in wet weather when they become next to impassable.

SIDE TRIP
(Km C-11) SAN QUINTIN TOURIST AREA — A paved access road leaves Highway 1 200 yards north of **Km C-11** and is signed for the Hotel La Pinta. This junction is on a relocated section of Highway 1. After 1.2 miles you will cross the original highway and an abandoned PEMEX station. This highway relocation no doubt throws a slight *kink* into all the kilometer points to the south and provides the perfect excuse if you find my distance figures slightly in error.

The area contains the Hotel La Pinta San Quintin and the Cielito Lindo Motel and Trailer Court. They are near an excellent Pacific beach. The Hotel La Pinta is the northernmost of the original *parador* hotels. I do not find it as nice as the other La Pinta hotels, but it will provide a fair idea of what to expect from its sister facilities to the south. The Cielito Lindo Motel is a pleasant place to stay, but the trailer court is suffering badly from lack of maintenance. The access road to Cielito Lindo can be impassable following storms. End **SIDE TRIP**.

SIDE TRIP
(Km C-15) EL PABELLON BEACH — Midway between **Km C-15** and C-16 a dirt road leaves to the right and in 1.1 miles arrives at El Pabellon Beach on the Pacific. There is a nearby trailer court which in 1992 bore the name El Pabellon (The name keeps changing). The camp provides full hookups for R.V.'s but is devoid of landscaping. The excellent nearby beach is its best feature, and many visitors choose to settle behind the sand dunes in this area. End **SIDE TRIP**.

(Km C-24 to C-41) PACIFIC COAST — After having entered the flat coastal plain at Colonet to the north, you will find that Highway 1 has been constructed some distance inland. Finally, at **Km C-24**, the road approaches the coast and parallels it within 1/4 to 1/2 mile until **Km C-41**. The ocean is in view along much of this section of highway, and there are numerous low standard dirt roads that may be used to reach camp spots on the low coastal bluffs. Sadly, this relatively unimpressive 10-mile section of road is the only place south of Ensenada where the Pacific Coast is in close view from the Transpeninsular Highway. Your next close encounter with salt water will be on the Sea of Cortez, more than 200 miles to the south, near Santa Rosalia.

The Hotel La Pinta San Quintin on the beach east of Bahia San Quintin.

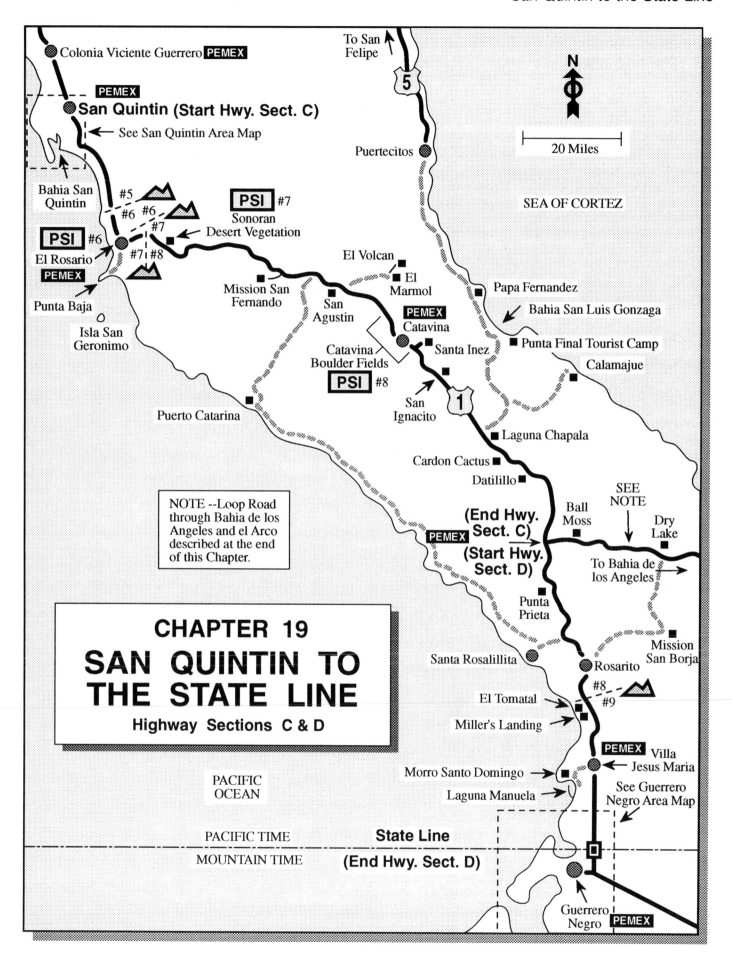

Colonia Viciente Guerrero **PEMEX**

PEMEX

San Quintin (Start Hwy. Sect. C)

← See San Quintin Area Map

To San Felipe ↑

5

Puertecitos

N

20 Miles

SEA OF CORTEZ

Bahia San Quintin

#5

#6 #6

#7

PSI #7

Sonoran Desert Vegetation

PSI #6

#7 #8

El Rosario

PEMEX

Punta Baja

Isla San Geronimo

El Volcan

El Marmol

Papa Fernandez

Bahia San Luis Gonzaga

Mission San Fernando

San Agustin

PEMEX Catavina

Santa Inez

Punta Final Tourist Camp

Calamajue

Catavina Boulder Fields

PSI #8

San Ignacito

1

Puerto Catarina

Laguna Chapala

Cardon Cactus

Datilillo

SEE NOTE

NOTE --Loop Road through Bahia de los Angeles and el Arco described at the end of this Chapter.

Ball Moss

Dry Lake

(End Hwy. Sect. C)

PEMEX

(Start Hwy. Sect. D)

To Bahia de los Angeles →

Punta Prieta

Mission San Borja

Santa Rosalillita

Rosarito

#8

#9

CHAPTER 19

SAN QUINTIN TO THE STATE LINE

Highway Sections C & D

El Tomatal

Miller's Landing

PEMEX Villa Jesus Maria

Morro Santo Domingo →

PACIFIC OCEAN

Laguna Manuela →

See Guerrero Negro Area Map

PACIFIC TIME

MOUNTAIN TIME

State Line

(End Hwy. Sect. D)

Guerrero Negro **PEMEX**

#5 △△ #6

(Km C-41) GEOGRAPHIC CHANGE — **Km C-41** brings the traveler to the southern end of Geographic Section No. 5. At this point the highway leaves the flat Continental Borderlands Province and reenters the Peninsular Range Mountains. Lying ahead is Geographic Section No. 6, a short 14 km (9 mile) mountainous segment ending at El Rosario.

At **Km C-41** the highway starts to wind its way uphill to a plateau area which levels out at **Km C-50** at an elevation of some 800 feet. After a few miles, it then descends rapidly to the town of El Rosario.

(Km C-41 to C-55) VEGETATION TRANSITION — Much of the original vegetation north of this point has been replaced or heavily modified by agricultural activities. At **Km C-41** the native chaparral becomes more evident, but it shares the hillsides with various types of cactus, century plants, and other species normally associated with the desert. You are traveling through a transitional vegetational zone between the *California Region* to the north and the *Sonoran Desert* to the south. The full change will become more apparent when the highway crosses to the south of the Rio del Rosario at **Km C-63**.

(Km C-55) EL ROSARIO — At the center of the community of El Rosario (The Rosary), the highway takes an abrupt 90-degree turn to the left (east) and proceeds up the northern edge of the flat valley lands of the Rio del Rosario. At this turn, a secondary road leaves the highway, to the right, and is the starting point for the trip to the mission ruins and Punta Baja. (See the EL ROSARIO AREA Map.)

There are two PEMEX stations on the highway. Be sure to obtain fuel here unless you are positive you can make it through

The author's camper in splendid isolation above the Pacific surf at Punta Baja.

the mountains and desert to Guerrero Negro. Near the 90-degree highway turn is Mama Espinosa's restaurant. It is famous for its lobster burritos and is well worth a visit.

As recently as the mid-1960s, El Rosario was portraied as "the end of the line." Roads to the south could only be described as primitive. Mail service and the weekly bus from Ensenada proceeded no further. The completion of the Transpeninsular Highway in 1973 was to alter El Rosario's place in the sun. Rather than the *end*, the town is now more properly looked upon as the *beginning*; for here the new highway starts its lengthy journey through the interior mountains and deserts of the peninsula.

El Rosario was also the point of beginning for Baja's Dominican friars, for it was here that they established their first mission in 1774, only two years after they took over administration of the peninsula's missionary activities from the Franciscans. It was to be the jumping-off point for the founding of eight additional missions between there and the international border.

The original mission site was up-river from the center of town. In 1882, it was moved about one and one-half miles downstream. Its ruins may be visited as part of the POINTS OF SPECIAL INTEREST Tour. A sign in front of the site notes, "1434 Christian Indians registered between 1774 and 1817. These were supported from products of desert, sea, cattle, sheep, goats, and plantings of cereals imported by the Spaniards." Many of these Indians were soon to die in the epidemics which accompanied the Spanish wherever they went.

PSI #6

SIDE TRIP
(Km C-55) MISSION RUINS AND PUNTA BAJA — Start at the 90-degree highway turn mentioned in the first paragraph of the section above and drive west, past the market.

0.1 Miles - Junction with dirt road marked on the SW corner by two sizeable tamarisk trees. Turn left taking this road. Take the left fork at a junction a short distance ahead.

1.0 Miles - Cross the Rio del Rosario. On my last visit in 1992 the river had been bridged with an earthen embankment and culvert, but high water may soon deposit these in the ocean. Use caution.

1.1 Miles - Junction with another dirt road paralleling the south side of the river. Turn right on this road and drive down-river.

1.6 Miles - To the right, on a bluff overlooking the valley, are the ruins of the mission which was founded in 1782. This is stop No. 6 on the POINTS OF SPECIAL INTEREST Tour. Continue past the mission ruins if you are heading for Punta Baja.

2.6 Miles - Junction with dirt road heading 90 degrees to the left. This road goes to Agua Blanca. For Punta Baja continue straight ahead through agricultural fields.

2.9 Miles - Junction with another dirt road heading 90 degrees to the left. Turn left on this road and promptly begin to climb up the face of a broad ridge.

8.3 Miles - Road breaks out on top of ridge with fine view of Punta Baja and the ocean.

9.6 Miles - Junction with road bearing sharply to the left. Continue straight ahead and remember not to stray onto this road on your return trip.

10.6 Miles - Punta Baja fishing village. Note the one-room school house, which was constructed in October 1980 by the Del Mar Rotary Club and dedicated to the children of Punta Baja.

11.9 Miles - Punta Baja navigation light, and the tip of the point. Almost all of Baja's navigation lights are now reliable and are powered by solar energy. Note the solar panels atop the Punta Baja light.

Punta Baja is one of the most prominent points of land on Baja's Pacific coast. It provides good protection from the ocean's prevailing NW swells. For this reason, it is an anchorage used by Mexican fishing craft and yachts making the Baja passage. Small class 4 boats may be launched over the rocky beach at the village by using a steep road cut through the bluffs by the local fishermen. Because this is the open Pacific, small boats should not stray far from the protection of the point.

From Punta Baja, you can see Isla San Geronimo lying in the Pacific some 8 miles to the SE. It supports a sizeable fish camp. Punta Baja is also a good place to watch for gray whale spouts during the annual migration. End **SIDE TRIP**.

#6 ⛰ #7
(Km C-55 to C-63) GEOGRAPHIC CHANGE RIO DEL ROSARIO VALLEY

This short 8 km (5 mile) section of Highway 1 passes through the valley of the Rio del Rosario (Geographic Section No.7). The highway passes along the northern edge of the valley, which has been cleared for agriculture since the arrival of the missionaries in 1774. It is one of the few places in the peninsula where there is sufficient surface water to support crops.

During heavy rain from late fall tropical storms, the river can become a roaring torrent. The Transpeninsular Highway was opened before many of its bridges were completed. The river crossing at **Km C-63** was the burial ground for many vehicles that tried to cross during such runoff periods. The present 0.6 miles of causeways and bridges are safe and the longest anywhere in Baja.

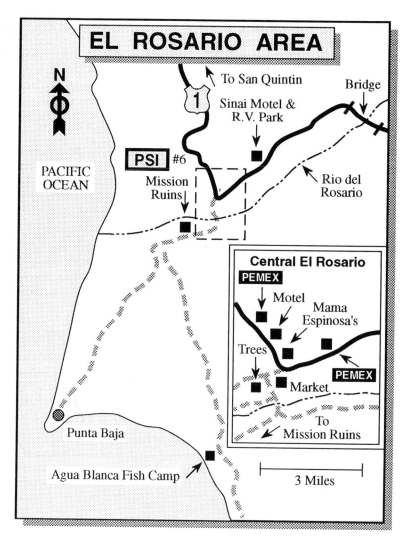

#7 ⛰ #8
(Km C-63) GEOGRAPHIC CHANGE — After crossing the Rio del Rosario, the highway enters the longest of its nineteen geographic sections (Geographic Section No. 8). For 287 kms (178 miles), the road passes through the mountains and plateaus that are typical of the gentle, westerly slopes of the Peninsular Range Mountains.

You might care to review the description of this range in Chapter 9 GEOLOGY. Highway 1 will cross over endless numbers of westerly draining arroyos without the aid of drainage structures. Rain water and debris must pass over the surface of the highway. To drive over these crossings (vados) at high speeds when they contain water or debris is to invite severe tire damage.

In many places the highway will pass over broad ridges with good scenic views. Also, there are extensive level stretches through intermountain valleys. In summary, the road conditions are not severe and reflect the relatively gentle terrain of the Peninsular Range's western slope.

South of the Rio del Rosario bridge, Highway 1 begins to gain elevation rapidly.

PSI #7

(Km C-63 to C-80) SONORAN DESERT VEGETATION
— Sonoran Desert vegetation begins after crossing the Rio del Rosario. The brush species you have been seeing to the north are still present, but true desert plants now become commonplace. Among them are many century plants and several species of cactus. Baja's most unique plant, the cirio, comes into view at about **Km C-69**. From **Km C-70** to **Km C-74** the highway passes through a broad valley where these plants are numerous. Although many of Baja's desert plants persist all the way to the peninsula's tip, you will see no more cirios after leaving Geographic Section No. 8.

At **Km C-80** the desert vegetation is particularly varied and plentiful and by now includes prickly pear cactus, galloping cactus, candelabra cactus, velvet cactus, giant cardon, and cirio. This is stop No. 7 on the POINTS OF SPECIAL INTEREST Tour. Linger here and seek the assistance of Chapter 10 VEGETATION in identifying the more common species and in investigating the characteristics of the desert plants which it describes.

SIDE TRIP
(Km C-114) MISSION SAN FERNANDO — Immediately south of **Km C-114** a low standard dirt road leaves Highway 1 to the right (west). It is level but narrow and is not recommended for larger R.V.'s. A journey of <u>3.2 miles</u> will bring you to the ruins of the only mission in the Baja peninsula that was founded by the Franciscan order. If you don't make the side trip, you might at least pause and reflect that here in this lonely and desolate place the Portola-Serra expedition passed through in

Adobe ruins of the Mission San Fernando founded by Junipero Serra in 1769. The flat valley behind the ruins provided the pasture which was the reason for founding the mission at this site.

1769 on its historic journey from Loreto to San Diego. See the story in Chapter 12 HISTORY.

The mission site lies on the north side of the Rio San Fernando. This location was selected because it provided good pasturage for the expedition's livestock. It is hard to believe that this remote outpost founded by Junipero Serra was developed by the succeeding Dominicans into the home of some 1,500 Indians. These people were decimated by epidemics in the years 1777-80, and by 1818 the mission was abandoned. End **SIDE TRIP**.

BOB & JEAN 4X4

(Km C-128) -- PACIFIC COAST LOOP — Here is trip #2, the longest of the "Bob and Jean 4x4" Recommendations noted in Chapter 3. Leave Highway 1 to the south about 8 miles NW of San Agustin. The road is signed for Puerto Catarina - 33 Km. The route travels about 35 miles south to Puerto Catarina (the former shipping port for the El Marmol onyx mine) and then some 100 miles SE along the coast to Santa Rosalillita. There are several unroaded gaps shown in this route on the AAA map, but Bob and Jean have driven it many times. Its all there. The return road to Highway 1 from Santa Rosalillita is noted in this chapter at **Km D-38**.

This coastal loop offers numerous outstanding camping spots, deserted beaches, and spectacular vistas of the Pacific. You may find yourself taking a few wrong turns discovering the main road along the coast, but the ever-present coastline will be your guide. Best travel with a buddy vehicle, for breakdowns in this seldom traveled region would mean a lot of walking.

(KM C-140) SAN AGUSTIN — There is an inoperative government-built trailer court at this point. The toilet and related facilities are abandoned and on my last visit the gate was locked shut. On other occasions I have been able to spend the night in its well-landscaped, pull-through trailer spaces.

SIDE TRIP
(Km C 144) EL MARMOL — It is a <u>9.8 mile</u> side trip over a good secondary road to the famous open-pit onyx mine at el Marmol (Marble) with its unique onyx block schoolhouse. It was the source of onyx that was hauled over 51-miles of rough dirt road for shipment by sea from Puerto Santo Catarina on the Pacific coast. The market for onyx is now greatly reduced because of the development of plastics. Quarried blocks of onyx may be seen lying about the mine area. Some small scale mining was observed in 1992.

One would expect a mine to be deep in the mountains. However, el Marmol is at the foot of the hills and the access road is passable even to larger R.V.'s. The initial 6-miles is totally flat with the remainder a bit more rolling. The road surface is relatively easy to drive over in comparison to most of Baja's secondary roads.

BOB & JEAN 4X4

NE from the schoolhouse, one can drive about 4.5 miles over rough roads to visit unique El Volcan, a mineral spring where water oozing from the ground results in new deposits of onyx. It is trip #3 of the "Bob and Jean" 4x4 Recommendations presented in Chapter 3. End **SIDE TRIP.**

PSI #8

(Km C-157 to C-179) CATAVINA BOULDER FIELD — The next 11 km (7 mile) segment of the Transpeninsular Highway is one of its most scenic and interesting. The highway has been constructed through an area of massive granite boulders and the desert vegetation is excellent. In particular, notice the elephant trees growing from the boulders south of **Km C-169**. It is stop No. 8 on the POINTS OF SPECIAL INTEREST Tour. Most vehicles can pull over at many places along the way. Even larger R.V.'s and trailers can pull off and turn around at a side road and blacktop mixing area a short distance north of **Km C-161** and also at **Km C-163**.

The Catavina Boulder Field and its impressive Sonoran Desert vegetation. Few places better befit the Norte Americano conception of the Wild-Wild West.

The thousands of rounded boulders that you will see are composed of granite rock. Please review the ROCK TYPE CLASSIFICATION Table in Chapter 9 GEOLOGY. Granite is an igneous—plutonic—intrusive rock. All this complicated terminology means that a mass of molten material was cooled slowly beneath (inside) the earth's surface. Because of the slow cooling, identifiable crystals of various minerals were able to form, and the rocks appear light in color. Pick up a piece of granite and you can readily see the individual crystals of quartz, feldspar, and mica. Take a piece with you to compare it with the fine-grained, darker colored igneous—volcanic—extrusive rocks that you will see to the south.

Observe the soil beneath your feet. It is made up of weathered particles of granite rock. This type of soil is universally known as **D-G**, *decomposed granite*. It is a road engineer's nightmare, as **D-G** soils are subject to severe erosion.

Many tourists ask "Where did the boulders come from?" The answer is that they were manufactured on the spot. Masses of granite rock tend to fracture vertically at the surface. These fractures are weathered by water and freezing temperatures, and the rock mass breaks up into blocks. With further weathering, the blocks are rounded into the boulders that you see.

(Km C-171 & C-175) PALM TREES — Within the Catavina Boulder Field Highway 1 crosses two substantial arroyos near **Km C-171** and C-175. Along these water courses you will see groves of native Washingtonia fan palms. Note that the leaves extend fan-like from the end of each stem. While palms are inhabitants of the desert, most species grow in places such as this arroyo bottom where there is water near the surface.

There are several species of palm that are native to the Baja peninsula. However, most of the trees that you will see are date palms introduced by the early missionaries. They are still found in great abundance in such towns as San Ignacio, Mulege, and Loreto. The leaves of this species project from both sides along the stem.

(Km C-174) CATAVINA — Cativina is a small development located near the highway in the heart of the Catavina Boulder Field. At **Km C-174**, adjoining the highway, are an R.V. park, PEMEX station and the attractive Hotel La Pinta Catavina. The latter is typical of the original parador hotels.

The R.V. park is also typical of those built throughout the peninsula. The white masonry structures housing the water and electrical outlets make these facilities look like cemeteries from a distance. Some of these courts have been abandoned. The one here was open during my last visit, but the restrooms were unusable. The PEMEX station has usually been open in recent years, and a second station (Magna Sin only) has been built at the hotel.

(Km C-175) SANTA INEZ — A blacktop road leaves Highway 1 to the left (east) south of **Km C-175**. It is 0.8 miles to an airstrip and the Rancho Santa Inez. The ranch has rooms for rent and a small cafe. An area near the cafe has been cleared and is used as an R.V. parking area. It offers a bit more seclusion than the park at Catavina.

Datilillo is one of the dominant plants along the southern portion of Highway 1 described in this chapter.

The Mission Santa Maria, established to the east in 1767, was the last of the chain of outposts built by the Jesuit fathers. At the time, it was the most northerly point of civilization on the peninsula and was the final jumping-off point for the Portola-Serra expedition to San Diego in 1769.

BOB & JEAN 4X4

A 14 mile private road was constructed some years ago from Rancho Santa Inez over the peninsular divide to the mission. This road is now in poor repair. Driving it is trip #4 of the "Bob and Jean 4x4" Recommendations presented in Chapter 3. Only the end walls and foundations of the mission remain, but its lovely palm canyon and the remote beauty of the area make this a rewarding adventure. Ask for directions at the Rancho Santa Inez.

Km C-187) SAN IGNACITO — Here, across the highway from the Rancho San Ignacito restaurant, is a brass plaque marking the point where the two ends of the Transpeninsular Highway came together, and where work on the road was finished in September 1973.

(Km C-206) EL PEDREGOSO — On the right (west) side of the highway can be seen a hill of grotesquely shaped granite boulders. It is named El Pedregoso (the rocky one). It is a boulder field in the process of development.

(KM C-229) HIGHWAY JUNCTION — The southern end of the new highway from San Feilpe joins Highway 1 at this point. It is built to highway standards but only the first 56-miles south from San Felipe are oiled (See Chapter 15 for a full description).

When completed, this highway will become a major new access route from the United States to Baja California. It will bypass all of the 324 miles of Highway 1 to the north of this point. In 1992 the road was signed to Calamajue, a Sea of Cortez fishing camp at the end of a branch off the main road.

(Km C-231) LAGUNA CHAPALA — Highway 1 passes along the western edge of a large dry lake bed, Laguna Chapala. This topographic depression is similar to many found in desert regions where water collects after heavy rains due to lack of a drainage outlet. Prior to the completion of the new highway, the road ran across the middle of the lake and provided rock-jostled drivers with a rare opportunity to gather speed. Following rain, the lake bed became a quagmire and vehicles had to be detoured around the eastern perimeter.

(Km C-241) A CARDONAL — The Transpeninsular Highway passes through an impressive *cardonal*, or forest of cardon (giant cactus). See Chapter 10 VEGETATION. Also present are numerous ocotillo and cirio.

(KM C-250) DATILILLO — At this point the traveler can see a scattering of datilillo trees. This species will become commonplace south to the state line and along the highway to Bahia de los Angeles. Datilillo means *little date,* although the plant is in the lily family and is not related to the date palm. These multitrunked plants closely resemble the Joshua tree found in the deserts east of the Los Angeles basin and in other places in SW United States.

(Km C-258) SIDE ROAD — South of **Km C-258** Highway 1 is joined on the left (east) by a low-standard road signed to San Felipe. This is an older road to San Felipe and should not be confused with the newer highway standard road noted above at **Km C-229**.

(Km C-280 & Km D-0) BAHIA DE LOS ANGELES JUNCTION — This is the breakpoint between Highway Sections **C** and **D** and the junction with the highway to Bahia de los Angeles. The government trailer court here is open for use but there are no operable facilities. The PEMEX station which has been abandoned in the past was open in 1992.

SIDE TRIP -- A loop road leaves Highway 1 at this point and travels 42 miles to Bahia de los Angeles, south along the Sea of Cortez, and then inland through el Arco to rejoin Highway 1 at **Km E-190**. Bahia de los Angeles is an important tourist area. The entire loop is described in a separate section at the end of this chapter. End **SIDE TRIP**.

(Km D-13) PUNTA PRIETA — A detachment of army personnel is based to the right (west) at a place named Punta Prieta. The area to the south is sometimes bathed in fog and low clouds rolling in from the Pacific Ocean. Starting at about **Km D-20**, note that many of the cirio trees are draped with flowing lichens which thrive in the often moisture-laden air.

(Km D-29) OCEAN VIEW — From this point on the highway, you will be able to see the Pacific Ocean many miles to the west if it is not obscured by fog. This will notify you that the Transpeninsular Highway is now rapidly approaching the Pacific coast. There will be three opportunities to make side trips to camping spots on the coast between here and the state line.

SIDE TRIP

(Km D-38) SANTA ROSALILLITA — Midway between **Km D-38** and **Km D-39** a secondary road leaves Highway 1 to the right (west) for the small fishing village of Santa Rosalillita, which is located directly on the Pacific shore. It is 16 km (10 miles) to the coast.

If you turn left (south) after reaching the town you will find places to camp on the bluffs overlooking the Pacific. A little further along on this same road is a beach where the fishermen launch their boats. Because the waters are very shallow at this point, launching is done with the aid of a trailer made from the rear axle and wheels of a car. It is an interesting operation to watch.

You can also work your vehicle over low standard roads to the beach in the cove north of the village. End **SIDE TRIP**.

(Km D-45) BALL MOSS — For a mile or so south of this point, you will see round masses surrounding the branches of the larger plants. These are ball moss. There is a far larger colony on the Highway to Bahia de los Angeles and on numerous secondary roads near the Pacific shore. The nature of this plant is described in Chapter 10 VEGETATION.

(Km D-51) ROSARITO — The town of Rosarito is of little interest to the traveler, and its PEMEX station and trailer court are abandoned.

(Km D-68) EL TOMATAL — A low standard road leaves Highway 1 to the right (west) midway between **Km D-68** and **Km D-69**. It is 2.9 miles to a camp spot in a grove of date palms at the inland edge of a small lagoon and some 100 yards from the beach. Approximately 0.2 miles past the palms and SE along the coast is the El Tomatal fish camp. The road is straight and flat but of low standard and is not recommended for large R.V.'s.

An even lower standard road branches south from the road to El Tomatal 0.4 miles before reaching the palm grove. This leads in 2.0 miles to Miller's Landing. Take the right fork along the way. Miller's Landing was a shipping point for onyx many decades ago. There are a dozen or so blocks of onyx and many smaller pieces lying about near the shingle beach.

#8 ▲ #9
(Km D-70) GEOGRAPHIC CHANGE DESIERTO DE VIZCAINO — Here, just south of the junction with the road to

El Tomatal, is the dividing line between the Peninsular Range Mountains (Geographic Section No. 8) to the north and the Desierto de Vizcaino (Geographic Section No. 9) to the south. The Desierto de Vizcaino is a portion of the Continental Borderlands Province. As in other places, this dividing line between geographic provinces is readily apparent. The highway now leaves the mountains and plateaus and will traverse flat terrain for the next 192 km (119 miles).

(Km D-80) LIVING FENCE — Notice that the fences along the highway starting near here are made of posts cut from the datilillo. Densely packed rows of posts also outline the yards of the dwellings in the upcoming town of Jesus Maria. Many of these take root and form living fences. This is an example of vegetative reproduction common with desert plants.

(Km D-96) VILLA JESUS MARIA — Villa Jesus Maria is a small community adjacent to the highway. A PEMEX station was operative on my last trip. If you look to the west you will see a small mountain, Morro Santo Domingo, the only one present in this otherwise flat area. Keep it in mind for it will guide you to the coast if you choose to take the side trip described in the following item.

SIDE TRIP

(Km D-96) LAGUNA MANUELA — A secondary road to the Pacific at Laguna Manuela leaves Highway 1 to the right (west) at Villa Jesus Maria, 200 yards north of **Km D-96**. Laguna Manuela is a saltwater estuary lying directly south of Morro Santo Domingo. The first 0.9 miles is a two-lane paved, road. At the 0.9 mile-point a wide, straight, gravel road veers off to the left and heads directly to the peak of the mountain. Taking this road for an additional 6.4 miles will bring you to the coast near the edge of Laguna Manuela. (Total 7.3 miles.) This road is straight and flat but with a washboard surface.

Local fishermen launch their boats into the protected lagoon and have developed its waters into an oyster farm. Tourists can find camp spots along the shore. The lagoon and adjoining ocean bay are protected from the Pacific swells by Morro Santo Domingo.

> **BOB & JEAN 4X4**

The camping spots adjoining Laguna Manuela leave something to be desired. Thus, if you have a 4x4 vehicle, you may take an excursion up the steep, sandy road that starts near the masonry buildings at the head of the lagoon and proceed westerly past the lighthouse to Morro Santo Domingo.

This is trip #5 of "Bob and Jean 4x4" Recommendations noted in Chapter 3. This short 3-mile drive traverses the cliffs above the Pacific and offers secluded camping sites with spectacular views of the surf below. End **SIDE TRIP**.

(Km D-128) PARALELO 28 (THE STATE LINE) — Starting about **Km D-117**, the huge, 135-foot tall Monumento Aguila (Eagle Monument) is in view rising above the desert

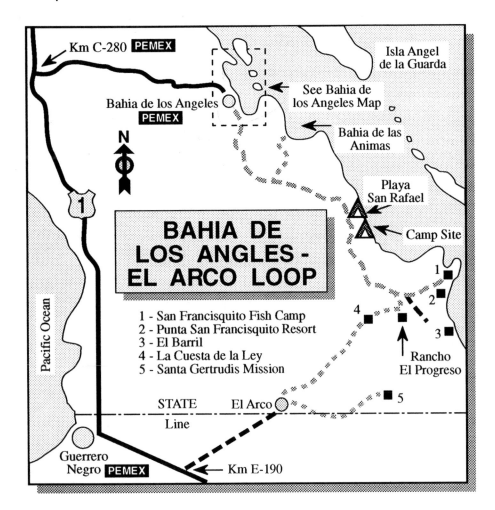

BAHIA DE LOS ANGLES - EL ARCO LOOP

1 - San Franciscquito Fish Camp
2 - Punta San Francisquito Resort
3 - El Barril
4 - La Cuesta de la Ley
5 - Santa Gertrudis Mission

floor. It marks *Paralelo 28*, the 28th parallel of north latitude, and the line between the states of Baja California and Baja California Sur.

Here is located another in the chain of parador developments that accompanied the completion of the Transpeninsular Highway. The Hotel La Pinta Guerrero Negro is well maintained and the adjoining trailer court is open. The PEMEX station and series of semi-underground shops built between the highway's divided lanes are closed. Part of the latter space has been converted into a school. There is now a gas pump at the hotel and there are gas stations in nearby Guerrero Negro.

Paralelo 28 is the division point between highway sections **C** and **D**. In the sections to the south, you will encounter the kilometer posts in reverse order (descending numbers heading south). Don't forget to move your watches ahead one hour as you are leaving the Pacific Time Zone and entering the Mountain Zone to the south.

BAHIA DE LOS ANGELES - EL ARCO LOOP

SIDE TRIP

This subsection of Chapter 19 will detail the loop road starting at the division point between Highway 1 sections **C** and **D** (**Km**

C-280 and **Km D-0**) and ending at **Km E-190**. It consists of four substantially different segments with a total distance of 181.4 miles.

(1) The initial 68 Km (42 miles) is a paved highway to the village of Bahia de los Angeles on the Sea of Cortez. En route it passes through desert vegetation that is varied and interesting. Fuel (no Magna Sin) is normally available at Bahia de los Angeles.

(2) The second segment is a 1 1/2 lane secondary road with a fairly rough surface. It connects Bahia de los Angeles with the El Progreso Ranch area and provides side trips to several places on the ocean. It is easily traveled by pickups and vans but travel time is slow due to the rough surface.

(3) From El Progreso to the town of El Arco is a narrow, low-standard dirt road. In most places travel speeds are actually faster than on segment (2) because of the smooth, sandy roadbed. With one exception the terrain is relatively level. The exception is La Cuesta de la Ley (Grade of the Law). It poses a segment of steep grades for both directions of travel. My standard drive pickup made it with no trouble going NE, but the opposite direction appeared more formidable. As few Mexicans have 4x4 vehicles it is no doubt passable to standard vehicles in both directions, but be prepared to grit your teeth.

(4) A paved highway was constructed from El Arco to **Km E-190** on Highway 1 when the latter route was completed. This was no doubt a concession to the community for being bypassed by the new highway. Virtually all of the original layer of paving has disappeared leaving a moderately washboarded travel surface. Most traffic uses a closely paralleling and smoother surfaced dirt road.

SEGMENT (1) — The highway to Bahia de los Angeles leaves Highway 1 to the left (east).

(Km-10) BALL MOSS — Starting at this point, you will see hundreds of six-to-eight-inch diameter, ball-shaped masses surrounding the branches of the cirio, datilillo, and other larger plants. This is ball moss (although it is not a moss). The plant makes its own food through photosynthesis and secures moisture from the air. It does not penetrate into the tissue of its host as is the case with mistletoe.

(Km-36) DRY LAKE — At this point, the highway enters the western edge of a dry lake bed some 5 miles in diameter. It is nearly surrounded by high, sparsely vegetated mountains.

(Km-49 to Km-52) CIRIO — Here, near the southern end of the dry lake, is an outstanding array of cirios. The individual plants are large and of many interesting shapes. A good spot for photography.

(Km-52) GEOGRAPHIC AND VEGETATIVE CHANGES — At this point, the traveler is rewarded with a vista of the Sea of Cortez and the highway begins its descent to sea level. From the Transpeninsular Highway to here, the terrain has been gentle, as one would expect of the westerly slopes of the Peninsular Range Mountains. Ahead lies the much steeper grade down the eastern escarpment.

There also occurs a prompt change in vegetation. The interesting and varied species of the Vizcaino Desert community are left behind and one enters the less attractive San Felipe Desert community composed mostly of creosote bush and other low shrubs. This scant plant growth clearly reflects the arid conditions of the rain shadow of the mountains.

(Km-58) OCEAN VIEW — A short distance past **Km 58**, Bahia de los Angeles and its close-in group of protecting islands are arrayed before you. Isla Angel de la Guarda, the second largest island in the Sea of Cortez, is in the background. These islands combine to make Bahia de los Angeles an extensive and well-protected boating area.

(Km-61) PUNTA LA GRINGA SHORTCUT -- An old dirt road leaves the highway about 200 yards downgrade (easterly) from Km-61. This is the shortcut route to Punta la Gringa. Its travel surface is smother than the main secondary road described in the next paragraph.

(Km-64) PUNTA LA GRINGA — To the left is a road junction at the northern edge of the village of Bahia de los Angeles. (See BAHIA DE LOS ANGELES Map.) You will no doubt wish to proceed straight ahead into town. Should you return to this Punta La Gringa road you will travel over it as follows: (A) 0.8 miles. Branch road left to the airport. (B) 1.3 miles. Branch road right to the government-constructed trailer court. The area is used as a camping site although its restrooms are not available to the public. (C) 7.8 miles. End of the road near a point of land, Punta La Gringa.

There is a fine beach where you may camp after paying a small fee. The area has extensive views of the bay and the towering escarpment of the mountains in the background. Many visitors find this a more enjoyable site than the trailer courts in the village.

(Km-64) VILLAGE OF BAHIA DE LOS ANGELES At this point you enter the village of Bahia de los Angeles. Here you will find the Casa Diaz Motel and Hotel Villa Vitta. Both of these establishments operate nearby R.V. parks. Guerrmo's Trailer Court lies between these first two. They offer little or no landscaping due to the areas dryness and thus appear a bit austere. Each court offers a hard-surfaced boat launching ramp.

To some people, the Bahia de los Angeles area suffers in charm because of its scant vegetation. To others, its near-barren mountains are beautiful to behold as the sun casts an ever-changing variety of shadow patterns on their slopes. Also on the positive side are its excellence as a boating and fishing area and the relatively short driving distance from the international border (405 miles).

The village of Bahia de los Angeles. The oiled highway can be seen entering town at the top of the photo. The secondary road heading south toward El Arco is visible at the bottom of the photo.

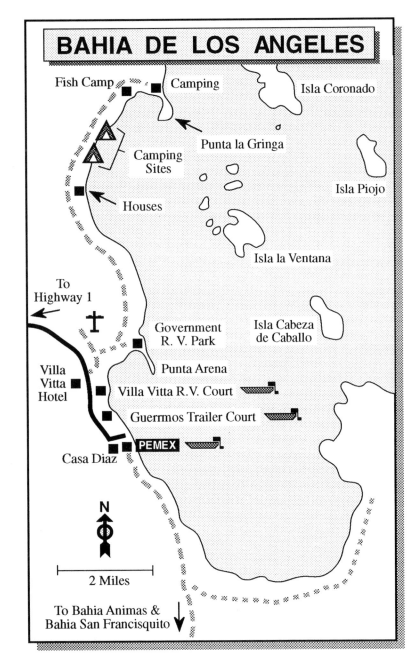

BAHIA DE LOS ANGELES

Fish Camp
Camping
Isla Coronado
Punta la Gringa
Camping Sites
Isla Piojo
Houses
To Highway 1
Isla la Ventana
Government R. V. Park
Isla Cabeza de Caballo
Villa Vitta Hotel
Punta Arena
Villa Vitta R.V. Court
Guerrmos Trailer Court
PEMEX
Casa Diaz
N
2 Miles
To Bahia Animas &
Bahia San Francisquito

Bahia de los Angeles can be particularly hard hit by the strong northern winds common to the upper Sea of Cortez in the late fall and winter. In addition gale force winds sometimes flow across the Baja peninsula from the west and strike the village area. Taking to sea in small boats becomes impossible and living conditions become most uncomfortable.

SEGMENT (2) — The Segment (2) secondary road leaves the Bahia de los Angeles village about 100 yards inland from the Casa Diaz Motel. (The mileages noted below start from 0.0 at this point.) The initial 3-4 miles parallels the shore of Bahia de los Angeles where tourists homes are being constructed. It then moves inland.

4.6 Miles — A low-standard dirt road heads east at this point, traverses a dirt airstrip and accesses a small group of tourist

houses and a good camping area at the SE corner of Bahia de los Angeles in about 5 miles.

27.6 Miles — Junction with side road to Bahia de las Animas. It is 10.7 miles to the first good camping spots on the edge of the bay and an additional 0.3 miles to the first of two fish camps. Most of this road is little more than two tracks in the sand but the terrain is level and regularly traveled by standard-drive vehicles. Portions of the route are in an arroyo bottom which could be impassable following rain. At the 7.1 mile point one has the choice of going straight ahead or turning 90 degrees to the left. The left turn is the proper choice.

There are several good camping sites on a narrow sandy beach. Be alert to numerous small sting rays that inhabit the shallow waters at the head of the bay. I was treated to my first, and hopefully last, sting from one of these *Moving Rocks* while cooling the beer in the ocean (one of the lesser known hazards of alcohol addiction).

41.6 Miles — Spur road east heading toward the coast. In about 1 mile it becomes very low standard and is best for 4x4 vehicles.

45.6 Miles — A short spur road leads east and in about 0.1 miles arrives at a camping spot at the north end of Playa San Rafael.

47.8 Miles — Spur road east leads in 0.1 miles to a fish camp at the south end of Playa San Rafael.

48.3 Miles — Spur road east accesses camping spots on a bluff overlooking a rocky shore. The San Lorenzo Island chain and the south end of Isla Angel de la Guarda are in view from here.

73.7 Miles — Junction with low standard road to the right (south) leading to Rancho el Progreso. This spur road is the beginning of Segment (3) of the loop route under discussion. However, the main secondary road continues eastward. Taking this latter route one encounters (1) a junction with another 2-lane road heading SE in 0.3 miles (see note below); (2) the junction with the road into the Punta San Francisquito Resort in an additional 11.8 miles; then arrives at the Bahia San Francisquito Fish Camp in an additional 0.4 miles. It is thus 86.2 miles from Bahia de los Angeles to Bahia San Francisquito.

The Punta San Francisquito Resort offers several modest sleeping cabins, central toilet and shower facilities, and a small restaurant. It caters primarily to patrons arriving at its nearby dirt airstrip. Aviation and regular fuel are available but it is expensive.

NOTE — I have not traveled the 2-lane road mentioned above but it appears to be being constructed to highway standards. It is no doubt heading toward El Barril, a private residential area on the coast about 7 miles distant. The standard of this road gives rise to speculation that it may become part of a coastal highway heading south to join Highway 1 near Santa Rosalia. Time will tell.

SEGMENT (3) — Return to the Rancho El Progreso junction noted above at <u>73.7 miles</u>.

<u>74.3 Miles</u> — The Rancho El Progreso and its well of fresh water lies on the south side of the road.

<u>82.7 Miles</u> — A gate in a cattle drift fence is built at the top of the steep La Cuesta de la Ley (See discussion at the start of this subsection). Between here and the rock corral noted below much of the road passes through an extensive burned over area indicatinging that travelers must be careful with fire even in the desert.

<u>92.0 Miles</u> — A large Rock corral lies adjacent to the road making an unmistakable landmark.

The Hotel Villa Vitta boat launching ramp at Bahia de los Angeles. The village may be seen in the background.

<u>106.5 Miles</u> — At this point one leaves the relatively level terrain and sandy soils prevailing to the NE and enters rolling hills. The travel surface becomes more rocky.

<u>112.8 Miles</u> — El Arco. In approaching El Arco from the reverse direction (west) one is tempted to turn right in the center of town. The correct course of action is to proceed straight ahead crossing an arroyo whereupon the road veers to the NE.

The main peninsular road passed through El Arco prior to construction of the Transpeninsular Highway. Gold was mined in the area by an American company, and during the 1920s over 1,000 people were employed. Gerhard and Gulick's *Lower California Guidebook* describes the town in 1960 as consisting of two groups of shacks on opposite sides of the arroyo with a population of about 150. By 1989 there had been a modest rejuvenation of the mining industry and the community was the base for a small detachment of federal soldiers. A lonely place for such duty.

SEGMENT (4) — It is <u>26.6 miles</u> from El Arco to Highway 1. The first <u>6 miles</u> SW from town passes through rolling terrain and one is compelled to drive on the main highway standard road and its washboarded surface. Beyond this point the land is level and the road is closely paralleled by a low-standard dirt road where a smoother surface makes it the most popular route of travel.

<u>139.4 Miles</u> — After many bumpy miles, the loop road joins Highway 1 near **Km E-190**. End **SIDE TRIP**.

CHAPTER 20
STATE LINE TO SANTA ROSALIA

Chapter 20 will guide you for 221 km (137 miles) in a journey completely across the peninsula from the Pacific Ocean to the Sea of Cortez. While very few tourists set out to visit this region, it nevertheless contains some of Baja's most intriguing points of interest. I hope you will not let the lure of the beaches ahead pull you through it with undue haste.

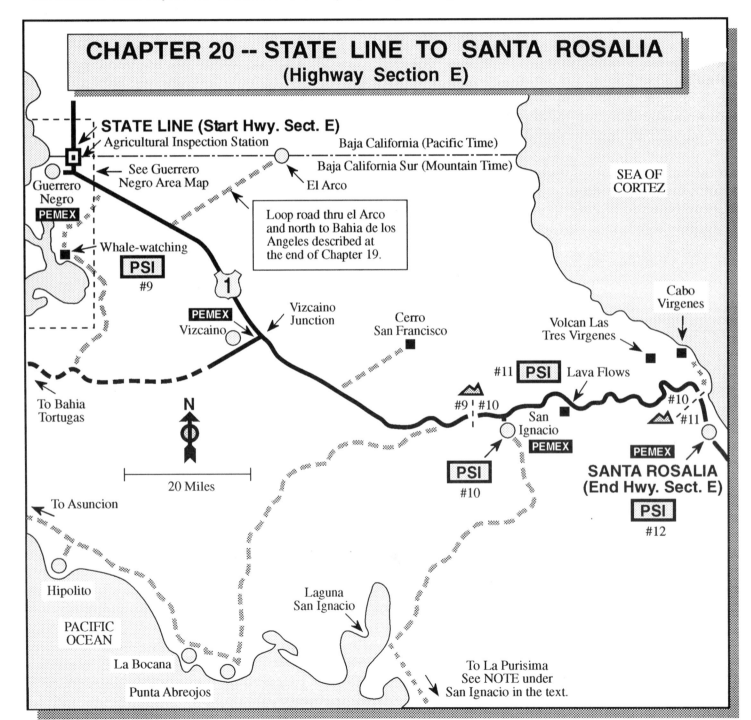

CHAPTER 20 -- STATE LINE TO SANTA ROSALIA
(Highway Section E)

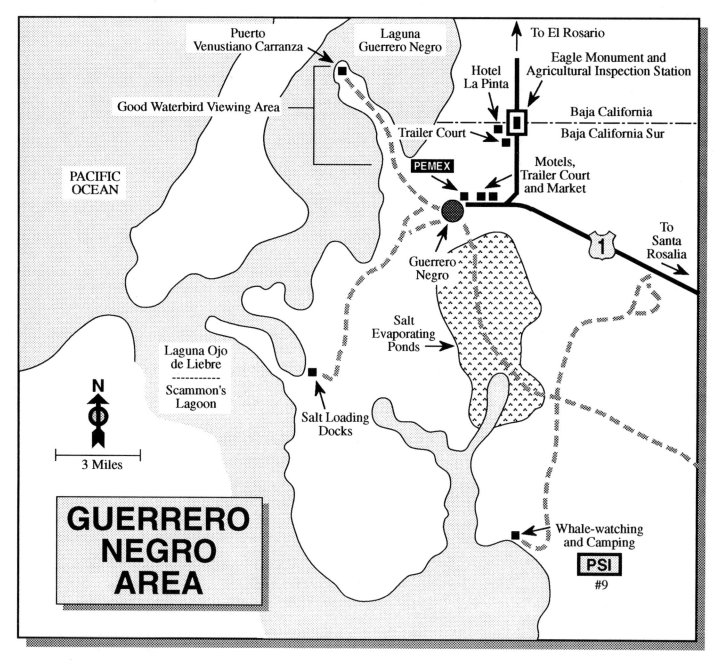

N
3 Miles

GUERRERO NEGRO AREA

Puerto Venustiano Carranza

Laguna Guerrero Negro

To El Rosario

Eagle Monument and Agricultural Inspection Station

Hotel La Pinta

Good Waterbird Viewing Area

Baja California

Baja California Sur

Trailer Court

PEMEX

Motels, Trailer Court and Market

PACIFIC OCEAN

Guerrero Negro

To Santa Rosalia

1

Salt Evaporating Ponds

Laguna Ojo de Liebre

Scammon's Lagoon

Salt Loading Docks

Whale-watching and Camping

PSI
#9

(Km E-217) GUERRERO NEGRO — At this point, Highway 1 veers to the left to begin its journey across the peninsula. Turn to the right, at the junction here, to enter the town of Guerrero Negro (Black Warrior). After 1.1 miles you will find the Malarrimo Restaurant and Trailer Court, and several motels, all on the right (north) side of the road. The Malarrimo restaurant (tourist hangout with live music) is very nice and the above motels are modest but adequate. Further into town are a supermercado and two PEMEX stations, one on each side of the road. Remember to pay them a visit before starting the long trip north on your way home.

SALT MANUFACTURING — Guerrero Negro is supported largely by the salt-producing industry. Large segments of the land to the south have been converted into salt-evaporation ponds, reportedly the largest such operation in the world. Sea water is introduced into these areas. After the sun has baked out sufficient layers, the salt is trucked to barges waiting at docks located west of town.

The shallow waters of the coastal estuaries near Guerrero Negro are unsuited for large ocean freighters. The barges are thus towed through a channel into the ocean and then to the shores of Isla Cedros some 70 miles away. Here, at a deep-water port, the salt is transferred into gigantic mounds where it awaits reloading into large ore carriers.

SIDE TRIP
PUERTO VENUSTIANO CARRANZA — A wide, two-lane road with a packed sand surface turns right (north) from the main street of Guerrero Negro in front of the salt company's headquarters. Travel over this road, as follows:

FIELD GUIDE To The GRAY WHALE

THE OCEANIC SOCIETY

**GRAY WHALE FACTS
GRAY WHALE LIFE CYCLE
WHALING & CONSERVATION
TIPS ON WHALE-WATCHING
(From Land & By Boat)
WHERE TO WHALE-WATCH**

Don't be fooled by its small size. This 50 page booklet was prepared by eminent gray whale experts under direction of The Oceanic Society. It contains all the essentials the Baja traveler needs to know concerning the peninsula's most interesting wildlife species.

Get your copy from the BAJA BOOKSHELF in the Appendix

1.2 Miles. Another wide, two lane, dirt road leads to the left (SW). Stay straight ahead for Puerto Venustiano Carranza. The road to the left leads in 6.8 miles to the gate of the salt-barge loading facilities on Scammon's Lagoon.

7.0 Miles. Arrive at the long-abandoned port facility that extends into Laguna Guerrero Negro. Mating gray whales may be present in this lagoon, but in some years they are unable to enter because the entrance is blocked with sand. I have not been able to view them from the dock area during my visits as they tend to congregate some distance away near the lagoon entrance. In the past, a sizeable boat took tourists to view the whales from here. It was not present in 1992. Contact the Malarrimo Restaurant or Hotel la Pinta concerning whale watching trips.

Bird lovers will wish to take this side trip to Puerto Venustiano Carranza, regardless of the presence of whales, as the road passes through 5 miles of excellent salt water marsh lands. The road lies atop a massive, 10-foot-high fill, so you can look down on the birds. See Chapter 11 WILDLIFE. End **SIDE TRIP**.

SIDE TRIP PSI #9
(Km E-208) SCAMMON'S LAGOON — Laguna Ojo de Liebre (Scammon's Lagoon) is one of the major breeding grounds for the California gray whale. Visiting the whales is stop No. 9 on the POINTS OF SPECIAL INTEREST Tour.

The whales are normally present from the end of December to early April. See Chapter 11 WILDLIFE for details concerning the whale, Scammon's Lagoon, and for observational techniques. (Also see the notice on this page for an excellent small book about the gray whale.) A whale-watching boat service was operating from the Scammon's Lagoon camping area in 1992. No reservations were required.

A sign on Highway 1 marks the junction with the road to Scammon's Lagoon 100 yards north of **Km E-208**. It reads "Laguna Oro de Liebre". It is 15 miles to the edge of the lagoon over a flat, natural surface road that is graded through the desert. The road may be washboarded but it is occasionally graded with equipment owned by the salt company.

The fishing village and small cove at Punta Eugenia.

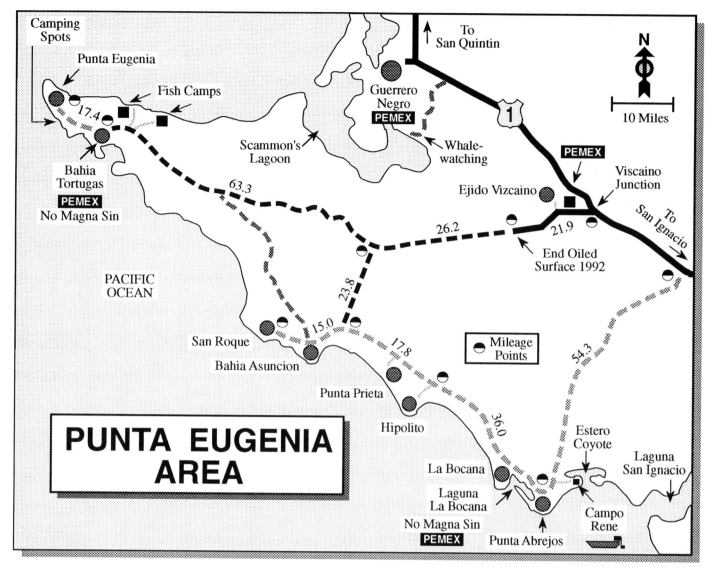

PUNTA EUGENIA AREA

Members of a local ejido collect a small fee for camping at the edge of the lagoon and operate the whale-watching boats. Facilities are limited to crude outhouses, but the area is kept clean, and the road from the highway is signed at points where you might go astray.

I recommend that you plan to camp overnight if you take this journey. It is a long trip in and out, and you need to let the sight and sounds of the whales make a proper impression on the senses. I fear you will be disappointed if you rush in and out and allow for only a short stay at the water's edge. End **SIDE TRIP**.

(Km E-190) HIGHWAY 18 — Between **Km E-189** and **Km E-190,** a road branches to the left. This is the southern end of the Bahia de los Angeles - el Arco loop road described at the end of Chapter 19. The mining town of el Arco is located some 26.6 miles to the east, at the base of the mountains which can be seen in this direction.

SIDE TRIP
(Km E-144) VIZCAINO JUNCTION AND ROAD TO PUNTA EUGENIA AREA There is a growing cluster of homes and a PEMEX station where a blacktopped highway leaves

Highway 1 to the right (west) exactly at **Km E-144**. (See the PUNTA EUGENIA AREA Map.) It is 5.4 miles to the turnoff to the village of Vizcaino. Vizcaino is surrounded by orderly plantings of grape vines and fig and citrus trees irrigated with well water. It is a good place to visit to see the Mexican people turn the desert into a productive farming area.

West of the Vizcaino junction, the oiled surface continues for an additional 16.5 miles. Further west, to Bahia Tortugas, the road has been constructed to highway standards, but as of 1992 was not yet oil surfaced. (The same is true of a 23.8 mile branch road leading to Asuncion.) Oil surfacing has been extended from Highway 1 a few miles in each of the last several years. Travelers can thus anticipate improved road conditions with the passage of time. For now, most of the roads shown on the PUNTA EUGENIA AREA Map are usable by large R.V.'s, although there is some washboarding. Because of the newness of the road construction and the relatively long distances involved, this area currently receives little tourist traffic.

In my 1992 survey I found that much of the road from Km E-98 on Highway 1 to Punta Abreojos had been completely rebuilt and was about 6-miles shorter than the old route. This road, and

Young men help a diver unload his catch of abalon (abalone) at the cove at Punta Eugenia.

most of the others shown on the PUNTA EUGENIA AREA Map, do not have a surface of rough imported gravel as do most other secondary roads in Baja. The travel surfaces are thus relatively smooth.

Each coastal town shown on the map is a sizeable communitiy with schools, fish-packing plants, and power generation facilities. There is a PEMEX station at Bahia Tortugas. A major water line has been constructed from wells near Vizcaino to all the coastal towns.

While many of the roads pass over flat desert lands, the coastline is mountainous, picturesque, and offers many places to camp. The only tourist facilities are the small Vera Cruz Motel at Bahia

The town of San Ignacio lies in a lava rimmed valley filled with palm trees.

Tortugas and the minimal facility resort named Campo Rene on the shores of Estero Coyote. For an extended trip, make a complete loop starting at the Vizcaino junction and ending at **Km E-98** on Highway 1. Also, take the side road to Punta Eugenia. End **SIDE TRIP**.

(Km E-144) POOR HIGHWAY CONDITIONS
— The worst road conditions on the Transpeninsular Highway have always been that portion through the Vizcaino Desert (Geographic section #9). As of 1992 much of this bad mileage has been upgraded with the only remaining poor section lying between the Vizcaino Junction (**Km E -144**) and the geographic change noted below. Here the highway is very narrow. Meeting oncoming vehicles is a trying experience. Never drive this section of highway after dark. Hopefully these conditions will be improved in the future.

BOB & JEAN 4X4

(KM E-119) CERRO SAN FRANCISCO — Between **Km E-119** and **E-118** a secondary road leaves Highway 1 to the left and may be seen climbing the mountains to the NE. A 23 mile drive brings one to a small village where a guide can be secured to take you on a short walk to overhanging cliffs and their red and black Indian cave paintings. This is trip #6 of the "Bob and Jean" 4x4 Recommendations presented in Chapter 3 even though the road to the cave paintings can actually be negotiated in standard drive vehicles. Primitive camping sites in the mountains are available.

(Km E-98) ROAD TO PUNTA ABREJOS -- Heading south at this point is the road to Punta Abrejos and Campo Rene. (See discussion of this road earlier in this chapter under ROAD TO PUNTA EUGENIA AREA.)

#9 **#10**
(Km E-84) GEOGRAPHIC CHANGE — Highway 1 has slowly gained in elevation, and in the vicinity of **Km E-84** the eastern edge of the Continental Borderlands blends with the beginning of a low pass through the Peninsular Range Mountains. This dividing line between geographic provinces is not as sharp as in other places, but it will soon be apparent that the highway has left the flat plains behind and enters more rugged terrain.

PSI **#10**
(Km E-74) SAN IGNACIO — There is a PEMEX station near the junction of the paved side road into the town of San Ignacio. An "Magna Sin" pump is also present at the Hotel la Pinta. Directly behind the station is another of the government-constructed trailer courts. I have always found it to be in operation.

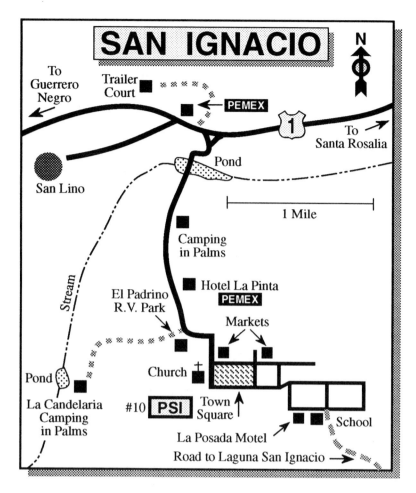

The square is completely shaded by six massive Indian laurel trees (Arbol de la India) with trunks three-to-four feet in diameter. You will find smaller examples of this broadleafed evergreen tree along the waterfront at La Paz and in many other places.

NOTE — The northern termini of the rough-surfaced secondary road leading in 32 miles to Laguna San Ignacio is shown on the SAN IGNACIO Map. Laguna San Ignacio is then linked by roads of various standards to the town of La Purisima. The road is then highway standard with some paving south to Ciudad Insurgentes. This entire San Ignacio to Ciudad Insurgentes route may eventually be a paved highway. Its present southern portion is described at the end of Chapter 21 under the LA PURISMA & CIUDAD INSURGENTES LOOP.

(Km E-71) SCHOOL BUILDINGS — To the right of the highway notice the modern, one-story school building. Most of the schools you will see in Baja offer primary education only. Here is one of an increasing number of secundaria-tecnico facilities built during recent years to improve the educational standards of rural Mexico. See the discussion of education in Chapter 13 OUR DEVELOPING COUNTRY NEIGHBOR.

(Km E-67) VOLCAN LAS TRES VIRGENES — After passing east of **Km E-67**, you will see a massive mountain ahead and to the left of the highway. This is the 6,547-foot-high Volcan las Tres Virgenes (Three Virgins Volcano). It was known to have erupted in 1746 and to have emitted smoke in 1857. When an area's principal mountains are dominant, more or less isolated peaks such as Las Tres Virgenes, it is a good sign that you are viewing mountains of volcanic origin.

SIDE TRIP -- San Ignacio is one of Baja's most charming towns and is surrounded by date palms introduced by the Jesuits more than 200 years ago. It is stop No. 10 on the POINTS OF SPECIAL INTEREST Tour. Even the largest of R.V.'s can make this trip and head back to the highway by circling the town square. However, to minimize traffic congestion, I suggest that trailers be parked near the hotel and their occupants walk the last few hundred yards. End **SIDE TRIP.**

It is 1.4 miles from Highway 1 to the town square. En route, you will pass R.V. parks in the palms, the Hotel La Pinta and the side road to La Candelaria, a delightful camping spot in the palms at the edge of a pool of cool water. Here is one of the few places to go swimming in the desert.

The town square is typical of such public places found throughout Spanish America. Here and elsewhere they are called *el zocalo* (the public square). At the west end of the zocalo is Mision San Ignacio, one of the finest churches in all of Baja. The mission, originally established by the Jesuits in 1728, was for twenty-four years the northernmost mission. At one time it served some 5,000 Indians. The present thick-walled stone church was completed many years later by the Dominicans, in 1786.

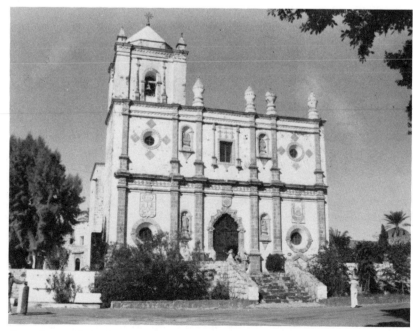

San Ignacio's famous Dominican-built church.

191

Starting near San Ignacio, you pass through an area made up of volcanic rock. Refer to the ROCK TYPE CLASSIFICATION Chart in Chapter 9 GEOLOGY. This igneous-volcanic-extrusive rock is called *basalt* and is formed when molten material is *extruded* at the surface of the earth. Because it cools rapidly, the rock is fine grained as no recognizable crystals have time to form. Note the reddish color typical of these formations. In some places, basalt is honeycombed with small holes formed by pockets of gas trapped at the time of solidification. Thus, from a distance, an observer can come to believe that basalt is coarse, rather than fine grained.

(Km E-62) DATILILLO — The datilillo is one of the most characteristic of the plants of the Sonoran Desert. The stand visible here in the mountains is the most robust seen anywhere along the Transpeninsular Highway. It is mixed with other attractive plant species.

PSI #11

(Km E-42 to E-38) LAVA FLOWS AND ELEPHANT TREES — For several miles the Transpeninsular Highway passes through an area of recent lava flows originating on the sides of Volcan las Tres Virgenes. Here, at stop No. 11 on the POINTS OF SPECIAL INTEREST Tour, I suggest that you pullover and take a closer look at these flows. A good turnout is just east of **Km E-41**. There are very few places along the highways of North America where you will have this opportunity. Walk a few feet onto a flow. There are few environments where you will have such a feeling of complete desolation.

Ironically, this most hostile of growing sites provides the preferred environment for the thick-trunked elephant tree (*Pachycormus discolor*). Some individuals growing on these flows are three feet in diameter at the base, and they are the sole

vegetation. In nearby deep-soiled areas you will find a species of very similar appearance but which is only distantly related to the trees on the lava flows. This is *bursera microphylla*. (See Chapter 10 VEGETATION for descriptions.) The fact that these two species look so much alike is a dramatic example of convergent evolution, as discussed in Chapter 10.

(Km E-35) GEOGRAPHIC NOTE — It is here that Highway 1 starts its descent down the steep, east-facing escarpment of the Peninsular Range Mountains. Contrast the considerable drop in elevation you will experience on the highway ahead to the almost effortless climb that has taken place over the gentle western slope behind you. See Chapter 9 GEOLOGY.

The dominant, dome-shaped mountain lying ahead is Cabo Virgenes (Virgin Cape). It marks the northern limits of the relatively gentle coastal lands through which you will be passing in the miles ahead and which contain the most extensive tourist area on the Sea of Cortez. The ruggedness of Cabo Virgenes and the mountains to the north forced highway engineers to route the Transpeninsular Highway across the peninsula through the inviting pass over which you have just traveled.

(Km E-17) SEA OF CORTEZ VISTA — Highway 1 renews its steep descent at this point. A section of highway known as The Devil's Grade lies ahead. It is the most dangerous section of mountain highway in Baja. At **Km E-17** the traveler is treated to the first significant view of the Sea of Cortez. In nine more kilometers you will be at its shore.

Directly ahead you can also see the first of many offshore islands that rim the peninsula's eastern shore. This is Isla Tortuga (Turtle Island). Like its mainland neighbors, it is also an extinct volcano, most of which lies below the surface of the sea.

The town of Santa Rosalia and its breakwater lined harbor.

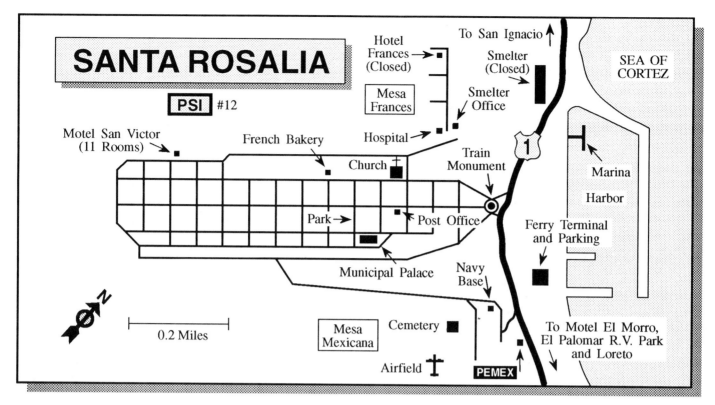

SANTA ROSALIA

PSI #12

Hotel Frances (Closed)

To San Ignacio ↑

Smelter (Closed) →

SEA OF CORTEZ

Mesa Frances

Smelter Office

Motel San Victor (11 Rooms) →

French Bakery

Hospital →

Train Monument

1

Church †

Marina

Harbor

Park →

Post Office

Ferry Terminal and Parking

Municipal Palace

Navy Base

N

0.2 Miles

Mesa Mexicana

Cemetery

To Motel El Morro, El Palomar R.V. Park and Loreto

Airfield †

PEMEX

#10 ⛰ #11

(Km E-8) THE SEA OF CORTEZ AT LAST — At long last, after a journey of 920 km (572 miles) from the international border, the Transpeninsular Highway overlooks the shore of the Sea of Cortez and turns south toward Santa Rosalia. This is the end of Geographic Section No.10 and the northern end of the gentle coastal lands lying along the Sea of Cortez.

Prior to reaching **Km E-7** a dirt road leaves Highway 1 to the north. It used to access a camping spot in 3.2 miles. This has now been taken over by a gypsum mining operation. The area is worth a visit only if you are interested in this industrial activity.

PSI #12

(Km E-0) SANTA ROSALIA — Santa Rosalia has received mixed reviews from previous travel book writers. Some even have said that it has little interest to the tourist. Nothing could be further from the truth, and I have placed this town of 14,000 people on the POINTS OF SPECIAL INTEREST Tour as stop No. 12.

Admittedly, it may not be a pretty place, for this was an industrial town where there is little vegetation and the surrounding hills bear the scars of more than a century of copper and manganese mining. But for uniqueness and historic interest it would be hard to surpass.

I said *was* an industrial town, as the old smelter closed, probably for the last time, about 1990. During my 1992 visit it was being extensively rebuilt, but even a retired forester like myself could see that this was probably socialistic nonsense. It was.

The town was built by the French (see Chapter 12 HISTORY for Santa Rosalia's background as a mining center) and as a result almost all of its buildings are made of imported lumber rather than masonry. Many have broad verandas, and the houses along the three main streets are closely packed in orderly lines. It is an interesting community. (During my last visit, the town had sprouted two traffic lights. Horrors, the place is going to hell.)

The Hotel Frances at Santa Rosalia. It is typical of many of the French-built wooden buildings in this historic town.

Smaller vehicles can be driven into town but trailers and large R.V.'s should be parked along the highway or in the parking lot at the ferry dock. Do your sightseeing on foot. I recommend you proceed as follows:

1. Walk about on the streets in the main section of town and notice the architecture and wooden construction of the buildings.

2. Visit the unique church designed by Gustave Eiffel (builder of the Eiffel tower in Paris). It was constructed from prefabricated galvanized iron as the the building was originally destined for a humid African country where resistance to termites was needed.

3. Starting in front of the church, proceed up the steep road that winds its way up to the Mesa Frances (French Mesa). Here you will find a broad street lined with large wooden buildings. Take note of the mining company office across from the hospital (closed along with the smelter). Visit the Hotel Frances, also closed with the passing of the smelter. During my last visit, one could look through the hotel windows and see its photo collection of sailing vessels adorning the walls. Santa Rosalia was one of the last ports in the world to be served by the age of sail. Outside the hotel, note the adjacent brick tunnel leading from the smelter to the smokestack high above town.

4. Look over the breakwater walls that form the harbor. They are made from blocks of slag left over from the smelting process. A small marina was completed about 1987 and attracts boaters most of whom cross the Sea of Cortez from San Carlos near Guaymas on the mainland shore.

5. If you can get inside the old smelter it is worth a visit. It contains an old French clock and loads of decades-old machinery. It should be made into a museum.

Santa Rosalia's famous metal church surrounded by many of the town's old wooden buildings.

The church interior. The prefabricated iron panels are easy to observe.

CHAPTER 21
SANTA ROSALIA TO LORETO

Chapter 21 describes the Sea of Cortez central coast, one of the six principal tourist areas introduced in Chapter 2 THE BIG PICTURE. It contains the peninsula's most heavily used beachside camping areas and the towns of Mulege and Loreto. Highway 1 will pass over a series of coastal benches and low hills lying at the base of the steep eastern escarpment of the Peninsular Range Mountains. This section of the mountains is called the Sierra Giganta (the Giant Range) and will treat you to the best scenery in view from the Transpeninsular Highway.

The fuel situation has improved along the Central Coast in recent years. There are PEMEX stations at Santa Rosalia, Mulege, Loreto and at press time, one was under construction at Puert Escondido. In addition there is a new, easy-to-access station about 3-miles south of Mulege on Highway 1. Thus, it is no longer necessary to enter the constricted street of this community to obtain fuel at the town station.

(Km F-195) HOTEL EL MORRO — On the cliffs overlooking the Sea of Cortez is the Hotel El Morro. It has a very nice restaurant.

Note the navigation light tower on the small rocky islet lying 200 yards offshore from the motel. You should become familiar with these aluminum towers and their solar-powered lights if you plan to use a boat in the Sea of Cortez. They are to be found in scores of locations and are reliable aids to navigation.

(Km F-193) EL PALOMAR R. V. PARK — There has long been need for a trailer park near Santa Rosalia as many people like to settle down for the night after the long journey through the desert to reach the Sea of Cortez. Also it is quite easy to spend many hours prowling about the historically interesting town.

This need has now been met a short distance south of Santa Rosalia by the El Palomar R. V. Park and cafe. It had just opened during my visit in 1992 and will no doubt be improved in future years.

(Km F-190) STATE PRISON — There are no signs on the large building at this point but there is little doubt about its function. There is relatively little crime in Baja California, but obviously there is some.

BOB & JEAN 4X4

CANDELARIA — Six miles south of Santa Rosalia a secondary road signed for Santa Agueda leaves Highway 1 to the west.

The village of Santa Agueda is reached in about _7 miles_. The additional 20 miles to the Rancho Candelaria is lower standard road along an arroyo bottom. Ask at the ranch for a guide for a walk to nearby Indian cave paintings. This is trip #7 of the "Bob and Jean 4x4" Recommendations as noted in Chapter 3.

SIDE TRIP
(Km F-182) CALETA SAN LUCAS — A dirt road leaves Highway 1 to the left (east). In 0.5 miles you will reach the shores of a shallow cove protected from the sea by a rocky bar. This is Caleta (little cove) San Lucas. Here you will find the San Lucas R.V. Park with its small cafe. A military detachment lies SW from the trailer court.

Near the cove's southern end another dirt road leaves Highway 1 at **Km F-180** and accesses many fine palm-shaded camp sites along the shore. See CALETA SAN LUCAS Map. In spring 1992 this road was fenced-off from public access, perhaps to induce people to use the San Lucas R. V. Park; perhaps to give the military a bit more elbow-room. Another sad loss of seaside camping access. Perhaps it will reopen. End **SIDE TRIP**.

ISLA SAN MARCOS — Isla San Marcos is in view offshore from this general area. Notice the light color of the land at the south end of the island. This light area is the barren slope of an open-pit gypsum mine. The workers' village, the mill, and port

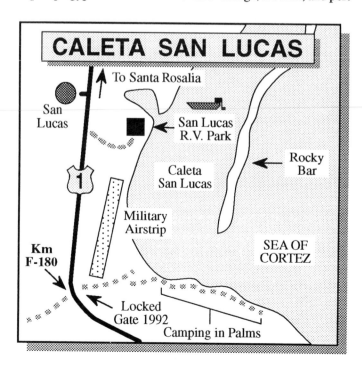

CALETA SAN LUCAS

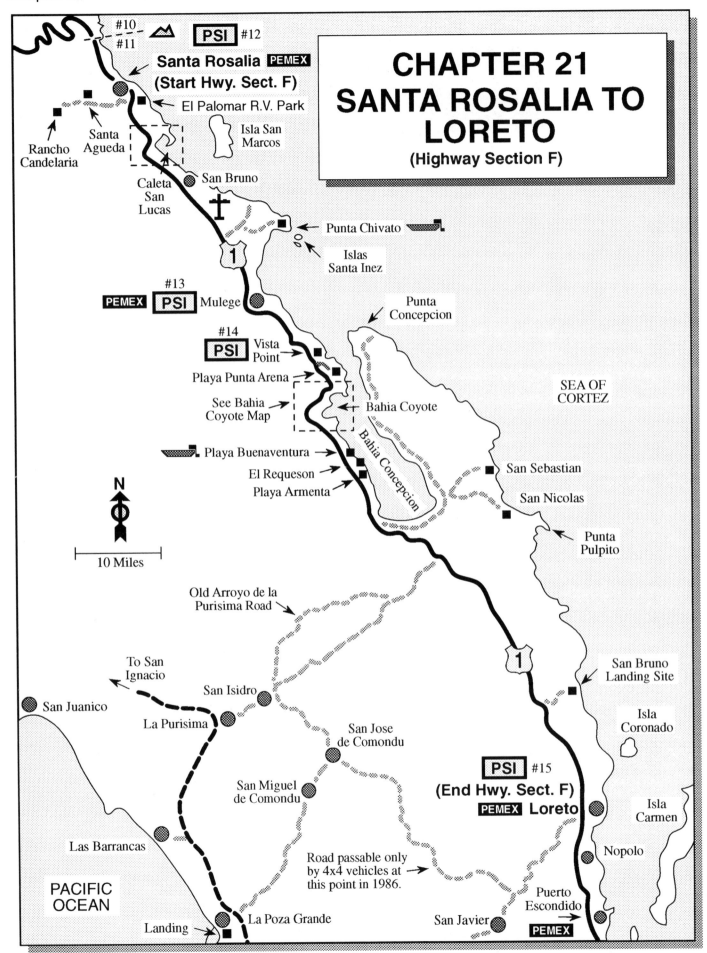

#10
#11
PSI #12
Santa Rosalia PEMEX
(Start Hwy. Sect. F)
El Palomar R.V. Park
Isla San Marcos
Santa Agueda
Rancho Candelaria
Caleta San Lucas
San Bruno

CHAPTER 21
SANTA ROSALIA TO LORETO
(Highway Section F)

Punta Chivato
Islas Santa Inez

1

#13
PEMEX PSI Mulege

Punta Concepcion

#14
PSI Vista Point
Playa Punta Arena
See Bahia Coyote Map

Bahia Coyote

SEA OF CORTEZ

Playa Buenaventura
El Requeson
Playa Armenta

Bahia Concepcion

San Sebastian
San Nicolas

Punta Pulpito

N

10 Miles

Old Arroyo de la Purisima Road

1

To San Ignacio

San Bruno Landing Site

San Juanico
San Isidro
La Purisima

San Jose de Comondu

Isla Coronado

San Miguel de Comondu

PSI #15
(End Hwy. Sect. F)
PEMEX **Loreto**

Isla Carmen

Las Barrancas

Nopolo

PACIFIC OCEAN

Road passable only by 4x4 vehicles at this point in 1986.

Puerto Escondido

Landing
La Poza Grande
San Javier
PEMEX

facilities can be seen faintly north of the mine. Gypsum is one the softest of minerals, and the San Marcos variety is light yellow in color. Many of the town's buildings have been constructed from foot-thick blocks of compressed gypsum despite the fact that you can scratch it with your fingernail. Walking through this almost totally yellow town is an interesting experience.

(Km F-173) SAN BRUNO — The town of San Bruno is in view on the shore to the left (east). A drive of 0.5 miles over a dirt road accesses a small trailer court occupied largely on a full-time basis. It has a few transient sites but I have not included it in the list of R.V. parks in Chapter 4. The town is fronted by a good sandy beach.

(Km F-162) SANTA ROSALIA AIRPORT — A jet airport and 1.6 mile oiled access road were completed east of this point in fall 1988. It will serve Santa Rosalia to the north and Mulege to the south but in 1992 it lay unused. Such projects illustrate one of the characteristics of a centralized, socialistic form of government. The international airport at Loreto and the resort area at Nopolo to the south are vastly underutilized. And yet, here, someone is contemplating a repeat performance. Perhaps new hotels and other tourist facilities will follow. Time will tell. In the meantime, the tarmac makes a fine R.V. parking area.

SIDE TRIP
(Km F-156) PUNTA CHIVATO — A sign at this road junction indicates that it is 20 km to Punta Chivato. (My odommeter recorded it at over 25 km (16 miles).) The small community of Palo Verde lies along the highway.

Taking this secondary road left (east) from Highway 1 leads in 5.5 miles to a Y junction. (This section of road seems to suffer from chronic washboarditis but Punta Chivato is worth the trip.) There is a line of about twenty-five palm trees in the crotch of the Y. There is little of interest to the tourist served by the left-hand branch.

Take the low standard, much smoother, dirt road to the right for Punta Chivato. An additional 10.0 miles will bring you to the camping area on the beach. Also in the area are the very fine Punta Chivato Hotel and a dirt airstrip. The access road leaves much to be desired but it provides a level trip and large R.V.'s and trailers make it on a regular basis.

End **SIDE TRIP**.

PSI #13

(Km F-136) MULEGE — Again, as at Santa Rosalia, I suggest that you take an hour or two and visit another of Baja's historic and intriguing communities. It is stop No. 13 on the POINTS OF SPECIAL INTEREST Tour. The two towns have little in common except that the river along which

The isolated Hotel Punta Chivato north of Mulege.

Mulege is built bears the name Rio Santa Rosalia. Santa Rosalia is also the name of Mulege's famous mission.

TOWN CENTER — The center of this community of 4,000 people is reached from a road leaving Highway 1 west of the highway bridge shown on the MULEGE Map. The town's streets are narrow so it is best to leave the big R.V.'s and trailers near the highway. Obtain gasoline at the PEMEX station 3-miles south of town on Highway 1.

If you drive into town, I suggest you park near the Hotel Las Casitas and savor the community on foot. Keep in mind that you are viewing a place that was founded sixty years before the first Europeans discovered San Francisco Bay.

Be sure to visit the massive thick-walled federal prison. It looks like a structure you would find in the Sahara Desert manned by

The historic federal prison at Mulege.

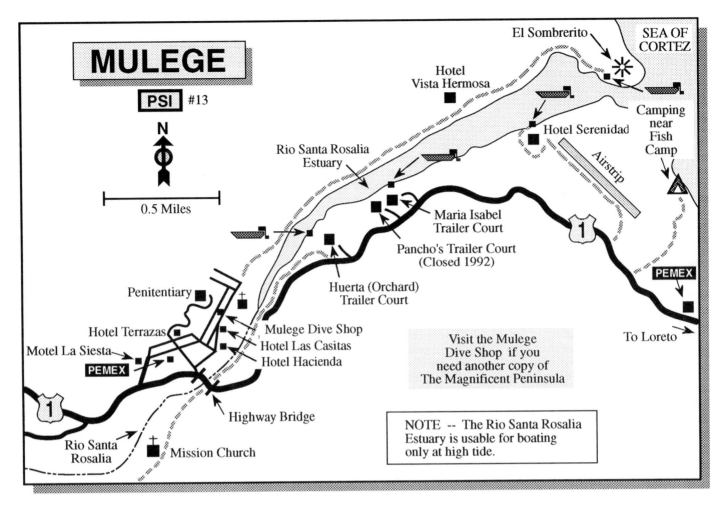

MULEGE

PSI #13

N

0.5 Miles

El Sombrerito

SEA OF CORTEZ

Hotel Vista Hermosa

Camping near Fish Camp

Hotel Serenidad

Airstrip

Rio Santa Rosalia Estuary

Maria Isabel Trailer Court

Pancho's Trailer Court (Closed 1992)

Huerta (Orchard) Trailer Court

Penitentiary

Hotel Terrazas

Motel La Siesta

PEMEX

Mulege Dive Shop

Hotel Las Casitas

Hotel Hacienda

Highway Bridge

Rio Santa Rosalia

Mission Church

PEMEX

To Loreto

Visit the Mulege Dive Shop if you need another copy of The Magnificent Peninsula

NOTE -- The Rio Santa Rosalia Estuary is usable for boating only at high tide.

the French Foreign Legion. Although it is no longer used as a federal prison, on occasion it is used to detain local law breakers. Sometimes it is open to the public and other times it is not.

The prison was famous for being operated on the honor system. The inmates worked or visited in town during the day but were required to return for the night. Misconduct by one prisoner was considered an infraction by all, and all were punished. It was no doubt a very orderly place.

If you have a small vehicle, drive down the dirt road along the palm-lined north bank of the river and visit the Hotel Vista Hermosa. True to its name, it offers a *vista hermosa* (beautiful view) of the mouth of the river, the Sea of Cortez, and a small hat-shaped hill which could only be named El Sombrerito (The Little Hat). In October 1847 it witnessed a battle during the Mexican-American War between local patriots and forces from the U.S. sloop *Dale*. See Chapter 12 HISTORY.

TRAILER COURTS — The SE side of the Rio Santa Rosalia is the main tourist area at Mulege. It may be reached by driving under the highway bridge at the SE end of the main section of town, or directly from the highway. There are two large R.V. parks among the palms along the river. They have boat ramps usable at high tide only. There is another smaller R.V. park adjoining the Hotel Serenidad.

MISSION — From under the highway bridge, drive upstream for 0.4 miles on a dirt road through palm groves along the SE bank of the river to the restored Mission Santa Rosalia de Mulege. (The towers of the church can be seen while crossing the bridge and from the highway entering town from the north.) Here, Jesuit missionaries founded their fourth mission in 1705, only eight years after they established themselves on the peninsula in 1697. It originally served an Indian population of some 2,000 persons.

Walk to the vista point on top of a point of rock located a few feet behind the mission. From here you can look over a sea of palm trees, a small reservoir, and the agricultural area upstream from Mulege.

NOTE -- See the aerial photo of the Mulege area on page 118.

SOUTH OF TOWN — At **Km F-132** a dirt road will bring you in 0.5 miles to the Hotel Serenidad. This attractive facility is located near the mouth of the river and directly adjacent to a dirt surface airstrip. Many of the hotel's patrons arrive by small private aircraft. Adjacent to the hotel is a small R.V. park.

Near the mouth of the river, and hidden from view by the hotel, is the Fisherman's Landing boat launching ramp. One must drive around three sides of the hotel on a narrow dirt road to arrive at the ramp. Boaters need to time their launching with the state of the tide as there is no water at the ramp when the sea is at low ebb.

About 0.1 miles south of the road to the Hotel Serenidad, another side road leaves to the left (east). After passing through the remains of a former dumping ground, this road arrives in 0.4 miles at a camping spot on a long sandy beach. On my last visit, the area contained a small fish camp and scattering of trash, and was less than one's vision of an idyllic tropical camping spot. However, it was here that my wife and I camped for ten days on our first trip to Baja and fell in love with the Magnificent Peninsula. We both agreed that we had never had such a relaxing vacation. After returning to the hectic life of the city, it was several days before I was aware that I was no longer smoking a pipe which had been a constant fixture in my mouth. I have never touched it again.

(Km F-131 PEMEX STATION — This station was constructed about 1990 to relieve traffic congestion caused by the old station on Mulege's narrow streets.

(Km F-126) VIEW OF PUNTA CONCEPCION — You are now approaching Bahia Concepcion, the largest protected body of water on the Sea of Cortez. To the SE from this point on the highway, you can see Punta Concepcion, the northern tip of the peninsula which forms the eastern shore of the bay. The channel into Bahia Concepcion lies between this peninsula and the promontory supporting a microwave tower, which is in view ahead and to the left.

Near this same point on the highway, a dirt road leaves to the left and in 0.4 miles arrives at a camping spot on the low bluffs above a shingle beach. There are also several other dirt road heading toward the Sea of Cortez between the new PEMEX station and the vista point noted below. I have not explored these so help yourselves.

PSI #14

SIDE TRIP
(Km F-124) VISTA POINT — There are few good vista points directly along Highway 1. I have therefore included a visit to the microwave tower, noted above, as stop No. 14 on the POINTS OF SPECIAL INTEREST Tour. It is signed for "Est. Microonades (Microwave Station) Tiburones." The last word on each microwave sign along the highway is the name of the individual station. In this case *Tiburones* means sharks.

The cobblestone road to the tower begins with two moderately steep switchbacks which are in view

The restored mission church on the banks of the Rio Santa Rosalia at Mulege. It was founded in 1705 by the Jesuits. The church was originally built in 1766 and has been remodeled many times.

from the highway. These are the main problem spots on the 0.8 mile drive to the tower. Because of these switchbacks and the lack of places to pass oncoming vehicles, this trip is not recommended for large R.V.'s. If you make the trip, you will find good turnaround spots at the end of the road or in a low saddle about 100 yards before reaching the tower. You will be rewarded with fine views of the entrance to Bahia Concepcion and the coastline. End **SIDE TRIP.**

(KM F- 121) VILLA DE MULEGE — It is 1.7 miles to the beach and an area being subdivided. There was a locked gate along the way during my last visit.

The entrance to Bahia Concepcion as seen from the vista point at **PSI** stop No. 14.

Bahia Coyote. The birdlimed island in the foreground is Isla Blanca. The J-shaped beach above and to the right of the island is Playa Santispac.

(Km F-119) PLAYA PUNTA ARENA — To the left, a dirt road leads in 2.6 miles to the end of the sandy beach camping area at Punta Arena (Sand Point). I recommend that you proceed to the Santispac area at the northern end of Bahia Concepcion if you have not visited this region before. However, should the crowds of people that are normally found there not be to your liking, you can consider Punta Arena as an alternative. There are usually fewer campers and the beach is excellent. Its negative features are the bumpy access road and its exposed location which provides little protection from the northerly winds that prevail in the early winter months.

(Km F-114 to F-108) BAHIA COYOTE — Bahia Coyote is the wind-protected bay lying at the NW corner of the much larger Bahia Concepcion. It is the most heavily used camping and boating area in the entire Baja Peninsula. During my 1992 survey, the number of tourists visiting Baja was down sharply, but the beach camping areas at Bahia Coyote were packed as usual.

Most of these camping areas have no facilities other than crude outhouses. R. V.'s simply line up at right-angles a few feet from the beach. See the photo on page 35.

There are five separate sections of the Bahia Coyote area, each served by a short side road from Highway 1. They are described in the order they are encountered along the highway from north to south. The exact operating conditions of these campgrounds will vary from year to year, but at most beaches you will be charged a small daily fee. At some places, this will entitle you to the use of a beach-side shelter called a *palapa*. They are made from poles and grass mats.

PLAYA SANTISPAC (**Km F-114**) — Standing at the beach at Santispac, one can readily come to the conclusion that most weary travelers from north of the border shout "This must be the place!" when they arrive at Santispac, for the beach is usually lined with vehicles of every description during the winter. Many travelers stay here for extended periods, others make it a one-night stopping point, for there is a busy influx of vehicles every evening and a sudden torrent of departees after breakfast. Be careful using the steep approach road and guard against the possibility of tipping over at its junction with the highway. The larger trailer rigs sometimes have to take a run to return to the highway.

NOTE -- See the photo of Playa Santispac on page 35

Shoreside vegetation has long ago yielded to the onslaught of campers. However, the protected cove is excellent for windsurfing, water-skiing, and swimming. There is a small restaurant, and your modest camping fee helps keep the area clean. A short walk to the west of the main beach, on a trail along the base of the highway, will bring you to a natural hot spring. Thus, if you enjoy beach bumming in close proximity to many other friendly folks doing the same thing, then your first assessment will prove correct and, in fact, *this must be the place.*

POSADA CONCEPCION (**Km F-112**) — Posada Concepcion is the domain of those who became enamored with this part of the world and decided to stay. Located here is a subdivision of winter homes and numerous trailer houses supplemented with adjoining grass-mat shelters. (There is also an R.V. and boat storage area.) You can arrange to park your R.V. by the day, but the permanent residents have the best locations.

LOS COCOS (Km F-111) — The access road from Highway 1 is 0.3 miles in length and leads to a fine beach and camping area.

LA BURRA (Km F-109) — Another good camping beach which is in full view from the highway. The access road leaves directly at the Km F-109 sign.

PLAYA El COYOTE (Km F-108) — The southernmost of the Bahia Coyote camping spots is a beach which bears the same name. A few feet after the side road leaves the highway, turn right and proceed along the water's edge and in 0.5 miles arrive at an excellent beach. At the far (south) end of this camping area,

a trail leads some 100 yards to a hot spring near the water's edge. (This is my favorite of the Bahia Coyote camping areas.) There is a sizeable trailer park on the other side of the highway, but it is very lightly used.

NOTE -- See photos of Playa el Coyote and El Requeson on pages 6 and 36.

Approximately 1 mile SE from Playa el Coyote is another fine beach in a deep cove. It is undeveloped as there is no access road. This cove provides an excellent picnic or camping site for small boat owners who can load up their gear and escape the crowded conditions at the other camping areas that rim Bahia Coyote. It is only a short distance over the protected waters of the bay from any of these areas.

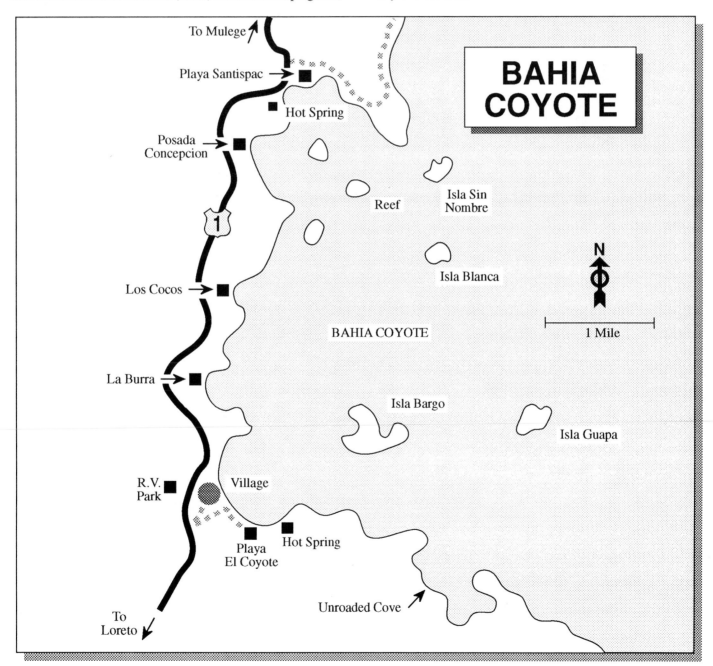

(Km F-94) PLAYA BUENAVENTURA — In the previous edition of this book I noted that between Km F-94 and F-95 there was a lesser quality, undeveloped, waterside camping area that would look pretty good to people tired of the crowded conditions to the north at Bahia Coyote. In fact, it looked so good, that an R.V. park and boat ramp has now been built here.

The park, Playa Buenaventura, is actually considerably nicer than those at Bahia Coyote but is more exposed to the wind. This is a problem in the cooler winter months, but might be a blessing as the warm summer set in. There is a nearby restaurant and bar.

(Km F-92) EL REQUESON — El Requeson is a small island lying between **Km F-93** and **Km F-92**. At low tide it is connected to the mainland by an isthmus of sand. The higher portion of this isthmus provides a fine camping spot, and it and the island form a small, well-protected but shallow bay. A good spot for launching class 4 boats over the beach. The entire area is in view from the highway, and the approach road is less than 0.1 miles in length.

(Km F-91) PLAYA ARMENTA — Playa Armenta is a small beach lying on the north side of a point of lava rock. It is fully exposed to the prevailing northerly wind but is a good camping spot during calm weather. The approach road is 0.6 miles in length and leaves Highway 1 between **Km F-91** and **Km F-90**. The beach cannot be seen from the junction point, but it and the approach road are in full view from the highway, a short distance to the south, should you care to look it over before driving in.

ADDITIONAL CAMPING SITES — Spur roads lead to several camping sites at (1) 200 yards north of **Km F-88**, (2) north of **Km F-84**, (3) just south of **Km F-82**, and (4) near **Km F-80**. These are not as good as the Bahia Coyote beaches, but some of us can suffer some shortcomings in exchange for not being herded into the larger developed areas.

The restored mission church at Loreto. A fine historical museum is housed in an adjoining building.

(Km F-77) BAHIA CONCEPCION (SOUTH AND EAST SHORE) — A dirt road leaves Highway 1 between **Km F-77** and **Km F-76** and closely follows the south shore of Bahia Concepcion. The terrain at the southern end is extremely low and flat. After a rain, the road in this vicinity becomes slick and impassable, but travel is easy and rapid in dry weather. There are numerous spurs that provide access to camping spots at the water's edge. A second, parallel road branches inland about 1/4 mile in from the highway. It traverses higher ground and is preferable in wet weather.

The area's principal shortcoming is that it is fully exposed to the northerly winds that funnel between the mountains that rim Bahia Concepcion on both sides. Near the junction with Highway 1 lies one of the abandoned cemetery-like trailer courts which have been previously mentioned. It was no doubt a victim of these windy conditions.

At the SE corner of Bahia Concepcion the traveler is offered three choices of travel (See the AAA map). Two roads proceed easterly to San Sebastian and San Nicolas on the Sea of Cortez shore. I have started out on both of these routes but turned back after several miles feeling they were a bit marginal for a standard drive pickup. I have been to both areas by sea and they are two of the most attractive of Baja's hidden coastal Shangri-las.

BOB & JEAN 4X4

A third road runs at the water's edge the full length of the eastern shore of Bahia Concepcion and passes over the divide ridge to the Sea of Cortez. At this point one may explore the extensive ruins of an abandoned manganese mine or take a trail north to Punta Concepcion. This is trip #8 of the "Bob and Jean 4x4" Recommendations presented in Chapter 3. Much of this road is suitable for standard drive vehicles but there are rough spots making extra traction advisable. End **SIDE TRIP**.

CARDON — The flat plain lying along the southern and eastern shore of Bahia Concepcion (just south of Km F-77) supports one of the finest *cardonals* of giant cardon cactus in view along the entire Transpeninsular Highway. It is a good area for photographing Baja's largest desert dweller.

(Km F-68) SIERRA GIGANTA — The base of the Sierra Giganta has been some distance inland since the Peninsular Range Mountains were crossed north of Santa Rosalia. In the vicinity of **Km F-68**, the range's steep eastern escarpment is closer to the coast and will provide you with the best scenery in view from the Transpeninsular Highway. Note the characteristic saw-toothed silhouette.

(Km F-60) ROAD TO LA PURISIMA — At this point, a secondary road leads right (west) to the historic towns of San Jose de Comondu and La

Loreto — An aerial view of Loreto. The town dock has now been expanded into a small breakwater-lined harbor. (See other photo on this page). The sizeable three-story building on the shore to the left is the Hotel Mision de Loreto.

Purisima, and eventually to Cuidad Insurgentes. It provides one of the most interesting back-road adventures in Baja. The full route is described at the end of this chapter. End **SIDE TRIP**.

(Km F-21) SAN BRUNO LANDING SITE From this portion of Highway 1, the Sea of Cortez is in view about 6 miles to the east. A low section of coast lies between mountains to both the north and south. It is along here that Padre Francisco Kino and Isidro de Atondo made their attempt to found a colony in 1683. This effort lasted only nineteen months but was a key step to the permanent settlement made in Loreto 14-years later, in 1697. (See Chapter 12 HISTORY). The dirt road to the area leaves the highway just north of **Km F-20**.

(Km F-6) SCENIC VIEW — Prior to **Km F-6** one can see the town of Loreto and its thousands of date palms lying along the shore at the eastern edge of a sizeable coastal plain. The large island south of town is Isla Carmen. The smaller island off its SW tip is Isla Danzante, with Puerto Escondido hidden along the peninsular shore to the west. (See map in Chapter 22.) It is apparent, toward the south, that the Sierra Giganta is sweeping to the coast and the offshore islands appear to be its seaward extension.

PSI **#15**

(Km F-0 and G-120) LORETO — Whenever you have visited a locality long

enough ago to be considered an *old-timer*, you must be prepared for the disappointments brought about by change. All Baja is changing rapidly, but it is particularly apparent at Loreto. While the town is the oldest permanent Spanish settlement in all of the Californias, it has probably never been among its most charming. Its flat terrain made it easy to design the town in conventional and uninspiring square blocks.

Now it has received a considerable face-lifting of new streets and buildings. Its western fringe was planned to be an extensive

The boat launching ramp and harbor at Loreto.

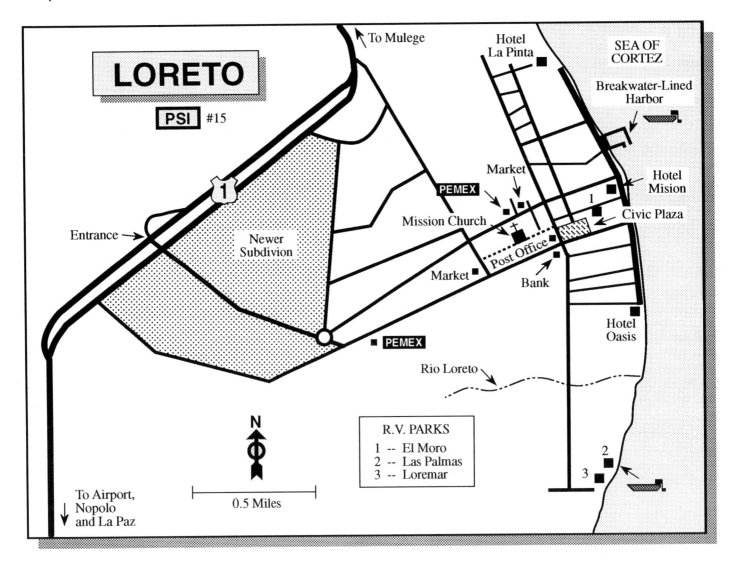

recreation home subdivision but the area elicited little or no interest from tourists. It is now being developed into housing for local citizens.

The most recent improvement has been construction of a small breakwater lined harbor, boat launching ramp, and parking area which incorporates the old town pier as its northerly leg. In addition the old earth surface waterfront street has been replaced by a handsome hard-surfaced boulevard complete with palm trees. A new charm has begun to emerge at Loreto.

Loreto finds a place on the POINTS OF SPECIAL INTEREST Tour as stop No. 15. Drive into town and peruse the civic plaza. The mission church and the adjoining historical museum are the most important places you should visit. The present church is the successor to Baja's original mission founded in 1697.

Loreto is where it all began. It was the base from which Junipero Serra started his expedition to settle Alta California, and Loreto was to serve as the military presidio, the residence of the Father Superior of the peninsula's missions and the seat of its civil government until 1829. In that year, the town was essentially destroyed by a hurricane and the capital moved to La Paz.

Loreto was to drift into oblivion but has now been given a new birth by the tourist industry. There are good R.V. parks and hotels at various locations. See the LORETO Map.

LOOP ROAD TO LA PURISIMA AND CIUDAD INSURGENTES

SIDE TRIP

Described from north to south in this subsection of Chapter 21 is a 111.6 mile loop road from Km F-60 on Highway 1 to Ciudad Insurgentes. Consult the CHAPTER Maps for Chapters 20, 21, and 22 concerning the material to be discussed.

The principal reasons for traveling this loop are (1) to visit the historic and picturesque towns of La Purisima-San Isidro and San Jose de Comondu-San Miguel de Comondu; and (2) to access sites for launching kayaks and other small boats near the north end of the Magdalena Lagoon System. The latter objective is best met by driving north from Ciudad Insurgentes.

The Baja peninsula offers several small communities that affect travelers as places that look like sleepy Mexican town ought to look. Among the best of these are San Ignacio, Mulege, and

Todos Santos. But each of these has been modified to one degree or the other by the presence of highways and the onslaught of tourism. The best advice I can offer is to say "You ain't seen nothen yet" until you visit the four towns noted in the paragraph above.

The road from **Km F-60** to San Isidro-La Purisima is a fairly rough secondary road, but is readily negotiable in pickups and vans. It is not suited for larger R.V.'s. Most of the 70.1 miles of road from La Purisima to Ciudad Insurgentes has been recently constructed to highway standards. Of this, 29.1 miles were paved in spring 1989. Addition paving should be anticipated in the future.

IMPORTANT NOTE — The highway standard road noted above continues north from La Purisima and is signed for San Juanico (45 Km) and San Jose de Gracia (98 Km). I have not made this trip. However, it seems logical to conclude that this road is destined to be a through highway from San Ignacio to Ciudad Insurgentes along the Pacific coast. If so, it will offer an alternative to driving Highway 1 between these two communities. It will be less scenic than Highway 1 but will allow tourists to travel down the peninsula on one road and to return north on the other.

(Km F-60) — The loop road leaves Highway 1 to the west 0.1 miles south of **Km F-60**. The peninsular divide of approximately 1,500 feet in elevation is reached in about 8 miles. West from here the roadbed lies in reasonably gentle terrain but can be badly damaged after heavy rains. Another 1,500 foot pass is encountered at the 31.5 mile point whereupon the road descends rapidly into the valley ahead.

BOB & JEAN 4X4

Approximately 13 miles SW from Highway 1 on the secondary road to San Isidro one encounters the junction with the old canyon road along Arroyo de la Purisima to San Isidro. Taking this 24 mile long route offers a scenic challenge with numerous arroyo crossings. Near its eastern end the road encounters the Rancho Ojo de Agua which is where the water rises that is eventually channeled into the palm covered valleys at San Isidro and La Purisima. This adventure through rugged terrain is trip #9 of the "Bob and Jean 4x4" Recommendations introduced in Chapter 3.

32.7 Miles — Encounter a T- intersection. The left branch is a single-lane, 19.5 mile, secondary road to San Jose de Comondu. It is readily passable to pickups and vans but travel speed is slow due to its rough, rocky surface. San Jose de Comondu and San

The beautiful valley of the Arroyo La Purisima between the communities of San Isidro and La Purisima.

Miguel de Comondu lie about 2 miles apart along a palm shaded valley surrounded by steep lava cliffs.

Jesuit padres established their fifth mission in 1708 at Comondu Viejo. It was moved to San Jose de Comondu in 1737. The present stone chapel is reported to be the missionaries house. San Miguel de Comondu is the site of a 1714 visiting station and cattle ranch for the San Javier mission to the SE.

BOB & JEAN 4X4

Taking off to the SE from San Jose de Comondu is a 26 mile long road to San Javier which passes through high desert terrain. (San Javier and its remarkable mission church are described in

The community of San Jose de Comondu nestled in its palm filled canyon.

Chapter 22.) Portions of this road have been built to secondary road standards but they have been damaged by storms and best suited for 4x4 vehicles. It is an additional 44 miles to the SW from San Javier to the highway near Santo Domingo along an arroyo and passing many ranches and camp sites. This 70 mile loop is trip #10 of the "Bob and Jean" 4x4 Recommendations (See Chapter 3).

A 23.8 mile secondary road runs from San Miguel de Comondu to the highway standard road near La Poza Grande. I have not taken this road but believe it would make a good route for proceeding south and avoiding the return trip to San Isidro. Something has to be left for the adventurous traveler.

35.1 Miles — Town center of San Isidro. At the east end of town a road forks to the north and crosses the Arroyo de la Purisima. A short distance further, a second road branches to the right providing access to numerous places to camp in the desert. There are few camp sites in the valley itself that are not a part of someone's home or garden.

37.6 Miles — Center of La Purisima. It is approximately a 6 mile drive through the two towns of San Isidro and La Purisima. The majority of the area is a valley some 1/2 miles in width completely covered with palms and other trees and numerous garden plots. There is surface water running in the stream and the overall atmosphere is most pleasant.

41.5 Miles — Junction with highway standard but as yet unpaved road. Take the left (south) fork to Ciudad Insurgentes. The right fork towards San Ignacio is of the same standard as far as the eye can see. I have not taken this route. Proceeding south from this point:

54.5 Miles — A side road leads in 5.2 miles to a solar experimental area. This sizeable facility built by the Mexican government was abandoned during my last visit.

69.4 Miles — A secondary road branches to the NE and accesses San Miguel de Comondu in 23.8 miles. I have not traveled this road. The 6.7 miles of the main road north of this junction was paved in spring 1989.

72.4 Miles — A two-lane dirt road branches to the west and in 2.0 miles arrives at the community of La Poza Grande. From the extreme southwest edge of town (at the end of the power line) a low standard, but level dirt road leads in 3.8 miles to a good landing and camping site (San Jorge) at the northern end of the Magdalena Lagoon System. Kayaks and small car-top boats may be launched over the shore for trips south through the lagoons. There are a few confusing side roads on the way to the lagoon, but perseverance, and the maintenance of a generally southwest direction will bring one to the water's edge. (San Jorge is shown mistakenly as being northwest of La Poza Grande on the Southern California Automobile Club map.)

92.4 Miles — A paved road branches to the west and arrives in 2.0 miles at Santo Domingo and its PEMEX station. The paved surface extended from Highway 1 at Ciudad Insurgentes to 3.2 miles north of this Santo Domingo junction in spring 1989.

It is 11.9 miles over a low-standard but level dirt road to a fishing and clamming village near the mouth of Boca de Santo Domingo. A concrete lighthouse marks the spot. Kayaks and car-top boats may be launched here for trips along the Magdalena Lagoon System. There are numerous branching roads along the way so this trip may involve some wrong turns and doubling back.

110.1 Miles — A paved highway to the right leads in 24.6 miles to Puerto Lopez Mateos. Because of this town's importance as a whale-watching center it is described as a side trip from Ciudad Insurgentes in Chapter 22.

111.6 Miles — Ciudad Insurgentes and the Transpeninsular Highway. End **SIDE TRIP**.

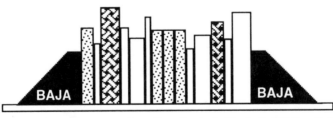

| See the BAJA BOOKSHELF in the Appendix | | See the BAJA BOOKSHELF in the Appendix |

BAJA   BAJA

BAJA BOOKSHELF

The BAJA BOOKSHELF offers the Baja Buff an array of publications concerning Baja California. Some were written specifically about the peninsula. Others are the best available books dealing with subjects related to Baja such as wildlife, Spanish, etc. Each represents my choice of the best title available on the subject.

Order books directly from the BAJA BOOKSHELF in the Appendix, or upon request we will send you more complete information on any book, including new titles that were not available when the THE MAGNIFICENT PENINSULA was published.

Jack Williams

CHAPTER 22
LORETO TO LA PAZ

Baja's Central Coast Tourist Area continues for 36 kms (22 miles) south of Loreto. It ends near Ligui on the shore of Ensenada Blanca. From this point south to La Paz, there are several interesting and challenging side trips, but the journey along Highway 1 itself is one of the peninsula's least inspiring.

SIDE TRIP

(Km G-118) SAN JAVIER — To the right (west), a secondary road leaves Highway 1 and crosses the Sierra Giganta to the village of San Javier. In this vicinity the Jesuits founded their second mission in 1699, only two years after landing in Loreto. In 1744, they began construction of a stone church at San Javier, which today is a small village of some 300 people. The building's stone masonry and its lava rock ornamentation are truly remarkable considering its location in what was one of the world's most remote and primitive places. Still in use today, it represents Baja's finest and best preserved of the Jesuit missions.

> NOTE -- See photo of the San Javier church on page 111.

The access road is well constructed, but because of its steep grades and rough surface it is best suited for lightly loaded vans and pickups. It passes through scenic mountain terrain.

9.4 Miles — Cross stream channel. A good camping spot.

12.5 Miles — Rancho Las Parras. A pleasant oasis of grape vines, figs, olives, and citrus trees.

13.7 Miles — Top of the divide after having climbed the steep eastern escarpment of the Sierra de la Giganta. The Sea of Cortez has been in sight to the east for some time.

19.4 Miles — Junction with a road to San Jose de Comondu. Steep grades and erosion reduced this road to four-wheel-drive status ten miles to the west in 1986.

23.1 Miles — San Javier. End **SIDE TRIP**.

(Km G-117) LORETO AIRPORT — An oiled road leaves Highway 1 to the left (east) and arrives at the Loreto airport in 0.5 miles. Here you will find a parking lot, modern waiting room, and an international airfield serving aircraft from the United States and the Mexican mainland. These facilities provide air access to Loreto, Nopolo, and Puerto Escondido. NOTE — Aero California Airlines had scheduled flights here in 1992, but at times in the past there has been no commercial air service.

SIDE TRIP

(Km G-114) PRIMER AGUA — Between **Km G-113** and **Km G-114** is a large electric transformer station . A secondary road leaves to the west, directly south of the station, and leads in 4.1 miles to Primer Agua. Here, near the base of the Sierra Giganta, lies a delightful oasis watered by a ditch-diverted stream. FONATUR has developed the area as a nursery to supply ornamental trees and shrubs for its developments. Trails lead through beds of a large variety of plants being reproduced from cuttings. There is also a pool of water and an adjoining barbecue area. It is a pleasant spot to visit if you are staying in the Loreto-Puerto Escondido area. It is open to the public on a charge basis. End **SIDE TRIP**.

PSI #16

(Km G-111) NOPOLO — Prior to 1977, this section of coast was a deserted beach providing isolated camp spots for a few people seeking solitude. Now you will find a one-half square-mile area laced with well landscaped roads waiting to serve future tourists. This is the FONATUR development at Nopolo. It has attracted very little attention and lags far behind similar developments at Cabo San Lucas and San Jose del Cabo to the south. For this reason it is a pleasant, unhurried place to visit.

In 1992 there were a scattering of residences and the Hotel Presidente Loreto, one of the peninsula's finest hotels. Across from the hotel are a large number of tennis courts and related facilities which it was hoped would attract international competition. A 9-hole golf course is also completed. Only the future knows the eventual success of this substantial undertaking, but certainly it will be one of the few places in Mexico where the tourist can enjoy golf, tennis, watersports, a fine hotel, and excellent scenery all at one location.

Nopolo is stop No. 16 on the POINTS OF SPECIAL INTEREST Tour. The hotel is worth a visit, and I believe a circle drive through the area will give you a quick vision of what the future holds for Baja. Even the largest of R.V.'s can easily make this tour. At least for the present, tourists are permitted to camp along the excellent sandy beach at the south end of the Nopolo development near Punta Nopolo. (If you ask at the FONATUR office you are told "No Camping," but self-contained R.V.s are tolerated.) A cobblestone road built parallel to the beach provides a good parking area.

(Km G-103) PLAYA NORTE — Playa Norte is a part sand and part shingle beach providing camping spots about 150 yards east of the highway.

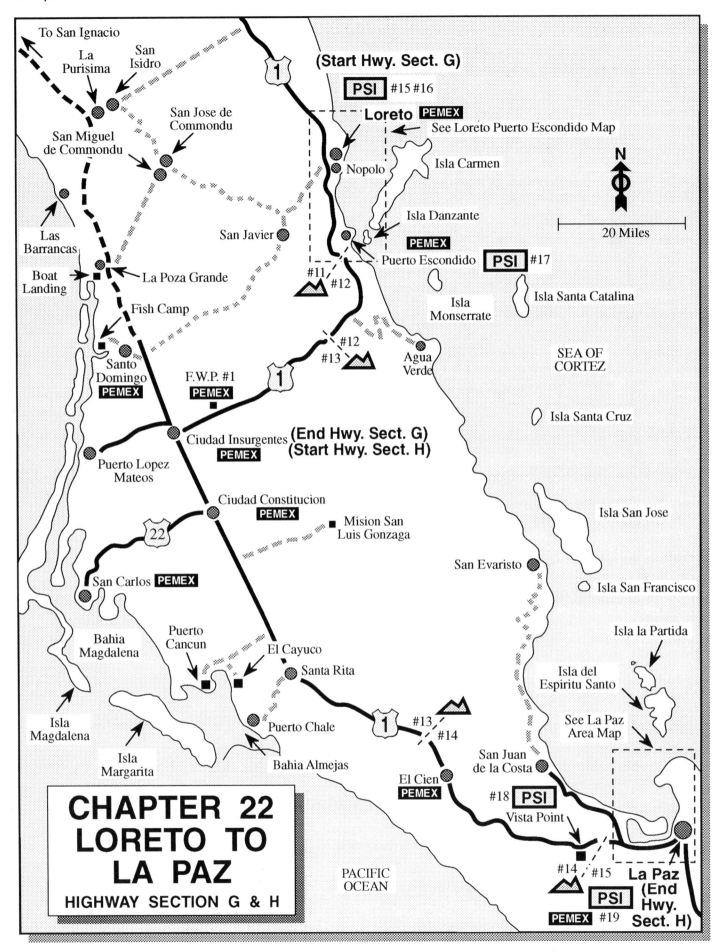

To San Ignacio
La Purisima
San Isidro
San Miguel de Commondu
San Jose de Commondu
Las Barrancas
San Javier
Boat Landing
La Poza Grande
Fish Camp
Santo Domingo **PEMEX**
F.W.P. #1 **PEMEX**
Puerto Lopez Mateos
Ciudad Insurgentes **PEMEX**
Ciudad Constitucion **PEMEX**
Mision San Luis Gonzaga
San Carlos **PEMEX**
Bahia Magdalena
Puerto Cancun
El Cayuco
Santa Rita
San Evaristo
Isla San Francisco
Isla Magdalena
Isla Margarita
Puerto Chale
Bahia Almejas
El Cien **PEMEX**
San Juan de la Costa
Isla la Partida
Isla del Espiritu Santo
See La Paz Area Map
#18 **PSI**
Vista Point
#14 #15
La Paz (End Hwy. Sect. H)
PSI
PEMEX #19

(Start Hwy. Sect. G)
PSI #15 #16
Loreto **PEMEX**
See Loreto Puerto Escondido Map
Nopolo
Isla Carmen
Isla Danzante
PEMEX
Puerto Escondido
PSI #17
#11 #12
#12 #13
Agua Verde
Isla Monserrate
Isla Santa Catalina
SEA OF CORTEZ
Isla Santa Cruz
Isla San Jose
(End Hwy. Sect. G)
(Start Hwy. Sect. H)
#13 #14

N
20 Miles

PACIFIC OCEAN

CHAPTER 22 LORETO TO LA PAZ
HIGHWAY SECTION G & H

(Km G-97) EL JUNCALITO — A low standard road leaves to the left (east) at this point. This road shortly divides with the left branch leading to the seaside village of el Juncalito. Proceeding straight ahead brings one in 0.5 miles to a grove of palms and a fine sandy beach. You may camp among the palms or along the 1/4 mile long beach. (I am advised that FONATUR plans some type of development here so look for the possibility of change.)

PSI #17

(Km G-94) PUERTO ESCONDIDO — Take the paved side road at this point 0.6 miles to Tripui and 0.9 miles farther to the inner harbor area. This is **PSI** stop No.17.

The shore of the almost totally land-locked bay at Puerto Escondido (Hidden Port) was long one of Baja's most heavily used camping spots. The area was then taken over by FONATUR for a massive Pueblo Nautico (Nautical Village). Planned for construction were hotels, dockside condominiums, marina, and other at-

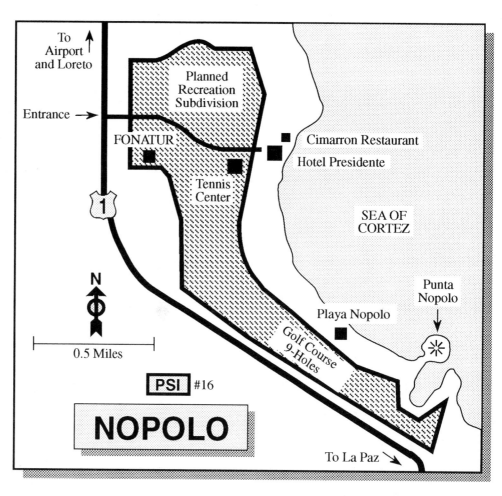

tractions. However, the past 5-years have seen very little progress, and as of spring 1992, the only usable facilities were a concrete boat ramp and rental sailboats. A PEMEX station was partially completed and showed signs of life. One could conclude that the balance of the development was an ill-conceived project from Mexico City. (God bless socialism.)

TRIPUI R.V. PARK — Many tourists regretted the passing of Puerto Escondido's beach-side camping area. But at least, here at Puerto Escondido, an excellent replacement facility was provided. An outstanding, attractively landscaped R.V. Park was constructed nearby and complemented with a swimming pool, showers, restrooms, laundry facilities, restaurant, store, small motel and sports facilities. While not at the water's edge, it offers splendid views of the Sierra Giganta and is surrounded by attractive desert vegetation.

The sad part is that the park has now been totally converted to full-time tenants with a guard at the gate to keep the rest of us out. Short-term R.V.'s are relegated to a fenced in parking area next to the road. So depending on your point of view, you will either love Tripui, or hate it.

Should a less expensive beachfront spot be more to your taste, return north to el Juncalito, or drive south to Ligui on Ensenada Blanca near Ligui.

CANYON HIKING — Directly across Highway 1 (and north of an electrical substation) from the blacktopped entrance to Puerto Escondido is a low standard dirt road paralleled by a power line. In 0.9 miles this road will bring you to a water pumping station at the base of the Sierra Giganta. There is a small turnaround area here, but you should leave large vehicles behind. Park at this spot and hike into the steep-walled canyon that dissects the cliffs a few yards north of the pumping station.

There is no developed trail but once you are between the steep cliffs it is impossible to lose your way. It takes 20 to 30 minutes of hiking along a cascading stream to arrive at a point where further progress is impeded by massive boulders. The rocks and canyon walls are of volcanic origin, and the stream bed is an enticing realm of small pools, palm trees, and other vegetation. Take along your bathing suit and enjoy an hour or so in this delightful rock-walled oasis.

(Km G-84) LIGUI (ENSENADA BLANCA) — A small school house and other buildings are located to the left (east) of Highway 1 north of **Km G-84**. This is Ligui. A low standard dirt road leaves the highway and in 2.1 miles arrives at the fishing village of Ensenada Blanca located on a fine sandy beach. An even lower standard road continues for some 1.1 miles around the edge of Ensenada Blanca to camping spots at the water's edge. There are also several spur roads to similar beach-side

To Mulege

Isla Coronados

N

#15
PSI
Loreto

To San Javier

To Primer Agua

PEMEX

LORETO PUERTO ESCONDIDO AREA

Loreto International Airport

Nopolo PSI #16

See Nopolo Map

Isla Carmen

Playa Norte

#17
PSI
Puerto Escondido

PEMEX

El Juncalito

Nautical Village Development

Tripui R.V. Park

△ Camping Spots

5 Miles

Isla Danzante

Ligui

#11
#12

Ensenada Blanca

---

hideaways between the highway and the village. These roads are level but unimproved.

Ligui is the southernmost area of level land on the Central Coast Tourist Area that began north of Santa Rosalia. Confronted with this topographic situation, the Jesuit missionaries located the Ligui mission here in 1705, only six years after arriving on the peninsula. It became the jumping-off point for missionary trails leading into the mountains of the interior and south along the coast, but the mission itself lasted only sixteen years.

#11 ⛰ #12

(KM G-83) GEOGRAPHIC CHANGE — The Sierra Giganta's presence at the Sea of Cortez coast forces the Transpeninsular Highway to ascend the steep eastern escarpment (Geographic Section No. 12). The road is winding, but grades are moderate, and the traveler is rewarded with fine mountain scenery, the last to be seen for many miles. This dramatic and rapid climb up the eastern face of the Peninsular Range Mountains, and the level and lengthy descent lying ahead on the western side provides the best examples you will see of the fault-block mountain structure presented in Chapter 9 GEOLOGY.

South of this point (**Km G-83**), the eastern coastline of the peninsula is steep, rocky, and majestic. It is best viewed by boat or from small private aircraft. However, portions of the area can be enjoyed by taking the side trips to Agua Verde and San Juan de la Costa described in this chapter.

SIDE TRIP

(Km G-63) AGUA VERDE — A secondary road heads left (south) from Highway 1 between **Km G-63** and **Km G-64** to the small fishing village of Agua Verde. Taking all or a portion of this 24-mile side trip will allow you to enjoy a portion of the dramatic eastern side of the Sierra Giganta, an area which is viewed by very few tourists.

<u>10.9 Miles</u> — You are greeted with an outstanding view of the Sea of Cortez, offshore islands, and the coastal mountains. There is a flat area for camping some 200 yards prior to reaching this vista for those who do not wish to proceed further. The road to this point passes over rolling desert lands and can be traveled by most R.V.'s.

The road ahead makes a steep, four-mile descent down the face of the eastern escarpment. I recommend that you park your vehicle at the vista point and walk ahead for <u>0.2 miles</u> to a place where the road descending the mountain is in view. From this spot, you can also look to the south and see a large pinnacle rock lying several hundred feet offshore. This is Roca Solitaria. It marks the entrance to the anchorage at Agua Verde. Having located this landmark and looked over the road, you can judge how far you will have to travel to Agua Verde and can make your decision as to whether to proceed. I alert you that it is not

Ensenada Blanca and its small off-lying islands. Note the steep face of the mountains directly along the shoreline.

a suitable trip for large R.V.'s or any vehicle that tends to be top heavy. However, if the road is in good repair it makes a fine trip for those in pickup trucks, vans, and other smaller vehicles.

14.6 Miles — You have reached the bottom of the grade and can start worrying about the return trip. A short distance ahead, a side road veers sharply to the left and in 200 yards arrives at a camping spot on a bluff overlooking the sea.

16.8 Miles — A side road leads for 0.5 miles to a camping spot along the banks of an arroyo near a shingle beach. There are also several other side roads which I have not explored between this point and the Agua Verde village .

25.4 Miles — Arrive at Agua Verde. You will find this village to be one of the most primitive in Baja, but one most abundantly supplied with goats. The new road built in the early 1980s will no doubt bring much change to Agua Verde. End **SIDE TRIP**.

(Km G-64 to G-45) VOLCANIC MOUNTAINS — This section of the highway is relatively flat but passes through massive mountains of volcanic rock. This is a good place to stop and examine these igneous volcanic rocks if you have not done so before. See the ROCK CLASSIFICATION Chart in Chapter 9 GEOLOGY. Note their dark reddish color, fine grain, and the numerous pockets formed by gases trapped in the molten mass as it cooled.

#12 ◿◿ #13

(Km G-45) GEOGRAPHIC CHANGE — It is here that you might ask, "What happened to the other side of the mountain?" You have arrived at the end of Geographic Section No.12, and the western side of the mountains simply blend with the Continental Borderlands Province ahead. This section of the province is the Llano de Magdalena (Magdalena Plain). It is Geographic Section No.13. You will be passing over its flat terrain for the next 164 km (102 miles).

Highway 1 passing through the mountains of Geographic Section No. 12 west of Ligui.

Puerto Lopez Mateos on the Magdalena Lagoons. The group of large buildings along the shore is the fish cannery. Whale-watching tours leave directly to the left of the cannery. The community is within the trees further inland.

Looking ahead on clear days, you will be able to see the mountains that rim the outer edges of Bahias Magdalena and Almejas on the Pacific coast. At other times, they, and the entire Magdalena Plain, may be shrouded in fog and low clouds. The straight stretch of highway between **Km G-39** and **Km G-32** points directly at this range.

(Km G-17) FEDERAL WATER PROJECT NO.1 —An easily accessed PEMEX station (no Magna Sin in 1992) lies at this point and serves the agricultural area you have just entered. Here or at Villa Insurgentes is a good places to fuel on the return trip north in order to avoid the congestion often encountered at the stations at Loreto and Mulege.

ZONA DE NEBLINA — At several places along the highways in this area you will see signs reading "Zona de Neblina" Neblina means fog and you are being alerted to the fact that layers of fog will sometimes restrict visibility. The fog also brings moisture to the desert plants. Many of the larger species become festooned with lichens and ball moss (See Chapter 10 VEGETATION). This situation may be seen along any of the side roads leading from Highway 1 to Bahia Magdalena.

(Km G-0) CIUDAD INSURGENTES — At this point, Highway 1 makes a 90-degree turn to the south. You have now reached the breakpoint between highway sections **G** and **H** and the edge of the town of Ciudad Insurgentes. A PEMEX station lies on the south side of the highway, a short distance east of this turning point. There is another PEMEX station in town on the west side of the main street.

Cuidad Insurgentes, a town of some 15,000 people, lies near the center of one of the largest agricultural areas in Baja. As noted in Chapter 12 HISTORY, development here was not able to start until 1933. Prior to this time, most of the peninsula's lands were encumbered with various foreign-dominated leases which produced little more than speculation. It is easy to understand why the Mexican government has, until recently, wanted to maintain control of all the country's enterprises.

SIDE-TRIP
PUERTO LOPEZ MATEOS — Cuidad Insurgentes is the starting point for a side trip to Puerto Lopez Mateos on the 70-mile-long coastal lagoon lying north of Bahia Magdalena. It is the most convienient site for viewing the California gray whale in Baja California. (Scammon's Lagoon is also popular but access is over a lenghty dirt road.) See pages 188 and 189 and Chapter 11 WILDLIFE for information about the gray whale.

From the Highway 1 90-degree turning point noted above, travel north through Cuidad Insurgentes for 1.5 miles. At this point, a blacktop highway leads to the left (west). It is 24.6 miles to Puerto Lopez Mateos.

Upon arrival at the port, proceed around the north side of the waterfront fish processing plant. Here is a public parking area from which you may sometimes view the whales. (This area is closed at night, but you may camp in a not to inviting area immediately outside.) Pangas are for hire to take you for a closer encounter with these marine giants at their calving areas about 5 miles distant.

Small boats and kayaks may also be launched over the beach for camping adventures along the lagoon. There is abundant bird life in addition to the whales. (Guided whale-watching trips to Puerto Lopez Mateos are available in La Paz.) End **SIDE TRIP**.

(Km H-211) CIUDAD CONSTITUCION — **Km H-211** marks the center of the largest community in the Llano Magdalena agricultural area. It has a population of 42,000. Upon entering town from the north, look for a small traffic circle on the right with a statue at its center. This is the junction with Highway 22, which leads to the port city of San Carlos and Bahia Magdalena.

South of this junction the main street of town turns into a palm-lined boulevard. There are two PEMEX stations on the west side of this boulevard. Two blocks south of the Highway 22 junction you will cross Olachea street. On the NE corner lies a three-story concrete building housing the Hotel Maribel. Two blocks east on Olachea is the smaller Hotel Casino. These are adequate facilities for an overnight stay but are not of the luxurious variety.

At **Km H-209** south of town a dirt road leads to the right (west) and in 0.6 miles arrives at the Campestre La Pila Trailer Court. This facility has full hookups. It is located adjoining a working farm and a large grassy area with swimming pools, picnic tables, and showers.

SIDE TRIP
(Km H-211) SAN CARLOS (BAHIA MAGDALENA) It is 57 km (35 miles) to San Carlos, a town of some 5,000 people, and the shores of Bahia Magdalena over straight and level Highway 22. (There is a statue within a small traffic circle at the junction point.) I recommend visiting this area if your principal aim is to take advantage of the best waters for using small trailer boats on Baja's Pacific coast. If, instead, you are seeking the best camping locations or hotels, you will be better served in other places.

At Km 52 (about 3 miles prior to reaching San Carlos) is a massive square building from which projects a stubby smoke stack. This is the most recent of Baja's three power generating plants. Its fuel is delivered by ship to the port of San Carlos, and then through a short pipeline to the plant. The building and its many lights provide a prominent landmark.

As you approach San Carlos you will begin to see marshy areas and the town itself is located on an island. These features are indicative of the fact that the western edge of the Continental Borderlands is sinking into the sea.

After arriving at the edge of San Carlos, you will see a sizeable wharf that has been built many hundreds of yards into the shallow waters of Bahia Magdalena to a point where deep-draft ships can be accommodated. This dock and its warehouses are the shipping points for cotton, grain, and other agricultural products grown in the interior. San Carlos and Ensenada to the north are the only deep-water commercial ports on the peninsula's Pacific coast. The PEMEX station is near the landward end of the port facility.

Bearing left at the PEMEX station it is 1.7 miles through town to the Las Palapas R.V. Park. Proceed into town, pass by the western side of the town square, and take the road paralleling the shore. What is called the Las Palapas R.V. Park was originally constructed as a tourist facility but its former rental cabins are being used as homes for Mexican fishermen. In 1992 the small restaurant was still serving meals and boats may be launched at mid to high tide at a nearby ramp. R.V.'s can park on the adjoining beach but there are no hookups. Be careful in picking your spot as some high tides will put your vehicle awash.

End **SIDE TRIP**.

BOB & JEAN 4X4

(Km H-195) SAN LUIS GONZAGA — Just south of **Km H-195** a secondary road leaves Highway 1 to the east. It is signed for a large dam named La Presa Iguajil which is about 21 miles distant. From the dam a road runs south to a grove of palms sheltering the stone Mision de San Luis Gonzaga and a ranch who's owners serve as caretakers for the mission. This is trip #11 of the "Bob and Jean 4x4" Recommendations (Chapter 3).

San Luis Gonzaga was founded in 1737 and was the fifteenth of Baja's Jesuit missions. Its oasis like setting is a welcome relief from some of the most barren landscape in the peninsula. Numerous other roads proceed easterly into the mountains from here, one of them reaching the Sea of Cortez shore at San Evaristo.

SIDE TRIP
(Km H-173) PUERTO CANCUN — You may have always longed to take your wife to exciting Cancun in Mexico. Here is your chance. Perhaps she will not notice that this is not the exotic resort area on the Caribbean coast. In any case, she will be consoled knowing that accommodations are a bit less expensive camping here on the shore of Bahia Almejas.

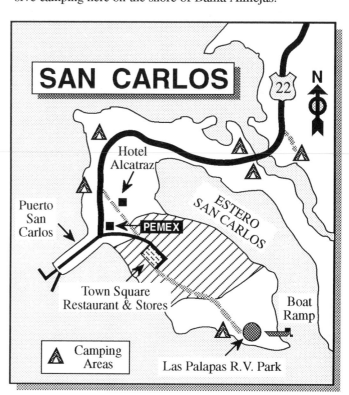

The secondary road to Puerto Cancun is straight, wide, level, and washboarded. At the 13.0 mile point a one-lane secondary road leads in 2.5 miles to the El Cayuco fishing village. It is a bit on the dirty side and camping space is limited unless you can negoiate low standard sandy roads along the shore.

Puerto Cancun is 19.9 miles from Highway 1. There are good camping spots on the bluffs above the beach west of the village. Almejas means clams, and there is no better place to find them than in the extremely shallow waters of Bahia Almejas here at Puerto Cancun. Low tide exposes sandy clamming grounds over 1/2 miles in width. End **SIDE TRIP**.

(Km H-169) MAGDALENA MOUNTAINS — Here, near a large microwave tower, is an excellent view to the west of the mountains which rim the outer edges of Bahias Magdalena and Almejas. (On some days they are hidden in fog and low clouds.) A gap in this range is the 2-mile-wide entrance to the bay from the Pacific Ocean. While passing through this rocky portal by boat, one is reminded very much of the Golden Gate at San Francisco. San Francisco Bay and Bahia Magdalena are the two finest natural harbors in the Californias.

SIDE TRIP
(Km H-157) PUERTO CHALE — Highway 1 makes a 45-degree turn to the left at the very small town of Santa Rita. At this turn is a junction with the secondary road to Puerto Chale. Puerto Chale lies on an estuary at the edge of Bahia Almejas. Here are located a small fishing village and an experimental shrimp farm. It is 14.6 miles to the water's edge over a straight, level road. End **SIDE TRIP**.

#13 ⛰ **#14**
(Km H-120) GEOGRAPHIC CHANGE — South of Santa Rita on Highway 1, the totally flat terrain through which you have been passing comes to an end and the land begins to roll. The highway slowly begins to gain elevation, and the Llano de Magdalena merges indistinctly with the gentle western slopes of the Peninsular Range Mountains. Thus, **Km H-120** is only an approximate dividing line between geographical sections. In a few miles, however, it will be apparent that you have left the plains of Geographic Section No. 13 and are in the plateaus of Section No. 14. Here you will be traveling for the next 89 km (55 miles).

The terrain in this section is composed of sandstone, shale, and other sedimentary rocks. Notice the horizontal banding of the rock layers in the highway cuts and surrounding hills.

(Km H-100) EL CIEN — El Cien is a small village whose chief claim to fame for the tourist is a PEMEX station, the only one between Ciudad Constitucion and La Paz. Appropriately, El Cien (cien means 100 in Spanish) lies exactly at the 100-kilometer point.

(Km H-82) PACIFIC VIEW — Near **Km H-82** there is a tall microwave tower. From this point, one can see the Pacific

Ocean far to the west. (There will be other such views between here and the Km H-35 Vista Point ahead.) A short distance south, near **Km H-80**, a side road leads to the coast at El Conejo. The coast is relatively uninviting in this area. Beginning south of the Magdalena Mountains and stretching for more than 100 miles to Todos Santos, the shore is basically one long sandy beach backed by monotonous low plains. The Pacific swells break heavily, making swimming and boating hazardous activities.

PSI **#18**
(Km H-35) VISTA POINT — On the right, near **Km H-35**, is a small monument bearing a cross. Even the largest R.V.'s can pull over here at POINTS OF SPECIAL INTEREST Tour stop No. 18 and enjoy one of the most rewarding views in Baja.

1. The vista point lies near the edge of the plateau area through which you have just passed. Lying below, to the south, stretches the Llano de La Paz, the southernmost portion of the Continental Borderlands Province. At this narrow point the peninsula is almost divided in half, providing clear evidence to geologists that it has been stretched linearly as noted in Chapter 9 GEOLOGY.

2. South of the plain lie the massive granite Sierra de la Laguna in the Cape Region.

A monument bearing a cross lies alongside the highway at **PSI** Stop No. 18. A visit here awards the traveler with fine views of the Sea of Cortez and the Llano de La Paz.

3. To the NE is Bahia de La Paz, a broad indentation in the Sea of Cortez. At the water's edge, near the base of the Sierra de la Laguna, the city of La Paz is in view.

4. Several miles into the Sea of Cortez rest Isla Espiritu del Santo and Isla la Partida. The two islands appear as one. They provide many snug coves frequented by yachtsmen. Here, and on the other Sea of Cortez islands to the north, the ocean cruisers are free from the activities of the peninsula's road builders.

#14 ▲▲ #15

(Km H-31) GEOGRAPHIC CHANGE — At approximately this point, the highway leaves the plateau lands (Geographic Section No. 14) and enters the level Llano de La Paz (Geographic Section No. 15).

A picturesque section of the highway between Highway 1 and San Juan de la Costa.

(Km H-27) SIERRA GIGANTA — From a slight rise in the highway near **Km H-27**, one may look to the north and see the southern terminus of the escarpment of the Sierra Giganta. This is the end of the steep-faced coastal mountain range that started at Ligui. Visible is a light pinkish band of volcanic ash. This band is not level, as viewed from here. Rather, it slopes downward below the earth's surface at its inland end, providing yet another indication of the downward westerly tilt of the fault-block mountain structure.

SIDE TRIP

(Km H-17) SAN JUAN DE LA COSTA — A trip to, and beyond, the phosphorus mining community of San Juan de la Costa is your second opportunity to experience the steep coastal section of the Sierra Giganta at close range. The road is oiled the first 26 miles into San Juan de la Costa and is constructed to highway standard, but not yet paved, for an additional 32.7 miles. The route offers some of the best coastal scenery in view from any of Baja's highways.

Further highway standard construction is planned and this route may eventually join with the coastal road to Agua Verde described earlier in this chapter.

12.5 Miles — The oiled road crosses the level Llano de La Paz and arrives at the base of the towering Sierra Giganta escarpment.

14.3 Miles — This point is the end of the flat plain and the site of an abandoned highway work center. Nearby are camp spots behind a coastal dune fronted by a fine sandy beach. There are additional places to reach the coast between here and San Juan de la Costa at points where the road dips to cross arroyos.

25.0 Miles — The main, but unpaved road, veers to the right toward the village of San Evaristo. The paved road continues straight ahead for one mile into San Juan de la Costa. This community is a mining company town with scores of homes built in neat rows on a level area several hundred feet above the sea.

I do not recommend the trip toward San Evaristo for larger R.V.'s. (Mileages continue to be from Highway 1 and do not include the side trip into San Juan de la Costa.)

27.7 Miles — At this point you arrive at the dock and conveyor system used to load ocean-going ore carriers. Inland are the processing facilities where raw earth containing about 10 percent phosphorus is enriched to 30 percent by leaching with sea water. After a fresh water rinse, it is dried for shipping and used as fertilizer.

The road ahead for the next three miles is extra-wide and well maintained but is heavily used by ore carrying equipment except on weekends. Between here and mileage point 57.7, the road is constructed to highway standards but is not yet oiled. There are several places to camp on the coast in the shadow of the magnificent Sierra Giganta mountains.

57.7 Miles — End highway standard road. Pickups and vans can readily make it ahead an additional 1.2 miles to a camping spot near a shingle beach. Beyond that point the road is best suited for 4x4 vehicles. In the past I have traversed this road in my standard drive pickup complete with camper but when last inspected in spring 1989, the surface had been badly eroded. Look for additional highway standard construction in this area in the future.

73.8 Miles — Arrive on the beach near the small fishing village of San Evaristo, another of the ocean cruiser's hideaways captured by the road builders. End **SIDE TRIP**.

(Km H-17) EL COMITAN — Immediately east of the highway to San Juan de la Costa, a dirt road leads to the left (north).

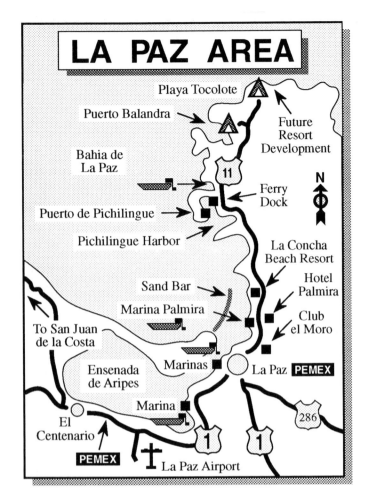

LA PAZ AREA

Playa Tocolote

Puerto Balandra

Bahia de La Paz

Future Resort Development

11

Ferry Dock

Puerto de Pichilingue

Pichilingue Harbor

N

La Concha Beach Resort

Hotel Palmira

Sand Bar

Marina Palmira

Club el Moro

To San Juan de la Costa

Ensenada de Aripes

Marinas

La Paz PEMEX

Marina

286

El Centenario

PEMEX La Paz Airport

1 1

In 0.8 miles it arrives at a beach-side camping spot at the western end of Ensenada de Aripes.

(Km H-17) ENSENADA DE ARIPES — From the San Juan de La Costa junction to La Paz, Highway 1 passes along the southern edge of a large lagoon (Ensenada de Aripes). It is separated from the Sea of Cortez by a spit of land whose eastern end is a sand bar that is awash only at low tide.

The city of La Paz and all of its tourist facilities are located along this almost fully enclosed body of water. The location protects the area from the open sea, but some tourists find that the lagoon's beaches, the quality of the water, and its overall aesthetic appeal are not as high quality as available in other areas. Please keep this situation in mind when evaluating the La Paz tourist accommodations presented in the balance of this chapter. In spite of these somewhat negative comments, La Paz is my favorite city in all of Mexico, and I am not alone in this assessment.

(Km H-15) EL CENTENARIO — Adjoining Highway 1 near the shallow western

end of Ensenada de Aripes is the small community of El Centenario. On a sandy beach lies the pleasant Oasis de Aripes R.V. park and restaurant. It is the only one of the La Paz area trailer courts directly on the waters edge.

Between **Km H-12** and **Km H-11** east of El Centenario is a PEMEX station with plenty of room for large R.V.'s. It is a good place to avoid the often hectic conditions at the stations in La Paz.

(Km H-9) LA PAZ AIRPORT — A blacktopped highway leads to the right for 2.0 miles to the La Paz Airport. This was the first of southern Baja's international airfields. It has modern terminal facilities. (There is almost continual urban development from this junction into the center of town.)

(Km H-7) DOVE OF PEACE STATUE — Just past **Km H-7** is a large, white, concrete statue of a bird. My notes say its a sea gull, but for a city named La Paz (The Peace) it must be a dove. It marks the junction of the old highway along the La Paz waterfront (to the left), and the newer divided bypass highway which skirts much of La Paz (to the right). Proceed accordingly. I don't know which of these routes is the official Highway 1, but I give the distinction to the old route on the map of La Paz.

(Km H-6) TOURISM DEPARTMENT — Between **Km H-6** and **Km H-5** is the office of the Secretaria de Turismo de Baja California Sur. Stop here for maps and travel information. There is another office downtown but parking is limited.

(Km H-4) LA PAZ R. V. Parks — There are three R.V. parks in La Paz. The El Cardon lies south of the highway at **Km H-4**. The La Paz park and the Aguamarina are located near, but not on the water front close to the highrise Hotel Gran Baja. See the LA PAZ MAP.

The giant Dove of Peace statue marking a major road junction as one enters La Paz from the west (See Text).

(Km H-0) LA PAZ — At last, the Transpeninsular Highway arrives at the city of peace, La Paz. It was here that Hernan Cortez stepped ashore on the third of May, 1535, only 43 years after Columbus discovered the Americas. See Chapter 12 HISTORY.

La Paz is a clean, modern city of over 100,000 people and the capital of the state of Baja California Sur. A walking tour of its waterfront and downtown area is stop No. 19 on the POINTS OF SPECIAL INTEREST Tour. While the city is growing in population, the downtown area is nicely settled down and there is little of the hectic growth apparent at Cabo San Lucas.

There are several fine resort hotels where sun worshippers can hibernate indefinitely. I strongly recommend them as destination points. However, I submit that if you choose a hotel in La Paz for your vacation, you should do so at least in part to enjoy the city itself; its weather, shopping, culture, and friendly people. If you are more interested in simply relaxing on the beach or around the swimming pool of a fine resort hotel, you probably will be more content at one of the fine hotels at the tip of the peninsula.

Near the heart of the downtown area, and across the street from the beach, is the Hotel los Arcos and its affiliated Cabanas de los Arcos. The restaurant is excellent, and while the Los Arcos is slightly less luxurious than some of the other hotels, it is located where you can readily enjoy the downtown area. The Hotel Perla is also located downtown on the waterfront but is a less auspicious establishment. In addition, there are a number of less expensive but fully acceptable hotels in or near the downtown area. The Hotel Gardenias is perhaps the best of these.

The tall building west of the downtown area on the waterfront is the Hotel Gran Baja. Nearby on the beach is the charming Hotel La Posada. North of town on the highway to Pichilingue are the Club el Morro, the La Concha Beach Resort and the Hotel Palmira. The latter is nicely landscaped but is separated from the beach by the highway.

SIDE TRIP
PICHILINGUE — Highway 11 travels <u>23 km (14 miles)</u> north from downtown La Paz to Pichilingue, which derived its name from the Dutch pirates who roamed the area in the 17th century.

As the long and narrow channel leading from the Sea of Cortez to La Paz is not suited for deep draft vessels, port facilities have been developed at the well-protected harbor at Pichilingue. Various industries requiring access to the sea are located in an industrial park surrounding the harbor. Also located here are (1) the terminal and parking lot for the ferries from La Paz to

The La Paz waterfront. The T-shaped pier to the left is the Commercial Wharf. The floating docks of the Marina de La Paz lie to the right.

Mazatlan and Topolobampo, and (2) a new passanger terminal developed to lure ocean cruise ships into La Paz.

PUERTO BALLANDRA AND TECOLOTE — To the north of Pichilingue there is presently almost no development. Here, facing the open Sea of Cortez are two beach areas heavily frequented by the people of La Paz on weekends. They also make good camping spots for tourists. These places are reached by taking a continuation of Highway 11 which was completed in 1991.

The new highway noted above was obviously constructed in anticipation of the development of a major new resort area at Tecolote, so brace for having another of Baja's idyllic beaches fall victim to economic progress. Its impact on the present hotels in La Paz is interesting to speculate.

4.4 Miles — An oiled side road to the left leads in 0.3 miles to the inner edge of the cove at Puerto Ballandra. (Continue ahead to Tecolote.) The shallow waters of the cove allow safe swimming, but its waters recede several hundred feet from the road at low tide.

5.7 Miles — At this point you arrive at the beach at Tecolote. It is far superior to the one at Puerto Ballandra although it is exposed to the wind and open sea. It is a fine location in calm weather. A low-standard road parallels the coast, for two miles to the east accessing numerous excellent camp sites.

The pool area of the La Concha Beach Resort.

CHAPTER 23
LA PAZ TO CABO SAN LUCAS VIA HIGHWAY 1

After traveling 1,483 km (922 miles) from the international border, your GRAND TOUR begins the final leg of the journey to the peninsula's tip at Cabo San Lucas. The scenery lying ahead is a considerable improvement over the rather unimpressive plains and low plateaus north of La Paz, as both of the highways to the south pass through or around the Sierra de la Laguna. The vegetation is also some of the most impressive to be encountered on the peninsula.

CAPE REGION CAMPING — Many of the locations along Highway 1 south of La Paz that were once popular beach-front camping areas have been usurped for residential and commercial purposes. This is particularly true in the "Corridor" between San Jose del Cabo and Cabo San Lucas where the last free beach camping area was closed to the public in 1991. It is also true in the Buena Vista-Los Barriles area. If beach camping is your objective, you need to consider taking one of the side trips described in this chapter. Excellent beach camping, and beach-side R.V. parks, are also available along Highway 19 on the Pacific coast. See Chapter 24.

PASSING THROUGH LA PAZ — On entering La Paz from the west, keep to the right at the Dove of Peace Statue (See Chapter 22). Taking this route will bypass the downtown section of La Paz.

SIDE TRIP
HIGHWAY 286 — The residential areas of La Paz are rapidly spreading to the south, so the junction of Highways 1 and 286 falls within the city. Be alert for the highway sign to S.J. de los Planes and position your vehicle to enable you to turn left from the busy, multilaned road. The junction is 1.3 miles from the intersection of 5 de Febrero and Forjadores Blvd. It is 58 km (36.5 miles) to Bahia de los Muertos.

Highway 286 is constructed through highly erosible granite soils. Thus, each side of the road has been provided with concrete-lined ditches to allow rain water to run off without damage to the travel surface. I have never observed this on any of Baja's other highways.

Km-23 — Highway 286 climbs through a region of low hills and reaches its maximum elevation near this point. As you descend to the east an excellent view unfolds and you will be able to see the Sea of Cortez and the southern end of mountainous Isla Cerralvo lying 7 miles off the shoreline.

Km-38 — A secondary road leads left (north) to the small towns of La Ventana (5.1 miles) and El Sargento (7.3 miles). A low standard road branches to the east between Kms 6 and 7 (1.2 miles south of the warehouse in La Ventana) and in 0.5 miles arrives at an excellent camping beach. I am advised that this road extends eastward to the Hotel las Arenas but is best suited for 4x4 vehicles due to sandy conditions. Campers can also find spots on the beach near both towns but there are no tourist facilities. During winter all of these locations are exposed to the prevailing northerly winds.

Km-41 — Between **Km 40** and **Km 41** a secondary road leads right (south) 14.3 miles to the town of San Antonio at Highway 1. It provides the opportunity of traveling south without returning to La Paz. The northerly 11.3 miles is a good, relatively level, one and one-half-lane secondary road. However, much of

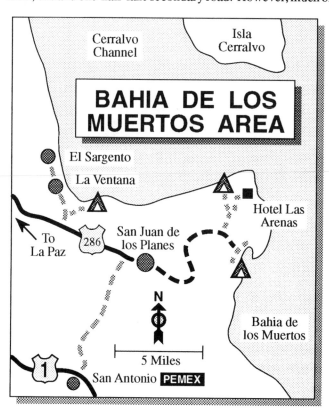

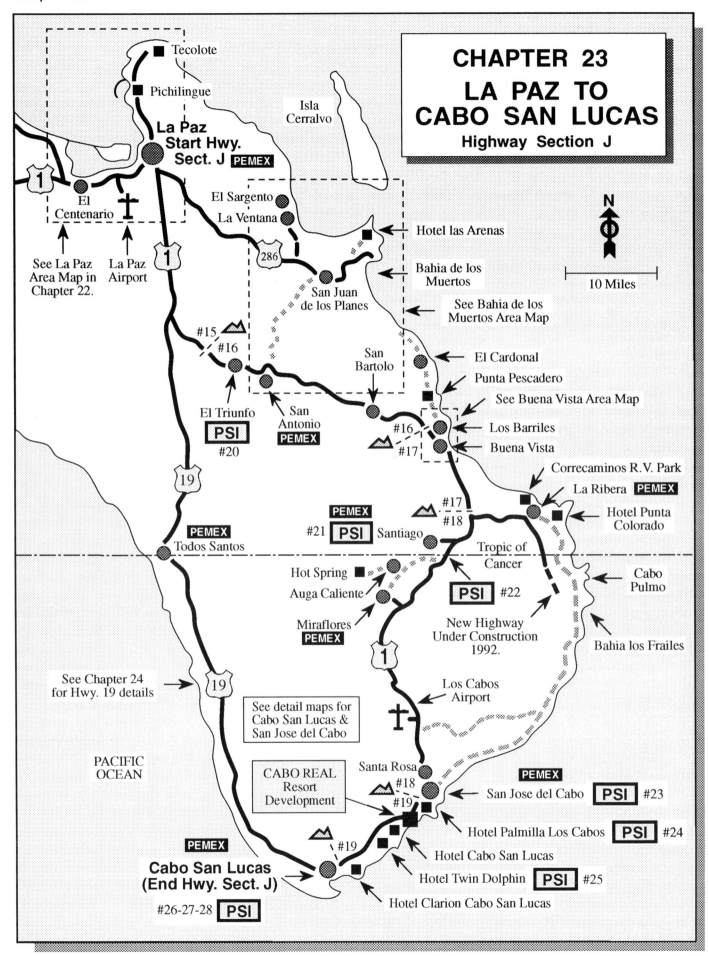

**CHAPTER 23
LA PAZ TO
CABO SAN LUCAS**
Highway Section J

Tecolote

Pichilingue

Isla
Cerralvo

**La Paz
Start Hwy.
Sect. J** PEMEX

El Sargento

La Ventana

El
Centenario

✝

See La Paz
Area Map in
Chapter 22.

La Paz
Airport

1

286

Hotel las Arenas

Bahia de los
Muertos

San Juan
de los Planes

See Bahia de los
Muertos Area Map

N

10 Miles

#15

#16

San
Bartolo

El Cardonal

Punta Pescadero

See Buena Vista Area Map

El Triunfo

PSI

#20

San
Antonio

PEMEX

#16

#17

Los Barriles

Buena Vista

Correcaminos R.V. Park

La Ribera PEMEX

19

PEMEX

Todos Santos

PEMEX

#21 **PSI** Santiago

#17

#18

Hotel Punta
Colorado

Tropic of
Cancer

PSI #22

Cabo
Pulmo

Hot Spring

Auga Caliente

Miraflores

PEMEX

New Highway
Under Construction
1992.

Bahia los Frailes

1

Los Cabos
Airport

✝

See Chapter 24
for Hwy. 19 details

19

PACIFIC
OCEAN

See detail maps for
Cabo San Lucas &
San Jose del Cabo

CABO REAL
Resort
Development

Santa Rosa

#18

#19

PEMEX

San Jose del Cabo **PSI** #23

Hotel Palmilla Los Cabos **PSI** #24

Hotel Cabo San Lucas

#19

PEMEX

**Cabo San Lucas
(End Hwy. Sect. J)**

Hotel Twin Dolphin **PSI** #25

#26-27-28 **PSI**

Hotel Clarion Cabo San Lucas

its remaining southerly portion has been located in the sandy bed of an arroyo and is of much lower standard. It can be in bad repair following storms.

Km-43 — Highway 286 passes through the center of the town of San Juan de los Planes. This community is the center of an agricultural region. The road from town to Bahia de los Muertos is constructed to the same standard as the balance of Highway 286 but was not paved in 1992.

Km 55 — About 0.1 miles west of **Km 55** a low standard but level road leads left (north) for 3.6 miles to the Hotel las Arenas. This is a first-class resort serving many guests who arrive in small private aircraft. Travelers arriving by road are also welcome. A short distance prior to reaching the hotel another road branches to the left and in 1.2 miles arrives at good camping spots on a sandy beach.

Recreation vehicles line the bluff overlooking Bahia de los Muertos.

Km-58 — Arrival at Bahia de los Muertos. The name means *The Bay of the Dead*, but there could not be a more pleasant spot, with camping along a low bluff overlooking the beach. The beach has reasonable protection from the prevailing northerly winds. End **SIDE TRIP**.

(Km J-185) HIGHWAY 19 JUNCTION — Highway 1 from La Paz to its junction with Highway 19 traverses the eastern edge of the Llano de la Paz. It is straight and level. At this junction you have a choice of two paved highways to Cabo San Lucas: 185 km (115 miles) via Highway 1, or 128 km (80 miles) over the shorter Highway 19. If this is your first trip to the area I recommend that you travel south on one route and return on the other. If you simply wish to proceed to Cabo San Lucas in the easiest manner, take Highway 19. It is shorter, does not require climbing over the Sierra de la Laguna, and there are fine views of the Pacific Ocean. See Chapter 24 for details.

A great majority of larger R.V.'s and commercial trucks now travel to the Cape area over Highway 19. This has removed almost all of the slow-moving traffic that once was a problem on Highway 1. The latter route is now far more enjoyable for recreation travel than it was in the past.

#15 #16

(Km J-170) GEOGRAPHIC CHANGE — SE from the Highway 19 junction, the Llano de la Paz (Geographic Section No. 15) begins rising to meet the mountains. At **Km J-170** the plains come to an end and the highway enters the Sierra de la Laguna (Geographic Section No. 16). You will be traveling in the mountains until arriving at the coast at Los Barriles; however, most of the curves and steeper grades are encountered during the first 17 km (10 miles).

DECOMPOSED GRANITE — The Sierra de la Laguna is composed of granitic rocks. If you will remember the discussion about the Catavina boulder fields in Chapter 19, you will recall

that granite rock breaks down into a very granular soil referred to as D.G. (decomposed granite). D.G. erodes readily. To complicate matters, the Cape Region receives much of its rainfall from intense storms related to tropical cyclones. The area's roads can suffer heavy damage during such storms. I have always found Highway 1 to be in good repair, but you may encounter washouts and detours when using lower standard roads. Be particularly cautious during and following heavy rains.

CAPE REGION VEGETATION — It is upon entering the Sierra de la Laguna that the characteristics of the Cape Region's Arid Tropical Forest vegetation become readily apparent. In the mountains between **Km J-170** and **Km J-50** several species of low trees become dominant, although many desert species are still present. The white-barked palo blanco is very abundant. This plant community has been described as an *impoverished tropical jungle*. South of **Km J-50** the trees are replaced by a variety of low shrubs, but the overall amount of vegetation remains far more dense than in the Sonoran Desert to the north.

PSI #20

(Km J-164) EL TRIUNFO — The mining community of El Triunfo (The Triumph) and its neighboring town of San Antonio lie in one of Baja's most historic areas. El Triunfo was the site of a cattle ranch in the early Jesuit period, and in 1748 silver was discovered in the mountains south of San Antonio. Many years later, in 1862, silver and gold were also located at El Triunfo. Believe it or not, the sleepy little town that you see today soon was to have a population of 10,000, making it the largest community in the southern peninsula.

El Triunfo is stop No. 20 on the POINTS OF SPECIAL INTEREST Tour. Even large R.V.'s can pull off the highway near the church. Take a short walk to the ruins of the old smelter. The smoke stacks are clearly in view from the highway. A few hundred feet SE of the larger stack lies a brick-walled enclosure

The mining ruins at the town of El Triunfo.

containing thirteen above-ground crypts. These reportedly contain the remains of American miners.

Be careful as you wander about, because present-day miners are using arsenic to reprocess the old mine tailings, as they seek what little metal remains. These areas are fenced and signed.

(Km J-159) SCENIC VIEW — Between **Km J-159** and **Km J-158** one may look out over the mountains to the plains around San Juan de los Planes. The Sea of Cortez and huge Isla Cerralvo are also in view on clear days. The island is separated from the mainland by a narrow channel. The Arid Tropical Forest vegetation is well developed in this area.

(Km J-156) SAN ANTONIO — San Antonio is a pleasant little town lying along the bottom of a sizeable arroyo. The town square and church lie 0.3 miles upstream to the south. There is a PEMEX station on the highway which I have found closed on some of my visits.

In 1748, silver mining started 5 miles south of here in the mountains at a place called Santa Ana. Look south into the rugged terrain and recall that Santa Ana was the site of one of the most important meetings in the history of the American West. In 1768, Jose de Galvez, personal representative of the King of Spain, made Santa Ana his headquarters. From here he sent for Junipero Serra, the newly arrived head of the Franciscan missionaries, and at this most unlikely of places they drew up the plans for the expeditions that resulted one year later in the founding of the missions in Alta California.

In 1828, Baja California's capital at Loreto was destroyed by flooding. Two years later the seat of power was moved to La Paz. During the brief interim, San Antonio served as the capital city.

(Km J-128) SAN BARTOLO — The town of San Bartolo lies along the highway above the banks of a deep canyon. The area contains numerous palms and a variety of large hardwood trees, a sight that is not often seen in Baja. Note the many light-colored granite rocks in view along the highway and contrast them with the darker basalt found to the north in the Sierra Giganta. Produce stands along the highway are a good place to stock up on fresh fruits and vegetables.

#16 ▲ #17
(Km J-112) GEOGRAPHIC CHANGE — Highway 1 arrives at the eastern edge of the Sierra de la Laguna (Geographic Section No. 16) and begins a short journey south along relatively level coastal flats (Geographic Section No. 17). The Sea of Cortez is in full view.

SIDE TRIP
(Km J-111) ROAD TO EL CARDONAL — A dirt road turns left (north) up the coast at this point. Immediately north of the town of los Barriles the road passes over the mouth of a broad alluvial plain. Campers can work their way to the beach at various places along here. The last 1.5 miles prior to the Hotel Punta Pescadero is steep and narrow and unsuited for larger R.V.'s

9.3 Miles — Arrival at the very pleasant Hotel Punta Pescadero, adjoining recreation homes, and a paved airstrip. The resort's fishing fleet is moored in a shallow bight to the south.

13.5 Miles — The small village of El Cardonal is located at this point. There are several places between here and the hotel from which to work your way from the road to the edge of the bluff overlooking the water. From El Cardonal, the campers on the beach at Bahia de los Muertos to the north are clearly in view. A road continues north from here to San Juan de los Planes but those who have used it report that portions are suitable only for the most rugged of 4x4 vehicles. End **SIDE TRIP**.

(Km J-110) LOS BARRILES — A good standard dirt road bears left (east) 0.2 miles north of **Km-J-110,** and Highway 1 swings to the south down the coast. Taking the former road brings you in a short distance to the hotels and R.V. parks in los Barriles. (See the LOS BARRILES - BUENA VISTA AREA Map.) If you proceed to the R.V. parks your route will have been joined by the road described in the item above, and you are headed for El Cardonal.

(Km J-108) BUENA VISTA — The community of Buena Vista lies along the shores of the Sea of Cortez and blends together with adjacent Los Barriles.

After passing an airstrip below the highway, a road turns to the left near **Km J-106** to the Rancho Buena Vista. This is a very pleasant resort hotel. A few yards south of the turnoff to the Rancho Buena Vista, a secondary road leads 0.5 miles to the right (west) up the hill to the Flag Monument. From there you can enjoy a good view of the coast in both directions.

A road leaves the highway to the left 0.2 miles near of **Km J-105** for the Hotel Spa Buena Vista and a subdivision development. From here south, Highway 1 starts to turn inland. At **Km J-104** another dirt road signed for the Rancho Leonero bears to the left (east) and in 1.5 miles reaches the Capilla R. V. Park on the beach. It is 4.6 miles on this same road to the Rancho Leonero hotel.

#17 ⛰ #18

(Km J-93) GEOGRAPHIC CHANGE — At this point Highway 1 leaves the flat coastal area (Geographic Section No. 17) and starts a 60 km (37 mile) journey over low hills and plateaus (Geographic Section No.18) between two ranges of mountains. To the right is that section of the Sierra de la Laguna that was the location of revolutionary battles from 1913 to 1915.

(Km J-93) EAST CAPE LOOP — An oiled highway leaves Highway 1 to the left (east) for the small coastal village of La Ribera, which is reached in 7.7 miles. This town is the northern terminus of a 100 km (62 mile) secondary, dirt road along the coast leading to San Jose Del Cabo. During spring 1992 the oiled highway from La Ribera was being extended southward with the obvious objective of also reaching San Jose del Cabo. Due to the length and diversity of these two paralleling routes (collectively referred to as the East Cape Loop, they are described in a separate subsection at the end of this chapter.

PSI #21

SIDE TRIP

(Km J-85) SANTIAGO — A blacktop road joins Highway 1 on the right (west) and leads to the historic town of Santiago, a pleasant village supported by small farms and ranching. It is stop No. 21 on the POINTS OF SPECIAL INTEREST Tour. Here the Jesuits founded their tenth mission in 1724. While the mission was maintained until 1795 (71 years), no traces of it remain.

Santiago was one of the sites of the 1734 Pericue Indian revolt described in Chapter 12 HISTORY. The missionary padre, two soldiers, and an Indian were killed here, and the uprising caused temporary abandonment of all the missions in the Cape Region and La Paz.

The town square and PEMEX station are 1.6 miles west of the highway. Proceed through the square, bear left, and take the main, tree-lined street to visit the charming Hotel Palomar, a museum, and the only zoological garden in Baja California. (See description in Chapter 11 WILDLIFE.) End **SIDE TRIP**.

BOB & JEAN 4X4

AGUA CALIENTE — Continuing westerly past the zoological garden in Santiago is an 11-mile-long road to the town of Miraflores noted below. Near the midpoint between Santiago and Miraflores is the village of Agua Caliente. Take a dirt road west from Agua Caliente to its end (about 2.5 miles) where you will be rewarded by a scenic camping spot in a canyon beside a large pool of water. A nearby hot spring fills a cement tub for your soaking enjoyment. There are other roads in this general area accessing the base of the Sierra de la Laguna. This area is trip #12 of the "Bob and Jean 4x4" Recommendations presented in Chapter 3.

PSI #22

(Km J-82) TROPIC OF CANCER — There is nothing fancy about the concrete sphere located by the road on the right, but most people from Canada and the United States never have the opportunity to stand exactly on the Tropic of Cancer (23 degrees 28 minutes north of the equator). This is stop No. 22 on the POINTS OF SPECIAL INTEREST Tour. I suggest you pause and stretch. You are now entering the world's tropical zone.

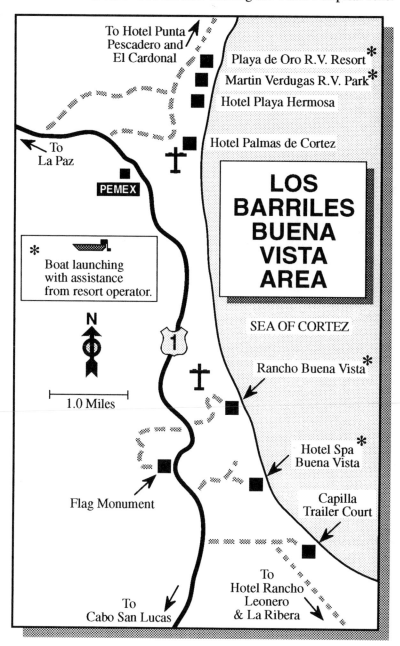

To Hotel Punta Pescadero and El Cardonal

Playa de Oro R.V. Resort *
Martin Verdugas R.V. Park *
Hotel Playa Hermosa
Hotel Palmas de Cortez

To La Paz

PEMEX

* Boat launching with assistance from resort operator.

N

1.0 Miles

LOS BARRILES BUENA VISTA AREA

SEA OF CORTEZ

Rancho Buena Vista *

Hotel Spa Buena Vista *

Capilla Trailer Court

Flag Monument

To Cabo San Lucas

To Hotel Rancho Leonero & La Ribera

The Los Barriles-Buena Vista area on the East Cape.

The section of highway between the Los Cabos Airport and San Jose del Cabo was in the final stages of being expanded to a 4-lane divided highway in spring 1992. By the time you read this you should be privileged to drive on the completed project. In that it is planned to extend this 4-lane standard all the way to Cabo San Lucas, you may also have the privilege of enduring additional construction farther along. Isn't progress wonderful?

#18 ⛰ #19 [PSI] #23

(Km J-33) SAN JOSE DEL CABO — San Jose del Cabo is a town of 10,000 people and the last geographic breakpoint. If you are in haste to reach the coast and Cabo San Lucas, stay straight ahead on the divided highway which passes west of the center of town. However, I suggest you turn left at the PEMEX station and take the three-sided loop through town. (See the SAN JOSE DEL CABO Map). San Jose del Cabo is stop No. 23 on the POINTS OF SPECIAL INTEREST Tour. This hard-surface loop will bring you back to Highway 1, near the coast, with no problems.

The town's history is one of the richest in the peninsula and includes the activities of the early Jesuit mission, visitations by numerous ships and famous captains, and an intensive battle in the Mexican-American War. The statue in the civic plaza is that of Naval Lieutenant Jose Antonio Mijares, who died here in 1847 while defending the town from takeover by the United States. Visit the church on the west side of the plaza. It was built in 1940 on the final site of the mission originally founded in 1730. A tile mosaic over its entrance depicts the slaying of the mission priest during the Indian uprising in 1734.

The town's major hotels are located along an outstanding beach south of town. The Hotel Stouffer Presidente is at the western edge of the coastal lagoon lying at the mouth

The sun moves in its yearly course between the Tropic of Cancer and the Tropic of Capricorn in the southern hemisphere.

(KM J-71) MIRAFLORES — A PEMEX station is located here at the junction of Highway 1 with a blacktop road that leads in 1.4 miles to the small town of Miraflores.

(Km J-44) LOS CABOS AIRPORT — The southernmost of Baja's international airports is reached in 0.8 miles over a blacktop road leading right (west). This is the entry point for tourists bound for Cabo San Lucas, San Jose del Cabo, and the Buena Vista area. There is a modern terminal, parking, and ample ground transportation. As of spring 1992 the airport had been expanded so as to accommodate jumbo jets. The Cape Area as entered the Big-Time.

The roadside monument at the Tropic of Cancer between Buena Vista and San Jose del Cabo.

of the Rio San Jose. There can be no more historic spot on the Magnificent Peninsula. The original 1730 mission was located between here and the cemetery, and the fresh water entering the lagoon was of critical importance to the crews of ships plying Pacific waters.

To the west of the Stouffer Presidente are three additional hotels. Inland from these is a golf course and residential and condominium area. All of this is a part of FONATUR's San Jose del Cabo development. A major marina project is planned for the estuary between San Jose del Cabo and the small community of La Playa. (Hold not your breath.)

I should note that the major new, privately-owned Cabo Real hotel and resort complex being developed ahead at **Km J-19** on Highway 1, appears to be having a dampening affect on FONATUR's San Jose del Cabo project. There have been no new hotels constructed here in over three years and some of the existing ones are suffering from lack of maintenance. The activity level here is in marked contrast to the feverish pace in evidence along the Cabo Corridor and at Cabo San Lucas.

On the beach SW of town, near **Km J-30,** is the Brisa del Mar, one of Baja's most popular R.V. parks. There are approximately 100 sites complemented by a bar, restaurant, pool, and a ten-room motel.

The next stop on the POINTS OF SPECIAL INTEREST Tour is the Hotel Palmilla Los Cabos. Its buildings may be seen near the end of the point of land projecting to sea several miles to the south. This promontory provides the only protection from Pacific Ocean swells in the San Jose del Cabo area.

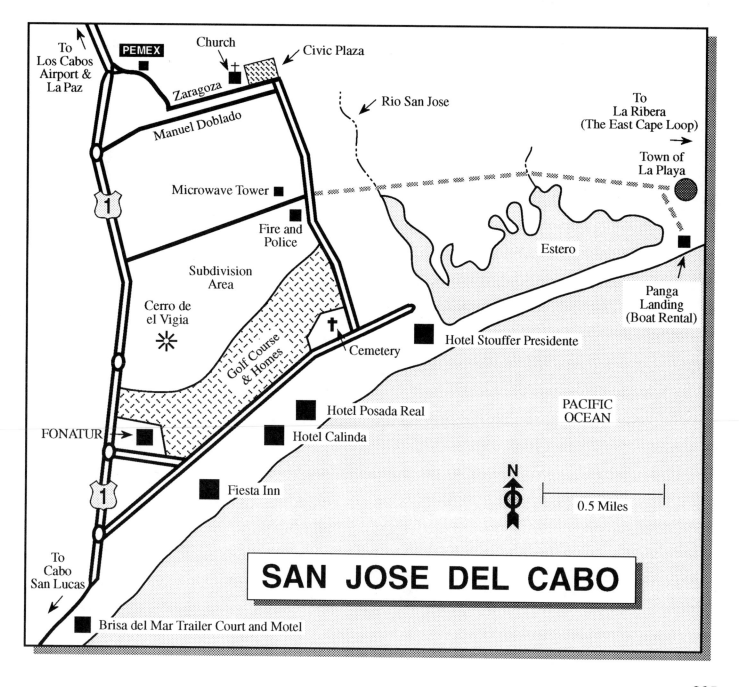

SAN JOSE DEL CABO

The church at the civic plaza at San Jose del Cabo. Take a close look at the mosaic over the entrance which depicts the 1734 Indian uprising.

Between here and Cabo San Lucas you will notice many residential developments which are not described. The road's right-of-way is fenced in most places, so there is limited access to the waterfront. There are now no areas where the parking of R.V.s or camping is possible along what is the finest stretch of coast in all Baja. On the positive side you will see some twenty-two "Accesso Playa" signs between San Jose del Cabo and Cabo San Lucas. A road leads from each of these and provides public access to the beach.

THE CABO CORRIDOR — The section of highway between San Jose del Cabo and Cabo San Lucas is referred to as "The Cabo Corridor", or simply "The Corridor". Within as recently as ten years ago there was very little development in this area. It is now only a matter of a few more years until it will be solid buildings of some variety. Construction of a new 4-lane highway paralleling the existing road will start soon, along with an additional fresh-water pipeline. Enjoy.

PSI #24

(Km J-25) HOTEL PALMILLA — Each time I visit the Magnificent Peninsula I am impressed that a different hotel seems to be the finest in all Baja, but the Pamilla Los Cabos is always in the competition. I include it as stop No. 24 on the POINTS OF SPECIAL INTEREST Tour. The drive in from the highway is about one-half mile. There is a small parking lot but the road is narrow and unsuited for large R.V.'s. This hotel has been here for many years and thus has excellent landscaping.

(Km J-19 CABO REAL — Here at Km J-19 is being constructed Cabo Real, the largest tourist development ever undertaken in Baja. It lies between Highway 1 and the ocean shore and is all on private land, in contrast to the government owned

The Cape Area coastline. The Hotel Pamilla Los Cabos lies on the prominent point of land at the left edge of the photo.

The Cabo San Lucas Area. The famous Cape itself is at the right side of the photo.

land at San Jose del Cabo and Cabo San Lucas. Everything is being done on a grand scale.

In spring 1992, the Hotel Melia and a nearby golf course were completed. Several other hotels and condominium developments were under construction. In future editions of this book I will no doubt have to include separate maps of the Cabo Corridor and Cabo Real. It is hard to keep up with what is occurring.

(Km J-15) HOTEL CABO SAN LUCAS — By now you must be aware that I believe my readers will be charmed, as I am, by Baja's fine hotels. Here is another one which is among the very best. The Hotel Cabo San Lucas was completed in 1962 and is surrounded by excellent landscaping. There is a sizeable parking lot, and the road is suitable for even large R.V.'s.

PSI #25

(Km J-11) HOTEL TWIN DOLPHIN — Here is another very fine hotel which may be easily visited by even the larger R.V.'s. Its landscaping was designed to feature native desert plants. It thus offers a unique atmosphere and has been placed on the POINTS OF SPECIAL INTEREST Tour as stop No. 25. (In recent years they have become a bit reclusive. The entrance sign reads only "Private Property").

(Km J-10) SHIPWRECK BEACH — Midway between **Km J-10** and **Km J-9** a dirt road used to lead left (south) for 0.5 miles to an undeveloped camping area on the slopes above a fine beach. The wreck of a sizeable ship lies stranded on the beach and gives rise to the area's name.

This was the last place in the Cape Area where beach camping and R.V. parking was permitted. It was finally closed in 1991, reportedly at the insistence of the Cabo San Lucas R.V. park owners who wanted the Shipwreck crowd as their paying guests. Pause here to mourn the passing of an era.

(Km J-6) VILLA SERENA R. V. PARK — Here lies Cabo's most recent R.V. park. It will probably prove to be its most popular as it offers fine ocean views and a pool area fit for a fancy hotel. It is a worthy replacement for Shipwreck beach, and no doubt the sanitation will be a considerable improvement.

(Km J-6) HOTEL CLARION CABO SAN LUCAS — A blacktop road leads left for 0.5 mile to the hotel. Most times I have paid it a visit it has a different name, so be prepared for something different. The Cabo Bella subdivision lies just to the west of this road. From the hotel you may look west across the outer harbor at Cabo San Lucas and see the peninsula's rocky tip

PSI #26

(Km J-5) CABO SAN LUCAS VISTA — Midway between **Km J-5** and **Km J-6** there used to be a simple concrete monument on the left side of the road. I designated this as POINTS OF SPECIAL INTEREST Tour stop No. 26 and recommended that you stop here for an excellent view of Cabo San Lucas. Nowadays its worth your life to stop along this busy highway, but you are still permitted to admire the view and congratulate all hands on having arrived within sight of the Magnificent Peninsula's most famous landmark. Let me add my own salute. Congratulations, you have reached *Finisterra* (Land's End). I hope you have not been led too far astray along the way.

(Km J-4 to J-2) TRAILER COURTS — There are four trailer courts with full hookups adjoining the highway in this

227

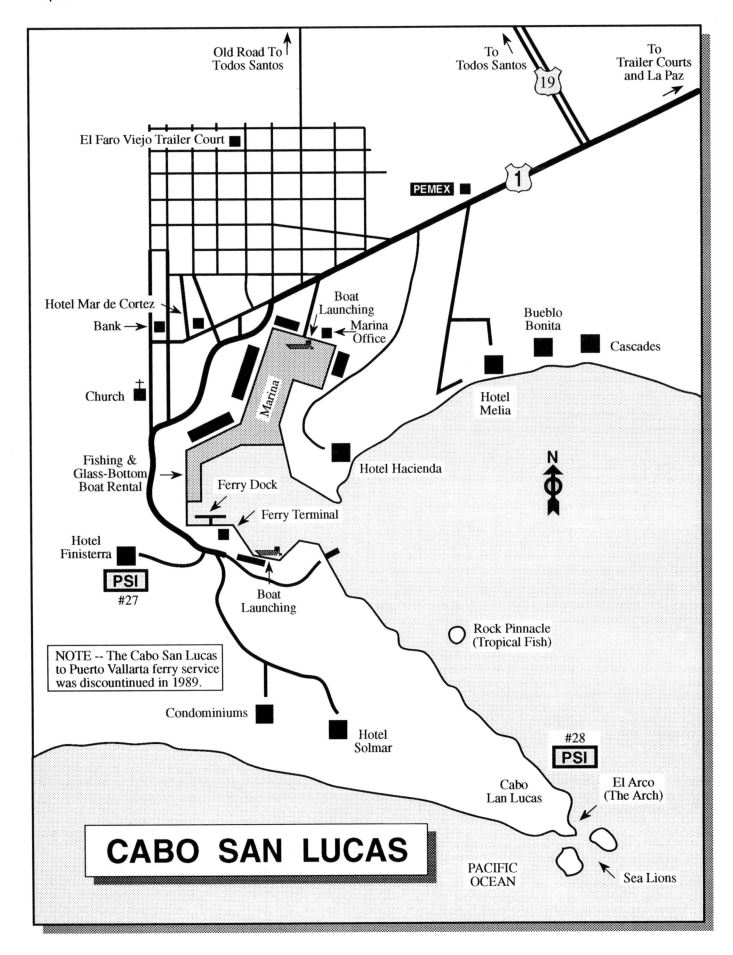

CABO SAN LUCAS

El Faro Viejo Trailer Court

Hotel Mar de Cortez

Bank →

Church

Fishing & Glass-Bottom Boat Rental →

Marina

Boat Launching

Marina Office

Ferry Dock

Ferry Terminal

Hotel Finisterra

PSI #27

NOTE -- The Cabo San Lucas to Puerto Vallarta ferry service was discountinued in 1989.

Boat Launching

Condominiums

Hotel Solmar

Old Road To Todos Santos

To Todos Santos

To Trailer Courts and La Paz

19

PEMEX

1

Bueblo Bonita

Cascades

Hotel Melia

Hotel Hacienda

N

Rock Pinnacle (Tropical Fish)

#28 **PSI**

Cabo Lan Lucas

El Arco (The Arch)

Sea Lions

PACIFIC OCEAN

The Bahia los Frailes Area along the East Cape Loop. Cabo los Frailes is the point of land in the top-right portion of the photo.

area. These are the El Arco above (north) of the highway and the Cabo Cielo, San Vicente, and Vagabundos del Mar below on the south side. A fifth court, the El Faro Viejo, is situated in the center of town.

(Km J-2) ENTERING CABO SAN LUCAS — Upon entering Cabo San Lucas note the junction with Highway 19 on the right (north). This highway skirts the community on its eastern edge. An easily accessible PEMEX station adjoins Highway 1 on the right.

(Km J-0) CABO SAN LUCAS — The zero kilometer post for the Transpeninsular Highway lies across from the town square. Let us hope that some of our gringo friends don't steal it. The latest town entrance sign claims 14,000 people, and the town is experiencing an enormous expansion of hotels, condominiums, and tourist oriented shops. In spring 1989 I described the place as hectic and bathed in construction activities. By 1992 it had settled down a little, but it will never again be the simple fishing village it once was.

There are many places of interest to the tourist in the Cabo San Lucas area. Here are some of the more important ones:

THE INNER HARBOR — It took over a decade to convert the waterfront area of Cabo San Lucas into a dredged, concrete-walled inner harbor. And now it has finally secured a first-class marina filled with the world's fanciest yachts. (Note - The aerial photo on page 227 was taken prior to development of this marina.) At the harbor's southern end are open-air gift shops. The harbor area will eventually be lined with hotels and condominiums. This was about 2/3 completed in 1992.

PSI #27

HOTEL FINISTERRA — Perched high on the cliffs south of the inner harbor is the Hotel Finisterra. It is stop No. 27 on the

POINTS OF SPECIAL INTEREST Tour. The hotel offers intriguing rock-masonry architecture, and from its entrance way the entire Cabo San Lucas community and harbor area are in view. Be sure to visit the Whale Watcher's Bar where the vista changes to the south and provides a commanding panorama of the Pacific Ocean The men's restroom is also one-of-a-kind.

HOTEL SOLMAR — If you love the beach, the Hotel Solmar is the place. It is in view from the Whale Watcher's Bar at the Finisterra, and its access road starts opposite the ferry terminal.

HACIENDA HOTEL — Yet another of Baja's very finest hotels adjoins the beach fronting the outer harbor. Its access road circles the inner harbor on its eastern side. If you like to swim in the ocean, this is the best place, as the beach here is protected from the main force of the Pacific swells.

HOTEL MELIA — Cabo's newest hotel all done in a "grand style." It lies immediately northeast of the Hotel Hacienda. Again the beach is readily used for swimming.

MAR DE CORTEZ HOTEL — A more modest, smaller, but very charming hotel lying in the business area of the community.

PSI #28

OUTER HARBOR TOUR — You have arrived at the town of Cabo San Lucas and have gazed seaward at the jagged finger of rock that forms the cape itself, but you haven't actually been there. The next challenge of the POINTS OF SPECIAL INTEREST Tour (stop No. 28) is to visit the natural arch and spires of rock at Land's End. (Stops No. 29 and 30 are along Highway 19 described in Chapter 24.)

There is also a pinnacle of rock in the bay near the cliffs some 0.3 miles south from the inner harbor entrance. Most of this formation lies underwater and attracts thousands of colorful tropical fish that are easily viewed with snorkeling equipment or from a glass-bottom boat. Small boats are for hire in the harbor or along the beach so you may accept this final challenge. Rent one with a glass bottom to see the fish.

EAST CAPE LOOP

SIDE TRIP

This subsection of Chapter 23 describes the road that closely follows the SE coast of the cape from Highway 1 south to San Jose del Cabo. The loop as described below is an oiled highway from Highway 1 to the town of Ribera, and a secondary, often badly washboarded, dirt road from there to San Jose del Cabo.

However, in spring 1992, a new highway was being rapidly pushed south from La Ribera, inland, and roughly paralleling, the secondary road. Seven-miles of hard-surface had been completed with many additional miles almost ready for oiling. The new highway will no doubt connect with the secondary road at various places. If you are headed south I recommend you take the new highway and use your best judgement on accessing the various coastal points. Stay tuned.

The old secondary road East Cape Loop is built through an area of decomposed granite; thus it is subject to erosion damage in the event of storms. On my most recent trip there was clear evidence that the eroded spots were being currently repaired. There are no steep grades, and barring storm damage there is nothing to stop larger R.V.'s from making the complete trip. However, its overall length and the roughness of the road surface will make it uninviting for most such vehicles.

Taking relatively short excursions into the camping spots which are concentrated at either end of the loop present alternatives to making the entire trip.

0.0 Miles — The East Cape Loop begins at the Transpeninsular Highway just south of **Km J-93.**

7.0 Miles — Highway junction. The new highway noted above bears right. Stay straight ahead for La Ribera and the balance of the route described below.

7.7 Miles — The oiled portion of the route arrives at the park in the small village of La Ribera. Take the road straight ahead and drive down a slope toward the sea.

7.8 Miles — At the base of the slope is a T intersection with the road to the left (north) leading to Buena Vista. At 0.4 miles along this road on the right is the Correcaminos R.V. Park nestled in a mangrove orchard. It is one of Baja's more pleasant R.V. parks and a short walk from the beach.

Turn right (south) at the T intersection down the coast and at 8.2 miles pass a PEMEX station on the right.

8.9 Miles — Road junction near a grove of tamarisk trees. The main road proceeds straight ahead. Taking a 90-degree turn left

toward the coast offers a slightly longer loop route, but it provides access in 2.6 miles to an excellent camping area along the northern edge of a lagoon bordered with low trees. A sand dune separates the camping area from an excellent sandy beach; and in an additional 1.6 miles one reaches the gate to the very pleasant Hotel Punta Colorado.

25.3 Miles — Arrive at spur road to Cabo Pulmo. There is a large area for R.V. parking at this point. The waters of Bahia Pulmo to the south of Cabo Pulmo support the only live coral reefs in the Sea of Cortez. It is thus a popular diving area.

28.3 Miles — A 0.9 miles spur leads to a ranch and camping area at the south end of Bahia Pulmo. This is the windy side of Cabo Frailes during the winter season.

30.4 Miles — A short spur road leads to the fine sandy beach at Bahia los Frailes. This is a good camping site, and the rocky point of land to the north provides some protection from northerly winds.

En route to Bahia los Frailes you will have passed a number of recreation home developments. Another is occurring at Bahia los Frailes. The sign reads Hotel los Frailes. In about 1987 it is reported that the friendly gringo owners burned out the Mexican fish camp and attempted to fence off the beach. Authorities were summoned from La Paz and the seaside land was affirmed as public property. As of 1992 the fish camp and tourist camping were still flurishing. However, the fence remains and the battle will no doubt be renewed. Stay tuned.

South of Bahia los Frailes the road narrows but has numerous sizeable cuts and fills. It is these fill sections that provide the East Cape Loop Road with its weak links because they are narrowed by erosion after storms. Proceed with caution.

44.8 Miles — A side road road leaves the East Cape Loop here and joins Highway 1 near the Los Cabos Airport in 23 miles. From here to the lighthouse at San Jose del Cabo I have observed over thirty places to camp near the water's edge, every one of them with one or more groups of people. Most of these are relatively small areas located by the sea below where an arroyo crosses the road. Some are on fine sand beaches, others on the bluffs overlooking the water. Access to these sites is most often over low standard "trails" where one can become mired down in the sand. Freedom has its price.

62.0 Miles — The East Cape Loop formally ends here, only a few feet from the lighthouse on the hill south of San Jose del Cabo. The road forks at this point, but either branch takes you through the small community of La Playa that lies on the east bank of the Rio San Jose. It is 2.0 miles from here, across the riverbed, to the boulevard south of the civic plaza at San Jose del Cabo. The junction is near the fire station and a tall microwave tower. If you plan to drive from San Jose del Cabo north on the East Cape Loop and have some difficulty getting started, look for the lighthouse and work your way to it as your point of departure. End **SIDE TRIP**.

CHAPTER 24
HIGHWAY 19

The northern junction of Highway 1 and Highway 19 is at **KM J-185** on Highway 1. There has long been a road between this point and Cabo San Lucas via Todos Santos and the Pacific coast, but completion of a modern highway took many years. In spring of 1984, the highway was opened to traffic for its full length. Highway 19 is easily traveled by all classes of vehicles and is the shortest and easiest route from La Paz to the tip of the peninsula.

Highway 19 will be described from north to south. Kilometer post numbers proceed in the same direction with 0 at the Highway 1 junction.

Taking Highway 19 offers the following advantages over traveling to Cabo San Lucas via Highway 1: (A) The 80-mile trip to Cabo San Lucas over Highway 19 is 35 miles shorter. (B) There are no steep mountainous sections such as the Sierra de la Laguna crossing on Highway 1. (C) There are many miles of highway offering fine views of the Pacific Ocean. Water views along Highway 1 are limited. (D) As the Sea of Cortez coast becomes overly hot in the summer the Pacific shore provides cooler weather.

(Km-10) CAPE REGION VEGETATION — You have now driven well into the area of Cape Region Vegetation, as shown on the map in Chapter 10 VEGETATION. It can be clearly seen that plant growth is far more dense than that encountered in the Sonoran Desert Region. The cardon cactus and many other desert species are still present, but note the dominance now of woody shrubs and small trees. Many of the trees are members of the pea family. They all have very small compound leaves and are armed with numerous spines.

(Km-31) GEOGRAPHIC CHANGE — The northerly 19 miles of Highway 19 crosses the flat southern end of the Llano de la Paz which can be seen stretching endlessly to the NW. In sharp contrast, the lofty peaks of the Sierra de la Laguna rise a short distance to the SW. At **Km-31** the highway begins to enter the low hills at the base of these mountains.

(Km-42) PRESA DE SANTA INEZ — At this point a secondary road leaves to the left (east) and in 3.6 miles arrives at the Presa de Santa Inez (Santa

Inez Dam). This large concrete dam was completed in 1983 to provide a more dependable water supply and flood control for the town of Todos Santos.

PSI **#29**

(Km-51) TODOS SANTOS — Enter Todos Santos, one of Baja's most entrancing towns. Note the trees and agricultural crops in the flat river valley to the right (west).

Park along the main street near the Hotel California and enjoy the town on foot. Todos Santos is stop No. 29 on the POINTS OF SPECIAL INTEREST Tour. It and Stop No. 30 are the only points not on Highway 1 but they have been included on the assumption that most travelers will use both Highways 1 and 19 in their visits to the Cape Region.

Todos Santos was established as a visiting station for the mission at La Paz in 1724. It became a separate mission in 1734 but was then destroyed in the Indian rebellion that started that same year. The site of this original mission is up the arroyo from the town but no ruins remain.

I suggest your visit include the following places:

1. Hotel California. The Hotel California was not built with the modern tourist in mind. Rather, it looks like what a hotel in an isolated western Mexican town should look like: thick walls,

The church and adjoining civic plaza at Todos Santos.

tile floors, and a balcony rounding its second story. Ownership changed about 1987 and a well landscaped swimming pool was added to provide a touch of moderism to its charms.

2. The village church, civic plaza, and municipal buildings overlook the flat fertile valley of the arroyo. In the 1950s, the valley was reported to be planted almost entirely with sugar cane. Today, the cane is gone and has been replaced with a variety of other crops. It is a welcome change to look out over abundant greenery after driving through many miles of desert.

3. Overlooking the valley are the ruins of one of the town's sugar mills fringed with a few remnants of cane.

4. Behind the PEMEX station is a well-landscaped trailer court. It adjoins another of the town's abandoned sugar mills and is appropriately named El Molino (The Mill). Its small restaurant is a popular gathering place for tourists and its speciality is Sunday brunch.

For the first 20 miles south of Todos Santos, Highway 19 will pass over gently sloping coastal benches, some of which have been cleared for agriculture.

(Km-54) PUNTA LOBOS — The Pacific Coast undergoes a significant geographic change at Todos Santos. North of the village, for over 100 miles, the shoreline is essentially one, long,

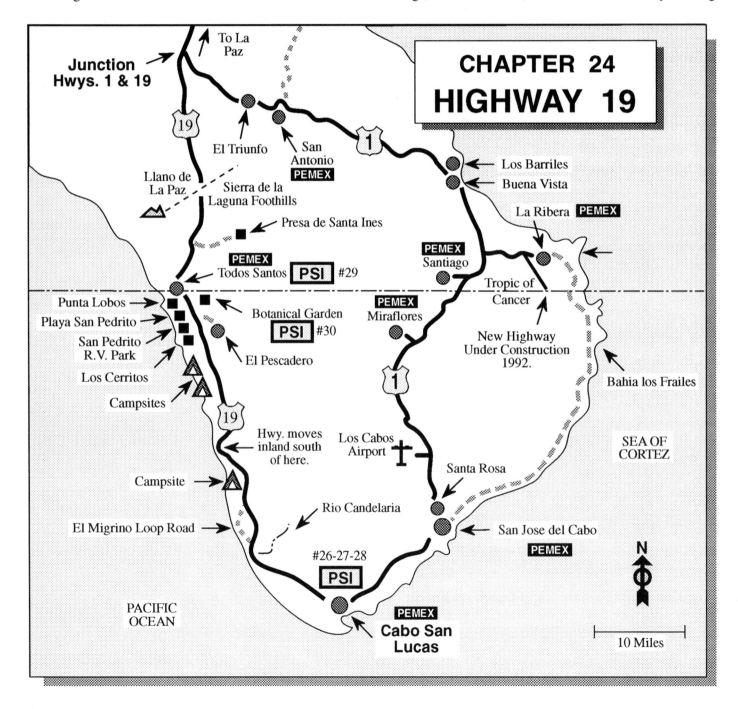

This is an excellent place to test whether you have properly identified the plants you have seen along the peninsula's highways. The garden is the final stop on the POINTS OF SPECIAL INTEREST TOUR. I hope you have visited many of the areas it highlights and that they have added to your enjoyment of the Magnificent Peninsula.

(KM-59) SAN PEDRITO R.V. PARK — A secondary road leaves the highway to the west 0.2 miles north of **Km-59** and in 1.9 miles arrives at the San Pedrito R.V. Park. This was the first tourist facility built along Highway 19 since it was completed. There is a restaurant, bar, swimming pool, a large number of full hookup units, and an excellent sandy beach. Tent campers are accommodated along the beach immediately south of the R.V. area. The R.V. parking area is a bit sterile but it will improve when the recently planted palm trees increase in size. The park's name is a bit confusing, as it is not at Playa San Pedrito, but it is devine to forgive.

(Km-60) RANCHO NUEVA VILLA — Many of the level lands between the mountains and sea in this area have been cleared for produce farming. About 100 yards prior to **Km-60** is a packing facility and retail sales stand selling organically grown vegatables. Several ladies have chastised me for not noting it in the first two editions of this book. I have a great

sandy beach backed by nearly level plains. To the south, the Sierra de la Laguna heavily influences the topography. Here the coast is frequently rocky and steep with mountains towering in the background. It is an attractive region through which to drive.

From Todos Santos, the northernmost of these rocky promontories is in view. This is Punta Lobos. (*Lobo* means wolf in Spanish but refers to sea lions when used in coastal place names.) Here, 200 yards north of **Km-54**, a dirt road to the right (west) leaves Highway 19, and in 1.0 miles arrives at a sandy beach. The local fishermen launch their boats over the beach immediately north of the point. The best campsites are at the end of a spur road near an abandoned building a few hundred yards to the north.

(Km-57) PLAYA SAN PEDRITO — Near **Km-57** a dirt road to the right (west) leads in 1.6 miles to a fine sandy beach, Playa San Pedrito. The junction point is directly opposite the botanical garden described below. The beach is backed by a large grove of native Washingtonia fan palms mixed with the introduced coconut palm. The combination of sea, sand, and palms makes this one of Baja's most pleasant camping spots. It is my personal favorite of all those in Baja. It is almost certain to fall prey to the hotel builders. The area is best suited for smaller vehicles.

PSI #30

(Km-57) BOTANICAL GARDEN — Opposite the road to Playa San Pedrito is the Campo Experimental Todos Santos. Here has been developed a fine array of desert plants from all regions of Baja. Many are marked with signs. This botanical garden adjoins the highway and is open to the public at no cost.

Ruins of one of the sugar cane mills at Todos Santos.

The palm-lined beach and cove at El Pedrito.

excuse. It wasn't there when they were published. But I have gotten the message. Be sure to stop and hope that the strawberries are in season.

(Km-61) EL PESCADERO — Between **Km-61** and **Km-62** a side road leads to the left (east) to the village of El Pescadero (the fish dealer). There are many palms and other trees in and around the community. It is a pleasant town but without tourist facilities other than a grocery store.

(Km-64) LOS CERRITOS — A 2-lane secondary road leads to the right (west) directly at **Km-64** and arrives at a fork in the road in 1.4 miles. The left turn brings one to another of the original government trailer courts. This one is now open and being improved. A short trip on the road to the right terminates at another excellent camping area near a fine sandy beach. A short point of land provides reasonable protection from both wind and swells. There are fine views of the coastline to the south.

(Km-82) GEOGRAPHIC CHANGE — Between here and Todos Santos, Highway 19 has remained within a short distance of the ocean and passed over mostly level coastal benches. At this point 0.2 miles north of Km-82, the highway gains elevation and moves inland over rolling plateau lands. Here is being developed the first of the subdivision tracts that are bound to blight the Highway 19 area in the future. Such is progress.

(Km-86) CAMP SITE — Here, 100 yards north of Km-86, Highway 19 crosses a dirt road at right angles. The road to the right (west) leads in 0.5 miles to a camping spot on a low headland with excellent views of the coastline in both directions.

(Km-94) EL MIGRINO LOOP NORTH END — Leading to the right (west) at a point 150 yards north of Km-94 is the northern end of a section of the old coastal road. It loops toward the Pacific and rejoins the Highway 1.7 miles ahead. The loop road is 2.5 miles in length and offers several excellent places to camp on low bluffs overlooking excellent sandy beaches. Near the middle of the loop are several steep dips. Larger R.V.'s should approach these with caution. (To my knowledge this loop area has no name but I call it El Migrino after a ranch bearing this name located near its southern end.)

There are no further coastal camping spots between here and Cabo San Lucas. Thus, this El Migrino area may become a very popular camping location now that beach sites in the Cabo San Lucas area on Highway 1 are all taken over by hotels and various private interests. You might care to look it over for future reference even if you do not plan to stay.

(Km-96) EL MIGRINO LOOP SOUTH END — Here, 0.2 miles south of Km-96 is the southern junction of the El Migrino loop road. The road leaves the highway to the right (west), passes through the Rancho El Migrino, and arrives at a T intersection. Take the right fork for the loop. The left fork leads to the edge of a large lagoon area which also offers camping spots.

(Km-97) RIO CANDELARIA — At this point, Highway 19 makes a long, low-water crossing of the Rio Candelaria. Clearly, this crossing could cause problems during and after storms. One might predict that it eventually will have to be bridged.

RIO CANDELARIA TO CABO SAN LUCAS — Highway 19 climbs inland south of the Rio Candelaria, with the Pacific Ocean occasionally in view in the distance. The vegetation you will encounter from about Km-110 southward is the best example of the Arid Tropical Forest found along Highway 19. In particular, note the cardonals (forests) of cardon cactus and the several species of low-branching trees. Among the largest is the palo blanco. Its light bark makes it easy to identify.

(Km-124) CABO SAN LUCAS — At the northern edge of Cabo, near the bullring, a new section of Highway 19 turns sharply to the left (east) and skirts the edge of the community. See Chapter 23 for details concerning the town's tourist attractions.

VAYA CON DIOS — I always hate books that abruptly come to an end without a parting word. While we have never met, we have been companions along the way, and it seems improper to leave without a brief farewell.

Former Los Angeles area television personality Ben Hunter wrote a book in 1978 about his experiences in Baja California titled *The Baja Feeling*. Thousands of Baja visitors join Ben in getting that feeling the minute they cross south of the border.

I sincerely hope you have shared in that feeling with us and that *The Magnificent Peninsula* has enhanced your journey. My wife Patty and I have worked diligently to bring you what we hope is the best guidebook available for Baja California. This 4th edition alone has taken over 8-months of our combined time.

Our greatest joy in producing it is knowing that we have helped others to better enjoy a brief time in their lives. If our paths should cross, please give us a yell so we can say hello. But for now, vaya con dios.

The Pacific beach at los Cerritos near Todos Santos. A small point of land out of sight to the right provides wind and swell protection.

OFFICIAL BAJA MOUSETRAP

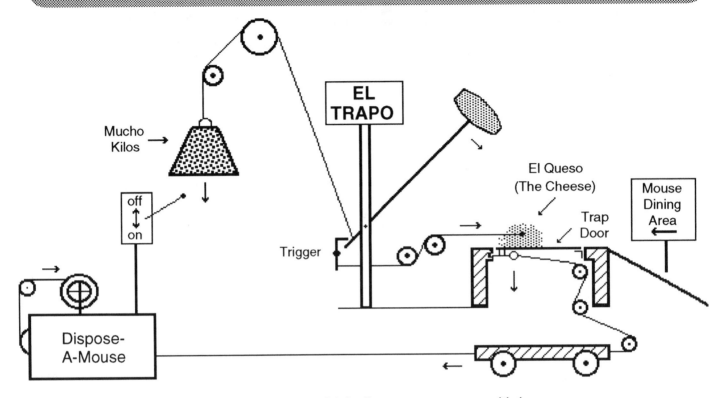

Dining mouse pulls trigger, which dispenses mouse with hammer
and activates trapdoor and Dispose-A-Mouse mechanism. Adios mouse.

It has been reported that if you build a better mousetrap the world will beat a path to your door. Sorry, we just sold the last trap, but we have just a few copies left of Baja's better guidebook. If you need another copy of THE MAGNIFICENT PENINSULA, see the BAJA BOOKSHLEF on page 242.

ABOUT THIS BOOK

People frequently ask various questions about how *The Magnificent Peninsula* was produced.

HOW LONG DID IT TAKE ? — That's a little hard to answer as the field investigations for this book were intermingled with those needed for the *Baja Boater's Guide*. But I estimate that I expended about four years of seven day-a-week work on the two books over a five year period. My wife Patty put in another three years during this same time. About half of this can be charged to *The Magnificent Peninsula*. The revision work for the 3rd and 4th editions each took an additional 8-months of our combined time.

HOW WAS IT PRODUCED ? — The book was produced on a recently acquired Macintosh IIsi computer. It was needed to generate the revised 4th edition maps and graphics. My aging 512K is now our back-up. In its custom-made trunk, it has made the sea voyage in my sailboat from San Francisco, completely around the Baja peninsula and return, and has withstood the washboard shock-treatment in the back of my pickup over thousands of miles of her worst roads.

The text was prepared on Microsoft Word 1.0 and 3.0, the maps and other graphics on Aldus FreeHand, and the type setting on

PageMaker 4.0. The camera ready pages were then printed on a Apple LazerWriter II NT. The basic process involved is generally referred to as Desk-Top-Publishing. All of this work took place in a spare room of our residence in Sausalito, California.

HAVE YOU MADE ANY MONEY ? — During the first two years most of the receipts went into computer equipment, printing, and other expenses, including those ever-present taxes. Since then this book and the *Baja Boater's Guide* have resulted in a nice profit which is providing the frosting on our economic cake.

There is a rather limited market for a book on Baja California, and this market must be shared with the competition. Thus, the secret to profitability has been to do everything possible ourselves, including assuming the role of publisher, and to scrounge most of the rest. Too bad we couldn't come upon up a cost-free printer.

WOULD YOU DO IT OVER AGAIN ? — Absolutely. I was going insane at my office job, and after retiring I would have died of boredom without this project. And if you are willing to work seven-days-a-week instead of five, perhaps you too might decide to write books.

A GLOSSARY

of Spanish words, trade names, and acronyms that
YOU WILL ACTUALLY SEE
while traveling in the Baja peninsula.

To learn Spanish, acquire a language textbook and an English-Spanish dictionary. But use the Glossary and the Road Sign listing to understand much of what you will constantly see on road signs, maps, store fronts, the side of buildings, and other places.

ACRONYMS AND ABBREVIATIONS

C and F —— Letters on water faucets made in Mexico. In the poorer establishments they reportedly stand for Cold and Freezing. In the better hotels, C is for CALIENTE (hot) and F for FRIO (cold). Sometimes Mexican faucets may be mixed with those made in the U.S.A. Thus, C (caliente) and C (cold) can be entertaining.

CONASUPO —— COMPANIA NACIONAL de SUBSISTENCIAS POPULARES. National Company of Popular Subsistences. Government stores selling basic commodities to assure that the public has access to essentials at reasonable prices. Drat, they don't sell beer.

DIF —— DESARROLLO INTEGRAL de la FAMILIA. A government agency concerned with the family. The acronym appears on many public buildings and in parks and playgrounds.

FONATUR —— FONDO NACIONAL de FOMENTO al TURISMO. National Fund for Tourism Development. Federal agency that is developing tourist facilities at Loreto, Bahia Escondido, & San Jose del Cabo.

IMSS —— INSTITUTO MEXICANO de SEGURO SOCIAL. Mexican Social Security Institute. Found on the front of hospitals and clinics.

PAN —— PARTIDO de ACCION NACIONAL. National Action Party. A principal political opposition party to the PRI.

PEMEX —— PETROLEOS MEXICANOS. Mexican Petroleum. The government company that produces all of Mexico's petroleum products and runs the retail gas stations.

PRI —— PARTIDO REVOLUCIONARIO INSTITUCION. Institutional Revolutionary Party. Mexico's dominant political party. Seen painted on buildings, rocks, and other places. It is possible to conclude that he who controls the paint brush controls the political destiny of Mexico.

S.A. —— SOCIEDAD ANONIMA. Literally translated, an anonymous company. It means incorporated. You will see it at the end of many company names. It does not refer to South America

SARH —— SECRETARIA de AGRICULTURA Y RECUSOS HIDRAULICOS. Secretary of Agriculture and Water Resources. The government agency that is developing new farming areas and related water sources.

SCT —— SECRETARIA de COMUNICACIONES y TRANSPORTAES. Secretary of Communications and Transportation. They are in charge of the highway and ferry systems. Look for the symbol on the side of highway maintenance trucks.

SEDUE —— SECRETARIA de DASARROLLO URBANO Y ECOLOGIA. Secretary of Urban and Ecological Development. The agency that adminsters parks, federal beaches, etc.

SRH —— SECRETARIA de RECURSOS HIDRAULICOS. Secretary of Water Resources. Seen on the side of water tanks.

ALCOHOLIC BEVERAGES

CERVEZA —— Beer. Common brands are:

Bavaria	Bohemia
Carta Blanca	Corona
Modelo	Negra Modelo
Pacifico	Superior
Tecate	XX Dos Equies
XXX Tres Equies	

GINEBRA —— Gin. A common brand is Oso Negro which means Black Bear. Look for the bear's picture on the bottle.

LICOR —— Liquor. Most liquor stores bear the name "Vinos y Licor." "Y" is the Spanish word for "and."

RON — Rum. A common beverage made from sugar cane which is grown in the tropical southern portion of mainland Mexico. Cuervo (crow) is the principal brand. Look for the picture of the black crow in many advertisments.

TEQUILA — Tequila.

VODKA — Vodka

VINO — Wine. Blanco (white). Tinto (Red). Rosado (Rose)

GEOGRAPHIC PLACE NAMES

BAHIA — Bay. Remember that the letter "H" is always silent in Spanish.

CABO — Cape. As in Cabo San Lucas.

ESTERO — Estuary. There is little practical difference between estero and laguna, which means lagoon.

ISLA — Island.

PLAYA — Beach.

PUNTA — Point, or projection of land protruding into the sea.

SIERRA — Mountain range. The word also means saw. The words CERRO or MONTE are used to refer to an individual peak or mount.

LICENSE PLATES

FRONT — FRONT is an abbreviation for FRONTERA, the Spanish word for frontier. It, along with state abbreviations, appears on the plates of the two states in the Baja peninsula and other Mexican states bordering the United States, for cars that are not manufactured in Mexico. Thus: FRONT B. C. indicates a foreign-manufactured car registered in the state of Baja California and FRONT B.C.S. a similar car registered in Baja California Sur.

MEX — MEX is an abbreviation for Mexico. It and a state abbreviation appear on the plates of any car manufactured in Mexico. Thus: B.C. MEX, B.C.S. MEX, SON (Sonora) MEX, etc.

CALIFORNIA — Plates from a foreign land to the north, severed from the Mexican Republic in 1848 through the force of arms. It is now being recaptured by the Mexican people through the more socially acceptable processes of nocturnal immigration and the willingness to work for a minimal wage. This latter affliction is readily cured upon obtaining U.S. citizenship or through contact with the civil rights movement.

SCHOOL TERMS

ESCUELA — School. Escuela is a feminine noun. Feminine nouns usually end in "A." Masculine nouns in "O."

JARDIN DE NINOS — Kindergarten. Literally, garden of children. The letter "J" in Spanish is pronounced as the English "H."

PRIMERIA — Primary. The word primeria is an adjective. Spanish adjectives end in A if they modify a feminine noun such as escuela. They end in O with masculine nouns.

SECUNDARIA — Secondary.

TECNICO — Technical.

SHOPS AND STORES

ABARROTES — Groceries or grocery store.

DISTRIBUIDORA — Distributor. Often the word is followed by the name of the products that are sold.

FARMACIA — Pharmacy. Mercifully this Spanish word starts with an "F" rather than the insane "Ph" of English. The names of many types of stores end in such letters as "eria" or "cia." Other common examples are:

LLANTERIA — Tire store or shop.

LUNCHERIA — A lunchroom or small restaurant. A word obviously derived from English.

MUEBLERIA — Furniture store.

PANADERIA — Bakery. PAN is the Spanish word for bread.

TORTILLERIA — Tortilla shop. A place where tortillas are baked and sold at very low prices.

MERCADO — Market.

SUPERMERCADO — Supermarket.

TALLER — Workshop. You can easily draw the conclusion in Baja that all mechanics are big lanky fellows as there are frequent signs reading TALLER MECANICO. They of course mean "mechanic shop" and not "taller mechanic."

TIENDA — Store.

NOTE: Three words in this list contain a "LL" which is a separate letter in Spanish. In Mexico and much of Latin America, the "LL" is pronounced like the "y" in "yes."

OTHER COMMONLY SEEN WORDS

ABIERTO — Open. Signs with this word, or CERRADO (closed) hang in store fronts.

ADUANA — Customs house. Watch for this word at the ports-of-entry and near the ferry docks.

BAJA — Baja is the feminine form of the adjective BAJO meaning "below."

BANCO — Bank. Look also for banking company names starting with BANCO or BAN.

BANO — Bath. Usually the sign reads LOS BANOS and refers to the rest rooms. This is one we all have to know, as we all have to go.

BASURA — Rubbish. Watch for this word on trash barrels and similar places.

CALLE — Street. Watch for signs on the sides of buildings at street corners.

CORREO — Post Office.

CRUZ ROJA — Red Cross. Most commonly seen on ambulances.

CUENTA — Restaurant check. This is the one word in this glossary that you rarely see, but if you can't ask for the check, "LA CUENTA." you may be stuck in Baja for the duration. The waiter normally does not bring the check until you request it. You can make believe you are writing on the palm of your hand with an invisible pencil, but that's tacky.

DINA — Mexico's truck and bus manufacturing company. The name appears on the front of these vehicles.

EJIDO — Common Land. An institution under Mexican law for the common ownership of land. See Chapter 13. The word, or the abbreviation EJ, is commonly seen as part of place names on road signs and maps.

EMPUJE — Push. The word appears on doors you are trying to open by pulling. JALE means "pull."

HOTEL — Hotel. One of several words that are spelled the same in English and Spanish but where the pronunciation is quite different. Remember, "H" is silent in Spanish.

INMIGRACION — Immigration.

LA PINTA — The Spot. The trade name of many of the original parador hotels seen along Highway 1. See Chapter 6.

LARGA DISTANCIA — Long Distance. Look for signs with these words and a picture of a telephone indicating offices where you can make long-distance phone calls.

MICROONDAS — Microwave. The word is usually preceded by EST, the abbreviation for estacion (station) You will see these words on signs marking the roads to the stations. The additional word or words on the sign name the particular station.

PALACIO MUNICIPAL — Municipal Palace. Look for these words on the front of town halls in communities that are the seats of local government. In the smaller towns the town hall will bear the words Delagado Municipal, (Municipal Delegate). See Chapter 12.

PALAPA — A shelter made of palm branches. Usually with no walls.

PANGA — A flat bottomed fishing boat.

PUENTE — Bridge. Highway bridges in Mexico are given names. The word Puente followed by the bridge name will be seen on signs on either side of the bridge.

RAMAL — Branch. The word is commonly seen on road signs and refers to a branch road to the place referred to on the sign.

RESTAURANTE — Restaurant. One of many words that are spelled almost the same in English and Spanish but where the pronunciation is considerably different. In Spanish the accent is on the "RAN" and the "R's" are rolled.

REGALOS — Gifts. You will see this word on the front of many stores.

ROPA — Clothing or clothes. Another word seen on store fronts.

SE VENDE — Derived from the verb vender (to sell). In effect, it means For Sale. It is frequently followed by the name of the product available.

SECRETARIA — Secretary. The word will be frequently seen as part of the name of various federal agencies, and in this context means "ministry."

TRES ESTRELLAS — The full name is TRES ESTRELLAS de ORO. Three Stars of Gold. This is the name of Mexico's largest bus company. Look for the name on all sides of the buses along with the three-star logo.

NOTE: Mexicans use a variety of hand and body signals. One of the most common is to hold up the hand with the thumb and index finger separated about one inch. It means "wait a minute." It is often used by waiters or others of whom you are requesting a service. In effect they are acknowledging your presence and indicating that you will be helped soon.

Carlos Salinas de Gortari   The man elected President of Mexico in July 1988. His name will be seen painted on the sides of walls and buildings in scores of places, usually in company with the PRI symbol. The name will remain until the next election.

BAJA BOOKSHELF

The BAJA BOOKSHELF offers the Baja Buff an array of publications concerning Baja California. Some were written specifically about the peninsula. Others are the best available books dealing with subjects related to Baja such as wildlife, Spanish, etc. Each represents my choice of the best title available on the subjects. Jack Williams

No.	TITLE	AUTHOR	PRICE	AD PAGE
1	The Magnificent Peninsula	Jack Williams	$15.95	---
2	Baja Boater's Guide - Volume I - Pacific Coast	Jack Williams	$24.95	37
3	Baja Boater's Guide - Volume II - Sea of Cortez	Jack Williams	$26.95	37
4	The Baja Catch	Niel Kelly & Gene Kira	$19.95	47
5	Baja California Plant Field Guide	Norman C. Roberts	$22.95	82
6	Spanish Lingo for the Savvy Gringo	Elizabeth Reid	$12.95	72
7	Baja California Diver's Guide	Michael & Lauren Farley	$12.95	45
8	Back Country Mexico - Guide & Phrase Book	Burleson & Riskind	$12.95	70
9	Distant Neighbors	Alan Riding	$ 9.00	128
10	The Baja Highway	John Minch & Thomas Leslie	$19.95	131
11	Into A Desert Place	Graham Mackintosh	$24.95	185
12	ChartGuide Mexico West	Ed Winlund and Others	$58.00	38
13	Launch Ramps of Baja California	Mike Bales	$ 6.95	235
14	Fileld Guide to the Gray Whale	Oceanic Society	$ 4.95	188
15	The Elephant Seal	Burney J. Le Boeuf	$ 4.50	50
16	A Field Guide to the Seabirds of the World	Peter Harrison	$24.95	95

Order By Phone (VISA or MASTERCARD)   (415) 332-8635
See Phone Ordering Instructions on Next Page (242).

Or, use this order form, or write your order on any piece of paper. Add 7.25 % sales tax for books shipped in California, plus $3.00 shipping for first book, $2.00 for each additional book. ------ Ship books to:

NAME _____

ADDRESS _____

CITY, STATE, ZIP _____

☐ VISA   ☐ MASTERCARD   Expiration Date

Account Number

Authorizing Signature

NUMBER	TITLE	PRICE	TAX	SHIP	TOTAL
_____	_____	$_____	$_____	$_____	$_____
_____	_____	$_____	$_____	$_____	$_____
_____	_____	$_____	$_____	$_____	$_____
				GRAND TOTAL	$_____

Make checks or money orders payable to H. J. Williams Publications, (U.S. dollars only), and mail to:

H. J. Williams Publications
P.O. Box 203 - B
Sausalito, CA 94966

Prices subject to change without notice.

There's a sign over my desk in the back room of our house. It reads, "H. J. Williams Publications -- International Headquarters." The place in question is also U.S. Headquarters, California Headquarters and the only headquarters of our enterprise. In otherwords, we ain't Rand McNally.

With this edition of *The Magnificent Peninsula,* we decided to list our phone number in the BAJA BOOKSHELF (see page 240) and take credit card orders. Everybody was calling us anyway, so why not go with the flow.

But, keep in mind that if we hire someone to answer the phone, our profits will drop from anemic to hemorrhage. So treat us with kindness and please observe the following Phone Ordering Instructions:

PHONE ORDERING INSTRUCTIONS

1 -- If nobody answers the phone, we ain't home (or are in bed). Please try again.

2 -- Sometimes we leave town for awhile. If you can't get through by phone, please make your order by mail. Someone is always watching the P. O. Box.

3 -- If you hear a baby crying in the background, you have the wrong number. We're over that.

4 -- If you get me, and I sound grumpy, I'm on the computer and trying to concentrate. Order a book and I'll cheer right up. If you're lucky, you will get Patty.

5 -- Don't call during 49er football games. Prices double. Consult your TV guide. If they don't win, wait awhile.

6 -- If the phone keeps ringing busy, Patty is talking to her brother in Nevada. Keep trying, they will tire after awhile, and Baja will still be there.

7 -- Ask all the questions you want about Baja, but remember, almost everything we know is "In the Book."

8 -- Q. Why don't you have an (800) number?
    A. People are always asking questions about Baja. We would go broke paying the phone bill.

Jack Williams and Patty

ROAD SIGNS

Some Mexican road signs are pictorially self-explanatory and use the diagonal slash to indicate NO (see the No Parking sign). However, the majority simply spell out their message in Spanish as shown on many of the signs in this exhibit.

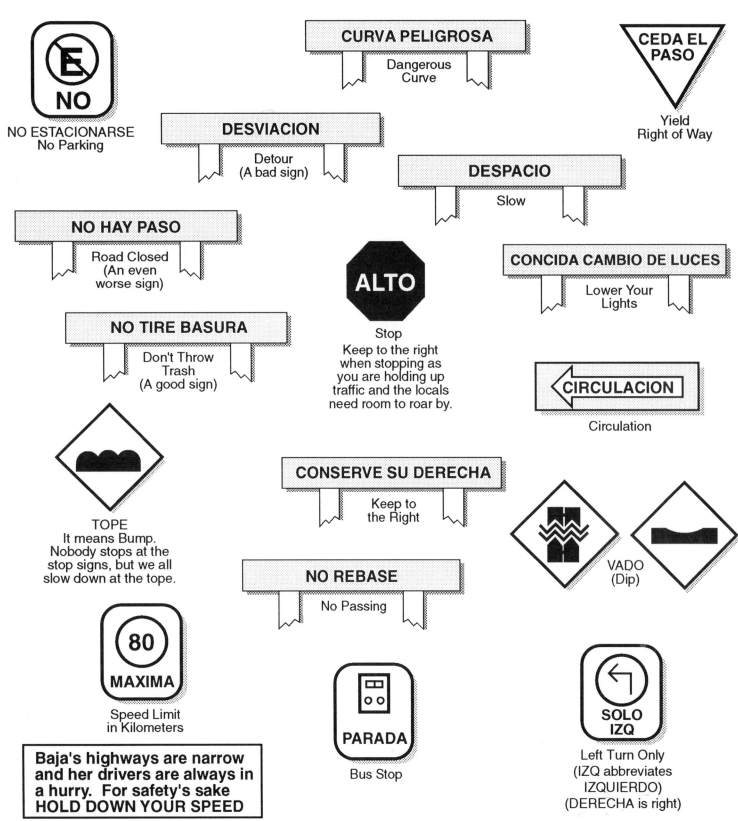

NO ESTACIONARSE
No Parking

CURVA PELIGROSA
Dangerous Curve

CEDA EL PASO
Yield
Right of Way

DESVIACION
Detour
(A bad sign)

DESPACIO
Slow

NO HAY PASO
Road Closed
(An even worse sign)

ALTO
Stop
Keep to the right when stopping as you are holding up traffic and the locals need room to roar by.

CONCIDA CAMBIO DE LUCES
Lower Your Lights

NO TIRE BASURA
Don't Throw Trash
(A good sign)

CIRCULACION
Circulation

TOPE
It means Bump. Nobody stops at the stop signs, but we all slow down at the tope.

CONSERVE SU DERECHA
Keep to the Right

NO REBASE
No Passing

VADO
(Dip)

80 MAXIMA
Speed Limit in Kilometers

PARADA
Bus Stop

SOLO IZQ
Left Turn Only
(IZQ abbreviates IZQUIERDO)
(DERECHA is right)

Baja's highways are narrow and her drivers are always in a hurry. For safety's sake HOLD DOWN YOUR SPEED

INDEX By Patty

Bold type indicates places found in the PART III GRAND TOUR, hotels found in Chapter 6 Hotel Descriptions, and plants found in Chapter 10 list of Common Plants.

Index

Index

VAGABUNDOS DEL MAR
A Full-Service Recreation and Travel Club

Auto - R.V. & Boat INSURANCE

Club members may acquire low-cost Mexican auto, R.V. and boat insurance through OSCAR PADILLA MEXICAN INSURANCE. See page 248 for details.

GO SAFE
in MEXICO with
OSCAR PADILLA
MEXICAN INSURANCE
REPRESENTING
MEXICO'S LARGEST
INSURANCE COMPANY

SPECIAL SERVICES

Available to club members are a monthly newsletter, Mexican Tourist Cards, boat permits, fishing licenses, travel advice and discount prices on maps, and guide books.

ACTIVITIES

Fun-filled, low-cost activities, led and organized by member volunteers. The Vagabundos del Mar is organized for fun, not profit. Excerpts from the monthly club newsletter (THE CHUBASCO) will give you the idea.

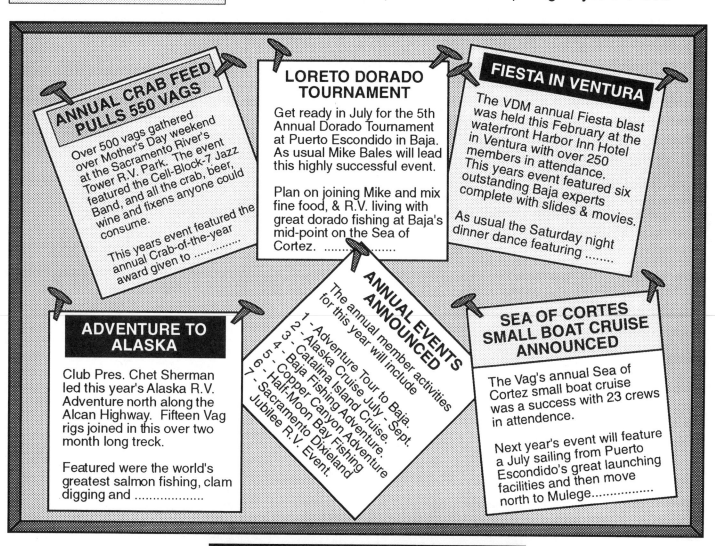

ANNUAL CRAB FEED PULLS 550 VAGS

Over 500 vags gathered over Mother's Day weekend at the Sacramento River's Tower R.V. Park. The event featured the Cell-Block-7 Jazz Band, and all the crab, beer, wine and fixens anyone could consume.

This years event featured the annual Crab-of-the-year award given to ....

LORETO DORADO TOURNAMENT

Get ready in July for the 5th Annual Dorado Tournament at Puerto Escondido in Baja. As usual Mike Bales will lead this highly successful event.

Plan on joining Mike and mix fine food, & R.V. living with great dorado fishing at Baja's mid-point on the Sea of Cortez. ....

FIESTA IN VENTURA

The VDM annual Fiesta blast was held this February at the waterfront Harbor Inn Hotel in Ventura with over 250 members in attendance. This years event featured six outstanding Baja experts complete with slides & movies.

As usual the Saturday night dinner dance featuring ....

ADVENTURE TO ALASKA

Club Pres. Chet Sherman led this year's Alaska R.V. Adventure north along the Alcan Highway. Fifteen Vag rigs joined in this over two month long treck.

Featured were the world's greatest salmon fishing, clam digging and ....

ANNUAL EVENTS ANNOUNCED

The annual member activities for this year will include

1 - Adventure Tour to Baja.
2 - Alaska Cruise July - Sept.
3 - Catalina Island Cruise.
4 - Baja Fishing Adventure.
5 - Copper Canyon Adventure.
6 - Half-Moon Bay Fishing
7 - Sacramento Dixieland Jubilee R.V. Event.

SEA OF CORTES SMALL BOAT CRUISE ANNOUNCED

The Vag's annual Sea of Cortez small boat cruise was a success with 23 crews in attendence.

Next year's event will feature a July sailing from Puerto Escondido's great launching facilities and then move north to Mulege.................

See Page 248 for more information.

VAGABUNDOS DEL MAR
Organized For Fun, Not Profit

A Great Combination

1 - Membership in the Vagabundos del Mar
Baja / Mexico's First and Foremost Travel Club.

2 - Major Savings in Mexican Insurance
For Vagabundo Members Only

The VAGABUNDOS DEL MAR is a nonprofit social club of some 11,000 members who have joined together for recreational boating and travel. The club organizes many activities each year in Alaska, the U.S. and Canadian Pacific Coasts, and western Mexico. Many take place in Baja.

Join now. 12 month membership includes newsletters, decals, the opportunity to make new friends, to participate in all activities and programs, and to enjoy many discounts.

VAGABUNDOS DEL MAR
MEMBERSHIP APPLICATION

Mail to P.O. Box 824, Isleton, CA 95641.

☐ Please enroll me (and my family) in the Vagabundos del Mar. First 12 months $45 (includes $35 annual dues)

_____
Name (include name of spouse)

_____
Address

_____
City - State or Province - Zip

Enclosed is my check for $_____

☐ Send information on our full-service marine insurance (includes Mexico).

☐ Include application for boat insurance.

M.P. 4th

MEXICAN INSURANCE RATES

AUTO FULL COVERAGE up to	BAJA and NW MEXICO	ALL OF MEXICO
$ 5,000	$ 88	$ 130
$ 10,000	$ 116	$ 144
$ 15,000	$ 132	$ 164
$ 20,000	$ 144	$ 177
$ 25,000	$ 161	$ 196

Full coverage available up to $150,000.

	BAJA and NW MEXICO	ALL OF MEXICO
Auto Liability Only	$ 53	$ 72
Boat Liability Only	$ 72	$ 72
Legal Service	$ 25	$ 25

Rates subject to change.

Vagabundos del Mar provides its members with California's OLDEST and LARGEST Mexican insurance service through OSCAR PADILLA MEXICAN INSURANCE. Started in 1951 as California's first Mexican insurance agency, Oscar Padilla now provides nine border offices and nearly 200 statewide agents.

Obtain club membership and insurance directly from Vagabundos del Mar. Call (707) 374-5511 (VISA and MASTERCARD accepted) or mail the adjoining membership application.

Avoid waiting at the border by acquiring insurance in advance. You will receive your insurance application as part of the reply to your completed Vagabundos del Mar membership application.

See additional information on page 247.